Sustainability of Rural Health Care and NGOs in India

Sustainability of Rural Health Care and NGOs in India

Manoj Kar

KALPAZ

First Published, 2021

Published by

Kalpaz Publications
C-30, Satyawati Nagar,
Delhi – 110052
Ph.: 011-47034999, 9811692060
www.kalpazpublications.com
E-mail: kalpaz@hotmail.com

Printed at: Gyan Press, Delhi.

Cataloging in Publication Data—DK
Courtesy: D.K. Agencies (P) Ltd. <docinfo@dkagencies.com>

Kar, Manoj, 1966- **author.**
Sustainability of rural health care and NGOs in India / Manoj Kar.
pages cm
Includes bibliographical references.
ISBN 9789353243135

1. Non-governmental organizations—India. 2. Rural health services and Public Health Policy —India. I. Title.

LCC RA529.K37 2021 | DDC 362.10954 23

DEDICATED TO MY PARENTS WHO INSPIRED ME TO DO THIS RESEARCH AND THE MEMBERS OF THE COMMUNITIES, HEALTH CARE WORKERS, NGOs & CIVIL SOCIETY ORGANIZATIONS WHO ALL PROVIDED INPUT TO THIS RESEARCH WORK

Contents

Foreword

It is with great pleasure that I write a Foreword for this book on *Sustainability of Rural Health Care and NGOs in India, written* by Manoj Kar. I have the opportunity of going through this book which I find very timely and relevant.

Some decades ago, India, perhaps, was at the crossroads between social transition and health care transformation through the phases of agrarian and industrial reforms and modernity, with its age old anchored system of indigenous practices and cultural traditions and its own unique ethos. As in all social spheres, "there is a human face" which is influencing human civilisation as well as functioning of civil society which are in turn affecting 'Health Culture', 'Health Care' and 'Sustainability'. It is in this context that the book intensely discusses the cross cutting issues and strategies which are central to the theme of Sustainability of Rural Health Care involving Non-governmental Organisations.

The author of this manuscript, in this scholarly analysis, amply illustrates the interdisciplinary aspects of Health Care Sustainability in rural cultural settings. This covers the sociology of health & ill-health, governance of health systems-planning & decentralization, human resources management of NGOs, centre-state relations, politico-administrative dimensions of health policy, and health care sustainability in rural India. The research thrust is on providing the reader a theoretical and conceptual framework on 'Health Care Sustainability' based on approaches of 'Primary Health Care'. The important highlights of this manuscript are;

- Problems of human development, poverty, ill-health and their determinants influence social policy, health policy, health care development and health outcomes
- Sustainability of Primary Health Care – opportunity for new public health and health systems strengthening
- Changing role of NGOs in the context of health care sustainability
- Interdisciplinary approaches in health policy and health care sustainability

Bal Rashmi Society, Jaipur, Mr. Ajay Singh Mehta, Chief Executive, Seva Mandir, Udaipur and Mr. S.P.Agarwal, Programme Director, Bhoruka Charitable Trust, Churu district in allowing me to undertake the case study and provided tremendous co-operation in the respective NGOs in the State of Rajasthan.

My special thank goes to the Director, IEC, Directorate of Health & Family Welfare, Government of Rajasthan, the Henderson Library and Information Centre - Indian Institute of Health Management Research (IIHMR), Jaipur, Rajasthan, and the Documentation Centre of each of the mentioned NGOs, Library and Documentation centre of the HCM - Rajasthan Institute of Public Administration, PRIA, VHAI, AVARD, New Delhi, NIHFW and Ford Foundation (India) -New Delhi for providing relevant data and sufficient information on the research topic. I would like to thank the Documentation Unit of the Centre for Social Medicine and Community Health, School of Social Sciences, (CSMCH-SSS), JNU for providing the required in time for finalising the present book.

Prof.(Dr.) S. Acharya, the then Director Institute of Development Studies, Jaipur, Rajasthan, has always encouraged me to keep up the writing process incorporating the missing link of the state of health and NGOs situation throughout the field-work. Prof.(Dr.) Rameswar Sharma, the founder Director of the Indian Institute of Health Management Research (IIHMR) and the then Director, State Institute of Health & Family Welfare, Jaipur, Rajasthan, has been a great help in carrying out this research in providing appropriate guidance in collecting state specific policy information in Health and Family Welfare. Prof. (Dr.) S.D.Gupta, visionary Public Health Leader and the then Director, IIHMR, Jaipur has always been a great encouragement for completing the present research. Dr. Ashok Agarwal, the Trustee, IIHMR & Bhorukha Charitable Trust - Jaipur, a nationally acclaim corporate philanthropist and futurist leader in Global Public Health remains an inspiration throughout this journey. Special mention goes to Mr.N.D.Sharma, Sr. Research Officer, IIHMR for providing valuable information and timely contribution towards the organisation of field based information collection.

I acknowledge the contribution of Mr.K.Gopalan, Director, Commodity Management Unit, CARE India, New Delhi, who taught me the subjective importance of strategic planning in the management of Inter-sectoral Action in Health programmes. The participation of Dr. S.Krishnaswamy, GM, Private Sector, SIFPSA (USAID), has enriched my research work. I am extremely grateful to Dr. Robert J. Kim-Farley, WHO Representative, India and Dr. T. S.Walia, Public Health Administrator, WHO India office, New

Delhi, for the professional and moral support they have provided to accomplish the present research. Their consistent interaction and value additions have helped me to develop the study.

I acknowledge the contribution of Professor Ghanshyam Shah, CSMCH-SSS,JNU who taught me the critical issues of 'Decentralised Planning' and its importance for the present research. The initial interaction with Prof. (Dr.) Rishikesh Maru, Head, Public Systems Management, IIM, Ahmedabad, who enlightened me the importance of 'NGO Management in Health Sector in Globalisation'. Prof.Dileep Mavalankar, Director, IIPH, Gandhinagar and Prime Minister's Mission Steering Group on National Rural Health Mission for his guidance on 'changing role of NGOs in Health Systems Strengthening' is worth mentioning. Late Dr. Santosh Sahu, cultural anthropologist in health research, CSMCH-SSS,JNU remains as a living spirit throughout the task of present study in the completed form. I acknowledge the tremendous leadership support received from Prof. (Dr.) S.Parasuraman, the then Director, TISS, Mumbai and my professional mentor Prof. (Dr.) B.R. Patil, an internationally renowned Sociologist and Social Communication expert in health sector. I am most grateful to my all-time mentor Prof. (Dr.) Bhagwanprakash, globally renowned expert in Public Systems Governance for his inspiration. I have rich memories of all of them. Initial support from the Indian Council of Social Science Research in the form of awarding research fellowship for a limited period of the study was the helpful source of financial assistance to accomplish this study.

Last but not the least, I am greatly indebted to Sir A.R. Nanda, former Secretary Health, GOI, who is not only an outstanding mentor, health policy leader, planner, strategist and an internationally renowned national human rights advocate in the human development process, but has also exhibited in his writing a deep insight into the problems of the disadvantaged especially in the areas of women's health rights, national health policy and national health development goals. Without naming each of them, I wish to acknowledge my grateful thanks to all my family members, friends, colleagues and especially to my research guides Prof. (Dr.) P. Ramalingaswamy and Prof. (Dr.) K.R. Nayar, CSMCH-SSS, JNU who all guided me. Special mentioning about Prof. Arun Adsool, our ever inspirational Chairman, Indian Institute of Education and former Vice Chancellor, SPPU, University of Pune and Dr. Jaysing Kalake, our motivational Vice-Chairman, Indian Institute of Education, Pune for their consistent encouragement and motivational support to complete this study in the present form. For the innumerable assistance given to me in little ways by various generous people, I acknowledge my gratitude to all of them.

Abbreviations

ACHAN	:	Asian Community Health Action Network
AIDS	:	Acquired Immune Deficiency Syndrome
AIIHPH	:	All India Institute of Hygiene and Public health
AIPEBM	:	Area Intensive Programme for Educationally Backward Minorities
AKF	:	Aga Khan Foundation
AKHS	:	Aga Khan Health Services
AKRSP	:	Aga Khan Rural Support Programme
ANM	:	Auxiliary Nurse Midwife
AOR	:	Action Oriented Research
ASFR	:	Age Specific Fertility Rate
AVARD	:	Association of Voluntary Agencies for Rural Development
AWARE	:	Action for Welfare and Awakening in Rural Environment
BASICS	:	Basic Support for Institutionalizing Child Survival
BINGO	:	Bilateral NGO
BMARU	:	Bihar, Madhya Pradesh, Rajasthan, Uttar Pradesh
BRAC	:	Bangladesh Rural Advancement Committee
BSA	:	Banwasi Sewa Ashram
CAH	:	Community Action in Health
CAN	:	Community Needs Assessment
CAPART	:	Council for Advancement for Peoples' Action and Rural Technology
CBD	:	Community Based contraceptive Distribution
CBO	:	Community Based Organisation
CBR	:	Crude Birth Rate
CDP	:	Community Development Programme
CDR	:	Crude Death Rate
CED	:	Chronic Energy Deficiency
CEDAW	:	Convention on the Elimination of All Forms of Discrimination Against Women

MHC	:	Mini Health Center
MMR	:	Maternal Mortality Rate
MO	:	Medical Officer
MOHFW	:	Ministry of Health and Family Welfare
MOs	:	Membership Organizations
MPW	:	Multi Purpose Worker
MSOs	:	Membership Support Organizations
NFHS	:	National Family Health Survey
NGO	:	Non Government Organisation
NGOs	:	Non-governmental Organizations
NIHFW	:	National Institute of Health and Family Welfare
NNGOs	:	Northern NGOs
NPA	:	New Policy Agenda
NPO	:	Non-Profit Organisation
ODA	:	Overseas Development Administration(UK)
ODI	:	Overseas Development Institute(UK)
OECD	:	Organisation for Economic Co-operation and Development
OPD	:	Out Door Patients
ORS	:	Oral Rehydration Salt
ORT	:	Oral Rehydration Therapy
PHC	:	Primary Health Centre/Care
PHC-MAP	:	Primary Health Care – Management Advancement Programme
PHN	:	Public Health Nurse
PRA	:	Participatory Rural Appraisal
PRIA	:	Participatory Research in Asia
PSC	:	Public Service Contractor
PSM	:	Preventive and Social Medicine
PSS	:	Parivar Seva Sanstha
PVO	:	Private Voluntary Organisations
PVOH	:	Private Voluntary Organizations in Health
QUANGOs	:	Quasi-NGOs (Sometimes a parastatal)
RcA	:	Research cum Action
RCH	:	Reproductive Health Care
RCO	:	Rural Community Organisers

RH	:	Reproductive Health
RHC	:	Rural Health Centre
RVHA	:	Rajasthan Voluntary Health Association
S&T	:	Science and Technology
SC/ST	:	Schedule Caste / Schedule Tribes
SCF	:	Save the Children Fund
SDGs	:	Sustainable Development Goals
SEWA	:	Self Employed Women's Association
SEWA-Rural	:	Society for Education Welfare and Action-Rural
SIDA	:	Swedish International Development Agency
SIET	:	Scientific Illustration and Educational Technology
SNGOs	:	Southern NGOs
STD	:	Sexually Transmitted Disease
SWRC	:	Social Work Research Centre
TAC	:	Technical Advisory Committess
TAU	:	Technical Assistance Unit
TB	:	Tuberclosis
TBA	:	Trained Birth Attendants
TT	:	Tetanus Toxoid
UHC	:	Universal Health Coverage
UN	:	United Nations
UNDP	:	United Nations Development Programme
UNFPA	:	United Nations Fund for Population Activities
UNICEF	:	United Nations International Chidren's Emergency Fund
UNRISD	:	United Nations Research Institute for Social Development
USA	:	United States of America
USAID	:	United States Agency for International Development
VHAI	:	Voluntary Health Association of India
VHC	:	Village Health Committee
VHS	:	Voluntary Health Services
VHW	:	Village Health workers
VOLAG	:	Voluntary Agency
VOs	:	Voluntary Organizations
WB	:	World Bank
WHO	:	World Health Organization

Chapter - I

Introduction

The concept of community involvement is a central feature of the health-for-all philosophy that has guided the focus of community health management during the past decades. As the fundamental linkages between health and development have become clearer, "community involvement in health" has been superseded by the notion of "community involvement in health development"- which emphasizes that community action for health is also community action for development. The concept and practice of development are subject to constant change as researchers and practitioners introduce new forms of analysis and enquiry and learn more about the causes and problems of underdevelopment, poverty and ill-health, these changes thus influence health development.

In brief, a new perspective on health development has emerged whereby health is seen as an essential component of sustainable development which requires concerted actions by all sectors of society viz. Government, Non-government Organizations, and Civil Society Institutions and International Donors agencies. The twenty-first century calls for a new health system, which is partnership-oriented, population-health based and proactive rather than reactive in its dimensions. The health sector must serve as a guide to and be a partner in these actions so that health concerns are addressed and represented appropriately at all stages of implementation. The health sector has an essential advocacy role to play in highlighting the linkages between underdevelopment, poverty and ill health in addressing the challenges of health concerns through concerted actions. Sustainability of community action in health development is based on these measures that promote health and development among those in greatest need.

The greatest single challenge for the governments in developing countries is health development, in spite of several initiatives including rural poverty alleviation. The developmental and ethical challenge of rural poverty has dominated development policies from the 1960s, when the

World Bank, in particular, made this the central component of its strategy. Yet, greater political will and large amounts of aid directed towards 'integrated rural development' a proxy for rural poverty have not substantially attended to the prospects of the poorest in rural areas.

However, after several decades of relative failure in health development in the context of rural poverty alleviation programmes a new consensus has emerged on what may be needed to assist the poorest to escape from the conditions of poverty. This revolves around four propositions: (1) Identification of opportunities for change comes most frequently from within the communities of the poor, and the way forward can only be found by working with the poor and obtaining their 'participation'. (2) This requires external agencies to become more flexible and innovative, as large project bureaucracies or government ministries cannot easily devise local approaches to assisting the poor. (3) Commitment and patience, and willingness to listen are essential for poverty alleviation. (4) A purely economic and technical approach lacks the social and political dimension and fails to recognize the need to encourage the poor to assert their rights, particularly through group action. Many talk of 'empowerment', especially in the context of stratified South Asian societies, where relative poverty been looked upon as a natural condition, and dependence and subservience as a requirement for maintaining social and economic order.

All these concerns together participation, flexibility, commitment, and a social dimension have led to a reexamination of the nongovernmental sector: (1) It has considerable advantages over governments and official agencies in addressing poverty. (2) It has a tradition of selectively working with the poor. (3) It has the ability to exclude the nonpoor in ways that governments do. (4) It lays relatively greater emphasis on smallscale projects. (5) It has a tradition of voluntarism and ethics as the basis for its activities. Hence, Non-governmental Organizations (NGOs) are seen as the natural partners of the rural poor. Among official donors there is now a trend to channel their aid through NGOs, to involve NGOs in implementing parts of their own programmes, and to incorporate the best of NGO practices into official programmes. The emphasis on the NGO approach has been reinforced by NGOs' own advocacy: their financial supporters are constantly reminded of successful work with the poor, and this has formed the basis of much of the fundraising effort of NGOs to achieve sustainability.

NGOs embrace a wide array of agencies within and across different countries of the world. Broadly, NGOs are agencies or groups, which are different from government bodies. However, they are distinctive in containing a voluntary component and not operating for profit. Development

NGOs are a category defined by their purpose of providing development support. In development parlance, the term 'NGO' is used to encompass a whole range of organizations, which differ in size, function, and geographical location. The term can be used to refer to small, locally based, and loosely established voluntary and largely grassroots type of associations, as well as large, national, and even transnational voluntary associations with formal constitutions, and employing hundreds of staff. They may be engaged in relief, emergency or longer term development work or a mixture of all three.

The term Non-Government Development Organisation (NGDO) is frequently used to describe the growing numbers of associations whose work is exclusively concerned with broader development concerns. A distinction is also commonly made between NGOs, which originated in and have their home base in the industrial countries, which are referred to as "northern" or "international" NGOs, and those which originate in and operate within developing countries, which are termed "southern" NGOs.

Over the past quarter century, there has been a rapid growth in the numbers of NGOs involved in development, in the numbers of voluntary agencies working in relief and development. The people working for NGOs, and in the amount of money flowing into greatest growth has been in new grass roots organisations (referred to as 'groups', of 'people's organisations', as in the UN Human Development Report, 1993) which have grown up locally some extending no further than one or two villages. However, there has also been a rapid growth in larger southern and northern NGOs. During this period, a number of the older NGOs have changed their role, the most common change being a shift from an exclusive concern with relief and rescue to broader development issues (Korten, 1990b). Close examination of the characteristics of these organizations, has led to a distinction between 'intermediary', or 'secondary', and 'primary' organizations.

On occasion, this growth has led to a blurring of the distinction between governmental and nongovernmental organisations, and even between nonprofit and for profit organisations. In more and more developing countries, it has now become common for government and state agencies or politicians to set up their own "non-governmental" organisations. In industrial countries, it is now common practice for governments to channel some of their aid funds to and through NGOs.

Despite the difficulties, this is a period of tremendous creativity, with NGOs forming alliances among themselves and increasing their international networking. There is renewed attention to policy related work, a greater attention to poverty and related issues including issues of good governance agenda, and increased NGO access to policymaking bodies at national and international levels. The NGO development agenda is moving away from the North South "Charity paradigm" to one based more firmly on the principles of justice, rights, equality, partnership and solidarity. Development, sustainable human development, is being increasingly perceived by NGOs as a global challenge albeit with local perspectives. It is no longer confined to the countries and societies of the developing world. It is of equal concern for the developed countries also.

In spite of increasing opulence in pockets and unprecedented rise level in per capita income in the world, millions of people die prematurely and abruptly from intermittent famines and every year from endemic undernourishment, poverty and deprivation linked health problems across the globe. Further, millions lead lives of persistent want and insecurity. Despite centralization of economic and political power, national or international control over mass media, and growing marginalization and exploitation of the poor, their capacity to organise themselves and wage struggles has been remarkable. The poor are asserting their rights throughout the world. The 1990s witnessed an increasing engagement of several streams of NGOs, involved in welfare, development and political activism, in public policy debates on global issues concerning local actions. As these trends gain momentum, NGOs of the North and the South addressing population, health, environment, human rights and women's concerns would require forging new alliances to address shared concerns. What then could be the potential role for NGOs in India? What tasks and roles need emphasis to achieve sustainability?

The causes and characteristics, of the maladies and possible remedies have not yet been clearly understood. Analytical as well as empirical investigations are needed to provide the background for policy making and action for eradicating health-related problems affecting development. The present study is an attempt in this direction.

The role of NGOs in managing development initiatives in developing countries has been very central in contemporary development aid discourse. According to some Western analysts the reasons for the emergence of development NGOs since the 1970s are several. Among them 'market failure' and 'state failure' or 'government failure' are considered the leading ones in developing countries (Anheier & Seibel 1990). Scholars argue that this growth of NGOs is a reflection of dissatisfaction with both state and market. On the other hand, the use of NGOs has been consistent with both the New Right aid policies of governments in the USA and UK and the 'alternative' aid policies of the consciences of the donor community in developing countries (Hulme 1994). Researcher and policy-makers have begun to re-examine decentralization and privatization and to consider the NGOs a possible remedy for the 'crisis of the welfare state' (Anheier and Seibel 1990). The restructuring policies of the World Bank and other influential donor institutions (e.g. in OECD countries) led to a planned reduction of the role of state in developing countries and increased space for development NGOs (Tvedt 1998).

Conceptual and terminological aspects of NGOs will be discussed in a following chapter. A belief in the comparative advantage of NGOs is often found in development aid literature. Development projects run by NGOs are assumed to be flexible, innovative, participatory, cost-effective and dedicated to the poor. Several social, political and cultural arguments exist to justify the advantages of NGOs. Some shortcomings of NGOs have been documented in several works and some of them have challenged the idea that NGOs are necessarily more effective and efficient than official channels (Korten, 1991). In addition, some shortcomings in the existing NGO literature have also been identified in their writings. Therefore, in this process of determining the comparative advantages or disadvantages of NGOs, their performance in strategizing development management plays a crucial role. If NGOs fail to produce better performance in their development initiatives or if they suffer from shortcomings similar to those believed to be common in government-led initiatives in developing countries – where is the justification to involve NGOs in development? Do NGOs have better administration capacities than the government agencies in the developing countries? Are their projects sustainable enough to face the challenges of the development world? These are the issues this study tries to investigate by focusing on the issues of sustainability and by limiting the study to selected NGOs involved under GOI and USAID funded Private Voluntary Organizations in Health (PVOH-II) project in the North-West part of the Indian State of Rajasthan. The assumptions are that if the state policies of the recipient countries and donor organizations and the capacity of management strategy of the NGOs are supportive and appropriate to community need, it helps to ensure the sustainability of NGOs initiative in health and social sector development.

As already mentioned, NGO-led development projects are often assumed to be flexible, innovative, participatory, cost-effective and directed to the poor, but the present study does not necessarily share all these views. In reality, these suggested advantages of NGOs in developing countries are already in question. Despite the increase involvement of donors over the past decades, NGO-led development has been disappointing, like the government-run development projects. They have had limited success, having failed largely in their efforts to reduce rural poverty by any significant amount (Kalimullah, 1990). The situation has not been developed in recent years. Although NGOs provide technology and funds like other international donors, their planning and implementation leave much to be desired, like government-run traditional development projects in developing countries. 'Management' has always been identified as a neglected factor in development project activities (Paul 1986). The same is true with the NGO-led development projects. It has been assumed that the reason for this disappointment is that they did not consider properly the work environment of the project area. Some have argued that the NGOs and their donors paid too little attention to the local needs, social norms, values and cultures of the project area and failed to plan and implement their development projects properly. That is why the sustainability of NGO-led development projects is in question among the donor and recipient countries. Questions about co-ordination, complementarities and the relative autonomy of the NGO with regard to the state and the market are the central issues that should be addressed both from the perspectives of the North and the South, by the donors and recipients alike.

In the present research the issues of NGO initiatives are understood to look into the broad aspects of sustainability within the context of donor supported NGO managed health care projects in social sector development. Thus the research is aimed at advancing understanding of the issues of sustainability, by assessing the effectiveness of NGO strategies in managing these issues under PVOH-II project. However following issues of the challenges and opportunities of NGO management are qualitatively analyzed and addressed in the context of sustainability.

- NGOs do not get a favorable environment to work in, due to the lack of proper grassroots policies and the oligarchic character of governments in most developing countries including India.
- The commitment of the donors and their policy of supporting NGOs are not yet stable enough in donor (e.g in OECD) and recipient countries. Thus NGO workers and activists are working with a degree of uncertainty in developing countries. And, finally,
- For various reasons the management capacity of NGOs in managing development initiatives is weak. Poor performance in project management makes the NGO-led development initiatives unsustainable.

The concept of sustainability in the present research is as follows: A development programme is considered sustainable when it is able to deliver and appropriate level of benefits for an extended period of time after major financial, managerial, and technical assistance from an external donor is terminated. The managerial capacity of NGOs plays a crucial role in this respect.

The specific objective of the research is the study of sustainability of NGO-led development initiatives in health. The general concept of development initiative in the study refers specifically to management of Community health projects. For analytical purposes, three influential issues have been identified that affect sustainability of NGO initiatives in health. These are:

- The overall and particular work environment of the NGOs in the target community;
- Policy support and the degree of commitment of the Government co-operation concerning NGOs;
- The overall management strategy of the operating NGOs.

These three factors are highlighted in the study, which includes analysis of the overall and particular working environment of the project in the target community; analysis of the policy and commitment of the donor as supported by the government; and analysis of the human resources management capacity of the concerned NGOs and their projects.

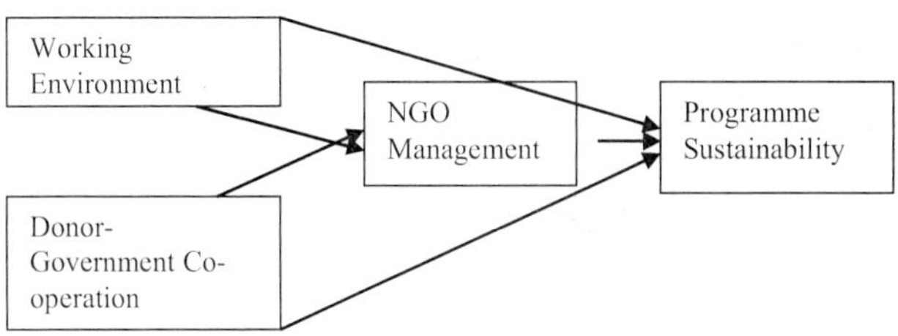

To assess sustainability, a qualitative analysis has been the focus of NGOs' management strategies involving their initiatives in health project. Their management strategies have been assessed by studying and observing their organizational effectiveness, local participation for example: understanding of contextual factors, operational factors and leadership factors through initiating case study methods. Their present management strategies has been analysed and assessed through qualitative observations. However, the focus was on the notion of sustainability in their health initiatives. As stated above, the notion of sustainability comprises facts and realities from the NGOs' state situation in the present study, and from the government – donor support and realities in the perspectives of operating

NGOs themselves. This is why the mode of inter-connectivity and interdependence has been considered and discussed as key implications for NGO government partnership in sustainable health development.

The sustainability of NGO-led development initiatives which has been questioned in the Social Science literature are understood from different angles. The NGO sector, in general, is facing many challenges in its development initiatives. Failing to overcome these challenges would gradually make NGO programmes less sustainable. The future key issues, implications, and challenges of this special sector of NGOs, operating development projects in developing countries (Salamon and Anheier, 1996), are to:

- Emerge from the shadows
- Establish legitimacy
- Establish meaningful collaborative relationships between NGOs and the State both in the North and in the South, and go beyond the paradigm of conflict;
- Redesign their role in development, from agent to partner

In order to address the central theme of sustainability by studying and analysing the working environment and the policy of the official donor, the central and state government in the study and the strategies of NGOs, a total of seven chapters have been prepared and presented in the study with the help of case study methods.

The first (present) chapter gives a study description. The chapter presents a theoretical basis and gives a detailed description of the study. Methodologically the chapter introduces different concepts and programmatically the research by focusing on the review and analysis of the existing literature in the field.

The chapter two discusses about the **issues of NGOs in Social Development.** This discusses on the position of NGOs in the alternative development paradigm in the context of Globalisation. This is followed by the theoretical standpoint of development administration, i.e., administration in development context. The chapter highlights the concept of development administration, analyses the role of NGOs in development and presents an overview on the NGO, state and donor co-operation in development initiative. Methodologically the chapter clarifies different concepts and theoretically describes the research by reviewing and analyzing the existing literature in the field of Social Development.

This is followed by the 'role of NGOs in health and social sector development in India' through the review of history, growth and evolution of NGOs through policy planning in health development. The third chapter presents a literature review on community action for sustainable health development, community involvement in health, experiences of community participation from developing countries, community action in Decentralised Health System, Key issues of Community Involvement in Health, Health sector reform involving Community Action. A specific literature survey on issues and challenges of community action in sustaining primary health care initiatives is stressed upon in this chapter. This is followed by the review of literature on sustainability of development initiatives with special emphasis on health and social sector in developing countries. This chapter focuses on conceptual framework of sustainability, sustainability of health systems development, sustainability: a client-driven approach in non-governmental health care focuses on sustainability of non-governmental health care. This chapter attempts to address the broad framework of sustainability within the contextual hostility of non-governmental health care in developing countries. The chapter four describes the following in brief; background of socio-demographic and health profile of Rajasthan. 'Health & Family Welfare' NGOs involved in the state government schemes - for community participation and NGO involvement in health & family welfare programmes. This is followed by the contextual review of programme sustainability: PVOH-II (Private Voluntary Organisations in Health Phase -II) in India, and with special emphasis on the study of NGOs in Rajasthan, the challenges of sustainability under PVOH-II project, and note on the research methodology followed in the present study. It was important further to examine different issues and literature available on sustainability of non-governmental health care in India. The methodology attempts to understand the processes involved in the effectiveness NGO management strategy to sustain the benefits of health initiative during project life through case study methods.

Chapter five describes the Study Design and Methodology used for case studies of NGOs in the state of Rajasthan. Effectiveness of NGO management strategy, findings from the project experiences, community assessment and perception, issues on management strategies on sustainability, key lessons learned with programmatic recommendations for the NGO are the major focus of the case study in this chapter.

Chapter six discusses the effectiveness of NGO capacity and qualitative assessment of NGO strategies to address the issues of sustainability during project life based on the qualitative observation and analysis of factors of sustainability. This is followed by a discussion on strategising of opportunity and challenges from the findings of the strengths and weaknesses in NGO strategies. The focus of this chapter is the understanding of NGO capacity on the road map of sustainability within the broad framework of contextual hostility. This chapter presents the definition of sustainability in development projects with special emphasis on health care in developing countries. A note on sustainability of non-governmental health care is presented.

Chapter seven discusses an overview of lessons learned and key strategies of NGO initiatives in health development with special emphasis on the problems and prospects identified in the study, more or less, in the whole NGO sector involved in health and social sector development in general, regardless of differences among them. The chapter makes a brief notes on the role of local governance, the state, the donor, on the NGOs in ensuring the sustainability of their development initiatives focusing community health programmes in general and PVOH-II project in particular.

In this last concluding chapter, an attempt is made to describe in nutshell the PVOH-II project and its various aspects, the key issues of sustainability as they emerged from three case-studies with lessons learned in brief and their programmatic and policy implications for NGOs and the Panchayats as well as for the state of Rajasthan and the MOHFW in the central government within the context of International Donors. The chapter ends with a conclusion on the findings of the whole study and gives insight into the future direction of NGO research by referring to other scholarly works that highlight the need for further systematic study on sustainability of health development.

The study has been made only to generate and promote academic understanding about the human resources and strategic functioning of development NGOs as operating in the health and social sector in the wider context of development studies. The findings will be useful in policy influencing and policy research in sustaining NGOs involvement in health systems development and health care for the rural India using the framework of Primary Health Care and Universal Health Coverage. This can contribute further to handhold multiple stakeholders, academia, researchers, civil society organisations, policy makers and health care practitioners from the government to build the bridges and alliances strengthening in health systems, research and management practices for the rural India as essential for achieving Universal Health Coverage under the United Nations global call for Sustainable Development Goals by 2030.

Chapter - II

Issues on NGOs in Social Development

NGOs in the Alternative Development Paradigm - Globalisation

This review attempts to draw some lessons from the functioning in the past five decades of development NGOs throughout the world. It starts by describing the meaning of alternative development paradigm as practised by NGOs. It then examines some of the major socio-political changes that have occurred in recent years, and their impact on development NGOs. Finally, it outlines some key dilemmas facing development NGOs, and their potential implications for their future roles and contributions at the turn of the millennium.

Voluntary association and development action' have been a part of the historical evolution of many societies. The framework of development, however, is essentially a post-World War-II phenomenon. Individuals and groups within the field of development derived, and continue to do so, their motivation from an ideological and spiritual commitment to social reform and change. It is this personal commitment to contribute to societal improvement that characterised such non-state actors in the mid-twentieth century. Development NGOs are a contemporary sub-set of the same tradition.

When development NGOs began to be noticed in the 1970s, it was for what was beginning to be called an alternative development paradigm. The identification of NGOs with this alternative development paradigm grew stronger over the next decade or so. What were the characteristics of this paradigm, which distinguished NGOs from mainstream development actors? Several significant characteristics can be identified. The alternative development paradigm implied local-level development, which was seen to be in contrast to the agenda of national-level development of newly liberated post-colonial nation-states after the World War II. These states tried to establish certain prorates which were to be uniformly agenda had local priorities, and looked at the individual village or a slum as a space for improving people's socio-economic situation (Korten, 1990).

A related characteristic was the small-scale nature of these development efforts, something reinforced by Schumacher's 'small is beautiful' ideas. This alternative approach emphasised looking at development itself as a problem of human development, which can be understood, managed, and monitored by small collectives of human beings. Small-scale development contrasted with the large-scale macro development programmes which were then being launched with a great deal of vigour and pride – large dams, hydroelectric power stations, mines, roads, industry, plantations etc.

The third dimension of the alternative development paradigm was an integrated approach which implied looking at the individual, her family, and community as an integrated whole and bringing together various development inputs to converge in an integrated fashion so that individuals, their families, and their communities could all benefit. This approach contrasted with the fragmented, sectoral development schemes run by most national governments, in which each scheme addressed one aspect of human existence - education, health, drinking water, sanitation, agriculture, rural development, roads, communication, electricity, etc. These schemes were at times mutually conflicting or contradictory and required enormous efforts to integrate them on the part of the individual, her family and her community (Korten, 1990).

The fourth and perhaps most dynamic characteristic of the alternative development paradigm was its participatory nature. This paradigm believed that development cannot be delivered from outside, that people can develop themselves, and that their own involvement, engagement, and contribution are an essential foundation for sustainable development. People's own participation can be enabled through drawing on local knowledge and local resources, and enhanced through a series of interventions leading to their collective empowerment. This dimension was nicely juxtaposed against the externally determined, government – led, functionary – delivered development programmes which characterised many government efforts in the 1970s and 1980s. In the 1970s people's participation was not on the agenda of most governments, nor was it considered relevant or in any case appropriate.

The final dimension of this alternative paradigm was its ideological and inspirational character, which looked at the needs of the subaltern groups in the context of social and economic transformation. Inspired largely by the sufferings and deprivations of the marginalised sections of society, and committed to bringing about socio-economic equality and justice, the alternative development approach relied substantially on concientisation and the collective mobilisation of the marginalised themselves. Non-formal education, community based Primary Health Care, community organising, and local leadership building were the kinds of interventions that this alternative development approach of NGOs signified. This contrasted with the mainstream development paradigm, which focussed on growth in GNP and macroeconomic development (John Clark, 1991).

The distribution and equity dimension of development was not a major concern of governments in those days. Development was seen as a technocratic professional challenge, which could be managed through expertise and input of resources from outside. 'The technocratic approach, with its emphasis on technological modernisation, managerial efficiency and growth in GNP, held the centre of the state for over two decades but is now in disrepute' (Mehta et al 1977). Clearly, the NGO development paradigm, described as an alternative development paradigm, contained within itself the seeds of significant future evolutions and had in itself a number of significant analytical dimensions.

The first dimension was to look at the role of the state. Most post-colonial states in Africa, Asia-Pacific, and Latin America and the Caribbean were single-party and authoritarian. Even where democratic forms of political systems were in existence, the hegemony of the state in determining development agendas, mobilising development resources, and delivering development, was almost total. The gap between the promise and the reality of how the state functioned, and its inability to change the situation of the poor and the weak in any meaningful way, lent itself easily to a major critique of the very function of the state.

The alternative development paradigm, therefore, was an alternative to the practice of the state. This critique was also influenced by emerging negative consequences of development on the lives and destines of the poor. In many parts of the developing world, large-scale development projects were resulting in the displacement of indigenous people, rural poor and urban slum-dwellers from their land, livelihood and community. The NGO development paradigm began to critique such development projects on the basis of who benefits from them and who bears the cost. It is this critique which subsequently led to what began to be called a 'rights approach' to development. These human rights were larger than civil and political rights and included the right to a decent livelihood, the right to life, and the right to life with dignity. 'Thousands and thousands of individuals and groups, all over the world – are engaged in practising such alternatives' (Raise et.al. 1997).

In the 1970s, the alternative approach also signified a relative indifference towards macroeconomic issues and the production of goods and services. The major focus of analysis was on equitable distribution and on social justice. Agricultural and industrial production was not a major focus of NGO attention. In most situations, private capital, large plantations, and private ownership of industry were considered somehow injurious to the interests of the vast majority of people in developing societies.

While inadequately conceptualised, there were a number of significant elements in this analytical critique which evolved through development NGO practice in the 1970s. These critiques resulted in the emergence of a new agenda in the development paradigm. This included concern for the environment, for ecologically balanced and inter-generationally sustainable development, and the rights of women and gender equity. It looked at the disparities between the Western societies characterised by North America and Western Europe, on the one hand, and the developing societies on the other. The global system was seen as unjust and perpetuating the 'development of under-development' in countries of Africa, Asia, and Latin America (Andre Gunder, Frank and Samir Amin).

Outcomes of Alternative Development Paradigm

After two decades of widespread acknowledgement of this unique alternative development paradigm which was associated with NGO work throughout the world, a number of significant outcomes could be observed in the practice and discourse of development by the mid – 1990s.

The first set of resources is of the NGOs themselves. Between 1970 and 1995, NGOs gained a high degree of visibility in almost every country in the world. Their roles and contributions began to be noticed. Their presence, their experience, and their point of view began to be heard by the developmentalists, nationally and internationally. National governments began to take stock of the NGOs in their own countries and of the international NGOs working in their societies. Over the period of last twenty-five years, there has also been a significant multi-fold increase in the flow of resources to NGOs from global institutions, private foundations in the form of 'development aid' to humanitarian and emergency services.

NGOs began to be part of the UN system and of the Bretton Woods institutions in the 1980s and 1990s while representing International conferences to influence policy formulations, development debates and alternative development approaches. This period also witnessed an enormous growth in the size and diversity of the NGO community. The nature of NGOs also began to develop a broader range of International differentiation – from service delivery to welfare, to emergency operations, to policy advocacy, to networking, to researches and capacity building. Describing this variety, David Korten presented the four-generation model of development NGOs: 'The voluntary organisation with a fourth generation strategy is essentially a service organisation to the people's movement it supports' (Korten 1990).

A second set of outcomes during this period was related to the nature of changes in the political system throughout the world (Korean, 1990). By the mid 1990s, many more countries had adopted some form of liberal democratic governance mechanism. As a result, there was an increase in pluralistic and competitive politics with direct popular participation. Countries, which had remained under authoritarian and dictatorial regimes, became democratic, as exemplified by Philippines, Chile and South Africa in three continents of Asia, Latin America and Africa respectively. NGOs were seen to have played a significant role in energising the peoples' democratic aspirations and the resulting democratic transition of these countries. Throughout the world, the experiences, voices and contribution of NGOs from Philippines, Chile and South Africa were presented as exemplars (Korten, 1990).

A third set of outcomes is related to the dramatic shifts in the former Soviet Union and the nature of the socialist regime. Eastern and central Europe went through a period of significant economic and political transformation with the abandonment of Soviet- style socialism. This had enormous consequences worldwide, because the Cold-War dynamics of East and West suddenly disappeared and a new dynamic between the North and the South began to take their place. The response of Warsaw Pact countries to the aspirations of developing countries in Asia, Africa and Latin America had presented a competitive situation for Western Europe and North America during the Cold War period. With the disappearance of the Soviet Union, the world became a unipolar, and therefore, a much more hegemonic political regime than before (Tandon 1991).

Another outcome of this period was the dramatic change in the status of development of many countries throughout the world. Many countries of Southeast Asia, East Asia and Latin America have experienced dynamic improvements in income levels and social development outcomes. As a result, there were significant reductions in poverty and marginalisation, and substantial improvements in education, health, and other social indicators in these contexts. This presented the possibility that the model of rapid economic development of these countries represented could be forged as the model development paradigm for the rest of the world (Korten, 1990).

The most significant outcome of this period perhaps was in the slow but significant transformation of the development agenda itself. National governments, UN agencies, the Bretton Woods institutions, development think-tanks – the entire development discourse by the mid - 1990s – began to create an impression that the mainstream development discourse had 'absorbed' the principles of the alternative development paradigm that were being put forward by NGOs in the 1970s(UN, 1995). Local level development initiatives, integrated interventions, mobilisation of the poor and their active participation have become the hallmark of development philosophy. The Declaration and Programme of Action of UN world summit for Social Development held at Copenhagen in March 1995 had governments agree to the following:

- Encouraging the fullest participation in society requires –
- Strengthening the capacities and opportunities for all people,
- Enabling institutions of civil society,
- Giving community organisations greater involvement in the design and implementations of local project…(United Nations 1995: 98-99)

Mainstream development discourse at the turn of the millennium looks not very different from the alternative development paradigm that was so enthusiastically put forwarded by NGOs in the 1970s. In some significant ways therefore, NGOs can claim to have been 'successful': they can claim to have influenced national and international development policies, priorities and discourse in the direction of their own experience. The big players of development have now incorporated the alternative principles espoused by NGOs more than two decades ago, and mainstream development now reflects that perspective – call for 'coalition for change' (J.D. Wolfesnohn, WB, 1999).

The fraternity of NGOs can take pride in the fact that as we enter the new millennium, the global development agenda has been significantly inspired by the practice and perspectives of hundreds of thousands of NGOs worldwide (UN, 1995). The discourse has changed, but the practice needs much more improvement. Therefore, the fear of co-option of the NGO agenda by the big players remains valid if mere language shifts are confused with actual practice on the ground. Hopefully, the challenge now is to hold these macro players accountable to their own rhetoric, not to take this or granted.

NGOs today operate in a significantly different context to the one prevalent in the 1970s and early 1980s. What are some of the key challenges facing NGOs in today's context and how do NGOs attempt, if at all to respond to the challenges? and what are some of the directions in which these challenges will shape the future of NGO initiatives in development? The haunting dilemmas would surely throw further reflections in understanding these queries.

NGOs Haunting Dilemmas in Changing Development Alternatives

At the start of the new century, NGOs are facing certain unresolved, still haunting, dilemmas. These are issues on which clarity of perspective and decisive action is not very common, though need for it is periodically emphasized. Following under-mentioned discussions are these dilemmas, which haunt NGOs even today.

2.1.2.1. Governance

In recent years, good governance has become a new fad in development discourse. However, as noted earlier, the alternative development paradigm of NGOs focused a great deal on the 'bottom-up' process of development, which was to be collectively constructed through participatory action. 'Putting people in the centre of development' implied getting the state and its agents out of that centre. Participatory development models proposed by NGOs challenged the state-led models of development practised in the post-World War II scenario. Therefore, a logical next step in that alternative development paradigm was to reduce the importance of the state in the governance of natural resources and local development, enabling organised collectives of local communities to become responsible for such governance issues. 'They [NGOs] should push for a redefinition of just development and good governance' (Clark 1991).

This, of course, implies that NGOs need to deal with the possibility to create a more efficient, more transparent, and more accountable apparatus of democratic governance in our societies. However, NGOs continue to struggle with the provision of sector-oriented programmes and services – health, education, drinking water, rural development, urban development, environment, gender, etc. The link between poverty eradication and programme sustainability, on the one hand, and transparent, accountable, and participatory democracy and governance on the other, has not yet been conceptually or emotionally accepted by NGOs:

Citizens, believe that a good society is one in which they can participate in public spheres to make their own contribution towards the public good.

Their voices are loud and clear on this. People want a society characterised by responsive and inclusive governance. They want to be heard and consulted on a regular and continuing basis, mot merely at the time of an election. They want more than a vote. They are asking for participation and inclusion in the decisions taken and policies made by public agencies and officials (The Commonwealth Foundation, 1999).

This raises the challenge of dealing with the formal political system in a given country in shaping policies of development administration. As a result, NGOs are unable to figure out whether they should talk to the political parties and political leaders at all, except those who are government ministers. The NGO fraternity has not embraced the growing worldwide trend towards local self- governance through the elected local bodies as yet. Questions about their own internal governance become relevant too. Just as government agencies and departments cannot bring in externally designed programmes for local bodies simply to accept, likewise the NGO programmes designed and funded through external resources cannot be implemented in local communities unless they are reviewed by local bodies to ensure that NGOs are properly accountable to them (John Clark, 1990).

Likewise, there is a question of growing government expenditure on militarisation and defence, and large-scale consumption of public budgets in overstaffed public agencies. Money spent on these areas is money taken away from social development and poverty eradication programmes. Not many NGOs see this link or are willing to take a stand on issues of militarisation and public sector staffing, for example. 'While it is time that the future of poor-people centred development programmes has to be approached through a fusion of government and NGO practices, it will be far from easy to bring this about when, to do so will erode the power and income of the government officials' (Hollway 1989).

At the heart of the governance issue is the political process. Politics of negotiation and consensus building across diversified interest groups and varied priorities is the basis of democratic governance in any society. But many NGOs neither understand the political process nor are in a position to deal with it.

Globalisation

In some significant ways, NGOs have benefited from the process of globalisation. Access to global resources and influence in global forums, are some areas mentioned earlier. UN conferences in the last fifteen years represent a force towards the globalisation of development discourse and development policy-making. On the other hand, there are trends in globalisation, which enforce existing inequalities across nations and peoples. New information technology (IT) opens up enormous possibilities to those who have access to its hardware and software. That access is extremely unevenly distributed in the world today, as described by UNDP's 1999 Human Development Report. Many NGOs, with access to IT are themselves parting of the privileged few in their societies and countries.

Equal participation in the WTO and the dominances of northern capital flows in the world speculation market are some of the other areas that concern NGOs a great deal. There is increasing evidence that the natural resource bases of the poor as well as of local industry in many parts of the world have become victims of lopsided and Northern-centric globalisation. The common NGO reaction has been to shun and reject globalisation. But restricting oneself to national boundaries as an option has peculiar socio-political implications, including a return to feudal and parochial systems. Globalisation also offers new possibilities. Widespread citizen aspiration for democratic governance is one such possibility that NGOs can support. The emergence of multilateral mechanisms at regional [European (EU), Southeast Asia (ASEAN), and North American (NAFTA)] and global levels (WTO, APEC, Davos Summit, etc.) are opportunities to counterbalance bilateralism between the strong and the weak. This ambivalence towards globalisation and its forces continues to paralyse NGOs and undermines their ability to take advantage of some aspects, while continuing to challenge, critique, and resist others. A more reasoned and analytical approach to the issues of globalisation is needed by NGOs:

> Social fragmentation, economic instability, and uncertainty about the future are breeding prejudice, intolerance, and racism. Peace and democracy are not compatible with ever increasing poverty and exclusion. The social and geographic segregation of a growing number of individuals can only fuel ethnic tensions and violence. From the moral and ethical standpoint, global apartheid is absolutely unacceptable (Darcy De Oliveria and Tandon, 1994).

Bridging civil society

NGOs are facing the dilemma of who to speak to, historically; they have been busy working with the poor and the marginalized. Occasionally, they related to development policy makers and ideologues. However, over the years, NGO conversations generally remained limited to the 'charmed circles of the already converted' (Tandon). As a result, only a small section of society in the countries in which they operate was familiar with their approaches and experiences. In some situations, NGOs saw themselves as the only activists in pursuit of such important societal goals. 'Micro movements around all over the place, but there is not enough of a dialogue between them' (Kothari, 1988).

NGOs tended neither to pay attention to nor develop any relationship with other civil society actors – religious institutions, traditional formations, community-based initiatives, trade unions, or social movement. This inward-looking tendency has been historically reinforced through donor policies and practices. Issues of accountability, impact and sustainability are now pushing NGOs to open up their horizons and deal with the rest of society. Talking about their experience and perspective beyond the coterie of the already converted has become an important challenge for NGOs. The role of NGOs in strengthening civil society to regain and retain hegemony over the state and private enterprise is a critical strategic function (Tandon, 1991).[12]

In the Third World itself, governmental officials, social movement activities, international donors and other actors adopt the dominant paradigm of the moment and take it out of the ivory tower and into play-using its framework to generate certain questions and answers, to direct (governmental, international and philanthropic) funds, and to advance certain programmatic priorities over others. In the 1990s, civil society is fast becoming one of these dominant paradigms (Bickford, 1995).

The difference between NGO and civil society organisation (CSO) is important because the policy and power implications are different. Rightly or wrongly, NGOs are often described in service-delivery roles, whereas CSOs are depicted as political agents. In his review of donor policy on civil society, Robinson writes:

> *The developmental emphasis on institution building and participatory development focuses attention on NGOs and local membership organisations, whereas a concern with democratic highlights the more political role played by civic organisations, such as trade unions, professional bodies and groups representing women, students and youth. The former* emphasises *the role of civil society in service provision and programme implementation, whereas the latter addresses the contribution of civic organisations to the process of democratisation and in holding governments to account for their policies and actions (Robinson, 1996).*

This broad – based public education task is also an essential foundation for bringing about societal transformation within a democratic framework.

More and more people have to be persuaded to see the value and the relevance of the work that NGOs are contributing to the strengthening of civil society. However, dealing with all these other sections of society may strain NGOs and take their resources and attention away from their traditional beneficiary 'target' groups – the poor and the marginalised themselves. It is certainly an issue that most international donors and external resource providers ask: are you spending my dollar in directly helping the poor or not? Thus, NGOs wanting to break ground and expand their experience of working with other civil society actors is largely limited. Building a broad – based consensus in society on issues that concern NGOs may require resolving this dilemma sooner rather than later. 'This effective, pluralistic and efficient functioning of development NGOs in the South itself becomes an expression of sustainability in development (Tandon, 1996).

Sustainability

A major dilemma facing NGOs is the question of their own resources. As intermediary agents in their societies, serving the poor and the marginalized, NGOs have historically relied on externally generated resources. Most of this, in many countries of the world, has come from development aid. As development aid from Northern OECD countries began to contribute greater resources to NGOs, more and more development NGOs gained access to and began to become dependent on it. In recent years, a large proportion of this development assistance has been routed through governments, and NGOs have used resources made available to them from large-scale government programmes. The access to large-scale development aid has many serious implications.

Traditional Northern donors of Southern development NGOs are asking them to demonstrate financial sustainability. As an increasingly popular prescription, NGOs are being exhorted to enter into partnerships with the corporate sector, as this represents another enormous potential source of sustained flows of financial resources to NGOs.

It is obvious that intermediaries of any kind require resources from those who can afford to provide them. On that principle, NGOs' contribution to society may not be fundable by their direct (and indirect) beneficiaries. Yet, contributions from the development- aid machinery are stagnant, if not declining. The dependence on that aid flow is making NGOs become service-providers in a restricted and narrow sense, and so depriving them of their ability to maintain autonomous, independent perspectives and positions on a wide range of socio-political and economic issues. As NGOs become more involved in large-scale service delivery and/or become more reliant on official funding, one might expect some fall-off in their flexibility, speed of response and ability to innovate. 'The orientation of accountability (to donors) away from the grassroots is a particular threat to NGOs' agenda of sustainability (Edward and Hume, 1995). How does one maintain a sustainable economic base, a material base, which allows NGOs' flexible funds and yet keeps them accountable to the society and the community in which they live, work, and practice?

NGO legitimacy and accountability are being increasingly linked to their resource base. Resource providers can demand a certain limited type of accountability, - that which has to do with efficient and purposive use of resources provided by them. By clearly, NGOs do not only exist to spend money that they occasionally receive from outside. Rather, they exist to pursue a particular vision and set of priorities of development. Therefore, their accountability mostly translate, into the reality in which they intervene, and local communities and society must be the interface through which NGOs define their accountability. It is a difficult and problematic dilemma to resolve, but one, which is increasingly, haunting NGOs as prescriptions and solutions for sustainability and local resource mobilisation are being offers in the market at a rapidly increasing rate.

Such an approach of local accountability would also enhance the identity and rootedness of NGOs in their own societies. As a result, the challenge of sustainability would no longer be posed merely in financial terms. Indeed, the sustainability of NGOs then would also include their intellectual and institutional contributions.

In essence, the future contributions of development NGOs are linked to their ability to deal with the dilemmas and challenges described above. The foundation for NGO action has historically been in advancing new practices and promoting creative solutions. The new millennium presents a qualitatively different set of opportunities and challenges for NGO action in broad field of social sector development development. With this background, the present review focuses on the theoretical aspects of the study of development NGOs in the larger context of Public Administration.

The Study of NGOs in the framework of Development Administration

'How does the study of development administration differ from the study of public administration in general, or even from the study of comparative administration? No clear answer to this question can be given...' (Riggs 1977). Traditionally the study of 'development administration' has been viewed as part of the study of public administration.

Development administration refers to the administration of development programmes, to the methods used by large-scale organizations, notably governments, to implement policies and plans designed to meet their development objectives. A second meaning associated with the term 'development administration' also involves the strengthening of administrative capabilities (Riggs 1977, 6). Thus the term 'development administration' refers to organised efforts to carry out programmes or projects thought by those involved to serve developmental objectives (Riggs 1977B, 73).

Development administration, like the public administration of which it is a part, is a subject matter in search of a discipline. There is no embracing theory of development administration, or of institution building. Indeed the term 'development administration is not conceptualised in any precise and generally accepted fashion. Siffin argues that the label identifies a loosely sensed interest, which exists because some people deem it important. Its significance does not depend upon a paradigm or a systematic array of theoretical knowledge. He further presents, true, many of our particular concerns with public administration's quest for good theory. It is equally true that there is no widespread agreement on the theoretical centre and boundaries of the field. There is more agreement on the premise that 'development administration' is part of the subject matter of public administration. (Siffin 1991, 6) Hussain (1994, 13-14) gives a comparative view of the claim that 'development administration is occasional ...' is arguable and cannot be theoretically justified.

The focus for an agenda of development administration ought to be very general question: How do administrative things work under conditions of uncertainty when the objective is to foster some sort of development? (Siffin 1991,11).Siffin, seems escapist about development administration, as in his view it is committed to involvement in matters outside the boundaries of conventional public administration. He describes, for example, the business of planning and managing rural development, a subject whose large and varied literature demonstrates the entwinement of administrative knowledge with applied science and information about particular socio-economic environments. There are also health delivery, family planning and population control, environmental protection, transportation and communications, and other matters of infrastructure development and maintenance. Administration is in intrinsic to all these fields, in addition to the old standbys of budgeting, personnel, and management. What a fascinating mess, all of it present (or absent) in a congeries of cultural and political settings! (Siffin 1991, 11-12) In addition to these presentations of large areas of development administration, he suggests to adopt a public policy prospective to simplify the complex formation of development administration.

Jreisat (1991, 19) further points out that satisfaction of these criteria requires informed application of conceptual frameworks to the real administrative processes and their effects on organisational performance. Reactions to the perceived shortcomings of comparative and development administration attempt to extol the advantages of one conceptual scheme or another to remedy deficiencies and improve the standing of the field with academicians as well as practitioners. Two orientations have been particularly prominent among recommendations that name substitutes, propose extensions, or suggest improvements of comparative / development administration.: program /project management, and policy analysis. (Jreisat 1991,20) In addition to these notes he also claims that comparative and development administration offers a rich heritage scholarly contributions that include studies of numerous countries, cultures, organisations, and groups. Public administration as a field of study is in the forefront of advocative values of participation, equality and justice in dispensing public policies and output to the society. Not only public development administration or comparative and development administration, but also other fields of social science are facing problems with their conceptual frameworks. Comparative and development administration concepts need validation and integration, governed by the quality and reliability of information used in the comparative organisational analysis.

Katz (1977, 120-121) has, rather, identified the borders between development administration and public administration. He argues the fact that development administration is similar to traditional public administration in its concern with how a government implements its rules, policies, and norms. In his opinion development administration differs in its objectives, scope and complexity from traditional public administration. According to him development administration is innovative since it is concerned with the societal changes involved in achieving developmental objectives. In its quest for change, the government becomes concerned with a wide scope of activities. No longer is it limited to the maintenance of law and order, the provision of some limited public services, and the collection of taxes; rather, it is specifically involved in the mobilisation of resources and their application to a great variety of development activities on a massive scale. Following from the greatly increased scope of activity are the widespread functional and structural differentiation of government and the consequent emergence of many interdependent, highly specialised activities which require a high degree of co-ordination'. The administrative functions of decision, specification, communication, and control may take different forms in development administration as compared with traditional public administration.' He also confirmed the idea that the feedback circuit is strong in development administration, whereas the feedback characteristics are weak or lacking in public administration.

NGOs in Development Studies

The pro-NGO literature tries to justify the idea that traditionally the NGOs were already rooted in different countries of Asia, Africa, Latin America, and other parts of the developing world.(e.g. Korten 1991, 26-29) But the academic world should understand that there is a high degree of difference between Mahatma Gandhi's good work for the poor in the 1920s and 1930s and the present–day donor-funded development NGOs. Modern – day donor sponsored development NGOs are very different from the traditional village self-help associations in Africa, and the mid-1960s Catholic Church in Latin America. No doubt, the good values of traditional philanthropic organisations were also adopted by the modern development NGOs. However, linking up the modern NGOs with traditional services confuses the development readers about the growth of this emerging sector, which began only around the 1970s in the developing world.

NGO studies in the development aid literature are comparatively recent, beginning mainly in the 1980s with its focus on the developing part of the world. On the other hand, public administration research was gradually losing interest in the concept of development administration in the 1980s. This is so, as already mentioned, because throughout the 1970s public administration was more aimed at 'administrative / local government reforms ' of national governments. Dating the 1980s public administration, as a discipline, was aiming more towards theorizing concepts like privatisation, public and private management, bureaucracy, public budgeting, aspects of public service, administrative ethics, and further some issues like intergovernmental relations (Shafritz & Hyde 1992, 455-550).

Therefore, as an independent discipline, public or development administration has very little focused on study of development NGOs. Until recently there has been a scarcity of administrative science research focused on development NGOs. The other approach of administrative science in studying NGOs, i.e., studies on 'non-profit' or 'third-sector' organisation perspectives in developing countries, the non-profit sector in developing countries is typically considerably more complex and diverse, but also far less understood. According to popular stereotypes in the West, philanthropy is essentially a Western phenomenon associated with the Judeo– Christian tradition and therefore far less prominent in other cultures or religious traditions. In fact, however, rich philanthropic traditions are evident in virtually every major religious culture – in the Islamic concept of Zakat, in the emphasis on voluntarism in pre-colonial India, in the charitable culture of Buddhist monasteries, and the Akan culture of western Africa (Salamon & Anheier 1996, 104.105)'. Despite the scope for scientific research in this area, research on the non-profit or third-sector has remained largely unaddressed.

As a matter of fact, the study of development administration 'refers to organised efforts to carry out programs or projects thought by those involved to serve development objectives (Riggs 1977B,73)' – and NGO research could have been very central to this broader scope of the science. The study of NGOs has direct relevance to Riggs's concept (1977, 87-95) of 'Social Organization and Development administration', although NGOs were absent from his domain of presentation. Both factors, i.e., the rise of NGOs and the fall of the concept of development administration in the 1980s, have created a gap to study the NGO sector from an administrative science perspective. Therefore, this generation of administrative science researchers has the scope to update the almost forgotten concept of development administration and strengthen NGO research in administrative science studies. The NGO concept possibly emerges as a strong component of development studies, but one might also see its relevance with other branches of administrative science such as development administration. In fact, in the present context, development administration deals with the processes in which public and non-profit organisations make their contribution (sometimes in a supplementary manner) to social change, modernisation and economic globalisation.

Conceptual Issues of NGOs in Social Development

Changing patterns of development co-operation: conceptualising Non-Governmental Organisations in Development

After the Second World War, Western governments have been strongly involved with development activities in developing countries. Initially these activities were mostly organised by the individual governments themselves, through their own governmental agencies or through the governments of the recipient countries. Alternatively the activities were organised through international intergovernmental organisations – like United Nations

Development Programme (UNDP), UNESCO, UNICEF, World Health Organisation (WHO), or the World Bank.

After the early years, characterised by what today can be called unrealistically high hopes and aspirations, it became gradually obvious that developmental activities are not easy to organise and manage. In many cases, developmental operations targeting the modernisation of the recipient countries proved to be much less effective than predicted. Instead of success, there were often unexpected setbacks, embarrassing mistakes, and failures. This, among other reasons, led Western countries to seek deeper understanding of developmental activities, and to seek better ways to organise and manage their developmental aid.

Changing patterns of Development Co-operation

Since 1970, many of the donor countries have organised the importance of certain types of non-governmental, no-profit –seeking organisations to development co-operation. In the new situation these organisations – widely called either non-governmental organisations (NGOs), private vouluntary organisations (PVOs), or non-profit organisations (NPOs) – are recognised as important 'new' partners in development activities. Instead of using only governmental agencies (i.e., public sector or public bureaucracies), on the one hand, and private, profit seeking corporations (private sector) on the other, many of the donor countries have started to rely more and more on these 'newly recognised', 'alternative', or 'third' types of (third sector) organisations. In development co-operation they are used in various different ways, to fulfil numerous separate functions (Korten 1990, Part 3; Carroll 1992, CH .1). Sometimes they are used as go-betweens to channel funds from donor governments and countries to local individuals, groups, or organisations working in the recipient countries; and sometimes, they are used as local or international operators through which developmental activities are launched and carried out even at the grassroots level.

Due to the increasing recognition and use of non-governmental, not-for – profit organisations as important partners in development co-operation, the international scene of Third World development administration has faced several important changes. From the organisational or institutional point of view the new situation can be characterised by three closely linked developments: (1) increasing institutional fragmentation, (2) increasing functional specialisation, and (3) increasing organisational interdependency between the various institutional actors. Moreover, from the managerial or administrative point of view, the changing situation can be characterised by (1) an increasing need to achieve co-operation among the different organisations, (2) increasing complexity in organising (or achieving) this co-operation, and as a result (3) increasing stress on a new managerial concept: management of co-operation among organisational networks.

Increasing institutional fragmentation is caused mainly by the increasing number of organisations working in the field of Third World development. Many of these, especially among the 'new' organisations, are small and voluntary. And many of them are working at the grassroots level either in donor countries, to collect support and funds, or in recipient countries – for example to initiate, organise or fund a certain special type of developmental activities (i.e., to work as catalyst, organiser, or funder) or to provide services (to work as a service provider). Sometimes a clear conceptual division is made between non-governmental, not-for-profit organisations working within the donor countries, called Northern NGOs, and NGOs based in the recipient countries, called Southern NGOs (Smillie 1993).

The second development trend, increasing functional specialization, is caused by the changing division of labour between different organisational actors. The fact that many of the 'newly recognised', 'alternative' organisations are small, means that in most cases they are not able and, often, are not even attempting to solve large – scale developmental problems. Instead, they are concentrating their efforts on more specific and more reachable tasks and goals. Instead of serving 'everyone', or doing 'everything', they are trying to specialise in serving certain more specific (i.e, narrower) target groups or in solving certain more specific problems. From the institutional point of view, this means that the division of labour between different institutional actors is now more complex and more fine-grained than earlier. This situation is furthermore complicated by the fact that along with the funds received from governments, most non-governmental and not-for-profit organisations are expected to seek also other sources for funds. Consequently also their funding arrangements and fiscal responsibilities have changed to become more complex.

Along with institutional fragmentation and functional specialisation, the third important developmental trend is the increasing organisational interdependency between the various institutional actors. Due to the two already mentioned trends, developmental activities are increasingly organised and managed not inside one or two organisations or inside a clearly defined, simple chain of organisations, but through a complex network of organisations, all fulfilling their special tasks and functions. In this type of situation the success or failure of the development activities is more and more often determined, not by the success or failure of an individual organisation, but by the success or failure in getting these different organisations – with their individual interests and needs – to work together in productive and coherent ways, by working together, small, specialised, voluntary organisations are able to overcome many of their individual limitations (e.g. of size and funds) and to achieve better results.

Problems with current knowledge

Even though the role and impact of the non-governmental, not-for-profit organisations in developmental work is increasingly recognised (Rice 1983; and Masoni 1985), and even though the research interest towards them is continuously increasing[1], the theoretical knowledge concerning the nature and role of these organisations is still not yet well developed. As pointed out by several previous scholars (e.g. Anheier 1990), the literature is full of questionable beliefs and doubtful generalisations concerning the potential merit, role and impact of these new organisations as compared to the traditional governmental agencies or private corporations.

Furthermore, what seems to be even more troublesome is the lack of theoretical interest, to study, in a comprehensive and systematic way, these organisations, their various types, functions and rationality, their networks, and their complex interactions within themselves and with other organisations working in the field of Third World development. This type of research should be based both on theoretical thinking and empirical analyses.

Although several important steps toward a more comprehensive and more theoretically motivated knowledge have recently been taken (e.g. Anheier 1990; Korten 1990; Carroll 1992; and Smillie, 1995), the current state of knowledge is still far from satisfactory. More effort is needed to:

- collect both empirical and theoretical information on NGOs,
- systematise and scrutinise this information,
- find its strengths and weaknesses and fill the gaps,
- theorise, i.e., to create frameworks, models, and hypotheses based on the available information,
- evaluate and test this emerging knowledge and
- refine the theories, models, and frameworks so as to gain an even greater theoretical understanding of the subject matter.

Without more profound efforts towards theoretically oriented, systematic and comprehensive research, there is no reason to expect any dramatic change in the current lack of theoretical knowledge concerning NGOs in Third World development. And without this knowledge it is more

total clarity of language is probably impossible to achieve, at least we may be able to increase our intentional control over these problems and thus keep them at a more acceptable level (Malkia 1994, ch3;or 997,ch,3, Riggs,Malkia & Budin 1997; Riggs 1979; 1986;1990;1991;1993; Satori, Riggs & Teune 1975; and Sartori 1984).

Secondly, we need better conceptual tools (i.e., better conceptualisations) to clarify the nature, types and roles of the various organisational actors and their networks, and interactions in the field of Third World development. We believe that this should be the first step towards creating better theoretical understanding (i.e., better theorising of the issues in question and in future to create better knowledge that would help us to manage the different developmental activities and to facilitate the organisational networks of Third World development in more effective and more productive ways.

And thirdly, we need also better terms (i.e., better linguistic designations to identify the various concepts required to describe the situation. Without better terms we are unable to maintain and communicate the important distinctions between different organisational actors and their distinctive roles in developmental activities. More understandable, unambiguous, and transparent terms are required in order to communicate our better understanding of the issues to others, thus increasing the possibilities for more structured exchange of ideas, and the possibilities for the growth of knowledge in the area of Third World development.

In the present section, the discussion on non-governmental, so called not-for –profit organisations or NGOs is so important to the current scenario of Third World development, including the basic arguments for the use of NGOs in Third World development co-operation.

The importance of NGOs

One of the major reasons for the increasing use of NGOs in developmental activities is to find an alternative and better channel for development aid in Third World countries. The aim of this review is to pluralise the actors or stakeholders involved in the developmental activities so that the 'poorest of the poor' could be reached more effectively, bypassing the oligarchic state structure of most of the developing countries. Thus disappointment with, and crticism of public sector performance, in both donor and recipient countries, has had an important impact on this development. From a more general perspective, the issue is also related to the continuously declining environment of Third World development, characterised by recurrent economic crises, population growth, environmental degradation, poor agricultural and industrial production, growing corruption, bureaucratic complexities, inadequate policies, lack of democratic exercise in domestic policies, and the politics of debt crisis in developing countries. As a reaction to this general context, the western donor countries and agencies are seeking better ways to implement their policies by considering the comparative advantages and disadvantages of the organisations that are involved in this process.

As already pointed out disappointment with public sector performance has played an important role in recent developments. While public sector activities continue to be heavily criticised for having contributed much to the present problematic situation in many developing countries, NGOs are receiving much credit and gaining a greater status in development work. Whereas disappointment with official government programs and projects are growing, the non-governmental, not-for-profit organisations have gained such prominence that development transfers through these types of organisations have become more or less obvious, from the donors' point of view (Anheier 1990). For example, in Norway, in the beginning of 1990's the share of bilateral aid to NGOs was 25 percent, with the percentage continuing to increase (Tvedt 1995). In the United States the government has announced that in future it is going to channel about 40 percent of its development assistance through NGOs (United Nations 1995). And, according to a recent calculation (Fowler 1992), the value of total resources from NGOs to Third World countries account for about 15 percent of total overseas development assistance.

In contrast to official development agencies, the non-governmental organisations are believed to have fewer overhead costs, to rely less on bureaucratic procedures, and to be less subject to political constraints (Anheier 1990). Furthermore, it is believed that the NGO led projects are innovative, participatory, flexible, better directed, and more reflective needs of the poor in Third World Societies.

Main Arguments in Favour of NGOs

In his impressive and thorough analysis, Helmut Anheier (1990) argues that there are actually four basic arguments in favour of comparative advantage of NGOs in Third World Development. These are social, economic, political and cultural arguments:

The Social argument comprises the idea that NGOs try to simulate the participation of the poor and are able to reach those strata of disadvantaged Third World Societies that are bypassed by public service delivery systems. This argument attaches greater social equity to private voluntary efforts than to the public sector. Because of shortage of public funds combined with cultural and social access problems, disadvantaged populations are difficult to reach by conventional service systems – a problem which is amplified by elite influences on governmental decision making. Thus NGOs are in a better position to reach the poor and the disadvantaged.

The economic argument claims that NGOs are able to carry out services more economically than governments. In addition, as they are not seeking profits out of their actions, they usually aim at self-reliance and self-sufficiency. Just as the social argument refers to equity, the economic argument addresses the greater efficiency of NGOs. Their efficiency could be a guarantee of their operational sustainability and credibility to the donors. Greater efficiency of NGOs is largely based on a major cost advantage, which is related to both labour costs and incomplete pricing that is not making provision for depreciation, relying on voluntary local inputs, not including transaction costs, etc. Moreover according to this type of argument, failures with NGO led projects (as compared to failures with government led ones) have much less impact on the economy as a whole, since nearly all NGO led development projects are designed and implemented at the micro level. Governments, on the other hand, are often working at the macro level.

The political argument suggests that NGOs are relatively immune from changing political tides, while government policies and agencies are subject to unexpected change. An extension of the political argument refers to the 'hidden agenda' and ultimately political motivation of official development assistance if we consider aid as a political tool in global politics. By using NGOs as local and international operators, the problems with hidden agendas can be better dealt with. Thus, in general, NGOs are believed to be more 'honest' and less guided by political considerations.

Finally, the cultural argument stipulates that NGOs, embedded in the local culture, are more sensitive to local needs and their articulation. Rather than replacing indigenous social structures by large-scale organisations, NGOs try to nurture local organisations within their own cultural context.

Even though many of the above mentioned arguments are often repeated in the recent NGO-and development aid literature, it should be stressed that there is actually very little or no clear or systematic empirical evidence for or against these claims. Case by case, some of these claims may be true or some of them may be false. But mostly they are based purely on general assumptions, expectations, feelings and beliefs. This lack of systematic evidence has also been recognised more and more often in the recent literature (Anheier 1990; UNDP 1993).

Typical Conceptions: NGOs as a residual category

Even though the developmental literature is full of general discussions about the 'emerging' new non-governmental and not-for-profit organisations, there are actually surprisingly few signs of any clear conceptual thinking and agreement of about what these organisations are really about, or how they should be defined (Anheier 1990, David Korten 1990, Ian Smillie 1993, 1995).

To sum up the current scholarly thinking, one can argue that in most cases the theoretical conceptions that are used to conceptualise these emerging new organisations are not well developed. Typical conceptions are based on questionable dichotomies and scrutinised assumptions about the differences between the so - called public and private sectors and their distinctive organisations; or sometimes between public, private and collective (i.e., third) sectors or organisations.

What seems to be most often agreed upon in the developmental literature is, that when we are talking about 'non-governmental', 'private voluntary', 'non-profit', or 'third sector' organisations, we are talking about developmental organisations which on the one hand are not governmental-meaning that they are not 'traditional' government agencies - and which, on the other hand, are not private, profit seeking corporations. An important point here is the fact that from this perspective the non-governmental, not-for-profit organisations are conceptualised not by what they are, but by what they are not. Thus, for most authors these organisations are just a residual category of organisations or a black box somewhere between – or somehow distinct from – 'traditional' governmental agencies (public 'bureaucracies') and private, profit –seeking corporations (profit maximisers). The most obvious problem with description is that this general category of organisations is by definition extremely broad. Besides voluntary, grassroots organisations – which are often understood as some kind of core group of or an archetype for NGOs – it may include organisations like private, not-for-profit schools and hospitals, and International humanitarian organisations (Save The Children), help and relief organisations like (The Red Cross, CARE), various types of membership associations, co-operatives and self-help organisations, and sometimes even organisations like labour unions, political parties, religious sects, and churches.

Furthermore, when the descriptors 'non-governmental', 'private, voluntary', 'not-for-profit', are scrutinised, it can also be said that too often the extension and the intention of the concept remains to be further unclear. Thus the borders of the concept remain open in both empirical and theoretical terms.

The next sections describe briefly some of the problems related to the descriptors 'non-governmental', 'private voluntary', and 'third sector'. Following which, more complex empirical and theoretical classifications and typologies of different types and subtypes of NGOs are emphasised on to the review.

NGOs as 'Non-Governmental' organizations

When the descriptions 'non-governmental' or 'non-governmental organisations' are used, the emphasis is on the difference between governmental and non-governmental sectors, organisations and activities. The hidden implication is that the core identity for the emerging, new organisations is their being separate from the 'government', 'governmental' or 'governmental agencies'.

Given that the term 'non- governmental' defines a residual category – in the broadest sense all organisations that are not considered as, 'governmental'-it is not surprising that a wide variety of organisations can be so classified. Thus there are actually several different areas (or breaking points) where the description 'non- governmental' may cause uncertainty, and lead leaders in a wrong on unintended direction.

When we think about the extension of the concept 'non- governmental', how should we consider for example private firms, foundations, and governmental corporations and what about intergovernmental organisations, organisations belonging indirectly to public administration, or quasi - non-governmental organisations (i.e., quangos)? should these organisations be classified as 'non- governmental', 'governmental', or what? And what about the intention of the concept: what are the specific attributes that define various organisations as either 'governmental' or 'non- governmental'? Is it there economic, legal, political, or administrative independence from the government that makes these organisations non- governmental? Or is it something else? – In the literature these types of questions are sometimes asked, but hardly ever answered.

To take just one concrete example, in both ordinary language usage and in most organisation theory literature, private, for-profit-organisations are often considered as part of 'non- governmental' organisations. However, in developmental literature this is hardly ever the case. We believe that this is based mainly on historical reasons : In the developmental context, non-governmental organisations are typically understood not as a second category between governmental and non governmental, but rather as a third category of organisations between the public and private, between the government and corporate, or more lately between State and market.

The historical development leading to this somewhat strange conception can be easily understood: as directly indicated, in the early days of official development co-operation, governmentally funded development projects were usually implemented by the governments in Third World countries. When modern non- governmental, not-for-profit organisations emerged and started to gain wider recognition, they were understood as important alternatives to government- based developmental activities. In this situation, the developmental activists started to call these new alternatives 'non-governmental'. The apparent attention was to stress the difference between the 'traditional', increasingly criticised government- run developmental work and the emerging, new organisational forms.

At first this categorisation was probably quite useful, especially in order to promote the use of these new organisations (cf. Brown 1990). The indication was that the new NGOs are everything that governmental agencies were not: they are effective, non-bureaucratic, flexible, innovative, non-corrupted, non-politicised, participatory and more reflective of the needs of the poor. This is also about how NGOs and NGO activist mostly see themselves (David Brown, 1990). Thus in the context of Third World development the term 'non- governmental organisation' became accepted as a proper and useful description for this emerging group of organisations.

Later on, as the diversity and complexity of the NGO field became more obvious, and when problems related with this initial dichotomic conception became understood, it was already too late to change the language. The term NGO was already accepted as a true description of the new type of organisation.

NGOs as 'Private Voluntary' Organizations (PVOs)

Another way to conceptualise the core meaning of the 'emerging', 'new' non- governmental and not-for-profit organisations in the context of Third World development is to understand them as private voluntary organizations (PVOs). This conceptualisation is common in the U.S.A., where the term PVO is used largely as a synonym for NGO (e.g. Korten 1990, 2; Smillie 1995, 22).

When the description 'private voluntary' is used, the emphasis is first on the fact that we are thinking about private instead of public sector organisations. As there are apparently several types of private sector organisations, the qualifier 'voluntary' is used in order to differentiate the intended category from other types of private organisations.

From the theoretical point of view, this conceptualisation may at first seem to be useful. At least, the target is now positively intended and not

the private, for – profit world and the government. This intermediary organisational universe is comprised of 'Third Sector' organizations (Anheier). In recent research works, both terms 'Third sector' organisations and NPOs have benn used as synonymous within the broad spectrum of 'Third Sector', where all these 'emerging' NGOs and NPOs could fit.

However, Norman Uphoff (1996) argues that NGOs should not be understood as 'Third Sector' organisations. This statement is based on the clear distinction between NGOs or PVOs, on the other hand, and people's associations, membership organisations and cooperatives, on the other. According to Uphoff, NGOs are service organisations belonging rather to the private than to the third sector as indicated by Anheier. For Uphoff, third sector refers to people's association, membership organisations, and cooperatives. For him the defining criterion is their being organisations engaged in serving their members.

NGOs on the other hand, are not – for – profit oriented service organisations, belonging to the private sector. Rather than members, they are serving clients or beneficiaries. And the persons receiving their services have no formal power or influence on deciding the goals, operative patterns, or administrative arrangements of these organisations. Thus the difference between them being clients of non-profit service organisation or customers for private enterprise is not significant. The clients and beneficiaries of NGOs are in a ' take it or leave it' relationship similar to that of customers and employees of private firms. For him this relationship is fundamentally different from that of persons who belong to and are served by a membership organisation or co-operative (Uphoff).

Based on the above discussions, these 'emerging', 'new' NGOs and NPOs as named as third sector may be considered problematic. At the same time, we have seen that there is a strong-need to develop more differentiated conceptions of these different organisations.

Towards more differentiated conceptions

An even more important problem than the question whether these new organisations should be conceptualised as NGOs, PVOs, NPOs or as third sector, is the lack of conceptual clarity about the different types of 'emerging' development organisations. Among these organisations there is a wide variety of differences in their origins, interests, activities, clients and beneficiaries, financial arrangements, management -patterns, work strategies, operational procedures, and working environments (etc.). In this type of context we need more differentiated conceptions of different types of development-oriented organisations, their roles, functions, and rationalities, their networks, and their complex interactions within themselves and with other organisations working in the fields of Third World development.

By identifying different types of organisations as NGOs or NPOs the conceptual systems fail to reflect the complexity of the world to be described and understood. Instead of analysing different types of NGOs or NPOs, with different functions and different roles in the functioning of the system, we are too often trying to analyse the world of Third World development by using broad conceptual categories, like NGOs as if all 'non-governmental' organisations would be the same, or even similar. Thus, instead of speaking about various types of trees, bushes, shrubs and plants in a forest and their roles and functions in the forest ecosystem, we are seeing and discussing only about the forest itself. Even if sometimes it may theoretically justified and meaningful to map issues at this high level of abstraction, more often than not the map will be just too abstract and general to give any deeper insights or guidance for people attempting to understand the Third World development scene.

In recent years in development aid literature there have been several initial attempts towards establishing more differentiated concepts. Among others, the most visible of them have been David Korten (1990) and Norman Uphoff (1996).

In this attempt to understand the complexities of NGO action in developing countries, David Korten (1990), has identified four generations of NGO strategies based on the changing role of NGO development. According to Korten, the first generation of NGO strategies is called relief and welfare strategies, are based on NGOs giving emergency assistance to local populations in the case of natural calamities. NGOs engaged in this kind of action are doers and main actors to solve the needs. Thus the focus is on giving relief to individuals or families in need and helping them to recover. When this is done relief based NGOs will change their locations and seek new beneficiaries or clients in need of similar help. The second generation of NGO strategies is based on NGOs arranging small-scale community development projects for neighborhoods or villages. As compared to first generation strategies, this type of strategies is based more on development orientation, but the projects are understood has having a short term life span. Thus the management orientation is project management, and the chief actors are NGOs along with the local community. Here the focus is on the capacity of the NGOs on developing the capability of the people to better meet their own needs through self-reliant local action.

The third generation of NGO strategies is based on sustainable systems development and has a longer time perspective. The time frame varies from 10 to 20 years, and the scope of the project is expanded to a region or nation. These strategies look beyond the individual community and seek changes in specific policies and institutions at local, national and global levels. The chief actors are all the relevant public and private institutions. The role of the NGO is as a catalyst, and the management orientation is strategic management.

The fourth generation of NGO strategies is based on people's movements, which have an indefinite time frame. The scope is national or global and the actors are loosely defined networks of people and organisations. The management orientation is coalescing and energising self-managing networks. Inside these networks different organisations have different roles to play in the development process in developing countries.

However, universal application of Korten's above analysis of four generations of NGO strategies is not absolutely relevant to the NGO reality in the developing countries, and therefore could prove to be wrong. For example, his perception about the fourth generation NGOs may be challenged, In fact, a large number of NGOs in developing countries are the other way round. They are not revolutionary, rather are market oriented. The relevance of Korten's analysis depends on the particular geopolitical and socio-economic structure of a given country.

According to Korten, all of these four generations of NGO strategies and NGOs engaged in them continuingly co-exist in the contemporary development scene. It is easy to understand that there is a bewildering variety of different NGOs that have little or nothing in common with one another.

Strategies of Development – Oriented NGOs: Four Generations (Korten, 1990)

	GENERATION			
	FIRST Relief and Welfare	***SECOND Community Development***	***THIRD Sustainable Systems Development***	***FOURTH Peoples' Movements***
Problem Definition	Shortage	Local Inertia	Institutional and Policy Constraints	Inadequate Mobilising Vision
Time Frame:	Immediate	Project Life	Ten to twenty years	Indefinite future
Scope:	Individual or Family	Neighbourhood or village	Region or nation	National or Global

(*Contd...*)

Chief Actors:	NGO	NGO plus Community	All relevant public and private Institutions	Loosely Defined Networks of People and Organisations
NGO Role:	Doer	Mobilser	Catalyst	Activist/Educator
Management Orientation	Logistics Management	Project Management	Stategic Management	Coalescing and Energising Self-Management Networks
Development Education :	Starving Children	Community Self-help	Constraining Policies and Institutions	Spaceship Earth

(1) Voluntary Organisations (VOs) that pursue a social mission driven by a commitment to shared values.

(2) Public service contractors (PSCs) that function as a market oriented no-profit business serving public purposes

(3) Peoples' Organisations (POs) that represents their member's interest, have member accountable leadership and are substantially self-reliant.

(4) Governmental non-governmental Organisations (GONGOs) that are creations of government and serve as instruments of government policy.

(5) Corporate bodies: Many development NGOs have turned into corporate bodies and gradually shifted their focus from social development to market operations. In fact, these NGOs are making their effort to raise income.

Identifying the various roles, or, functions of NGOs in development could, also generate more systematic classifications. This is done, for example, when some scholars make a difference between Northern and Southern NGOs. These two types of NGOs play a very different role in development. Usually the Northern NGOs (NNGOs) are described as partners or donors to southern NGOs (SNGOs); SNGOs are seen mainly as local action organisations, and thus more grassroots based than NNGOs (Smillie & Helmich, 1993). If this is the case, then the difference between these two types of NGOs is basically the difference between top-down and bottom-up approaches in development. On the other hand, this may not always be true. Some of the NNGOs may have even more grassroots approaches than some 'opportunistic' SNGOs. Thus the grassroots affiliation depends on NGOs and their relationship with target groups irrespective of their origin.

It should be mentioned here that the working definition of NGOs in this study is non-profit-oriented NGDOs which seeks to empower poor people through provision of health and social service activities, strengthen democracy, protect human rights, ensure pluralism, bring gender balance in social development, and improve environmental standards incorporating sustainable implementation strategies.

Dynamics or Drawbacks - The Basis of NGO Research

It has been discussed earlier that despite claims about the advantages and disadvantages of the role of NGOs in development, the academic literature on these issues remains limited, narrowly focussed and full of unjustified generalisations. However, documenting the comparative advantage or disadvantage of NGOs plays a crucial role in development management. If NGOs are failing to achieve better performance in their development initiatives, or if they suffer from those of shortcomings like government - led development initiatives – where is the justification to involve NGOs in development? Do NGOs have better administrative capacity than the government agencies in the South? Are their projects sustainable enough in order to face the future challenges of the developing world? —No single answer to these questions would be easy to find and generalise. The heterogeneous nature of the special sector of NPOs also makes it more difficult to generalise the achieved findings of any specific research. However, research on these issues has vital importance. Similarly, it is also important to study systematically the impact and relevance of NGO operations, specifically in different countries and studies should target the social, economic and cultural context of the beneficiaries in developing countries.

NGO dynamics in development management have been discussed in a previous part of the study. Discussions in this part cover the drawbacks of the NGO sector as identified by different scholars. The section also tries to analyse the relevance of NGOs in development management, their administrative capacity and sustainability of their projects.

Drawbacks of NGOs: notes from the existing literature

It has been said that the wisdom of the comparative advantage of NGOs is now under question for various reasons. Among the most obvious ones for this have been observations that previous understanding of the roles and relative advantages of NGOs have been sharply challenged: They are not necessarily more effective or efficient than official channels. It has been argued that, the cost of NGO operations have been under reported and the real volume of resource flows through NGOs are not known. NGOs do not necessarily reach the poor and meet their needs at the grassroots level any better than the official assistance (Vuorela, Airaksinen & Ulvila 1996). About the cost-effectiveness of NGO operations, it has been claimed and argued that basically at the project level the cost of NGO operations is much higher than the government's (Aminizzaman, 1997). The relationships between official and NGO channel in development cooperation are also undergoing rigorous changes. The NGOs retain their interests in remaining different and autonomous. Questions about coordinations, complementarity, and relative autonomy of the NGO field with regard to the State, and the market are central issues to be addressed both from the perspectives of the North and the South, donors and the recipients alike (Vuorela, Airaksinen & Ulvila, 1996).

NGOs merit attention because of the light that they can throw on weaknesses of the State and the market as mechanisms for meeting the need of society (Hulme, 1994). This statement becomes relevant in the case of Third World countries due to their existence as weak States, with their scarcity of services for the larger population. It has been claimed that these organisations try to stimulate the participation of the poor and try to reach those strata of the Third World societies that are bypassed by the public service delivery systems (Anheier, 1990). On the contrary, the NGO reality in development countries suggests that most of the NGOs are headed by middle class and upper middle class educated people or by the local elite. This phenomenon is common also in Africa (Anheier, 1990). Often unemployed educated youth establishes NGOs in order to be employed and they certainly have also the right to do that. With their nationality these Southern NGO (SNGO) leaders might represent their society; but considering their economic and social position in Southern societies, they do not necessarily represent the disadvantaged rural poor or the poorer segment of the society. However, these SNGOs are at the heart of voluntary sector development activities. They are the operational, catalytic and indigenous units of NNGOs at national or regional levels in the South. Basically they implement projects, promote and support membership organisations (MOs) or clients and lobby national governments (Hulme, 1994). These SNGOs are the most important intermediary actors between NNGOs and MOs. Thus the wisdom pf employing NGOs in development-work very much depend on the nature of SNGOs. The 'opportunistic' charesteristic of the educated, unemployed middle or upper middle-class and often the Southern elite- class indicate that this sector has become an alternative source of employment. When the State capacity to offer public positions has reduced significantly due to the reduction of public services, this sector has really employed a large number of Southern job seekers (Hulme, 1994).

leading or executive members. The participation of women is very often ignored, which may raise questions about gender equality in organisations. Therefore, in many cases it looks odd that these organisations are building awareness in equality, gender–equality, participation, democratic exercise, empowerment etc. in Southern countries but it seems to be the case that they do not practice it themselves. For example, NGOs often advocate participation and local capacity development but failed to translate this into action. The result is low levels of participation of intended beneficiaries in project planning, implementation and evaluation because of their lack of skills, unwillingness to surrender power and resources. Usually, at a central level and 'executive board' consisting of a few members selected (often understood as elected) by a few more members, which designs, plans, and implements the whole process of the organisation. Therefore, the target group does not feel attached to the activities of the organisation. Often they consider NGOs a source from which to receive services or benefits. Yet participation must be seen as an exercise of giving the rural poor means to have a direct involvement in development projects (Oakley & Marsden 1990). The IIRR also states that most of the NGOs exercise leadership without basic management skills. Very often the organisational structure is weak with the problems of unclear role, weak administration and poor communication. They put emphasis on rapid responses rather than long-term solutions. Another limitation of their organisational culture is the 'founder's traps', especially in recently founded organisations. Founders may be unwilling to surrender control over the organisation. Activities are structured around strong personalities instead of organisational functions. So the donor's target to reach the 'pooerst' by involving NGOs and by bypassing the Southern government does not always work. Southern governments also follow the recent trend of forming the government – organised NGOs (GONGOs) as a substitute for real NGOs. For example the wife or daughter of any influential minister could chair the National Women's Association of a certain country or the relatives of the regional governors could chair regional organisations. At the same time donors – NGOs (DONGOs) have also been created in many Southern societies (Brown and Korten 1991).

The conventional belief stipulates that NGOs, embedded in the local culture, are more sensitive to the local needs and their articulation. Rather than replacing indigenous social structures by large-scale organisations, NGOs try to nurture local organisations within their own cultural context (Anehier, 1990). The NGO sector has a wealth of knowledge about the nature and operations of local elites, about strategies for by-passing, weakening, co-opting or coping with elites, and about the responses of those elites to such strategies (Hulme, 1994). These arguments might be true in the case of indigenous organisations but in case of foreign or international NGOs sometimes the Southern authorities could be very suspicious. At the same time the above – mentioned arguments might not be relevant in case of religious (i.e. Christian, Muslim, etc.) NGOs, whose primary mission is to preach their own religion philosophy to the target group. In this context, their might be a need to differentiate between religious missions in which the workers' main motivation is that their religion teaches them to serve the poor, feed the hungry, etc. The lack of ability to differentiate between these two sorts of motivations often causes misunderstandings to arise among ordinary policy-makers in different societies. However, the development activities might become a secondary priority to some religious organisations. The entrepreneurship for non-profit provision of education, health care and social services historically, has come from religious (or other ideological groups). It is important to note that, service-providing non-profits are typically not motivated by individual entrepreneurs, but by religious or other ideologically motivated organisations; by providing education, health, and other vital social services, they hope to maximise faith and adherents rather than profits (James 1990). Sometimes, foreign religious organisations may bring confusion and conflicts in their work with local societies in developing countries. Such confusion and conflicts are often visible in Bangladesh, Nepal and India in the region of South Asia.

Future Issues: Popular notion on NGOs in Development

Several issues have been receiving attention in seminars and conferences on NGOs organised by different donors, NGOs and research institutes including universities in developing countries. Some of them remain unanswered – It is also difficult to get academic understanding from popular debates and discussions. Academic research may contribute to a proper understanding of these following discussed issues:

Direct foreign funding to local initiatives- it is argued that direct funding usually from the embassies is a violation of diplomatic norms and values and may contain political risks to the governments in developing countries. Also the movement – oriented organisations claim that direct funding may destroy the commitment of their work and it has a direct effect on their workers. Research on this issues, may generate well-founded academic knowledge.

Accountability of NGOs- this has been a leading issue in different popular debates and discussions. Due to financial dependency on foreign donors, the NGO sector has a degree of loyalty and accountability to their foreign funding agencies. This loyalty or accountability often confuses the governments in developing countries, as these organisations perform responsibilities that are also the domain of the public sector. It has also been difficult for the governments in developing countries to establish an effective mechanism to make these organisations accountable to the government. The mismanagement in keeping the office record of NGOs and stated that 'the records are not kept for use in the local office, but to justify themselves to head office, and ultimately to demonstrate accountability to donors'. This practice 'reflects tensions between different levels of NGO management and the funding and operating NGOs. While the terminology is of partnership, the equality and mutual trust, which this implies are a great deal harder to achieve within hierarchical organisations or funding relationships. Progress towards fuller partnership would seem to be an important corollary of more satisfactory forms of record-keeping being instituted'. The area needs further academic understanding in developing countries and also in donor countries.

The NGO-Government relation- is another area where academic research may contribute a lot. There have been a few studies done on the theme, but such studies need further continuation – since the nature of the NGO sector changes rapidly and from time to time governments also change in development countries. For example, the involvement of NGOs in credit business, house-building finance, banking, etc. needs to be documented properly and their mode of partnership with the public and private sector also need to be addressed by academic research.

NGO-local government relations- this is taking collaborative form in some places in some developing countries. With NGO support in technology, marketing and management, rural local government institutions and municipalities are making good progress in implementing a number of projects in areas such as social forestry, environment, fishery, health and sanitation and alternative dispute resolution. In some places, NGOs have succeeded in imparting management development training and social awareness programmes for the local government councillors, officials and extension workers.

Voluntary vs. Professionalism – this aspect is also a leading dilemma in the NGO community. Career oriented professionals seem to be better performing in NGO operations and the idealistic volunteers are found to be weak in their managerial practices. Therefore, in recent development management the NGO sector has a dilemma with better performing highly paid professionals and low performing idealistic good volunteers. The well functioning NGOs often employ graduates and ignore the volunteers in project management. Thus the sector is also having the nature of recruiting professionals like other private and public agencies. Many argue that the NGOs should reorient their philanthropic base. Study on this issue may contribute new dimensions to community projects managed by voluntary organisations or NGOs.

Politics vs. development - - this could be one important domain of academic research. Usually, NGOs justify their operations as anti-poverty organisations. Several decades have already passed but the said global poverty scenario has not improved. For example Bangladeshi Grameen Bank's micro-credit programme has been appreciated by international donors and replicated in many developing countries. But the majority of the Bangladeshi population remains largely poor. As a result, NGOs are also seen as a tool of modernisation in developing countries – that create a market for Western products. Another giant NGO, Proshika, has recently launched their new enterprise for marketing water purification equipment in collaboration with a Canadian company. In traditional villages in Nepal, fresh water streams have been flowing from generations ago and satisfying the villager's thirst, but in these days people are being acquainted with mineral water, Coca Cola, Pepsi, etc. which add a new taste to life- at the same time they also add a new degree of complexity in village life. Empirical research on the impact of modernisation and the role of NGOs could discover well-grounded knowledge on the politics of development aid.

Cost-effectiveness of NGO operations – this is of vital importance to the relevance of NGO management. Surprisingly, very little research has been done on the issues of NGOs' cost effectiveness compare to the government agencies. Neither NGOs nor the pro-NGO agencies would probably do such research – thus there is a great need to accomplish such study.

NGOs in Globalisation – The role of NGOs in the modern globalised world are questioned from different aspects. The NGO sector in general is facing many challenges in development initiatives. The future key issues, implications and challenges of this special sector of NGOs in development projects in developing countries are;

(a) Coming, out of the shadows;

(b) Establishing, legitimacy

(c) Establishing, meaningful collaborative relationships between NGOs and the State, both in the North and the South, going beyond the paradigm of conflict;

(Smillie and Helmich, 1993), and over the same period the total spending of these NGOs has risen from US$2.8 billion to US$5.7 billion in current prices (OBCD, 1994). The 176 International NGOs' of 1909 had blossomed into 28 900 by 1993 (Commission on Global Governance, 1995)! Similar figures have been reported in many countries in the 'South' with a particularly rapid increase over the last five years. For example, the number of NGOs registered with the government in Nepal rose from 220 in 1990 to 1210 in 1993 (Rademacher and Tamang, 1993-94); in Bolivia the figure increased from around 100 in 1980 to 530 twelve years later (Arellano-Lopez and Petras, 1994:562): and in Tunisia there were 5186 NGOs registered in 1991 compared with only 1886 in 1998 (Marzouk).

Parallel to this increase in overall numbers has been the growth of some individual NGOs to cover the provision of health, education and credit services to millions of people in thousands of communities, especially in South Asia. For example, the Bangladesh Rural Advancement Committee (BRAC) now has more than 12 000 staff and has plans to work with over three million people (AKF/NOVIB, 1993) – it operates a field office in East Africa; in India, the Self-Employed Women's Association (SEWA) has over one million clients in its credit programs; Sarvodaya in Sri Lanka works in 7000 villages (Perera). The access of NGOs to decision-makers in both North and South is greater than ever before, as their advocacy role continues to expand and they are courted in debates over policy and practice. Grassroots organizations (GROs) have a lower public profile, but they have also experienced considerable growth over the last decade and are beginning to recognize themselves much more at the national and international levels (Korten, 1990; CIVICUS, 1994). Clearly, something significant is happening in the world of international development.

Beyond these figures the public image of NGOs and GROs has amplified in recent years. Their high visibility at the 1992 UN Earth Summit at Rio was eclipsed by events at Beijing in 1995 where the NGOs forum got greater news coverage than the official UN Women's Conference. For the general public in countries such as the UK development is what OXFAM, CARE-International, Save the Children Fund and the like do – who has ever heard of the Overseas Development Administration? On the television when a snatch of development or relief footage is required it is an NGO project we see, a tired Concern or *Medecin Sans Frontieres* worker who tells us what is happening or a small-scale project which is used to illustrate 'successful development.

The rise of NGOs and GROs on the world scene is an important phenomenon, which has implications for the development prospects of poor people, for the future of these organizations themselves, and for the wider political economy of which they form a small but growing part. But what lies behind these trends? The rise of NGOs is not an accident; nor is it solely a response to local initiative and voluntary action. Equally important is the increasing popularity of NGOs with governments and official aid agencies, which is itself a response to recent developments in economic and political thinking. Over the last fifteen years and particularly since the end of the Cold War, development policy and aid transfers have come to be dominated by what Robinson (1993) calls a 'New Policy Agenda'. This Agenda is not monolithic: its details vary from one official aid agency to another, but in all cases it is driven by beliefs organized around the twin poles of neo-liberal economics democratic theory (Moore, 1993).

First, markets and private initiative are seen as the most efficient mechanisms for achieving economic growth and providing most services to most people (Colclough and Manor, 1991). Government 'enable' private provision but should minimize their direct role in the economy; because of their supposed cost-effectiveness in reaching the poorest, official agencies support NGOs in providing welfare services to those who cannot be reached through markets (Fowler, 1988; Meyer, 1992). Of course, NGOs have a long history of providing welfare services to poor people in countries where governments lacked the resources to ensure universal coverage in health and education; the difference is that now they are seen as the preferred channel for service-provision in deliberate substitution for the state.

Second, under the New Policy Agenda NGOs and GROs are seen as vehicles for 'democratisation' and essential components of thriving 'civil society', which in turn are seen as essential to the success of the Agenda's economic dimension (Moore, 1993). NGOs and GROs are supposed to act as a counterweight to state power by opening up channels of communication and participation, providing training grounds for activists promoting pluralism and by protecting human rights. The rise of citizens' movements around the world documented by Korten (1990) and crystallized most recently in the establishment of CIVICUS (1994), the 'World Alliance for Citizen Participation', may not be a result of developments in official aid, but it cannot be separated entirely from the economic and political ideals that underpin the New Policy Agenda.

This context has fostered increased volumes of official aid being made available to NGOs and, to a lesser degree GROs. They are seen as one means for operationalising the New Policy Agenda's economic and political goals. Nerfin (1987) may have got it wrong-for some donors, NGOs are seen as being both 'prince and merchant'! Their relationship with the 'people' is seen as giving them greater public legitimacy than government while their managerial features are seen as permitting private sector levels of cost control and efficiency.

Published OECD data indicate that the volume of its members' aid going to NGOs increased from 0.7 percent of the total in 1975 to 3.6 percent in 1985 and 5.0 percent in 1993/94. However, these published figures grossly underestimate the true volume (Overseas Development Institute 1995: 1) as they exclude NGOs funding from the US government (perhaps US$1 to US$2 billion in 1993/94), multilateral donors such as the World Bank, European Union, UN agencies and the like, and official aid projects that are implemented by NGOs (estimated at US$640 million in 1994). The OECD estimate of US$5.7 billion for 1993, mentioned earlier, is certainly an underestimate, perhaps by as much as US$3 billion according to one World Bank estimate. Channelling funds to NGOs is big business!

This growth in official support has transformed the composition of NGO finances. The World Bank estimates that in the early 1970s about 1.5 percent of total income for development NGOs derived from donors: by the mid-1990s, this had risen to around 30 percent (Overseas Development Institute, 1995:1). In the UK, the five largest development NGOs are all increasingly dependent on government funding, with ratios varying from 20 to 55 percent in the mid-1990s. Figures vary greatly from country to country, however, depending upon bilateral aid agency policy. In Austria around 10 percent of NGO income is from official sources. The figure increases to 34 percent for Australia, 66 percent for the USA and 70 percent for Canada. For Sweden the figure reaches a staggering 85 percent (ibid.: 2). If Canadian NGOs reach for the Vitamin C when CIDA (the Canadian International Development Agency) sneezes (Smillie, 1995) then Swedish NGOs are likely to be admitted into intensive care units when SIDA (Swedish International Development Authority) has a snuffle! Of course, the Swedes may never catch a cold, but the potential havoc that can be wrought to dependent NGOs if government policy changes, is clear.

Comparative figures for Southern NGOs are not available, but all the evidence points to even higher rates of dependency on official funds, particularly for the larger NGOs in the South. As mentioned already, NGOs in Nepal, Bolivia and Tunisia have grown rapidly in numbers in the early 1990s because of a donor, 'spending spree' (Rademacher and Tamang, 1993). In Bangladesh, BRAC and Proshika have negotiated aid packages with donor consortia in excess of US$50 million at a time, and the Working Women's Forum in India is funded mainly by UNFPA (Ramesh, 1995). The recently-announced 'Consultative Group to Assist the Poorest (CGAP), housed in the World Bank, will provide US$200 million or more from bilateral and multilateral donors to NGO micro finance programs in the South. Our personal experience in Bangladesh, Sri Lanka, Kenya and Nepal indicates that a dependency of 80 to 95 percent on official funds is common, though often at second or third-hand as funds are channeled via Northern NGOs or other institutions.

Role of NGOs, State And Donor Cooperation

The relationships outlined in the previous section have and are being reshaped by the New Policy Agenda and other forces. The promises that this holds out for NGOs, in terms of finance and seats at important for a, might indicate that this is a time of unbridled opportunity. However, as the sub-title of this review indicates, we also perceive that the contribution of NGOs to development is under threat. Increased organizational scale and influence for NGOs can only be valued when it contributes to the achievement of developmental goals. If expansion and recognition mean diverting an agency from its mission, then there may be a higher price to pay. While the empirical evidence shows that the influences of the New Policy Agenda on NGOs are many and various, we concur with Smillie (1995) that the 'alms bazaar' of which NGOs are now a part increases the likelihood that they are becoming the implementers of donor policies.

The most obvious pressures for co-option arise from the availability of aid finance: 'he who pays the piper calls the tune'. While funds are important it must be recognized that the influence of utilizing such funds goes well beyond simple finance. The acceptance of increasing volumes of foreign aid involves entering into agreements about what is done, and how it is to be reported and accounted for. This fosters and emphasis on certain forms of activity at the expense of others, on upward accountability (rather than downward accountability to members or beneficiaries), and on particular techniques and donor definitions of 'achievement' throughout the organization (Edwards and Hulme, 1995). Not surprisingly, as NGOs get closer to donors they become more like donors (Jorgensen et al., 1993 for a discussion of the ways in which Danish NGOs have become a reflection of DANIDA). Unit costs, quantifiable outputs, logical frameworks and detailed specifications of what 'partners' are to do, become organizational norms. In themselves there is nothings inherently wrong with such approaches, but they are quite inconsistent with operations of organizations that claim to be promoting qualitative change, to believe that development planning and management are a learning process rather than a blueprint and who claim to treat their 'partners' as equals. Even more importantly, donor approaches to beneficiary participation became instrumentalist (ODA, 1995; Bhatnagar and Williams, 1992): this is incompatible with the proclaimed vision of the vast majority of NGOs who conceptualise participation as a means to empower the poor and disadvantaged, not simply to achieve short-term project goals.

Refection on NGOs, State and Donor Relationships

At the heart of the present discussion lie questions about the relationships between NGOs, developing-country states and donors, and in particular about the control or influence that each of these parties might have over the other. The relationships between the actors central to the present review can be represented schematically (Figure 2.1). Such an approach risks oversimplifying complex linkages, but it facilitates the discussion of the key elements of these relationships and permits the reader to identify the particular emphases, and omissions, in this literature.

This conceptualisation views relationships between NGOs, states and donors in terms of bargaining and negotiation, although at times coercion is a possible strategy. While one actor may dominate any particular bilateral relationship it recognizes that each actor will attempt to influence the behaviors of the others. Relationships are seen as having two main dimensions. The first concerns the particular objectives that an actor seeks to achieve through interacting with others. These are likely to be a combination of officially states goals (for example, assisting the people of poorer nations, promoting national economic development) and hidden objectives (for example, opening up new export markets, staying in government). The second dimension relates to the levers that an actor may use to control or influence other actors: these range from persuading by argument, through offering financial inducements, to direct coercion. Such mechanisms may be formal (financial transfers, accounting, contracts, reporting systems and registration) or informal (information flows, staff exchanges, patronage, and seminars or discussions).

Central to this review is the argument that both donors and developing-country states are taking a much greater interest in NGO activity, and are making greater efforts to influence it directly and indirectly.

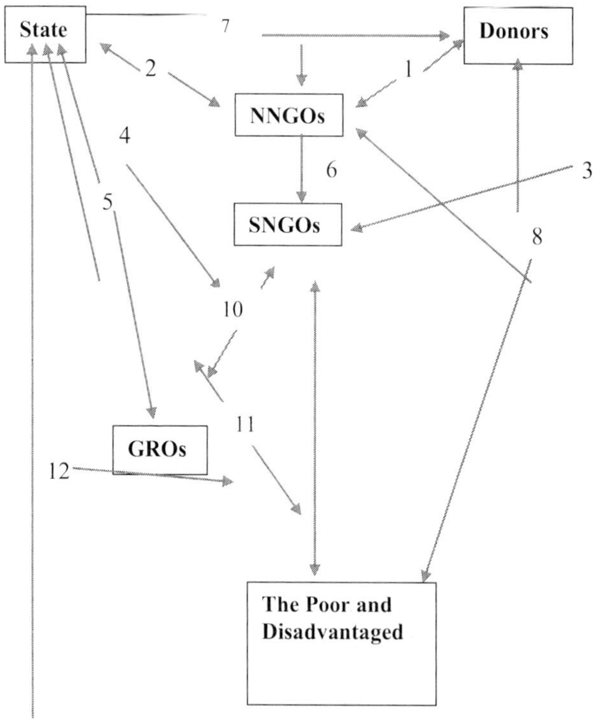

Figure 2.1 NGO. State and Donor Relationships: a schematic representation

For donors this interest derives from the New Policy Agenda and the principles that underpin it. For developing country states it derives from a response to donor initiatives and a desire to ensure that state (and often regime) legitimacy is not weakened.

The State, the NGO Sector and Popular Participation

Whether these contributions of NGOs to contemporary development issues be fully realized, given their emphasis and importance on poverty reduction, environmental conservation and participatory- development?

When a government endeavours to give greater weight to reducing poverty, to redressing gender or ethnic biases, to combating environmental degradation, or to involving the poor and their communities in development decision-making and resource allocation, it is likely to find its normal macro instruments inadequate. Economic policy, the provision of services and infrastructure, regulations and market mechanisms are rarely sharply directed towards vulnerable groups. Participatory development approaches are required.

Non-governmental organizations (NGOs) may provide instruments which, whether invited or not by governments, emphasize the participation of the poor. This is by no means uniform and depends on the NGO, the government and other factors. NGOs may keep their distance from the state and run their projects parallel to those of state; in some countries NGOs effectively play an oppositional role; while elsewhere NGOs seek to represent the voice of the weak and help them organize in their communities to achieve a more powerful voice in the making of decisions and the allocation of the resources. The latter NGOs are emerging as critical ingredients of civil society. They are moving beyond a 'supply-side' approach, concentrating on the delivery of the services or development projects, to a 'demand-side' emphasis, helping the community articulate their preferences and concerns so as to become active participants in the development process.

This is not an either/or situation. Some of the most effective operational NGOs (such as BRAC – the Bangladesh Rural Advancement Committee, the Philippines Rural Reconstruction Movement and the Worldwide Fund for Nature) are becoming effective in challenging development orthodoxy and promoting new people-centred approaches while they are increasing the scope of their own programs.

Many argue (OECD, 1988; Elliot, 1987; Fernandez, 1987; Garilao, 1987; Bhatnagar and Williams, 1992) that NGOs may be best placed for the tasks of fostering popular participation which include articulating the needs of the weak, working in remote areas, changing attitudes and practices of the local officials, and nurturing the productive capacity of the most vulnerable groups such as the disabled or the landless. In some countries, there may be a rigid divide between the voluntary, public and private sectors whereas elsewhere there is a high degree of interaction. It appears (Tandon, 1991) that where the interaction is high the climate is most favourable for poverty reduction and the other social priorities, though cause and effect may be difficult to separate. Whether a strong NGO sector encourages governments to pursue such priorities, or assists them to do so, this vehicle of civil society has potential importance, which has hitherto been largely neglected.

In many countries the voluntary sector concentrates on operating its own projects (Fowler, 1992, Bratton, 1989 and 1990) improving local situations but doing little to bring its experience to bear on the government's service delivery or policy making. It appears that where the voluntary sector is not only sizeable but also where it interacts with the public and private sector it is able to achieve a significant multiplier effects on its own efforts (Bratton, 1988and 1990).

NGOs may interact closely with local government and play a strong role in local development activities even where the central government have weak links with NGOs. Studies of decentralization and land reform programs in a range of countries have demonstrated that the active involvement of local organizations is a key factor in influencing the degree of benefits reaching to poorer citizens (Fisher, 1993).

'Scaling-up' of NGO experience has been the subject of considerable study in recent years (see, for example, ANGOC 1988 for a report of the Manila conference, and Edwards and Hulme, 1992). In addition to increasing its size by building up its capacity as an interactive provider of services and development projects, the voluntary sector can influence mainstream development in the following ways (Clark, 1991):

- Encouraging, official aid agencies and government ministries to adopt successful approaches developed within the voluntary sector;
- Educating, and sensitising the public as to their rights and entitlements under state programs;
- Attuning, official programs to public needs through acting as a conduit for the public opinion and local experience;
- Operational, collaboration with official bodies;
- Influencing, local development policies of national and international institutions including decentralization and municipal reforms (Rithcie-Vance, 1991); and
- Helping, government and donors fashion a more effective development strategy through strengthening institutions, staff training and improving management capacity.

The moving beyond the development 'supply-side' to 'demand-side' activities require that NGOs develop new skills, partnerships and ways of working in order to help communities articulate their concerns and preferences, to manoeuvre into a negotiating position with official bodies, and to mix technical operational skills with 'information age' communication, advocacy and networking skills. The literature that describes this evolution (Tandon, 1992; Clark, 1991; Edward and Hume, 1992) sees NGOs as becoming important agents of the civil society.

Governments do not necessarily resist this trend. For example, in the late 1980s the municipal reform program of the Colombian government erode their political power or even threaten national security (Fowler, 1992). And NGOs mistrust the motivation of the government and its officials.

Though controversial and risky, many of the more strategic NGOs are overcoming their inhibitions and are seeking closer collaboration with governments (Fernandez, 1987; Tondon, 1991; ANGOC, 1988; Garilao, 1987, Aga Khan Foundation, 1988). By so doing, NGOs believe, they will be better able to contribute to participatory development as described above, and they will be able to expose the government to a grassroots perspective, which might otherwise be neglected. However, there might be increased risk of corruption, reduced independence, and financial dependency.

The planning of projects and policies can be strongly influenced by inviting NGO leaders to serve on government commissions or by holding public consultations in which grassroots organizations are able to voice their concern and experience. As Michael Bratton commented (1990): 'Once the question was "how can development agencies reach the poor majority?", now it is "how can the poor majority reach the makers of public policy ?"'

World Bank experience (Cernea, 1988) drawn from a survey of 25 Bank-financed- projects, indicates a strong correlation between project success and the participation of grassroots organizations. More recently the Bank is deriving important insights from the public consultations included in Environmental Assessments in which NGOs often play major roles. Such consultations are effective where all parties are prepared to be objective and to learn from each other. Where NGOs use selective reportage or distortion in order to heighten criticism of the government, or where the government is not receptive to outside advice, 'consultations' are likely to be no more than confrontations.

Conversely, dialogue with NGOs may be unproductive where the state-NGO relationship is too cosy. NGOs may then accept too readily the government's information and its role in coordinating all development activities, including those of NGOs, and be too prepared to fill the gaps as directed by the authorities. In not questioning state activities, they fail to inject the grassroots perspective. A degree of financial autonomy of the NGO sector is necessary to insure their independence.

NGOs are often described as offering 'development alternatives but this is misleading. The dictionary defines 'alternative' as meaning 'either of two or more possible courses; ...mutually exclusive'. The population of any country does not have a choice between the development model offered by government and that by NGOs. NGOs can play an important role in helping certain population groups, or filling the gap in state services, or in pressing for a change in the national development strategy, but they rarely offer realistic pathways. Their innovations may test out new approaches, but these only become sustainable or of significant scale if they influence national development. If they achieved this then they may be commissioned by the government to continue providing services (for example, with BRAC in Bangladesh), or the NGO approach may be adopted by the government as a model of replication, as with the Escuela Nueva education program in Colombia (Ritchie-Vance, 1991) or the National Rural Support Program in Pakistan (based on the Aga Khan Rural Support Program). In such situation the NGO approach becomes mainstream rather alternative.

When both parties look too complimentary rather than the competing contributions, collaboration becomes possible, even though they may harbour very different goals. The government may be keen to harness foreign funds and the NGOs' capacity for service delivery. The NGOs may seek to reorient development priorities toward poverty reduction.

By offering or withholding support, official aid agencies can clearly have a major impact on the NGO sector. Through their projects and policy dialogue with governments, they are also able to influence the state- NGO relationship, perhaps enhancing the political will for constructive engagement. Some are realizing, in promoting participation and 'good governance' that the growth of a healthy NGO sectors an important contribution to development. The health of NGO-state relationship is sector-specific. Steps to improve the quality of relationship will also, therefore, be sector-specific (see, for example, discussion of NGOs in the agricultural sector in Bebbington and Farrington, 1992 and 1992/3b).

Factors to Healthy NGO-State Relationship

The following factors, identified by a range of commentators, are the major determinants of the health of the relationship between governments and NGOs (A. Flower, 1988 and 1992; Salamon and Anheier, 1991 and 1992; Bratton, 1988; Clark, 1991; Edwards, 1991; Tendler, 1982; Tandon, 1987 and 1992; Brown, 1988; Elliot, 1987; Broadhead and Herbert-Copley, 1988).

Policy Environment -NGOs often fall in the opposition camp while the government or the ruling party may see itself as the sole legitimate voice of the people. In such highly politicized policy environment neither party would have sufficient trust in the other to be able to work together, nor would they desire to do so. NGOs would not seek to the delivery of public services to the people or even make official development programs more participatory if by so doing they would increase the government's popularity.

merely an attempt to shape civil society in ways that external actors believe is desirable? Will it promote sustainable forms of democracy or call forth a backlash against foreign interference (Howell and Wanigaratne)? Successful civil societies develop their own systems and structures, norms and sanctions, over hundreds of year: by and large, they take care of their own strengthening (Robert Puttnam, 1993, has argued for Italy).

Nevertheless, the 'market plus civil society will yield development' myth has clearly favoured NGOs and GROs, and (for the time being at least) this myth seems here to stay. The key question for this opinion is: what implication does this have for NGOs and GROs themselves, and for wider question of political economy such as overcoming poverty and state-society relations? What do the chapters in this review tell us about the impact of current trends in NGO-state-donor relations in these crucial areas?

If NGOs, have indeed moved too close to donors, the danger is that in so doing they will have helped external interests to promulgate a myth of developments which, like all the others before it, will not only fail to resolve the problems of poverty and injustice in the world but will in important respects make long-term, sustainable progress more difficult to achieve. These 'side-effects' include the erosion of government capacity to care for the mass of it s citizens the distortion of civil society as NGOs and GROs become less independent, and the disenfranchisement of citizens as state provision is privatised and accountability is reduced further (Wood).

The evidence in this review shows that there have been a variety of experiences. While Bangladesh appears to be pursuing the current myth and state functions are 'franchised' out (Wood) the international picture reveals little documentary evidence of NGOs converting wholesale into public sector contractors as Korten (1990) warned (Robinson). What does seem to be happening, however, is a more gradual and less visible process in which a significant proportion of NGOs move closer and closer to donors and to the support of donor interests. It commences with the agreement to use aid monies: progresses with the adoption of donor techniques for programming, implementing, monitoring and accounting for performance (Edwards and Hulme, 1995); subsequently it, moves on to shaping the nature of appointments and the internal structures of NGOs with the recruitment of English speaking, local framework experts and information departments which function as public relation units; eventually the organizational culture is attuned to donors – and the local, indigenous and informal features that have underpinned NGO and GRO activities are lost (Pratten and Ali Baldo, 1995). Rather than a rapid deterioration in the patient's condition, we are witnessing a gradual hardening of arteries in the NGO world as the organizations become more bureaucratic and less prone to take risks or bear the cost of listening to those who they seek to assist. Vision becomes just another agenda item in an endless series of meetings, sandwiched somewhere between Matters Arising and Any other Business. 'In the absence of vision, pettiness prevails.' Many readers (especially staff from the large international and southern NGOs) will be familiar with this depressing story.

This process is generally identified as a gradual, but potentially catastrophic, weakening of NGO roots – both in the North (supporters) and in the South (members and beneficiaries) and in relation to the NGO's stated mission and values, vision and inspiration, independent voice and perspective.

Trends in NGO Activities

Health care and education were prominent among the initial concerns for social development, of many NGOs in the 1950s and 1960s. Increasingly, however, NGOs have moved into projects directly targeted at alleviating poverty and raising the incomes of the poor. Projects aimed at increasing poor farmers' incomes became fashionable in the 1970s, manifest in a growing concern with income generation, supply of credit, and crop production. These were often accompanied by measures designed to improve the rural infrastructure in the shape of minor irrigation schemes, and construction of schools, community buildings, local roads, etc.

A different trend also emerged in the 1970s, where the emphasis, was not so much on service delivery or development programmes, but on organising the poor with a view to enabling them to exercise greater influence over decisions affecting their lives. This 'empowerment' approach has its roots in the view that, literacy can often become a means by which the poor can reflect on the causes of their poverty and find ways of tackling them, usually by forming activist groups to put pressure on governments to reassess their policies, or to persuade the rich to redistribute power and resources in favor of the poor.

In the 1980s, new concerns, such as gender and environment, came to the fore with social forestry and soil conservation prominent among the environmental concerns. These reflect a concern about how projects affect the wider setting in which the poor live. Part of the reason for this extension of interests comes from another characteristics, which NGOs emphasize, innovation. NGOs pride themselves on being innovative in the sense of introducing new techniques and in fostering novel forms of social organization. As regards the former, this has centered on the development of appropriate, low-cost, technologies, which are accessible to the poor. Similarly, some NGOs claim to be innovative in their organizational approach, in that they promote participation, and forge new cooperative alliances among the poor through formation of grassroots organizations.

The 1990s witnessed further changes in the nature of NGO activities. Work in the areas of gender and environment has been widened, deepened, and in many ways integrated under the umbrella of 'sustainable development'. Additionally, some NGOs have focused their efforts on initiatives aimed at strengthening the power and influence of different (poorer) groups in civil society, and in a range of projects and programmes to build the capacity of local organisations.

Cutting across these concerns has been a growing interest in sustainability. There are two reasons for this. One stems from a concern with cost recovery, and the desire among NGOs (especially northern NGOs), to transfer the recurring costs of project management to the community following the withdrawal of the support agency. This is based on the belief that development- interventions can be sustained over the longer term only if the community assumes ownership of the project or programmed. The second reason for the interest in sustainability is bound up with the desire to avoid promoting dependence on external agencies. This is based in part on the NGOs not wishing to be perceived as benevolent patrons, especially when external dependence merely replaces the influence of locally dominant elites without addressing the structural reasons for such dominance.

In conclusion, we present not a set of answers but a set of strategic questions that arise from the review in its entirety. For donors the key questions must be: why are we exaggerating the role that NGOs play within civil society? Would not a more realistic analysis of what they can contribute help us to work with NGOs? In addition they should also ponder why their citizens (for bilaterals) and constituencies (for multilateral) do not provide them with support: have they an educational function in the north which they have singularly failed to achieve to date?

For those who control state power the questions are complex, given their great diversity, the short-term pressure they face and the fact that some lack genuine legitimacy. The obvious question, though, is whether NGOs contribute a threat to state power or whether a more laissez-faire stance to their activities (except on the issue of probity) might not be likely to generate more benefits to them than costs.

NGOs and their staff – if they are prepared to seize the initiative, ask difficult questions and act strategically –has the greatest room for maneuver about the nature of NGO-state-donor relationships. NNGOs need to analyse carefully their current situations and ask whether it is not time to scale down, refocus and concentrate on a smaller number of objectives. Prime among these must be action in their own societies where they can be most effective. This could mean 'alternative trading', specialist advice and support to southern partners, participation in global alliances for lobbying and advocacy, domestic development and work, and greater attention to encouraging values and attitudes of service, voluntarism and sustainable living. It certainly means more attention to development education: raising the awareness and knowledge of northern publics so that they appreciate the consequences of not demanding that their governments assist poor people in poorer countries more effectively. This is an old debate among NNGOs, but not a sterile one: the growing strength of the NGOs in the South provides a new context in which to return to old but crucial questions with renewed vigor.

For SNGOs, perhaps the time has come for a re-evaluation of the role of exogenous and endogenous factors in their programming and future direction. These would be no single answers to the questions raised by such a re-evaluation, but for many SNGOs it would surely mean returning to their roots: their ultimate achievements are not their scale, budgets or reputation, but their capacity to support effective association at the local level.

Embarrassing those in positions of power has always been a hallmark of NGO activity; the problem is that many NGOs themselves have now become the powerful, with depressing consequences for their ability to be self-critical, honest and courageous about the future. Perhaps now is the time to turn the spotlight on NGOs themselves; after all, there is nothing predetermined about the trends outlined in this review – NGOs have choices about what they do, how they do it and how it is financed. There is no inherent benefit in size and growth, nor is there one model of NGO activity which all must follow. Of course NGOs must work constructively and creatively with sources of funding, centers of influence, and those in political authority. But if they grow 'too close for comfort', NGOs, like I care us before them, may plummet to the ground when the heat of the donors melt the wax in their wings. Against the background of this literature on the Third World nongovernmental development initiatives, it is important to study the same in the Indian context.

NGOs in INDIAN Context:

Voluntary agencies or Non-Governmental Organisations (NGOs) in India have a history of involvement in a wide range of social welfare and development work which stretches back to the last century. In this respect, they have firmer foundations than their counterparts in most other developing countries. India is also of interest because of its intractable problems of rural poverty and the apparent limitations of government poverty alleviation programmes concerning health development.

There is widespread agreement among development practitioners, government officials, and foreign donors that NGOs play an important role in helping to alleviate rural poverty in India, complementary to that of government, in terms of both providing additional resources and making government health and related development programmes more effective. This view has formed the basis for a sustained increase in the level of funding from government sources and official aid donors. It is also a view shared by many NGOs, although some see their role in terms of empowering the poor rather than in implementing development programmes.

In a country the size of India, with major differences between individual states and regions, NGOs are characterized by a rich diversity of approaches, traditions, and activities, rendering the task of generalization problematic, if not impossible. They cover most geographical areas of the country and their activities affect a significant proportion of the population living in poverty. A number of studies have identified a particular set of attributes with which they are associated, but there is relatively little information on their aggregate impact in alleviating poverty concerning health development.

Estimates of the number of NGOs active in rural development in India range from less than 10,000 to several hundred thousand depending on their types of classification that are used. Nearly 20,000 organisations are registered with the Ministry of Home Affairs, for foreign funding, although the list does not distinguish between religious organisations (such as mosques and temple management committees), commercial bodies, and voluntary agencies; only half of these fall into the NGO category. In addition, there are many others which derive their financial support from internal sources, such as businesses and private -donations. A realistic estimate of the number of NGOs actively engaged in rural development in India would be in the 1520,000 range, including local and regional branches of national organizations, which operate as NGOs in their own right.

Aggregate numbers reveal only part of the picture as there are significant variations in the number of voluntary agencies in different states, with a marked concentration in the south of the country. For example, a directory produced by the 'Council for Advancement of People's Action and Rural Technology' (CAPART) in 1990 listed 470 NGOs in West Bengal and 373 in Tamil Nadu as compared to 77 in Madhya Pradesh and 11 in Jammu & Kakshmir. To some extent, these reflect differing patterns of poverty, but also historical factors (such as areas of Christian missionary influence or Gandhian activity) and the priorities of foreign donors. Some districts possess dense networks of NGOs, which overlap and compete for clients, while in others there are hardly any NGOs active on the ground. NGOs in India can be grouped into six categories according to their scale of operations and the location of their head offices:

- large indigenous NGOs working in several states in different parts of the country;
- large indigenous NGOs working in most districts of one state; *mediumsized indigenous NGOs working in a large number of villages in one or two districts of one state;
- small indigenous NGOs working in a group of villages in one locality (the most common type);
- large international NGOs with incountry representation providing funding and support to indigenous NGOs;
- small international NGOs working directly in one or two localities.

Comparatively few posses the staff or financial resources to work intensively at the state and national levels, although it is these organisations, which are best-known in the government and among the donor circle. A number of the larger NGOs perform an intermediary role in channeling resources from donor agencies to small local NGOs, and are generally not involved in actual project implementation. Most international NGOs have no direct representation in the country, and prefer to work through intermediaries, although several have regional offices.

NGOs are generally reluctant to divulge detailed accounts, but some of the larger national ones have budgets amounting to tens of millions of rupees. One survey reported fiftyfour NGOs with annual turnovers in excess of Rs. 1m., although this is probably an underestimate. The same survey found that nearly half the respondents had budgets below Rs. 250,000, which provides some support for the view that the majority of Indian NGOs are small scale and localised (Nath, 1989).

Recent estimates suggest that the amount of foreign funds coming into the country for use by NGOs each year is in the region of Rs.90bn. (US$ 520m.), up from Rs. 5bn. in the mid1980s. In quantitative terms, this is equivalent to approximately 20 percent of official aid flows, which stood at $2.4bn. in 1991. A further Rs. 500700m, is provided by the government. When individual and corporate donations are added, an annual income figure of Rs. 10bn. would seem a reasonable estimate of the total available resources, although this does not take into account unofficial payments or contributions in kind by project - beneficiaries. This figure is double the government's annual expenditure on IRDP, and 10 percent of its overall budget for poverty alleviation and service provision, which indicates that the resources mobilised by NGOs are important, but essentially supplement those provided by the government.

Historical Perspective of NGOs in Health & Social Sector Development

India's Complexity as a country lies in its religious, political, ethnic, social and cultural diversity as well as in its long history of civilization[1]. Therefore defining the Non-governmental sector in India is a different task because no single underlying theme or pattern can characterise the development of the Non-Governmental sector. Hence this chapter uses a historical perspective as an analytical tool to describe definitions-both conceptual and legal, that are then related to the structural/operational definition of the 'non-governmental sector' suggested by Salamon and Anheier (1992)[2]. This sector and the various terms used to describe it are analyzed in the context of the broader political economy at various periods of history to uncover underlying themes that are useful to understand its present and past role

It is important to divide the development of modern voluntarism[3] and the Indian non-governmental sector after the 'Earlier period' and 'Early British period; into four different periods; the Mid to Late colonial period (1810s & to 1947); the Early post independence period (1947 to the Late 1950s); the period between (1960s and 1980s): and the more recent past since then. Each period is characterised by a number of distinct themes or patterns that are vital to understand the development of the non-governmental sector in India.

Historical Development of NGOs in India

Voluntarism has long been an integral part of the Indian Society, dating back to 1,500 BC when it was mentioned in the 'Rig Vedas'[4]. Voluntarism was the main source of welfare and development except for those few empires with a well- developed public welfare system[5]. The role of political regimes was mainly restricted to promoting moral, aesthetic, and spiritual progress of the civilization, in addition to enduring exploitation by the monarch, the aristocracy, and Government officials. Naturally, voluntarism played an important role in social and economic development of the Civilization. It operated in the fields of health, education, cultural-promotion and in crises such as droughts, floods, and epidemics, and the poor were taken care of by social mechanisms outside the state - through the joint-family, caste, solidarity of colleagues, guilds, and individual religious philanthropy. The relationship between individual philanthropy and religion is explained by the mandates regarding charity laid down by predominant religions -Hinduism and Islam, as well as other religions: Buddhism, Jainism, Zoroastrianism (Dadrawala, 1991)[6], and Sikhism.

The Mid To Late Colonial Period (1810s-1947)

The Era of Church, National Bourgeoisie, Gandhian Philanthropy and Separatist Movements

The first voluntary efforts in social development were initiated by Christian missionaries in the early 1810s (Pande, 1967; Terry, 1983; Baig, 1985; Bhattacharya, 1987; Inamder, 1987; Tandon, 1988)[7]. Although their principal objective was propagating Christianity, they started to build schools, colleges, dispensaries and orphanages around the 1810s and 1820s (Natarajan, 1962; Singh, 1968)[8]. Parallel to their efforts in the urban areas; christian missionaries formed rural colonies from the 1860s until the 1940s with an emphasis on modernisation efforts focused on self- help, and the establishment of cooperative credit societies, health care, and training facilities, whereas the empowerment component consisted of adult literacy classes and the establishment of Panchayats (Local village councils) to solve local problems while dealing with a chain of events during this era culminating into the contemporary voluntary action, It would be pertinent to mention a number of socio-religious movements that emerged to grapple with various issues afflicting the society. Notable among those movements were Brahmo Samaj (1818 AD); Prarthana Samaj (1867 AD) Arya samaj (1875 AD) and Ramakrishna Mission, Satyahodhak Samaj and Indian National Social Conference began to emerge from these social movements (PRIA - 1991)[9]. Even though each of these had its own thrust and concerns with various points of difference, they together covered a wide variety of social and religious issues such as opposing caste system, Sati system, child- marriage superstition, idolatry, polytheism, rituals, hereditary, priesthood and hegemony of priests and social and legal inequalities, propagating modern education, equal right to women window remarriage, prohibition, freedom of individuals social integration and regeneration reinterpretation of scriptures and above all nationalism.

Alongside the above socio-religious movements, there were various other protests and movements against colonial rulers such as uprisings of peasantry in many areas against the unjust settlement practices and exploitative and oppressive revenue fixation and collection; protests and movements by forest dwellers against restricting their access to forests; protests against commercial plantations and mono culture and protests against restrictions of fishing and navigation rights.[10] Evidently, many such protests and movements became an integral part of the national freedom movement and made vital contribution to accelerate the process to win freedom.

The most important organisational offshoot of the nineteenth century reform movement and subsequent national consciousness was the establishment of the Indian National Congress in 1885. Liberal Minded British officials and businessmen assisted the modern Indian elite in establishing the congress which became the official platform for expressing growing national consciousness (Kochavek, 1947; D' Cruz, 1988; PRIA, 1991)[11].

There have been some other strands of voluntary action visible in Indian society. Charity, relief and welfare by religious bodies and other socially concerned institutions and groups have all along been visible there in it ; Like in most other societies. Such a self-less voluntary action which even though informal and unorganised, Covers the entire grant of rural life and keeps the communities going; thus greatly facilitates organised NGO actions.

The voluntary movement received the maximum impetus and incentive from Gandhi, who believed that voluntary action was the only path to India's development. Gandhi's concept of development included all aspects of Life; social, political, economic, cultural, and spiritual, (Chaturvedi, 1987)[12]. His notion of rural development was constructing self-supporting, self-governing and self-reliant village communities where everyone's needs were satisfied and everyone lived in harmony and cooperation. To achieve this goal, Gandhi introduced a 'constructive programme' to achieve egalitarianism in Indian society by introducing basic education and sanitation, and by eradicating 'untouchability'.

Thus the emphasis was on empowerment and transformation of the society and acquired a political context, instead of issue- based voluntarism of the nineteenth century. Also the demands made by various classes to further their social, political or economic interests as exhibited by the formation of business and caste associations.

The Early Post - Independence Period (1947s To The Late 1950s): The Era of Religion - Based And Gandhian NGOs

Two types of NGOs were predominant in this period of history; Gandhian NGOs and religion-based NGOs (Including both Christian and non-christian NGOs). Concurrent with these trends, older types of NGOs continued to exist in the sector. The primary activities of the Gandhian NGOs in this period were development and empowerment, while those of religion based NGOs were welfare and empowerment. For Gandhi, the constructive programme was the truthful and non-violent way of winning complete Independence It was designed to build up the Nation from the very bottom upward. Apart from being deeply transformative it was a strategic instrument for mass mobilisation for the National freedom movement, as envisaged it eventually became mass scale voluntary action. The out standing significance of this effort, however lies in the fact that it gave birth, space and substance to a socially conscious and participatory, politically aware, change and active, and ideologically secular and transformative voluntary action movement in India.

During this period, Gandhian NGOs were also requested to train govt. Officials employed in development projects, for example, the ministry of Community Development involved Gandhian NGOs to organise and conduct training programmes for its extension workers. Another example is the training of health workers undertaken by Gandhian-NGOs at the request of the Ministry of Health (Muttalib, 1987; Tandon, 1988)[13]. In the process of the mentioned constructive programme, there was considerable institution building, giving birth to a number of specialised All India Voluntary Organisation spread across the country, such as All India Spinners Association (1925); upliftment of the untouchable; Later 'Bharatiya Adimayati Sevak Sangh' (1948) for the upliftment of the tribals and similar bodies to promote prohibition, languages, eradication of leprosy, cattle etc. These constructive work organisations provided a solid base to the freedom struggle.

Some other voluntary organisations such as servants of India Society (1905) and Servants of People Society (1921) emerged during or around the same period[14]. Yet another notable aspect of Non-Governmental development action during the late pre-Independence period was some innovative initiatives and experiments by eminent socially concerned persons such as Rabindranath Tagore in Sriniketan and Jagatram and Dave in Vedchi.[15]

The welfare component of most religions based NGOs in this period is reflected in their effort to provide relief for refugees and flood and famine victims; and provision of health and nutrition services for the poor. The empowerment component is located in their educational activities.

The primary motive of the religion-based NGOs was religious philanthropy, while those of the post-Independence Gandhians that formed NGOs was to ensure a secure financial future (Sethi, 1988)[16]. Kothari writes that, NGOs headed by Gandhians with financial assistance from the state continued Gandhi's constructive programme. He suggested that Gandhians who did not or could not join the ruling party or the government worked closely with the government to set up handicrafts and village industries, rural development agencies, credit cooperatives and educational institutions.

The emergence of a large number of NGOs is perhaps, attributable to the initiative taken by the newly independent Indian state in promoting NGOs in development work, for example, the government took the initiative to form the central social welfare Board (SWB) in 1953 to promote and fund NGOs, setting aside 30 million rupees (approximate 1990 value = 410 million rupees or US$22 million) for funding them (Paul Chowdhury, 1987; Inamder, 1987)[17]. Paul Chowdhury states that planners under the leadership of Jawaharlal Nehru and voluntary social worker Durgabai Deshmukh felt that social work should be left to the voluntary sector with the state providing technical and financial support[18]. In the following year, the CSWB created the State Social Welfare Advisory Boards (SSWAB) for the purpose of strengthening existing NGOs and establishing new ones in the project areas that did not yet have them (Jagganadham, 1987)[19]. According to Chaturvedi (1987), the creation of CSWB and the SSWABs gave a new lease on life to the stagnating Gandhian NGOs. Seth and Sethi (1991) View the close relationship and dependence of the Gandhian NGOs on the state as a devise of vibrant sector of Gandhian organisations[20].

The Post Independence Period - The 1960s and 1970s:

The types of NGOs that existed in this period include welfare oriented NGOs, indigenous NGOs formed by international NGOs and Welfare Wings of Churches (WCO), NGOs formed by the middle class professionals; NGOs known as non, party political formations or action groups, Community, Based Organisations (CBO) formed by the poor with help of other types of NGOs or the local Government. Concurrent with these newer trends, the older types of NGOs continued to exist in the sector.

The welfare-oriented NGOs that emerged in the 1960s and to a certain extent in the early 1970s were mainly involved in providing relief to victims of disasters such as famines, floods, cyclones. Indigenous NGOs formed in the mid-1960s by International NGOs were primarily development-oriented with an element of empowerment. The NGOs formed by the middle class professionals in the late 1960s and early 1970s were capable of a high degree of specialisation in development work while including empowerment. The NGOs known as action groups or non-party political formations began to emerge in late 1960s and their numbers began to grow after mid 1970s. The primary emphasis of these NGOs was empowerment, although some of them mixed empowerment with development. CBOs that were formed in the early and mid-1970s undertook various developmental and empowerment oriented projects. Corporate philanthropy consisted of development programmes in rural areas (Franda, 1983; Terry, 1983)[21]. The NGOs formed by the Government were also development oriented (Franda, 1983; Kothari, 1986)[22].

The founders of NGOs in 1960s and 1970s had different motivations. The welfare-oriented NGOs, formed by the middle class and action-groups were most likely products of the socio- economic and political conditions of this period. These are discussed in detail in the next sub-section. International NGOs formed Indian NGOs out of a compassion for the poor in the developing world CBOs were formed by the poor who felt a need to serve their community often with outside intervention from the local state or NGOs assistance. Corporate philanthropy emerged because of tax incentives provided by the state, while the state sponsored NGOs were formed to develop appropriate technology.

The emergence of a large number of the welfare-oriented NGOs in the 1960s in the 1960s and to a certain extent the early 1970s is attributable to two factors (Franda, 1983; Terry, 1983; Fernandes, 1986)[23]. First, there was a need for relief work because of the regular occurrence of disasters such as famines, floods and cyclones in this period of Indian history. The need for relief work was exacerbated by the Bangladesh war, in 1971, which led to a massive influx of refugees into India. Second, western funding for relief work increased considerably during this period of history.

Emergence of NGOs in the late 1960s and early 1970s was conceivably due to the lack of jobs among the educated youth (Kaul, 1972; Sharma and Apte, 1976), as well as growing dissatisfaction with the existing institutional arrangements in India.[24]

The 1980s And 1990s : The Predominance of NGOs

Major factors, which deeply influenced the characteristics and growth of voluntary action in India during the post Independence period are discussed as follows[25].

1. After Independence the National Government initiated a process of planed development on the Western model. Most of the unjust oppressive and exploitative socio-economic institutions and legal framework inherited from the colonial rulers continued. Many restrictive laws were enacted and policies proclaimed, of course, with exception of legislation for Zamindari abolition, land reforms etc. Big projects such as irrigation, dams, power plants and industries displaced a large number of people, mostly the tribals, creating a new sizable category of ecological refugees[26]. A small minority of affluent benefited at the expense of a large majority of the poor. And all these activities were performed in the name of development and in 'public interest' for national reconstruction. Massive community Development programme launched for rural development could hardly create much impact for wants of popular participation. There were also sporadic organised protests against such types of development. Public debate against 'trickle down' theory of development and 'rich becoming richer, poor poorer' had started well within the first development decade by late 1950s. However, craze for 'nation building' and catching up with the West marked by hope and promise was so fascinating and charisma of the freedom movement graduated national leadership in power was initially so overwhelming that it took almost two decades for the basic issues of people centred development to surface and start gaining momentum on a sustainable basis, notwithstanding its strand being present all through since pre-Independence and national freedom movement days. During this phase, the state and the Government, thus assumed the principal responsibility and role of development and social change severely circumscribing the scope of voluntary action. In this situation, NGOs continued with conventional charity and welfare work and had only peripheral involvement in Government's development action.
2. After Independence a large number of freedom fighters inspired by Gandhi renounced power politics and joined non-Governmental Gandhian constructive work stream. This stream continuing as one of the largest, made notable contribution to the growth of NGOs sector during the post-Independence period. Apart from various constructive programmes, Bhoodan/Gramdan, (Land gift/ village gift) movements launched by this stream under the leadership Vinoba Bhave as a part of the Sarvodaya Movement

during first phase[27]. Conceptually these movements together represented an attempt towards non-violent rural reconstruction and social transformation, basically different from the prevailing charity/welfare approach during that phase with the achievement or failure, it has been one of the most significant Non-Governmental interventions in rural reconstruction for development during the post independence period.

3. As the public critique of centralised growth - centred development pursued by the Government became sharper from late sixties onwards, the Government responded with a number of 'target-group' and 'problem-area' focused programmes. By late seventies and through eighties the process culminated into a plethora of antipoverty programmes in which considerably increased involvement of NGOs was also sought. It implied increased funding of NGOs by the Government. In the process, it was but natural that a large number of new NGOs emerged and they along with most of the existing ones started implementing various Government programmes; generally in a more cost-effective, efficient and participatory manner, It is believed that weakening bureaucratic development delivery mechanism of the Government also contributed to and facilitated the expansion of NGO-sector during this period.
4. The issues relating to popular participation, equity and sustainability, linked with those of environment, Dalits and gender, arose from the persisting social, economic and political situation and came into focus, particularly during late seventies through eighties. Expansion of communication system for rising awareness, locally as well as globally, stimulated and accelerated the process. The issues and NGO strategies in response to them contributed a great deal to qualitative change in voluntary action; which sharpened and strengthened its transformative strand and activism. This has also been the period of deeper social concern especially among the youth and intellectuals. Increasing impact, visibility and credibility of NGOs coupled with increasing attention and assistance to them by the donor agencies during this very period has also made significant contribution to the growth of NGO sector.

Finally, in between various other factors have influenced the NGO sector one way or the other. Natural disasters and recognition of the need of poverty alleviation programmes for development action to minimise them, emphasis on professionalisation of NGOs and assistance needed for the purpose, initiatives taken by business and industry as a part of their social responsibility; networking needs, and clashing sectarian interests may be mentioned in this regard[28].

The above description seems to suggest that voluntary action in different parts of India was rooted in a specific socio political context and was inspired by the emergence and continuity of social reforms, social change and political movements in different parts of the country. All these facts contributed to the growth process of NGO sector in India, bringing it to its present stage.

Nomenclature of Indian NGOs

According to Literature (Seth; 1982; Franda, 1983, Sethi, 1984; Sethi and Kothari, 1984; Frenandes and Lobo, 1986; Jain 1986; Kothari, 1986; PRIA, 1987; Seth and Sethi 1991)[29], the terms used to refer to the NGOs in India are: voluntary associations; voluntary organisations; voluntary agencies; philanthropic organisations; welfare organisation; action groups; women's organisation; non-governmental organisations, Government organised NOGs; church organisation; religious groups; and Community Based Organisations (CBOs). The most commonly used acronym in India is VOLAG (voluntary Agency), which is unique to India. This sector is generally referred to as the voluntary sector or the non-governmental sector.[30]

Voluntary associations and related terms are traditional 'Indian English' terms. In Hindi language, NGOs are referred to as Sweshcha Sevi Sangathans/ sanghatans.[31]

With the exception of the term Government organised NGOs for example National Dairy Development Board and CAPART, all the above terms refer to empowerment oriented NGOs that emerged from the 1960 onwards.

The term NGO is a catchy phrase which fails to capture the wide array of institutions which share common features with such organisations (Salamon and Anheier, 1992)[32]. NGOs are generally formed by professionals from the middle class to serve the poor and have salaried employees (pardon, 1987; May 1989)[33]. Today NGOs are defined as humanitarian organisations and are recognised as having 'NGO status' by intergovernmental organisations such as the united Nations (UN) or European community (EC) by NGOs in developed countries or by national governments (Borghese, 1987; May, 1989). It is however, difficult to single out Indian NGOs because there is no accepted method for recognising whether or not a particular organisation has NGO status. Generally large and medium sized developmental and empowerment-oriented non-profit organisations, which receive foreign funds, are categorized as NGOs in India. According to a popular NGO-Society for Participatory Research in Asia the term 'NGO' is a negative and non-explanatory label because it includes private sector formations, development corporations, welfare boards etc.

According to PRIA, the terms 'Voluntary Development Organisations' should be used rather than NGO to define developmental organisations. There is no general consensus about the time of emergence of the term in India.[34]

Typology of NGOs working for Social Sector in India

The experience of voluntary development organisations through NGOs in India has become so diverse and multifaceted that there is a need to systematise and classify this vast range.

The purpose of evolving a typology is to attempt a classification of the range of Development NGOs India today. It is an attempt to describe through certain categories what exists in this field and differentiating between one type of NGO with another to understand their implications. Thus it follows with the classification of NGOs in India on certain dimensions which have both a descriptive as well as an analytical value in enhancing the understanding of their nature and functions. These typologies are as based on the following discussed parameters:

1. Inspiration

   One of the most important sources of differentiation in NGOs, is mostly about the nature of the inspiration of the Founder or Founders. This inspiration provides the philosophical perspective as well as analytical framework in viewing the social reality and thereby becomes the basis for evolving a set of actions by a given NGO. The inspiration takes various forms -it may be philosophical, intellectual, religious or ideological inspiration. Different types have quite different implications for the manner in which these organisations get established and the manner in which they function. Some of these types are discussed below.

   Historically, one of the most significant inspirations has been the Gandhian- school built on the experience of the freedom Straggle and Mahatma Gandhi's call for constructive social work, to help rural mass to achieve their own economic-social regeneration. The keystone of such organisations has been village reconstruction to reestablish traditional handicraft industries and create pride in 'Swadeshi or 'Indianness' e.g. Sewapuri case[35].

A second school, also historically are quite active, which could be called as Socialistic School. This inspiration can be best typified in the leadership of Purushottam Das Tandon, Ram Manohar Lohia and Jaya Prakash Narayan. Chattra Yuva Sanghars Vahini as an outcome of the J.P. movement in Bihar and other parts of North India during mid-70s is a typical example of this inspiration[36].

A third type of inspiration is the Marxist and neo-Marxist perspective. Several organisations inspired by this left ideologies were from the outcome of the left political parties. Some people who were involved in ultra-left movements, like the Naxalite Struggle, after some time changed their course and also set-up voluntary organisations.

Historically, the church has been a major source of inspiration and the teachings of Christianity have been used to inspire whole generations of missionaries to serve the poor and the needy. Likewise the influence of Islamic, Buddhist and other traditions has also been quite viable. Also the Ramakrishna Mission through its countrywide network of missionary development initiatives is a case in point. Its contemporary version is a voluntary development NGO - the Lok Shiksha Parishad. (Tandon, 1991)[37].

2. Rationale

The second parameter could be called the rationale for initiating voluntary action through NGOs. It is almost like a universal-view. The literature available for examining the range of NGOs in the country under the category could be of four distinct types as emerged till date[38]; which are as follows:

The first type is based on the rational that people need help that poor, down-trodden, weak need assistance and help. Most NGOs operating on a charity and welfare perspective carry this rationale. They provide relief and rehabilitation during events of disaster, droughts, cyclone, floods, earth-quake etc; which also operate under this underlying assumption.

The second type comprises an universal view that could be called as developmentalist. Here the focus is on people who could do the work on their own but with 'NGO' support particularly in the form of programmes, resources, ideas and skills. Under this category the programmes of health, agriculture, irrigation, economic activities, appropriate technology etc. is included.

The third type is based on the theme of empowerment. It assumes that the poor need to get organised and struggle in order for appropriate change to occur. The focus of intervention, therefore because on the conscientisation and organisation of certain sections, poor tribals, dalits, landless, women etc. The ultimate purpose of the strategy is empowerment. The struggle of the poor may be catalysed through a variety of such activities which may focus on acquisition of assets, wages, implementation of certain progressive legislations, education, etc.

And the fourth type is the need for support and influence at different levels not merely struggle by the poor directly and their organisations but struggle at the level of influencing policy, struggle at the level of ideas, struggle at the local, district, state, national and international levels. This perspective assumes that with growing modernisation of our societies and economical, forces of oppression and marginalisation operate from different levels and need to be countered and confronted at those levels. Therefore the support and influence will take different forms at different levels. It is here that institutions engaged in advocacy research networking documentation, training federating etc. came into the picture (support - organisation)[39].

There four types tend to describe a wide variety of programmes and activities that NGOs undertaken. Therefore, it is observed that a health programme carried out with the first rationale of help tends to provide medicines and treatments, while another are carried out with the rationale of development tends to educate people and solve other non-health related problems in an integrated manner. Thus these distinctions are important not merely in their underlying belief but in the outcome as reflected in the manner in which programmes and activities are carried out by such NGOs. Further differentiation does occur on the basis of the strategy of intervention. For example some organisations focus on one sector, like health, education, income generation etc. some organisations are multi-sectoral or integrated in their approach. Some NGOs focus on one constituency e.g. tribals or landless in a given geographical area. Some NGOs focus on multiple constituencies. These variations of sector and constituency also get further amplified within the rationale and the universal view described above. Thus it is possible to find different types of NGOs, carrying out the same sectoral work with similar constituencies but having totally different orientation, approach and activities.

3. Size

   In the present context, size has become one of the main parameters, which explains the differences among NGOs[40]. Size can be classified in various ways such as; one dimension is the area of coverage. Many NGOs are covering one or two villages or slums; some are national in their coverage. Another dimension of NGOs size, in terms of their full-time, part-time staff and their overall budgets and resources. Thus it is possible to develop various categories within these parameters of size of NGOs.

   The first category of small organisations is the most predominant are in the Indian context. These are the organisations (NGOs) which work in a few villages within a block of a district or in a few slums in one part of the city. Most of their funds are based in local resources, some contributed by members of the NGOs themselves, though they may occasionally receive some funds from outside on an informal or intermittent basis.

   The second category of medium size NGOs tends to cover a block or two in rural areas or several slums in a city and could also cover larger cluster if the nature of their work is at other levels than grassroots. Their fund arrangements are from national or international donor agencies.

   The third category of big NGOs, would be those who have project budgets varying from 5 to 20 lakhs of rupees per annum. They love wider area, several districts or cities and they operate on a regular programme basis.

   The last category could be called larger size NGOs which are fewer in number in India at present. They would have a budget around or above fifty lakhs per annum based on project grants from several sources.

Implications of Typologies of NGOs

A classification would be helpful to describe and understand the nature of NGOs in India today. This fact further can be analyzed by considering the following issues:

The first implication of this classification is that when 'universal view' rationales are mixed with a single organisation it creates confusion about identity. Thus when a NGO based on the rationale of help and charity also takes on a developmental perspective different segments and people within the organisation behave and react differently, thereby causing internal tensions and confusion externally.

The second implication is that the nature of the 'universal view' and rationale for setting up an organisation may end up defining its reflections with others in society. This fact tends to provide a definite space to NGOs in the socio political arena of the country. For example, those set up with the rational of help may find no conflict with the Government or the political parties, while those set up with the rationale of empowerment may find themselves in conflict with both.

A third implication is that, growth in size implies several institutional demands and forces, which are different from other parameters. And that independent of inspiration and rationale for setting-up of an organisation, and its growth in size brings similar pressures and demands.

Thus the present section on elaborating the history and evolution of NGOs has clearly highlighted the significance of understanding regional variations in a country like India. Regional variations have affected evolution of types of non-governmental organisations as well. Certain inspirations are more available in certain parts of the country as was discussed early in this section. The classification of the above type would help us to explore greater depth, the kinds of roles, functions and potentiality (fund available), scope of NGOs in India.

Roles: Based on the roles played by NGOs as the literature shows[41] the three distinct types are: a) Field level (implementing) NGOs, b) Support level (Service -provider) NGOs; c) Associations/ Networks NGOs. As obvious, the first type includes micro-level NGOs, whereas the last two types are macro level NGOs.

Earlier, the NGOs associations/networks combined both 'association functions' and 'service functions' and they were the ones which provided need-based services to NGOs affiliated to them and also to non-affiliated NGOs, as far as possible. Most of the associations are old as well as new ones, continuing with the above two pronged functions. However during the 1970s and 80s number of support organisations have emerged to provide various kinds of services to NGOs. Examples are PRIA, PRADAN, AFFORD, and ACORD in New Delhi, AFARM in Pune, CHETNA in Ahmedabad, XISS in Ranchi, ADITHI in Patna, AIRD and SEARCH in Bangalore, RDAS in Hyderabad, SPIAD and LSP in West Bengal GNK in Ghaziabad (Up) are only a few many of such support NGOs, filling in wide gaps left by the associations/networks[42].

There are support NGOs also in many other fields such as technology, communication skills and materials, and marketing promotion. Action research, building up knowledge-base relevant to NGOs' development action and clearing house and documentation are among very vital areas in which a number of support NGOs and networks have been active.

Quite a few of the networks and support NGOs also undertake their own experimental field projects to test and /or evolve innovative approaches and learn from direct experience. Some of the support NGOs eventually seek affiliation of NGOs served by them and thus try to acquire networking character for contacts, convenience in serving and legitimacy. Some of the support NGOs and apex bodies assist foreign funding agencies in identifying grassroots NGO partners, formulation and appraisal of project proposals channeling of funds, monitoring and evaluation of implementation and training in a much more cost effective manner.

On the other hand, quite a few of the competent field level NGOs, apart from implementing their own projects, have been performing the functions of support NGOs and networks. This is due to pressure from the needy NGOs as well as to gain leadership and influence. However this is a very cost effective and essential way to multiply need-based support to grassroots-level NGOs spread across the country.

Objectively, the above trends have their roots in the situation prevailing in the NGO sector. However, lately, Finding agencies, particularly foreign ones have been trying to promote certain networks and support NGOs with noble as well as ignoble intentions, more often simply to have amenable NGOs. On the whole, there is a wide variety of NGOs reflecting manifestation of diversities in the country.

Popular Participation: NGOs in India are generally committed to popular participation. It is a very positive aspect of their development initiatives. It is well recognised that popular participation in decision making is essential not merely for the success and sustainability of development programmes but basically because people have a right to shape their destinies according to their own needs, aspirations, priorities and perceptions.

NGOs have been devising and adopting appropriate strategies of popular participation in diverse situations. They have been trying to involve people actively in planning, implementing, monitoring and evaluation of people centred projects and programmes. However, apart from variations in strategies and approaches, popular participation in practice varies in degree from NGO to NGO and from project to project[43].

Activist NGOs have been far more successful in generating effective popular participation especially of the poor and disadvantaged sections. They usually do it through a sustained process of awareness. raising organisation and peaceful struggle on people centered issues, focus in their work is on structural change. However, NGOs work with the people in the unorganised sectors where there is no regular organised institutional base to enable people to participate through it. So exceptions apart, popular participation generated by NGOs is generally through improvised adhoc peoples' organisations such as all inclusive Gram Sabhas (village assemblies) and Lok Samities (peoples committees) or sectoral interest groups, especially of the poor and disadvantaged sections with appropriate networking at higher levels[44]. However there are also a few successful NGO initiatives of organising trade unions and cooperatives of workers in the unorganised sector. Panchayati Raj Bodies were conceived as peoples' own institutions at the village/primary community level, intermediate level and district level, to harness people's creative energies for their self-development. But for want of genuine democratic decentralisation, these institutions hardly have any powers, functions and resources and have therefore remained crippled, ineffective and defunct in most of the states in the country. In some of the states such as Karnataka and West Bengal experience of involving these institutions in development even it to a limited extent has been happy. Even where panchayati Raj bodies exist and function, NGOs reach out further down to small cohesive groups of the poor at the hamlet level, living together, and endeavoring together to facilitate more effective direct participation of the disadvantaged sections[45].

Repeated failures of centralised planning and development in India have created a situation where Government is now more receptive to the rationale of democratic decentralisation and popular participation. Numerous successful examples set and tremendous pressure generated by NGOs have also considerably contributed to improvement in the policy environment for popular participation. Thus NGOs' rich and varied experience, despite its limitations and handicaps, offers valuable insights, into strategies to generate and sustain popular participation.

Associations/Networks

Associations / networks of NGOs in India are as old and diverse as NGOs themselves although the term network is comparatively recent in origin[46]. Associations such as All India Spinners Association, All India Village Industries Association, and All India Women's Conference were formed during the pre-Independence period; 1920s and 30s. Christian missionaries also and had their own networks. This process continued through the early post-independence period. 'Sarv Seva Sangh' and 'Association of Voluntary Agencies for Rural Development' (AVARD) were formed in 1948 and 1958 respectively[47]. 'Bharatiya Adimjati Sevak Sangh' and 'Harijan Sevak Sangh' also belong to early period. Based on territorial jurisdiction, sectoral concerns, and persuasions, associations networks NGOs in India can be categorised as follows;

(i) Territorial Jurisdiction: National (all-India), Zonal (inter-state), State, Sub-state district.

(ii) Sectoral concerns: sectoral, multisectoral

(iii) Persuasion: persuasion wise, open/secular.

Considering the size of the country, inter-state diversities, convergence of various development functions and activities at the state level, and the need of a forum to promote friendship, cooperation and interaction among the NGOs at that level, a number of state networks have emerged during late seventies through eighties. Some of the national networks took initiative to promote such state networks. AVARD's planned efforts to promote state networks in AP, Bihar. Gujarat, Madhya Pradesh, Rajasthan, UP and West Bengal and Zonal network in North East deserve special mention in this regard[48]. Some of the national networks, especially sectoral ones such as voluntary Health Association of India (VHAI) have their state level branches or networks in most or some other states. In larger states such as Bihar, UP, Sub-state networks have emerged to cope with interstate diversities. Networking has gone further down to the district level; such networks, one each of Howrah district in West Bengal and Phulbani district in Odisha are cases in point[49].

NGOs in science and technology have their own networks: All India Peoples Science Congress at the national level and state level bodies in most of the states. Kerala Sastra Sahitya Parishad (KSSP) is an example of state level network[50]. Thus the networks/associations role in stimulating and strengthening the NGO sector has however been notable.

As mentioned earlier, there are cases of implementing NGOs and support NGOs performing networking function; this is on the increase especially because existing networks are unable to cope with the vast needs of the NGOs but to a considerable extent also due to unhealthy competition for leadership, There are a number of self appointed leaders of NGOs vying with one another. Bottom-up democratic and top-down not so democratic both the processes are seen as regards formation of networks. To some extent Governmental foreign funding agencies have been instrumental in promoting their own amenable NGO networks/ nodal agencies and leaders as well as unhealthy competition among them.

However, formal networks at various levels need to strengthen their institutional capabilities a great deal to improve their performance in 'networking' as well as support functions. In coming years, as obvious trend visible is for an increasing number of forceful informal strategic, networks coming up to spearhead various movements and campaigns for people centered development and against anti-people Governmental policies.

Activities and Scopes of NGOs

NGOs in India are engaged in all conceivable activities for cultural educational, health, economic and social development in their respective areas of operation. While planning and undertaking such activities they try to respond to local situations, needs, perceptions and priorities. Well planned, systematic and strategic interventions by NGOs have been increasing over the years particularly during the past two decades[51]. Impact and visibility of NGOs has also been increasing. Activism and professionalisation of NGOs have greatly contributed to their impact, visibility, and media accessible. NGO sector also has its share of elitism; since for the last two decades, more articulate and sophisticated NGOs and NGO leaders have been emerging; they have greater access to existing information system, powers that be and resources. This is no doubt a positive development, some of its weaknesses notwithstanding. On the other hand less articulate, less visible and less known grassroots NGOs remain the backbone of NGO sector.

However there is still a long way to go in this regard, Most of the NGO interventions are adhoc, haphazard and often determined by availability of resources and therefore donor driven. Nature of activities and interventions also depends on level of awareness capability, perception, priority, persuasion, and approach of the NGOs concerned. However NGOS have shown tremendous potential to learn and grow with the work.

NGO community in India can be compared with a tree having all round prolific growth while casting off its yellow leaves in the growth process. As indicated earlier, NGOS of different hues perceive, determine, and play their roles differently. However, there is consensus of the following scopes over the roles of NGOs[52];

(i) **Facilitating Participatory Process:** This is a multi-faceted scope. It involves a sustained process of animation, organisation, motivation, facilitation action and progress. In practice only a small number of NGOS are able to play their role in this scientific manner. Various awareness raising, training, and development education initiatives form a part of this role.

(ii) **Generating Alternatives:** It involves continuous experimentation and action research with innovative ideas and approaches in people centered and people led development; especially at the micro-level. Flexibility, freedom of action, openness, and intimate contact and intensive interaction with local people and situations help NGOs a great deal in generating better replicable development alternatives. NGOs in India have made notable contribution in this regard, set examples and shown the way.

(iii) **Monitoring the Effects of Development Actions and Highlighting Their contributions:** It includes monitoring of development actions by Government and private sector (business and industry) as well as by NGOs themselves. This kind of monitoring and constructive criticism is essential for corrective and transformative steps. It is in this way that NGOs have been able to bring to the fore issues relating to environment, women, Dalits (downtrodden) etc.

(iv) **Advocating causes:** Policy advocacy in favour of the disadvantaged sections of the society and for structural changes is vital, especially in a democratic set up. This kind of advocacy by NGOs has been increasing and becoming more forceful over the years.

(v) **Supporting peaceful struggles of people for their Empowerment and against Injustice, Exploitation and Oppression:** It is becoming very common with social activist groups. This role also has been assuming greater importance in the situation prevailing in India and with the growing awareness among the masses.

(vi) **Protection, upholding and Nourishing values:** It calls for deeper thought and understanding, but is important for NGOs, particularly in a miliu reolete with betrayals and conspiratorial tactics in society and governance and power-politics. Moral regeneration is considered extremely vital. While playing this role, NGOs themselves practise what they preach.

(vii) **Strengthening Democratic Institutions:** The stronger the involvement of democratic institutions, the greater the possibility of people-centered development interventions. Hence it is vital for NGOs to strengthen these institutions. These scopes of NGOs together capture various roles perceived and played including training and development education, professional assistance, constructive work, action-research, monitoring, activism and structural transformation. In democratic set-up in India where public -opinion plays an important role over the Governmental policies and programmes; the focus has been shifting towards generating from bottom enlightened and forceful people's opinion and peaceful action to bring about the desired changes.

Funding Pattern of NGOs

Historically, NGOs have been funded by different Governmental, non-institutional charity organisation at both the national and international level. In the post independence period, the non-institutional funding is the form of donation from the community, richer section of the society or from philanthropists etc. The most dominant sources of funding for NGOs in India till date have been international sources and the Government funding[54]. These sources are discussed funding as follows;

International Sources of Funding: The International contribution or foreign contributions in India is denoted as the donation, delivery or transfer made by any foreign source of any article, currency or foreign security, This is divided into the following categories;

(i) **Bilateral Institutional Funding:** Bilateral funding includes aid from agencies, department and ministries of the developed countries such as U.S.A., U.K., Japan, Sweden, Denmark, Norway, Canada and Australia etc. However, the substantial portion of this aid is made available to the Governmental sponsored programmes, while a very small proportion is made available to NGOs under the approval of the Government for the specific programme and largely regulated by the Government.

(ii) **Multilateral Institutional Funding:** The multilateral funding includes funds from various agencies of United Nations system like WHO, UNESCO, UNICEF, FAO, UNFPA, UNDP, ILO, UNEP etc. The other multilateral institutions like World Bank, IMF also provide funding to the NGOs in India under the overall supervision and regulation of the Government. It is mainly project based or scheme based. This type of funding is very limited and is confined largely to the major NGOs in India.

(iii) **International NGOs:** Private and NGOs of the developed nations primarily the European and American institutions foundations like Ford Foundation, the Rockefeller Foundation etc. provide support to the NGOs in India. Also a major source of funding comes to Indian NGOs from International Non-governmental sector. This funding is restricted to specialised institutions or available by the approval of the Government of India.

The major thrust areas of the international funding have been in the sectors like health, environment, family welfare, women and children, education, rural development and science and technology coming under the overall development programmes. The limitation in this type of funding is being temporary in nature and for short duration, action-oriented[55].

A Governmental legislation was passed in 1976, to regulate the flow of foreign contribution to the Non-governmental sector in India. For receiving any kind of assistance from the International Donors, the NGOs are required to register under the Foreign Contribution and Regulation Act (FCRA), 1976, under the Ministry of Home Affairs, Government of India[56].

Governmental Funding in India: For supporting the policy initiatives of encouragement of NGOs in Development sector the Government of India provided different programmes of financial assistance to the NGOs through grants-in-aid. Limited funding is available with the State Government and at the local institutional level. Many Government agencies like National Children's Fund, Central Social Welfare Board, Family Associations of India, CAPART etc. provide funding for NGOs. They are for specific purpose and in a limited scale[57].

At the local level, funds are provided largely through the District rural Development Agencies (DRDAS), Zilla Parishads, Panchayati Raj Institutions etc. At the central Government Level, Grants-in-aid are given to NGOs by various departments and ministries such as ministry of 'Human Resource Development', Department of Education, Department of Women and Child Development, Ministry of Welfare, Rural Development, Environment and Forest and Science and technology etc. The basic motto behind grants-in-aid is to encourage and promote NGOs in India and particularly in the areas where governmental action is rather limited. The rules of administration of grants-in-aid flow largely from the General Financial Rules, 1963 of Government of India[58].

NGOs in Health Sector Development:

The present section discusses the NGOs experience and approach to the health sector as a part of the development paradigm in India. In development terms, NGOs have provided an alternative and in many cases, a supplement to Government programmes. In several instances, NGOs have addressed the needs of the poor who are not served by Government programmes further, a vigorous non-Government sector as is present in India, is indicative on the part of Government, that some social functions are outside its legitimate control, thus reinforcing the role of NGOs for the pluralisation of society. With this backdrop the present analysis proceeds for a better understanding of NGOs performance in the health sector in a historical set up.

Although the state accepted responsibility for public health, in the mid 19th century, early efforts were almost entirely urban oriented with a strong emphasis on curative services; rural areas received attention mostly in times of epidemics. Only in 1946 was the concept of community based primary health care for both rural and urban areas brought to the forefront of Government attention by the Bhore committee on public health[59]. Among other things, it recommended the provision of primary health care through a three tiered system with a primary health unit for a population of 20, 000, emphasis on preventive health care through health education, immunisation programmes and environmental public health measures; training of support health personnel to guide people and reoriented medical education to cater to rural needs.

After Independence, the state took on the primary role in initiating and implementing development activities including the provision of health care and the recommendations of the Bhore committee as well as those of the several other committees subsequently appointed by Government on various aspects of community health were incorporated in the Five Year Plans and implemented through different Government programmes. Though the health situation improved considerably a result of these efforts, it was still far from satisfactory as late as 80s[60].

The 'Health and Development' field has been aided particularly by Non-governmental sector in spite of government's remaining as a major patron, especially since Independence. What is noteworthy is that the NGO sector was in contrast to the government, able to demonstrate significant reductions in mortality and fertility amongst its client groups, largely because many of the successful non-governmental organisations addressed themselves directly to the problems outlined earlier. Through trial and error and conscious innovations over a period, they (NGOs) evolved an approach to community health which worked altogether. It was an approach combining commitment and close involvement with the community at the grassroots, specific targeting of the poor and disadvantaged and organisational innovations. As a result, the NGO sector has built up a body of knowledge and practices how to identify the poorest in a community and how to involve them in the process of development which can be considered as an alternative approach to development. Because of this, there is a growing interest among governments, academics, social activists and donors (domestic or international) in the development initiatives of the NGO sector in Health, the objective being to learn from the diverse experiences of NGOs[61].

In India, NGOs working for community welfare were the result of a desire for social service associated with charity. The revival of Hinduism in the early Nineteenth century associated with the Christian missionaries and their activity were responsible for much of the early community welfare work. A large number of organisations came into existence between 1920 and 1947 as part of India's freedom struggle, as Indian patriots, enlightened officials and quasi missionary (YMCA) realised the need to up-lift the poor if self-government was to have any meaning[62]. Most of these NGOs were engaged in ameliorative work of relieve distress rather than developmental work to bring about long-term changes. An important part of this welfare way to offer medical aid, the approach being to set-up a hospsital or dispensary at the taluka (district/sub-district) level or in a densely populated village on an accessible route; with major emphasis on curative than the preventive or promotive aspects of health care[63].

However, there were three important exceptions to this pattern, which were to provide alternate models to non-Governmental Grassroots work in later years. These were the Martandam Rural Demonstration centre in Trivandrum set up by the Christian missionary organisation, the YMCA and the various projects for rural regeneration set up by Gandhiji and his followers such as the Sewagram project and Anand Niketan Ashram and Rabindranath Tagore's Sriniketan Institute of Rural Reconstruction, they all believed in long term development rather than temporary poverty alleviation[64]. They emphasised self-help to develop self -reliance in communities changing attitudes and social consciousness through education to make a long term impact and integrated development of the community by simultaneous efforts on many fronts[65].

In post Independence India, there was a phenomenal growth in the number of NGOs. Many were started as charities for relief work in the wake of droughts and floods but later turned to developmental work for long-term solutions to the problem of poverty. Others came about due to disenchantment with official development efforts which they felt were too slow or too corrupt or unable to reach the neediest. In this first phase (1947- 1960) most of the NGOs were conformist in their approach working within the established social framework and containing and resolving the conflicts within the existing socio-political structure[66].

In the mid- 60s, many realized that charity was not enough. Development, whereby local resources were to be used for the community's-development, has to replace welfare; their emphasis therefore shifted from charity to promoting self-reliance[67]. This phase marked the growth of social & consciousness among the educated, for many professionals, economists, sociologists, doctors, graduated to the NGO sector. It also reflected a growing impatience not only with the Government's slow functioning its inefficiency, corruption, and its development strategies which had failed to bridge the gap between the rich and poor, but also with the apathy and the dependent mentality of the masses who waited for the Government to solve all their problems rather than take any initiative themselves.

It was in the field of health that this new orientations first emerged. Experiments, at Narangwal in the late 1960s showed the way but its consolidation took place in Maharashtra with the Jamkhed, Mandwa, Miraj and Kara projects taking the lead[68]. The new approach had three main characteristics:

It was against giving anything free of charge, because if given free it ceases to have value for the people, creates a feudal relationship and paternalistic attitude to development along with a sense dependency among the beneficiaries;

- It was characterized by a project -based involvement
- It was professional in character.

Following the WHO-UNICEF Alma Ata declaration on primary health care, which advocates Health for All by the year. 2000 A.D; there was also a switch in emphasis from the purely curative to a balanced mix of preventive and curative services[69]. However, curative services remained and continue to remain an important component of health care offered by NGOs because they establish an organisations credibility in the community and lend it high visibility, facilitating later work in preventive health or other developmental areas.

Public recognition of the effectiveness of NGOs in grassroots development, including community health care, and the post 1977 official support extended to it by the Governmental and international agencies-bilateral, multilateral and private led to the rapid multiplication and involvement of NGOs in rural regeneration. The post 1970 years were characterised as being change or people oriented. Poverty was regarded not merely as a question of income generation but of attitudinal and value changes and of reorienting the social and political structure. The catchwords thus become conscientisation, participatory development; people's organisation etc and many NGOs were established to protest against socio-political abuses. Thus NGO health projects were characterised by[70]:

- An increasing involvement of the community in all aspects of programming.,

- adaptation of local health service personnel to primary health care,
- closer links between health and general development so that many way NGO focusing on health alone diversified into another development activities such as agricultural development and employment projects for women,
- a greater demand for rational resources and political will to support primary health care
- after 1975, when the women's movement had led to a recognition of the role of women in development, a greater concern with the health of women with a greater recognition of their potential as agents of change for health and development in the community.

Within this historical perspective of NGOs in Health and social sector development, the discussion further continue to understand their growth through different policy planning existed in India since Independence to exploit the early mentioned objectives to the maximum extent.

Growth of NGOs through Health Sector Policy Planning

The growth and development of various NGOs in India provided a good amount of insights how the NGOs have soldiered the responsibility in various sectors to make available fruits of development to the underprivileged exploited and marginalised communities in different stages of Indian developmental history. But questions arise, how the different policy decisions have given importance from time to time to the various NGOs to come forward to share responsibility in developmental measures. Unless an attempt is made to analyse how various developmental policy provided sufficient scope to play significant role to the NGOs, the direction of their future role in development as well as health sector cannot be accused properly.

There are several alternatives to the present mode of development, but those who bear the onus of influencing developmental policies do not seem to pay sufficient attention to the models already developed by scores of NGOs, based on their grassroots experiences. To a certain extent, the NGOs themselves are responsible for their own neglect, for most are so involved in their day-to-day efforts, as to become isolated from their Socio-political environment and to let their experiences, however unique, remain largely unrecorded and unheard[71].

Thus the contribution of the NGO sector is often unrecognised in evolving Policy, whereas it could provide a most useful basis for evolving more effective alternatives. NGO experiences are at times devalued because they are evaluated against a present criteria of development and not in terms intrinsic to their existence[72]. However, for our Policy makers who have fixed paradigms of development often not in tune with realities faced by the majority of our countrymen; NGO experiences can provide valuable ground level realities and facts. NGOs can no longer be dismissed as mere experiments considering the long period of tried and tested interventions. This does not imply a blind faith in NGO assertions but an acknowledgement of their contributions when defining developmental issues.

NGOs in India Function in both rural and urban areas, in one or more development sectors like health, education and employment, with activities ranging from providing services to advocacy and having charity, welfare, religious, political or corporate affiliations. Most of these NGOs are registered as non-profit-private trusts or societies funded from private, government, corporate or international agencies.

An estimated more than 5,000 organisations received international funding[73]. More than 100 field projects in rural areas concerned with health programmes have been identified in Maharashtra alone, where NGOs have a higher concentration in the least developed ones[74]. The NGO culture is also more marked in the developed states like Maharashtra, Gujarat, Kerala etc., compared to the less developed states in northern India. Activist groups are also largely concentrated in Southern India - Maharashtra, Karnataka, Tamil Nadu and Andhra Pradesh with a few in Bengal and Bihar[75]. The work of missionaries is also concentrated in these Southern States[76]. The Gandhian/Sarvodaya organisations made maximum impact after Independence till the mid-sixties, when voluntary action and NGOs joined together with government for nation building[77]. This resulted in both co-option and also formalisation of NGO work mainly in education, health and economic activities.

After Independence many NGO experiments and models became replicas that government used for formulating its own development strategy. Thus, the community Development Program-Projects of the government that began in Etawah, U.P. and the YMCA in Martandam, Tamil Nadu successful experiments with the community health approach by NGOs in the first half of the 1970s led to their being assigned an important role by the govt. in development planning and implementation and marked the culmination of an interaction which had begun with the First Five year plan. The plan had stated [78]; "Any plan for social and economic regeneration should take into account the services rendered by these agencies and the state should give them maximum co-operation in strengthening their efforts.

Public co-operation through voluntary service organisations is capable of yielding valuable results in channeling private efforts for the promotion of social welfare".

The result was that the government began to provide grants to NGOs to enable them to carry out their new development tasks, but the quantum of funding till the mid-60s was not very significant, and NGOs were not accorded any official states in the implementation of development programmes. Further development was the setting up of institutions for training young people in social work. The next phase between the 60s and early 70s was when a critique of the development model followed by the government began to emerge. In this period, the students' and Naxalite movements also gained momentum. There was simultaneously a change in strategy to area development programmes involving people's participation in government schemes. Many NGOs, which had started only with health interventions, went on to enter other areas like employment, agriculture and education to evolve as comprehensive development projects. Some of these NGOs took up government schemes for implementation. Other developments were the World Bank's support of anti-poverty programmes; and the corporate sector also became involved in altruism, of which house of TATA's was an example. However, the growing disenchantment with the government's development strategy in contrast to the NGOs' success in reaching the poorest, and the government's own realisation that it could not handle the enormous task of alleviating poverty single handedly, NGOs were given an increasingly important role from the Third Five Year Plan onwards. Each plan provided a growing amount to be channeled through NGOs for development programmes.

NGOs Growth in Fourth and Fifth Five Year Plans

The 1970s saw a great mushrooming of NGOs for various reasons. Firstly, the government was encouraging them by giving grants or permitting them to receive foreign funds directly. Secondly, the corporate sector in partnership with the government was encouraging and supporting NGOs, especially in the rural areas. Thirdly, new tax deductions to donors for providing funds for rural development and social services to NGOs were introduced in the Income Tax Act, therefore, increasing willingness to donate funds to NGOs. And finally, the professionalisation of the NGO sector provided opportunities to committed and motivated individuals to take up careers in 'development'[79].

Further, in the fifth-plan period the government began encouraging NGOs to take over, on a contractual basis for managing the programmes of the government in the social services sector. This was certainly a major policy shift from being earlier only a grant-giver. In the health sector the government, began giving its primary health centres to the NGOs to run them; also, certain national programmes (e.g. leprosy) in a specified area would be given to NGOs to implement. Under the Sixth Five-year plan this process was accelerated. In addition NGO representatives were made official advisors or nominated as experts in government committees and bodies, including the planning commission, indicating that NGO business were also official business. From the late 70s, ideas of conscientisation and people's participation began to emerge. The next phase in the 80s witnessed involvement with issues like environment and women's concerns. It has also seen the emergence of support organisations specialising in training, research, advocacy, documentation etc.

In health, the charity orientation gave way to emphasis on self-reliance and people's involvement in their own development. While the early initiatives were in setting up hospitals, giving free service, or distributing free medicines, the emphasis, particularly from early seventies, was on health care at the doorsteps of the rural workers. The new approach made several innovative experiments in primary health care.

In rural field projects, village health workers, locally selected and field trained, were employed for health services, reducing the almost total dependency on the professionals. Preventive and promotive health services involving community involvement like antenatal care, care of pre-school children, early detection and follow up of communicable diseases, were given importance besides including oral rehydration, immunisation and the concept of essential medicine. An epidemiological basis to the analysis of health and a community orientation to the resolution of health problems was adopted[80]. Health education was given due importance. Experiments at Banwasi Sewa Ashram set up in the 50s in U.P., Narangwal (Punjab) in the late 60s were forerunners; later many rural, field oriented health projects were set up around the early 70s like the Jamkhed, Mandwa, Miraj and Kasa projects which consolidated this health approach. Also during this period attempts have been made to find alternate source of financing health care particularly through community financing, which has also evoked strong opposition from some sections of health activities.

In Urban areas also, there were a few NGOs working with health care in the slums. A number of research and documentation centers, advocacy groups and movements and health related publications, began functioning. Support organisations for NGOs in health were also set up. In the 80s there have been many efforts to relate health to the macro-system. Health related issues like health policy, health expenditure, medical education, privatisation, rational drug and essential drugs, amniocentesis, have been taken up in a number of forms. Health culture, health economical and politics have been studied, including health in Panchayati Raj. A section of NGOs have been involved revitalising the indigenous systems of medicine and folk medicine traditions.

NGOs During Sixth Five Year Plan And After

During the sixth plan period NGO representatives lobbied the government with all its might and its impact can be seen in the National Health Policy statement and the seventh five-year plan. The 80s saw a consolidation of the NGO strengths, with their representatives getting place in government policy-making bodies effectively asserting their position, both in government bodies and through public platforms. The health section in the sixth five year plan document was heavily influenced by NGO methodology and the rural infrastructure prescribed was founded on recommendations, based on NGO experiences, as stated in ICSSR/ICMR report, 'Health for All: An Alternate strategy'. For the first time the government declaration of the 'National Health Policy' acknowledged the importance of NGOs. The seventh five year plan asserted the increasing reliance on the NGO sector to achieve the goal of 'Health for All'. The policy statement in the National Developing council was approved the role of NGOs which could play in planning and implementation of their own schemes since they had developed expertise to do so, particularly in the health sector. The active participation of rural agencies had been encouraged in a number of areas like improvement of primary health care, control of communicable diseases, MCH services, Sanitation, Rehabilitation of handicapped, reduction of infant mortality and family welfare. The Prime Minister's Technology Mission on drinking water literacy and immunisation envisaged a more effective role of NGOs. A Mission Director (Voluntary Agencies) on Technology Mission had been appointed by the office of the Adviser to the Prime Minister, for better co-ordination and effective implementation[81].

The Approach papers of the seventh five year plan calling for greater participation from NGOs, stated: " Non- governmental organisations will have to be associated more closely and actively than hither to with the programmes for reduction of poverty and with the efforts to make the minimum needs available to the population for improving their quality of life. This will be incorporated as part of the overall strategy for a augmenting such programmes meant for the poor, as also an alternative feedback mechanism for ascertaining whether the target groups have received the benefits meant for them "(GOI-1984)"[82]. It further adds that, 'Achieving active community participation and involvement in health and health related development programmes should also be part of the strategy. In particular, active community participation and involvement of NGOs in a massive health education effort is urgently needed....,with a view to reducing government expenditure and fully utilising untapped resources, planned programmes may be designed, related to the local requirements and potentials, to encourage establishment of practice by private medical professionals, increased investment by non- government. organisations in establishing curative centers and by offering organised logistical, financial and technical support to voluntary agencies active in the health field.'

The Ministry of Health and family welfare (MOHFW) is in full agreement with the planning commission on the issue of greater involvement of NGOs in the field of health care. In a government of India published (1985) document it was stated that, "The government has envisaged a very prominent role of NGOs in the implementation of these (health, family welfare and 20 point) programmes. In October 1982, directives were issued that NGOs be involved in the implementation of anti-poverty and minimum needs programmes which contain all the important health programmes like health education, drinking water facilities, immunisation, etc. and consultative groups be formed in all the states headed by a senior officer of the state. Also, NGOs involved in running hospitals and dispensaries outside the purview of government health sectors"[83].

Even the National Health Policy of 1983 recognised the need for greater reliance on the NGO and private sectors for achieving the goals of "Health for All by the year 2000 A.D". Thus the statement therein is [84] – "The policy envisages a very constructive and supportive relationship between the public and private sectors in the area of health by providing a corrective to re-establish the position of the private health sector".

The above statements make it appear that:

- The government has accepted its inability to provide adequate health care,
- The active participation of the NGOs is most necessary for achieving goals of the health sector and,
- Privatisation of the health sector will result in better provision of health services.

These perspectives, mostly suite both the government and private health care sector. The government succumbs to historical evidence of the failure of all its anti-poverty programmes including those of the health sector and invites the private sector to take charge the fight against poverty and disease. The private sector which is mainly responsible for the poverty-ill-health, malnutrition, poor-housing and sanitation, etc.- has over the years demonstrated to the government; through 'NGO-efforts', that it can do a better job even if 'development'! That is to be assessed in further analysis of the fact.

The government has thus been increasingly acknowledging the expertise and the innovative nature of NGO- intervention, and shown keenness to replicate innovative schemes already tried and tested in the field as well as readiness to reformulate old schemes, just as the NGO sector has sought to influence government policies on the basis of its expertise and experiences. The meeting of these two efforts however has not always been too happy. Whenever the government has tried to incorporate NGO initiatives within its rigid policies and infrastructure, the original innovation has been largely co-opted, only to become part of the traditional government machinery. Thus village health workers, the very basis of NGOs' rural health projects, were reduced to the undervalued lowest rung in the health hierarchy of the rural public health system. The original community Health centre, which was to be the centre of comprehensive health for 100,000 population, was reduced to yet another curative hospital rather than the centre for comprehensive health activities at 100,000 level[85]. The government was accused of following the NGO experiments twisted out of context.

The Rural Health Project of the king Edward Memorial Hospital (KEM Project) was consciously structured as a partnership between the government and an NGO to innovate and experiment within existing public health policies so that the government could test its own health tenants and, if successful, introduce them on a wider scale[86]. The KEM-Project was given the responsibility of managing the health care of Vadu block in Pune district of Maharashtra, using the government 's own health staff for that block. But here, the government surrenders only technical control and retained administrative control over the staff. However, the government went further in one instance, transferring the entire management responsibility - technical and administrative - to an NGO. The complete responsibility for the health care of Jhagadia block in Bharuch district of Gujarat state, has been transferred to the society for education welfare and Action - Rural (SEWA - Rural) - another of the Anubhav projects (financed by ford foundation) - by the government of India, the government of Gujarat and the district panchayat (village unit), the three agencies virtually involved in the various health programmes for the block[87].

Thus a self-fulfilling prophecy is generated regarding NGOs involvement in government - health - development programmes that;

- the government is inefficient, complacent and too bureaucratised and therefore cannot reach the people with its development programmes howsoever well planned; and
- the private sector is efficient, cost - effective, flexible and non-formal and therefore it can successfully execute the programmes of development taking it to population groups for whom they are really meant.

All this is clearly indicative of the close nexus between the private sector, NGOs and government policy making. The role played by the private sector in building up its socially more acceptable image through the NGO sector emerges clearly. How the government is used by the private sector for strengthening itself has also been established.

Policy Analysis of NGOs in Health Sector Development

Today, in the health and social sector development, we see a great boom in privatisation both independently as well as through the NGO sector. For which, diagnostic centers, corporate hospitals, health insurance and the like one on the uptrend, egged by the present government's policies to 're-established the private-sector'. What is meant by it ? What are the aims of such a strategy? Whom and what does it involve? How is it to be set about? What criteria may be used to judge whether it has been 'operationalised' or results achieved? Although National Health Policy Statement (GOI, 1982a)[88] invokes the private sector on several counts, there are no readily available answers to these questions. Thus the present section intend to review the basis of such a strategy which would enquire the desirability in connection with possibilities thereto in the present context of development.

Besides joining hands with the private sector for primary health care, the government also wishes to increase investment by private agencies in curative medical centers, particularly in 'specialty' and 'super-specialty' facilities, to ensure that they are adequately available within the country. The objective is to reduce government spending on these, so that more money becomes available for basic health services and existing government curative facilities are eventually used to treat the needy, underprivileged. To achieve this, it is proposed in the government policy-statements that the government has to offer logistic, financial and technical support to the private health sector. Thus in a spirit of 'privatisation', the government is devolving on the private sector same responsibilities which have been its preview to date. The several modalities enunciated pay due heed to the plurality of the private health sector: the private-NGOs in health sector is to participate in the extension of primary health care while private commercial interests invest in curative and specially facilities[89]. In this way, a more focused role seems to be envisioned for the government in the provision of health services. If the health sector is viewed as a conventional pyramidal structure, government services would be limited to the intermediate levels, while private agencies occupy the top and bottom of the pyramid. Their situation implies that both community -based voluntary agencies and sophisticated urban medical organisations will have interfaces' with the government health system. It is the nature of these interfaces – 'private-public' or 'government NGO' collaborates that is of immediate in the policy of privatisation.

However, the proposal for 'privatisation' can be viewed in a number of ways. At its most straight forward, it can signify the government's desire to expand private enterprise in all spheres of health in order to increase people's access to health care. By the absorption of private agencies and personal in state policy and programmes, the joint health sector may receive a fillip so that it becomes bigger, more varied and more effective, the inclusion of indigenous practitioners in the strategy suggests that no system are barred in the effort to expand health coverage, although the exclusion of private allopathic practitioners is puzzling in this regard. In any case, the scenario is one of "a hundred flowers are blooming", albeit at the periphery of government health services.

At this level, 'privatisation' may be part of a strategy for decentralisation, necessary to achieve better results in health, just as in other development sectors such as education or agriculture. Within the standard of governmental approach of policy making and planning at the centre and service delivery at the 'grassroots', with privatisation the implementation of programmes at the local-level would simply be entrusted to NGOs. This may help to circumvent a major problem, encountered in governmental efforts to decentralise the reluctance of state-level leaders to devolve power on the district, block and village-levels. The locus of conflict is shifted from centre – state, or state - district etc. to NGOs – state relations.

In the view of 'privatisation' the desire of government to involve NGOs in National Health development can be seen to stem from its admitted inability to meet policy and planning objectives and targets and to the implement programmes either the desired characteristics (e.g. community participation) or coverage (e.g. in remote areas where government doctors will not go). The decentralised and sociality committed nature of NGOs and its superior ability to organise people composed with bureaucratic structures are given as reasons for 'privatistations'[90].In this context, the government perhaps views itself as providing 'legal sanction' and 'back up' to the NGOs to fulfill mandate to spearhead social change. Another less-favorable interpretation of privatisation which finds currency in radical analysis of the government's courtship of NGOs (e.g.Sethi, 1984)[91]; is that privatisation is a strategy to co-opt the NGOs in order to quell shouts about bureaucratic inefficiency, corruption etc. and to dilute threats to existing power structures.

In this concern, the provision of funds and technical assistance to NGOs, the placement of private sector leaders on governmental committees or giving consultancies to them, are considered tactics of diffusion. Although the government appears to be 'decentralising' the co-operation view holds that the devolution of responsibilities on the NGOs is nominal rather than real. It becomes real in another possible interpretation of privatisation in which the term is taken to be akin to 'denationalisation'[92]. This fact may stem from the fact the realisation that, despite the immense resources the state has sunk into health services over the past fifty years of independence, it still fails to reach the majority of population. In contrast, the 'success' of the private sector is invoked. The corollary of 'denationalisation' is greater 'privatisation of the state', that is increasing reservation of government health services for 'the few', so that ultimately public services are made private[93]. Which of these interpretations of the strategy of privatisation is desirable? And also, as well as possible ? For understanding these facts the strengths and weaknesses of NGOs in health and social sector development must be examined.

Strength and Weakness of NGOs in Health and Social Sector Development

The potential for 'privatisation' or for collaboration between the government and the NGOs will be delimited by the strengths and weakness of both. NGOs in health sector are considered to have succeeded where government structures have failed. What have been the ingredients of the success? What have been the 'stress points'? The following facts very well discuss these queries.

NGOs have at one certain advantages and constraints to government programmes and their contributions and failures have to be seen in this context. The advantages are more clearly known: the motivation, dedication and commitment of the leadership and staff; the greater good will and receptiveness of the community in response to the close and intimate contact developed by NGOs, and the flexibility in operations, including an ability to experiment with new ideas and discard old ones that is afforded by their small size and non-bureaucratic structuring. Some NGOs have the advantage of the backup and support of large organisations or institutions such as medical college or hospital, a business organisation or a professional association, which undoubtedly contributes to their success. The disadvantages are many and more complex but rooted primarily in smaller and more uncertain resources in terms of both money and skills, though there are other problems, which need elaboration.

Both government and NGOs face some challenges because the problems of poverty, illiteracy and unemployment are so pervasive[94]. A streehitakarini found to its dismay, its biggest problem is the environment itself. The congesting and overcrowding, the lack of sanitation and clean drinking water and the lack of homogeneity in an urban slums composed of many caste, religions and languages make it difficult to plan for and spread health education. Migration in and out of the slum makes continuous monitoring impossible and the high levels of unemployed ensure that despite acceptance of health messages, and there is neither money nor facility to practice them, with far fewer resources NGOs can easily get overwhelmed by these problems.

A weak financial base is one of the major hurdles faced by NGOs which have to depend heavily on funds from government or foreign agencies[95]. Even the Anubhav NGOs, which are larger and more affluent than the average ones, are dependent heavily on these sources; for some almost half their budget comes from foreign donor agencies (as in case of CINI, the Pachod project, AWARE) or from the government (SEWA - Rural). This severely restricts their freedom and independence though it may not be openly admitted.

Because of uncertainty in funding, NGOs often have to compromise either in the activities they take on or in the manner of implementing them in order to conform to the funding agency's requirements. On the other hand, a good NGO is often under pressure to accept funds from several sources and ends up biting off more than it can chew comfortably, or loses programme cohesiveness by having to rely on too many desperate sources. Without continuous assured funding, long term perspective planning becomes difficult. The low incomes of the client groups also mean that self-supporting projects remain a distant mirage. The question of funding is thus one of the knottiest problems faced by an NGO.

There are other difficulties created by the NGO - government interface. Red-tapism and administrative bottle necks have led to delayed receipt of grants and supplier of drugs from the government. Some NGOs implementing government programmes in a particular area have faced difficulties in meeting the recurring requirements laid down by the government In some cases, duplication of health services has also been experienced, as in the VHS programme, since the bureaucracy has been slow to withdraw its own personnel from the areas where MHCs are operating in spite of government instructions to do so[96].

In both the RUHSA and KEM projects, where the government has surrendered only technical and not administrative control over the staff which placed under the NGO for health programme implementation, dual control has posed problems of co-ordination in administrative, management and supervisor issues[97]. Recruitment and training of staff have also proved more difficult because of consequent divided loyalties.

Even where total managerial controls, administrative and technical, have been invested in the NGOs, as in the case of SEWA-Rural, there have been problems. A lot of reporting, record keeping and follow up is required for the government can be a distraction and a strain. Further much less flexibility is evident or forth coming in respect of individual budgeted heads of expenditure, hampering innovation and a pragmatic approach to spending.

Despite the considerable effort, sensitivity and patience on the part of both the government and the NGO that require to achieve a harmonious relationship most desiring to co-operate with the government believe, that it can be done. Even as agency like AWARE, whose prime function is to conscientise the largest population to make demands on the government system to secure what's their due, and which can therefore be expected to come into conflict with the establishment frequently, has managed to keep such occasions to the minimum and has been able to co-operate closely with government. Functionaries[98]. Once an NGO establishes its credentials with the government and the people, there is less likelihood of the government being heavy-headed and strictly regulatory.

Sociological barriers are another constraints faced by NGOs. By and large, the traditionally conservative attitudes about women's roles and their illiteracy, itself a result of those attitudes, has meant that projects, especially in north India, have found it very difficult to hire women as community health workers or as higher functionaries. And without them it has been twice as difficult to reach poor women with health or other developmental programmes. Additionally, programmes directed at raising the status of women such as those undertaken by RUHSA, have met with resistance from the community because of deep-seated fears that they will change the established men-women relationship within the family and the community,

In RUSHA's experience husbands did not like even the midwives to talk much to their wives for fear that it could trigger irreversible thought processes[99]. The solution adopted by RUSHA to remove such traditional attitudes was to educate men, especially in women's issues.

The personnel problem faced by these NGOs has not been confined to recruiting women alone, but applies to the recruitment of doctors, other health functionaries and professional staff because of difficult rural living conditions, the major gap between urban and rural opportunities for earning high incomes and for professional advancement and the lack of personnel in rural areas. While the sociological barriers and recruitment problems are common to government and NGO programmes, staff recruitment problems faced by NGOs been compounded by their inability to pay high salaries to offer job securities due to uncertain funding or upward mobility because of the relatively small size of their operations.

The limits to NGOs success have come not only from constraints internal to NGOs but also from their external environment, which includes conditions which have already been discussed earlier, and the nature of the non-governmental voluntary sector itself. Indian voluntarism is fragmented and there are internal dimensions and factions. Thus it is not always possible to support, over a sufficient period of time, a common cause, which would improve impact. To this extent, these grass roots experiments do not constitute a monolithic movement of people's participation and self-reliance. Also, as the VHS experience has highlighted, there are the difficulties created by lack of horizontal co-ordination within the health sector, leading to duplication and overlapping.

First, there is the lack of co-ordination between the various units of the health department in the state government which deal separately with public health, family welfare, medical services, and medical education and so on, thus effecting policies towards NGOs. Second, there is lack of co-ordination between the state government and NGOs, especially as it related to information on government schemes and funds for NGOs, and accountability and auditing the operations of NGOs and the release of funds. Finally, there is lack of co-ordination between NGOs who could benefit by sharing their experiences. Often, they live isolated lives, cut off from other similar agencies and from the larger Socio-political environment. The situation is made worse by the lack of umbrella organisation, which could co-ordinate, represent and service the NGOs[100].

Collaboration between Government and NGOs

The issue of privatisation or collaboration between government and NGOs must be viewed in the light of the common features, differences and problems and possibilities of NGOs for which it is necessary to analyse the present policy on the subject concerned.

As already discussed, the National Health Policy Statement suggests that government interest in collaborating immediate cause, the inability of the public health system to deal effectively with national health problems. A partnership between government and NGOs is expected to overcome some of the structural weaknesses of the macro health system and to result in better utilisation of the government resources.

However, close security of some other government documents reveal a somewhat confused view of the relationship between government and NGOs. A publication of the Ministry of Health and Family Welfare (MOHFW, 1985)[101] stresses the steps the government has taken to date to support the NGOs and refers repeatedly to the fact that non-governmental agencies 'supplement' government efforts. This view is expanded somewhat in the following statement of the National Institute of Health and family welfare (1977)[102]: These agencies (NGOs) are mainly engaged to supplement the work of official organisations, to explore ways and means of doing new things, such as the spearheading of family planning movement in India and putting up demonstration and experimental projects.

Recently, the Approach paper to the VIII plan (1984) translated the recommendations of the National Health Policy to involve NGOs into a broad action strategy. It identified the areas of family planning, health education and curative medicine as important and suggested five ways in which NGOs can participate in planning, education, service provision, resource supplementation and innovation.

Thus, the government view of collaboration with the NGOs is largely one of encouraging the latter to fill the cracks between government health programmes, to undertake experimentation, and to provide resources. This is accompanied by the belief that government support and reinforcement will serve to give the NGOs the additional momentum it requires.

A somewhat complementary attitude exists in some quarters of the NGOs. For example, an editorial in a newsletter of the Asian Community Health Action Network, which includes some Indian Voluntary health groups, proclaiming, 'co-operation between governments and NGOs??- is unlikely to be very effective unless a significant portion of the initiative and the creativity in this relationship comes from the government (ACHAN, 1982)[103].

Another instance of this perception is provided by a national networking agency. At a seminar conducted by the VHAI (New Delhi) to discuss the

National Health Policy Statement, the main objectives set were the "dissemination of the policy and identification of modalities for collaboration with the Government in its implementation at every level". Although the associations has recently been concerned with issues relating to the demedicalisation of health care (such as low cost drugs, health education and the integration of health and development programmes), it does not seem to see a role for itself, as a pressure groups on the government. to adopt favorable strategies, norms or policies in this regard. "The report on Independent commission on health in India" is a supportive document towards this end.

Thus, it appears that NGOs are perceived both by themselves and the government as playing a supportive and not a lead or 'forceful' role. Not only can they not 'push or instruct government,' (ACHAN, 1982)[104], but their creative instruct have apparently to give way to government ones. Along these lines as extreme suggestion has been provided by ROY (1985) who states that-because the voluntary sector is 'demoralised and splintered' and suspicious of its fellow members on account of 'irregularities' and politicisation within it, the government is the only agency capable of bringing factions together[105].

There is another more complex perception emanates from the gap that existed between the GO-NGO collaboration that the government's avowed recognition the NGOs should be involved in the national health effort and its positive action in this direction. While higher echelons of government believe that the earlier attitude of government as 'patron' and NGOs as 'clients' has changed into one of equal partnership (MOHFW, 1985)[106]; NGOs allege that this change has not permitted lower level of government with which they deal more frequently (Roy, 1983)[107]. This attitude arises in part from governmental perceptions of NGOs as 'competitors' or as redundant entities.

Govt. Assistance to NGOs in Health Sector

According to the Ministry of Health and Family Welfare (MOHFW, 1985)[108], the government has taken several steps to date to 'collaborate' with NGOs in Health Sector. In the 1950s, a Board of Inspection was established in the Ministry of Health & Family Welfare, to visit voluntary medical organisations and encourage them to 'supplement' government effort. The Board was instrumental in recommending financial assistance to these agencies, and indeed the grant of funds has been the premier mode of collaboration between government and NGOs. Also NGOs are assisted specifically to promote voluntary blood donation, organise eye camps and promote family planning.

But, how do the NGOs view this modality? The issue of taking funds from government has perhaps been divisive. On the one hand, there is the feeling that government funds are public funds and so the government should make more available to the organisations, who are in touch with the people (Roy, 1983)[109]. In turn, some NGOs feel that taking government funds ensures credibility to with the government and the people, and accountability to them. While reporting that his experience with government funding has been encouraging, Roy (1983)[110] laments that a NGO becomes committed to "a straight, tangibly-oriented programmes, that has no room for improvisation or initiative" if it takes funds from government. In general, Roy perceives the 'attitudes and approaches' of government officials towards NGOs may cause problems for voluntary groups; thus driving them to seek. Their funding elsewhere; "A foreign donor agency comes with a human face; the governments in many cases think they are doing us a favor. The favor comes as an equal and is prepared to consider the agency efficient unless proved otherwise; the latter does not believe in equal partnership and in 80% percent of the cases considers NGOs guilty of corruption, of irregularities, of inefficiency........" (Roy, 1983)[111]. By the amendment of the Foreign contributions Act (1985)[112], now requires (NGOs) organisations receiving foreign donations to obtain prior clearance from the Home Ministry.

Despite the contractual nature of funding agreements, 'misunderstanding'- either genuine or 'engineered'- can lead to the application of adhoc decision; which lead many NGOs to stay away from government grants, which perhaps explains why funds meant for private programmes often go unutilised. Thus the 'communication and credibility gap' remains a major constraint to the Government.-NGO collaboration.

Critical Issues

It seems clear that the criticality of the NGOs to national health lies not in its size-which is small in terms of its coverage of the nation's population, but in the nature of its experience with primary health care, which however has been only faintly 'evaluated'. Despite the government's dependence in private sector experimentation, the lessons of NGOs' experience have had a limited applicability to the macro health system[113]. This constrained reality contrasts markedly with the policy prescription for 'privatisation', which implies large-scale difference on the part of the public health system to the private health sector.

Another attribute of the NGOs in health sector that puts pay to the possibility of 'privatisation' is its considerable heterogeneity 'charity-oriented', 'developmental' and 'political-activities', agencies make different contributions and would require different approaches on the part of government[114]. In the absence of a 'particular-standard' but effective approach, the government may find its interactions with NGOs in health sector too costly. Indeed, despite the changed orientation of NGOs' activity from 'social welfare to development', a look at its interaction with government reveals no new modalities.

Thus, any governmental attempt to decentralise health services through the NGOs in health sector (using micro-level projects to deliver macro-programmes') would be severely limited by its small size and heterogeneity. The government's hope to increase people's access to primary health care through the 'private sector' therefore, will have to take the form either of increasing size of the voluntary health sector several fold, or of markedly improving the capacity of government health services to 'absorb' its significant lessons. The first of these options clearly has limited potential, given the very special needs (besides finances and technical know-how) of Voluntary health-action; (e.g. dedicated leaders, community rapport) which cannot be 'produced' on demand by the government or anyone else. The second option, therefore, is for more important if collaboration between the government and NGOs is to have any meaning to the national health effort. Although this fact leads to the conclusion that NGOs must help the government to gain 'know-how' with regard to delivering primary health care and to improve the functioning of its health services, thereby enhancing its efforts and maximising the effectiveness of its resources, the tendency to date has been to concentrate on how the government must help the NGOs. Specifically, the following activities can be envisioned which would be fruitful but not detrimental to the 'national health policy' effort:

- Continued 'experimentation' by NGOs to develop approach and methods relevant to the macro-health system in the country.
- Pressure from the NGOs in Health Sector on the government (i) to improve its services so that more people enjoy access to them, and (ii) to develop structures capable of 'replicating' proven approaches on a larger scale,
- Funds from the govt. to NGOs for specific project inputs and relevant research,
- The collection and dissemination of information on both private and public health programmes, and networking of' actors' in both fields, undertaken by both public and private institutions,

- Interaction between the two sets of actors to foster a greater effort to educate the public, particularly by government institutions and large 'national' NGOs,

Finally, some modalities that are rejected by the present analysis must be of important facts to be mentioned. First, the attraction of private-sector resources into public programmes (except through health insurance schemes in the organised sector) would seem to be barking up the wrong tree. Second, the establishment of any 'code of conduct' (Roy, 1985)[115] by government for the NGOs in health-sector would likely to restrict voluntary action and may become an instrument of repression. As Baxi has argued (1985)[116], if governments' administrative or legal procedure which contradicts dialogue between government and NGOs' must concentrate on creating space for 'voluntary health action', rather than circumscribing it. Third, the creation of a 'semi-autonomous government department for social-service'-GONGO, (suggested by Chandra, 1985)[117] would make NGOs extensions of the government machinery and destroy their dynamism. The govt. should concentrate on planning for its own health service system to take into account the lessons of the private sector.

Fourth, while government should encourage the private voluntary sector, 'denationalisation' would work against the interests of national health. Although bids may be made by the private sector to take over government programmes, there are many reasons why health care cannot be left to the private sector alone, whether one considers 'commercial' or 'Voluntary' organisations, together or separately. These reasons are as follows:

- The private sector cannot spread widely and densely enough over the country to adequately meet the rural health needs,
- It lacks steady resource base and widespread infra structure that the government has,
- Its Voluntary component depends on the funds from external agencies and other uncertain sources,
- Its profit-making segment will not perform well in rural areas, even given Robin Hood methods,
- Nor will it provide the public health, preventive and promotive services required, as these are perceived to take away from its livelihood.

Majority of Indian, in need of health care, need free services because they cannot afford, even the 'highly-subsidised' ones. In this concern health care remains a social and community service and cannot become fully commercial enterprise (Basu, 1983)[118]

The inadequacies of the private-sector health care, are clearly demonstrated by the situation in urban areas where, despite a glut of private practitioners, clinics, hospitals. The poor flack to govt. hospitals and charitable clinics. The heavy demands on these urban facilities may suggest that they should be expanded, but perhaps more important, is the need to reserve these free public services for those who need them most, keeping out the affluent who can well afford to patronise the private sector. At best, the private sector can contribute to the national health effort by providing special services, generating knowledge, mobilising people and exerting pressure on government, through its voluntary effort by NGOs to fulfill its objective as well as responsibility. NGO initiatives in Health Care has vital importance to the current development discourse in terms of promoting community involvement, participation and their empowerment to achieve sustainability. The ongoing review further focuses on understanding community action and community involvement in strengthening health sector reforms in hastening programme sustainability in developing countries.

Chapter - III

Sustainability of Development Initiatives

Defining sustainability: common tools practiced by the donors

'Sustainability'- as a term and as a concept is broadly understood in two different ways in recent development aid literature. These are:

(a) Environmental sustainability - emphasising the environmentally sustainable aspects of development projects or interventions. The definition of this notion of sustainability is: Sustainable development is development that meets the needs of the present without compromising the ability of future generations to meet their own needs (Brundtland Commission, 1987). A development initiative is considered sustainable when it is economically and financially sustainable in terms of growth, capital maintenance and efficient use of resources and investments. But it has also to be ecologically sustainable, which means ecosystem integrity, carrying capacity and conservation of natural resources including bio-diversity. However, equally important is, the social side, for example, equity, social mobility, social cohesion, participation, empowerment, cultural identity and institutional development (Serageldin, 1996). So, the concept of sustainability in sustainable development implies balancing environmental protection with generation of increased opportunities for employment and improved livelihoods.

(b) Sustainability as Viability – This notion of sustainability, which this research is considering as its central concept, is emphasising the viability or sustainability (ability to survive) of certain development projects or interventions after the external support has been withdrawn. OECD's 'general definition' of this notion of sustainability is:

"While there is no universally accepted definition, in general terms sustainability is the survival of projects and programmes after the initial period of investment – financial, physical, and technological. In international development assistance, sustainability refers to the continuation of projects and programmes after the termination of assistance from an external donor. The concept, however must be expressed more precisely if managers of development are to understand what is required during the investment period to achieve sustained development activity activity"(OECD, 1989). To that end the following definition provides a more explicit basis for discussing the characteristics of the sustainability of development programmes.

Some of the key points of these definitions are;

- The focus is on sustaining the flow of benefits – the results or impact of a programme – that are relevant to a developing country's priority needs and the interest of decision- makers and beneficiaries.
- Projects are specific interventions of donors for assisting a developing country to achieve sustainable benefits and maintain supporting activities and institutions.
- The appropriate level of benefits and the time period will need to be defined in each instance taking into account the country's development objectives, the initial investments and recurrent costs and the creation of a permanent institutional capacity within the community.
- The termination of major external assistance assumes the developing country will provide the financial, technical and managerial resources required to sustain the programme. Continuing relations with external technical groups and supplementary financing of commodities may often be desirable.

The arrival of both notions of sustainability with the above definitions (a. and b.) in development and literature happened during very recent decades- when both of them got priority in policies regarding aid conditionality of the donors. Theoretical development of 'environmental sustainability' has been progressing well in the recent academic and professional research (Clayton and Radcliffe, 1996). But the other notion of sustainability, i.e, the project sustainability got very little attention in academic and professional research. In recent years, due to the practical matter that research and sustainability development programmes needs in depth field study on particular projects – also with a focus on the larger context of the development intervention (FINNIDA 1994). Often it is very difficult to generalise issues related to sustainability by consulting only data and information from secondary sources. The study of sustainability is also a time-consuming process, needing empirical evidence on each project – before anything can be theorised on the topic. Each of the above evaluation reports emphasised the need for further study on sustainability for development projects.

The present study only refers to the notion of sustainability of development projects, with a particular focus on NGO - led development initiatives. It is easy to understand from the previous definition that sustainability of development projects depends on certain factors, related to the project management. The factors of sustainability mentioned below are the abbreviated form presented by OECD study on 'Sustainability in development programmes, a compendium of evaluation experience':

Factors of Sustainability

The factors fall under the following headings: government policies, management, organisation and local participation; technology, socio-culture environment and ecology, and external political and economic circumstances. The relative importance of the complex of effects and activity under each of these seven headings to the sustainability of development programmes cannot be established except from an examination of each situation. The highlights of these seven factors are as follows:

(a) Host government policies – development projects operate within the context of national policies. Government commitment and policies that support project activities are critical to the sustainability of development programmes. Developing country commitment to a programme is one of the most commonly identified factors affecting sustainability. Analyses of this commitment take into account the agreement on objectives, the breadth and depth of support within the responsible organisations and from various political, bureaucratic, private and local community groups and the willingness to provide financial and personnel resources. Country commitment is also shaped by perceptions of mutuality of interest versus perception of predominantly donor-driven interests. Therefore, the analysis of the importance and effects of various government policies for programme performance and sustainability are desirable and where feasible, applied in promoting policy reforms.

(b) Management, Organisation and local participation – This include considerations of managerial leadership, administrative systems and the involvement of beneficiary communities. Programme management encompasses responsibility of shaping policy and technological applications, setting goals, and mobilising support from political leaders, complementary organisations, and beneficiaries, as well as directing internal administration. When project objectives are well matched with an organisation's administrative capability – existing or expanding-over time – sustainability is enhanced. For many programmes, where the benefits are directly associated with local community, participation becomes critical to sustainability. Community participation is an integral part of continuing the flow of benefits after termination of a donor's assistance.

(c) Financial factors: A major impediment to sustainability has been the inability to achieve continued, regular funding of annual operating costs. Experience shows that unless developing – country financial support is phased in while external support is still being provided it is unlikely that it will be continued after such support ends. Where the financing of recurrent costs is a chronic problem, donors nay have to cover a portion of these costs for an extended period. The prospects of sustainability are often greater for programmes that do not depend on general public funds for all of their recurrent costs. User fees, community financing and village contribution are desirable ways to shift some of the cost burden as well as establish the demand for services. An understanding by local communities of the nature and scale of this costs is important from the early stages of project activity. In general, the decentralisation of development activity to local communities and private enterprise can strengthen commitment and help to mobilise resources for sustainability that otherwise would not be available.

(d) Technological factors - The technology chosen for the programme must be appropriate both to the developing countrries -financial and institutional- capabilities and to the programme goals. A simple technology i.e., precisely focused on the needs of the task at hand and is of uniform origin enables counterpart staff to master it quickly. The costs of providing and maintaining the technology must not be excessive relative to benefits generated. Developing countries need to have the capability to develop and adapt new technologies as circumstance change. As per the development and application of 'soft' technologies such as organisation structure and management, personnel and training practices are important to facilitate the assimilation of new 'hard' technologies.

(e) Socio-cultural factors-the integration of a programme with the socio-cultural setting of its beneficiaries and operating circumstances becomes especially important if the activity is not to be rejected after assistance ends. Programmes which attempt to function in ways that are inconsistent with local traditions or assume changes in behaviour patterns, have a high risk of failure. The involvement of local communities can promote sustainability by building a base of support and fostering a sense of local ownership of the programme.

Gender – specific data that help to define the differences between the roles, responsibilities and opportunities of women and men can assist managers in strengthening the sustainability of programme benefits.

(f) Environmental and ecological factors- population pressures and poor management of natural resources is threatening to the ecological balance of many developing countries. Unplanned development, in some cases, has accelerated the depletion of natural resources, threatening the ability of the environment to renew itself and affecting program sustainability. Regulatory controls are often required to prevent environmental abuse for encouraging changes in behavior patterns to enhance sustainability.

(g) External factors – development programmes operate within the context of existing political economic and cultural circumstances that are beyond their control and influence. Yet, their sustainability can be deeply affected by these circumstances. Where the development programme or other forces cannot bring about changes in the external circumstances to create a more positive setting, copying mechanisms may need to be built into program management. Even where, programs and their benefits are deeply embedded in local institutions, their chance for coping with adverse circumstances, and thus, their sustainability is better ensured.

(h) Donor Support – sustainability is a subject very closely linked with donor policy and support. Development initiatives involving NGOs are usually not sustainable due to the following factors:

- NGOs do not get a favorable environment to work in, due to the lack of proper grassroots policies and bureaucratic dominance-nature of government functioning in most developing countries.

- The commitment of donors and their policies to support NGOs is not yet stable enough in donor and in recipient countries, by which NGO workers and staff members are working with a degree of uncertainty in developing countries.
- For various reasons, the management capacity of NGOs in managing developing countries is weak. This makes the NGO led development initiatives unsustainable.

With this backdrop on the literature on sustainability of development initiatives, the health care sustainability becomes vital to proceed further in reviewing the present study in the context of developing country.

Health Care Sustainability in Developing Countries

For aid agencies, unsustainable investments became a serious threat to institutional credibility. An implicit assumption of foreign assistance is that it should 'make the recipient capable of becoming autonomous at some point in the future'.(Bossert T, 1990). Yet, during the 1980's economic conditions dictated that the need for aid was increasing rather than decreasing. Many countries were struggling to run their existing services and were increasingly unable to maintain new investments without continued external support. Thus, during the 1980's donors began to question the long-term effectiveness of their own investments. This was reflected in discussing the following questions:

- Why do so many projects and programmes fail to continue after the initial investment is made?
- What happens after the donor money is spent?
- What can be done to improve project sustainability? (Bossert T, 1990, Buzzard S, 1987)

Until this time few questions were ever raised about sustainability in the health sector. But new conditions forced donors to begin to confront the issue. In addition to the financing crisis in developing countries, the 1980's brought a major shift in the dominant political ideologies of donor governments that changed perceptions and expectations of foreign aid. Fueled by the end of the cold war, western governments began openly promoting 'free markets' and 'good governance' in many new aid - packages. Economic values, in particular, filtered into the health sector in an explicit preference for private sector solutions (by some donor institutions) and increased use of economic indicators (World Bank, 1987). Cost-effectiveness and 'value for money' were increasingly used as the *sine qua non* of successful development assistance. Second, and related to these changes in success criteria, this period was also marked by an enormous push to justify aid spending. As resources became tighter in donor countries, aid donors came under increased pressure to optimize spending and demonstrate the utility of aid more clearly. Demands for evaluations increased and sustainability was introduced, along with other criteria, as a measure of aid effectiveness (Save the Children Fund, 1990).

Donor officials report that both the shift in aid goals and increased pressure to achieve them are linked to the decline of aid of budgets that was mentioned above. Most bilateral donor agencies reported a distinct decline in the popularity of foreign aid (and the security of aid budgets) throughout the 1980s. It is possible that the rigorous scrutiny of aid is a result of this decline. But it is equally possible that perceived- ineffectiveness is the cause. Whatever its sources, donors soon learned that their response to the health financing crisis in recipient countries were critical to their survival as institutions. Unless they could show that aid could be spent efficiently, they risked further budget cuts and continue erosion of support.

The combined effect of fewer aid resources, weakened (developing country) public sector capacity, and pressure to demonstrate the utility of investment (in economic terms) placed donor institutions in a difficult position. Demonstrating a lasting impact from aid had become increasingly difficult. Current approaches to investing in health appeared no longer valid. To cope with these pressures and preserve aid budgets health donors were forced to look for new ways to invest in health.

Despite these pressures, the PHC agenda was not abandoned. It was, however, re-interpreted and revised as the inevitable repercussions of economic recession and pressure on aid budgets became clearer. Realizing, the potential long-term effects of economic decline on developing countries, donors looked for strategies, that would work under economic adversity but at the same time satisfy the demand of their funding sources. Around the mid 1980s,many donors changed their approach to investment in health by narrowing on delivering specific cost-effective health interventions (e.g. immunization and oral rehydration therapy ORT). A statement from UNICEF recalls the problems facing many donors:

> *The disastrous consequences of the recession prompted UNICEF to re-examine its work with a view to exploring and reordering its priorities at times when resources are limited amidst increasing demands and needs. This led to the adoption of low-cost, high-impact measures which would contribute to child survival and development. They are now referred to as measures for CSDR : the Child Survival and Development Revolution and viewed as the core of a cost-effective and high impact*

programme which could ultimately lead to the development of primary health care (UNICEF, 1988)

Ironically, international development goals for health remained ambitious throughout the decade. Major health 'movements' such as the Child Survival Development Revolution were launched during this period and many donors committed themselves to achieving Universal Child Immunization by 1990. As stated by one aid official: 'We were asked to do more and more with fewer and fewer resources.' Unfortunately this initial response to the sustainability dilemma proved no more compatible with the goals of sustainable development than earlier approaches. In the poorer countries, it soon became evident that even single health interventions would require long-term support. Concerns were raised about the sustainability of this new investment strategy while donors struggled to find an answer to the recurrent cost problem.

Defining Sustainability of Health Systems Development

Sustainability is a subjective concept. While donors' investment experience in the 1980s was instrumental in placing the issue of sustainability on the agenda, their perception of sustainability and the sustainability problem) reflects only one perspective. This traditional notion of sustainability derives from the system for providing international assistance to poor countries. It is 'rooted in the development mode which relies on temporary projects using outside resources' (Honadle G and Van Sant J, 1985) to produce changes in health care activity and health status. International aid usually comes in the form of time-limited 'packages' designed for a specific purpose. The classic- project provides resources and advice for erecting a hospital or health center. A variation of an aid project introduces new health activities through training and supplying initial equipment and commodities. Through these interventions, aid projects aim to stimulate positive changes in health system performance.

For the most part, all external investment strategies are of the same basic design. They are predicated on the assumption that once initial 'start–up' costs are met, donors will 'hand over' all project responsibilities to government. Ordinarily these responsibilities consist of operational costs and support activities such as supervision and management. According to the traditional definition sustainability occurs when government absorbs these responsibilities and is able to maintain project benefits. Though it may be expressed in different ways by different donor agencies, the basic thrust of the concept revolves around the continuity and success of external investments. The majority of donor perceptions of sustainability are reflected in the following definition employed by the United States Agency for International Development (USAID):

Sustainability is the ability of a health project or programme to deliver health services or sustain benefits after major technical, managerial and financial support has ceased.

Donors adhere to this idea of sustainability due to reluctance to take on long-term recurrent cost support for health activities. They perceive recurrent funding as government's responsibility and are required to stimulate or invest in new services rather than prop up existing activities.

Sustainability, in the donor sense is an artifact of the dominant development paradigm. It is therefore only useful as a measure of the effect of external investment in health. This approach to sustainability was found to be inadequate in the following ways. First, it is focussed on the sustainability of single investments. Second, it reflects the narrow concerns of external agencies rather than the problem facing national governments. From the perspective of country level respondents, anxiety about sustainability was expressed in terms which were very different to those used by donors. Government officials reported that they were concerned about the entire health system, not simply a collection of donor projects. Ghanaian health managers felt that government's job is to secure resources and use them effectively to improve the capacity of the system as a whole. Donors are but one source of resources in this process. Though external funds may cover a substantial proportion of the health budget, ministries of health must be capable of maximizing all resources, which come into the sector to sustain and improve the entire system. Many of the developing country health officials interviewed for this research felt that donors began to employ the term sustainability to provide them, with an excuse to 'pull out' of projects even when government was in no position to carry on project activities.

The Director of the External Aid Coordinating Committee in the Ghanaian 'Ministry of Health' summarizes the difference between government, and donor perceptions of sustainability:

Sustainability is an important principle to both the Government of Ghana and the donors but it probably does not mean the same thing to both. Usually define sustainability to mean being able, after a period, to withdraw completely and have the system remain operational. We must remember that Ghana is not a rich country and that for a while yet we are going to need significant external support. With this provision, we have no alternative but to consider sustainability in terms of organisational development and systematic growth, confidence building and improved efficiency in the use of resources (MOH, Ghana 1993).

This reflection of the sustainability problem clearly indicates that the donors' notion of sustainability is at least one step removed from the sustainability problem that countries themselves are facing. Donors, pay more attention to the life of the project than to the contribution that project might be making to health system development. Evidence suggests, however, that the persistent demise of externally-financed activities is just a symptom of a deeper sustainability facing health systems throughout the developing world. Despite 14 years of investment in PHC, health systems in low- income countries continue to suffer from misallocation of resources, inequity, inefficiency and exploding costs (World Bank, 1993). The search for the key to 'donor project sustainability' must therefore yield to the following mentioned, more important questions:

- How best to ensure the sustainability of the entire health system?
- Why is the totality of investment in health not overcoming the obstacles to sustainable development?
- Why is it failing to improve local capacity to deliver health care?

The definition that guides the discussion of sustainability – *the capacity of the health system to function effectively over time with a minimum of external input was chosen to address the shortcomings of traditional concepts of* sustainability. Sustainability is used in a much broader sense, focusing on developing countries rather than donors. While the effectiveness of singular investments is important for health system development, sustainability will not result from a series of sustainable projects or interventions. At some point all investments must come together in a coordinated fashion to enable the establishment and survival of the whole health system. Having broadened the definition, the next challenge is to identify a way of measuring system sustainability.

Measuring Sustainability

The difficulties of measuring sustainability are legion. In contrast to other characteristics of a health system, such as effectiveness and efficiency, there are no standard or even proxy indicators of sustainability. The absence of tools to evaluate sustainability testifies to its 'slipperness' as a concept and may explain why it is interpreted and used in many different ways. What makes it so difficult to pin down is that sustainability represents a process rather than a static quality. There is a 'time element' that must be factored in to any measurement. Brinkerhoff and Goldsmith note that 'sustainability is not an end state but an ongoing input – output process' (Brikerhoff D and Goldsmith A, 1992). Indicators of sustainability must therefore capture this movement over time or capacity for continuity. In the case of health systems, sustainability indicates a capacity to continue to transform resource inputs into health outputs on a continuous basis.

For sustainability to be achieved, however, continuity alone is not sufficient. The perpetuation of a health system, which fails to meet health needs, is of little value. According to the definition above, a sustainable health system must 'function- effectively over time', meaning, in this case, being able to guarantee to all citizens access to health services at levels of quality defined by international standards. Thus, any appraisal of sustainability must include indicators of effectiveness as well as continuity. Effectiveness is not synonymous with an improvement in sustainability; nor should a functioning health system comprising of services, which are ineffective be considered sustainable.

Accessing sustainability is further complicated by the absence of an agreed normative definition of a health system. Neither, the structure or function, of what should be sustained in each country is universally recognized. This is not only problematic for studies of sustainability. It also confuses the way in which governments and donors develop health systems. Since there are no standard blueprints for the 'ideal' structure and function of a health system, investors in the same country may not share a common vision of the health system they are building. In the last fourteen years, only the Alma Ata declaration has offered any guiding principles. The primary health care approach called for universally accessible, appropriate and affordable health services. However, because these qualities themselves are also vague, they have been interpreted in different ways, resulting in considerable confusion and conflict. Three or four different concepts of primary health care might be applied within the same country at the same time. Even if there is agreement to develop a health system according to these principles, the strategy for reaching these goals is often disputed.

Clearly, defining the 'ideal health system' is beyond the scope of this review. Underlying the basic standards of continuity and effectiveness, the appropriate six- shape and functions of a health system are context-sensitive and must be determined according to country circumstances and local values. Nevertheless, for the empirical examination of sustainability, it was necessary to define some basic features of a health system that enable it to function effectively over time. These features are outlined in relation to two types of capacity as mentioned below the:

- Capacity to secure sufficient resources locally; and
- Capacity to use resources effectively and efficiently to meet health need.

For sustainability to be achieved, a health system must be able to perform both these functions on a continuos basis. These two capacities were chosen as the minimum basic requirements for the effective transformation of resource inputs into health outputs over time, without which a health system could not be deemed sustainable.

The capacity to secure resources locally pertains to the financial resource base for health – an area that has received unprecedented attention in the last decade due to the effects of economic recession on health spending – and the methods for raising revenue for the health system. The scale and complexity of the health services, which can be sustained depends on the absolute level of resources available and the ease with which the health system can secure them. A pattern of effective basic service provision, which costs $10 per person per year, cannot be sustained with financing of only $2 per person. Similarly, even if sufficient resources exist, unless they are made available to the health sector, sustaining basic levels of services will improve impossible. The amount of health benefit, which the health system produces over time, also depends on how those resources are used. The mix of services, the efficiency of delivery and the distribution of benefits among the population all influence the level of health output that can be sustained within a given budget, as well as the quality of care provided.

Before moving on from these basic requirements to discuss the determinants of health system capacity, a final dimension of sustainability must be introduced. The definition calls for a capacity to function effectively over time with minimum external input. This aspect of the definition is often viewed with trepidation since the discussion is focused on some of the poorest countries in the world. They are countries which will continue to rely heavily on international aid resources for developing and maintaining health services and are perhaps the least likely to achieve financial self-reliance, as do autonomy in planning and policy-making. Health systems may go through stages of increasingly greater self-reliance before they become fully autonomous. Investment strategies should lend equal weight to achieving effectiveness, continuity and self-reliance.

Sustainability-A Conceptual Framework

According to the proxy indicators above (the two capacities) most health systems in developing countries are not yet sustainable. They lack competence in specific operational areas that enable effective and continuos health care delivery: financial management skills for raising revenue, and planning and management skills for effective and efficient resource use. While the absence of these skills testifies to poor health system capacity, addressing these problems requires a deeper understanding of why they persist. The conceptual framework used in terms of the following mentioned factors;

- What has been the experience of health system development over the past decade?
- What aspects of this experience affected sustainability?
- Why did expected changes in health system capacity fail to happen?

Health systems develop in response to different influences, internal and external. Two broad areas of investigation were chosen to examine these determinants of sustainable health system development:

- The context or environment of development; and
- Investment patterns.

CONCEPTUAL FRAMEWORK

Determinants of Sustainable Health System

Context

Exogenous variables
(Economics, politics)
Actors
(Central government, health
ministry, donors, people)

↓

Investment → → **System capacity/ sustainability**

Process variables
(Logic, strategies,
methods, patterns)

Capacity to secure resources and use them effectively for long-term health – care delivery
(Effectiveness, continuity, self–reliance)

Health systems in developing countries do not develop in a vacuum. Their development path often passes through particularly hostile environments that directly and indirectly influence health system survival and effectiveness. Context is used here to denote the political, economic and organisational structures and actors, which act upon health systems. Exogeneous influences range from economic volatility to trends in international aid policies and practices. The period under discussion loosely defined as the 1980s and early 1990s, witnessed dramatic changes in these areas. Both governments and donors seemed to spend much of their time reacting and adjusting to the changes wrought by economic recession (in the early 1980s) and political change (in the early 1990s).

In terms of major international trends in health services system, there have been two major transitions in emphasis. The period began with a challenge to the primary health care movement by advocates of a narrower, more selective approach. By the middle of the decade talk of accessible, affordable and appropriate health systems had been muted by major drives for increased access to two basic health technologies: immunization and oral rehydration therapy. Eyes were also fixed on health economics and financing issues in an attempt to offset the effects of economic decline. Towards the early 1990s the position on health and development strategies began to shift away from these single interventions to emphasize again the importance of health system development. Only recently have major investors in health been able to pause to consider the effect of these rapid changes on strategies and methods of investment in health.

There are also internal environmental factors, which have an impact on the health system. The market for health may encourage investors to develop the most costly health care, leading to waste of scarce resources. Moreover, health may rank low on the governments' agenda or represent a profitable industry for special interests. Without consistent and appropriate internal support for health from providers, users and stakeholders, the health system may develop in unsustainable directions.

In addition to wider development trends, the way health system investment occurs within a particular country is equally important for sustainability. In this case, investment is the intentional use of resources for stimulating improvement in health status and health system capacity. It is used in its broadest sense, embracing the variety of activities and processes, which determine how resources are employed for health system development.

Health systems depend on the investment process to obtain resource inputs and generate helath outputs. This process is central to health system development because it is the place where all the major players come together to influence priorities, resource allocation and management. Chief among these players are health ministries, their governments and aid donors.

The quality of the investment process is judged according to its effect on health- capacity. What kinds of resource inputs lead to stronger local capacity to produce health outputs over the long-term? Does investment act as a catalyst for sustainable health system development or a deterrent? Even in poor countries not all investments are good investments when sustainability is the issue.

> *Managers must consider the possibility that the processes they use to apply resources, deliver goods and services and evoke response (in beneficiaries) may, in fact, lower the possibility that these processes will continue after investment is made (Honadle G and Vant Sant J, 1985).*

Analyzing the investment process raises questions about the actors or institutions, which are responsible for investing in health. Are the actors and methods of investment suited to the developmental needs of the health system? Most investment plans are made and implemented within organisational settings. Health ministries and donors experience pressures, which have a bearing on investment practices. While investment strategies and methods may appear to respond to the needs of the health system, they also reflect the culture and the structures of the institutions, which practice them. Understanding the motives and methods of investors (as well as their actions) helps to build a complete picture of the investment process.

Sustainability: Client-Driven Approach in Non-governmental Health Care

"Sustainability" is neither a new, nor an especially obscure concept in social development.[1] Buzzard's discussion paper, "Development Assistance and Health Programs: Issues of Sustainability," which reviewed USAID's worldwide experience with health service projects in order to identify factors necessary to their sustainability, appeared in 1987.[2] This review coincided with the initial stages of a USAID-sponsored review, conducted from 1986 to 1989, of U.S. government funded projects in health, population and nutrition in five countries for the purpose of beginning to develop guidelines for the design of sustainable projects.[3] The World Bank was also undertaking its first reviews of project sustainability in several sectors at this time,[4] although the issue of ensuring the continued flow of development activity benefits to intended populations beyond the completion of a project — while not using the term "sustainability" — was a matter of concern in the previous decade.[5]

Sustainability refers to the *probability* that an organization's activities will continue to produce outcomes of sufficient value for their intended client population(s) so that they generate adequate local resources to support the continuation of benefits at a steady or growing level. [6] Although this definition of sustainability is firmly rooted in a continuing dialogue within the development community that stretches back more than two decades, the particular approach approach to promoting sustainability that is described below is innovative and represents a departure from the conventional approaches typically followed by donor organizations.

The Conventional Approach: A Project-Based Model of Sustainability

The common project-based approach to development, which has been predominantly focused on public sector interventions, has framed most discussions of sustainability. Given that a project, by its very nature, is time-limited, the question of what would continue beyond the end of a project, i.e. what would be "sustained," typically distinguished between that project's *activities* and their resultant *benefits* for intended populations.[7] This applies equally to projects supporting public sector interventions, which has been the predominant focus of donor development assistance, and to projects undertaken by nongovernmental organizations (NGOs), which have gained increasing favor as implementation vehicles for donor-driven development activities.[8] In both cases, the sustainability of *activities* becomes an issue of how they can be transferred or absorbed by existing administrative structures. It is this issue that has dominated conventional approaches to sustainability. Discussions of the continuation of benefits that are not dependent on specific activities are less frequently encountered.[9]

Consequently, this traditional approach focuses primarily on the strengthening of internal management systems — planning, personnel, training, supervision, financial, logistical, and information.[10] Sustainability is equated with good management and is typically assumed to be an achievable end-state of a process of organizational development.[11] The project's external environment is taken into account in terms of its role within each of these systems (e.g. health needs, demographic structure of the community, regulatory environment), and as a source of resources and constraints to which the project or organization must adapt.[12] Moreover, such adaptation is typically conceived of as *homeostatic* in nature — directed to returning an organization to a state of stable equilibrium with its environment.[13]

The public sector context within which this approach has evolved yields analyses that are likely to be sub-optimal for non-governmental programs, for which a sustainability strategy should not be one of how best to transfer activities to established administrative structures, but of how to sustain the benefits derived from independent operations — whether self-contained or part of a larger network. For this, a more dynamic approach is required — one that combines the useful elements of the conventional approach above with those *specifically appropriate* to private sector organizations, both commercial and not-for-profit.

Our alternative approach to sustainability focuses on the organization that is producing the benefits that are intended to be continued. In doing so, it is less concerned with an organization's status as a non-profit or for-profit, than with its potential to function effectively as a *social enterprise* — an organization that combines the pursuit of a mission to contribute to some aspect of the common good with operations that utilize many traditional business practices.[14] This introduces a range of analytical tools that have not found a place within current approaches to sustainability.[15]

A focus on the organization (NGO), as a social enterprise includes several key capacities included in the more conventional approach to sustainability, e.g. the abilities to mobilize production inputs, and to organize and manage production, but it also includes the ability to correctly identify "entrepreneurial opportunities." This is as relevant for not-for-profit organizations as it is for commercial firms.[16]

This focus leads to a client-driven analysis of an organization's external environment is based less on a traditionally abstract input/output systems model, than on an analysis of market structure and competitive advantage.[17] While many elements are common to both approaches (e.g. the proximity of other suppliers of similar health care services), the latter analysis emphasizes their dynamic interrelationships (e.g. the extent to which the proximity of these other suppliers block new entrants to the marketplace, threaten to introduce substitute products or services, affect the bargaining power of organizational clients and resource suppliers).[18] Similarly, the marketing function becomes the critical operation within an organization, focusing its attention and efforts on the identification of clients' definition of their problem, not the provider's definition of the solution. It is in this sense that this alternative approach is *client-driven* (Ibid).

Thus, our approach to sustainability combines elements of the development community's experiences in *institutional development (or strengthening)*, and in *private sector development*. The former approach focuses on the enhancement of institutional capacities to attract and manage the resources needed to achieve organizational goals. These capacities typically include planning, the management of financial and human resources, and operations and information management. Strengthening these capacities also figures prominently in the private sector development approach, but primarily in terms of enabling the organization to respond effectively to market opportunities to generate a profit. Accordingly, organizational strengthening activities within the private sector development approach are frequently referred to as *business skills development*.

The gain from melding these approaches is more than semantic. Their combination yields a *synergistic* model of organizational functioning that firmly roots its sustainability in its interaction with the economic and political markets in which it operates. Consequently, the emphasis is placed on the manner and extent to which strengthening a particular functional area contributes to the organization's *adaptability* to the changing needs of its intended clients — that is, the extent to which it is a client-driven, client-centered enterprise, regardless of whether it is for-profit or not. It is this dynamic aspect of the "private sector" approach to non-governmental organization sustainability that distinguishes it from the more static, quasi-academic approach to sustainability traditionally followed in development projects.

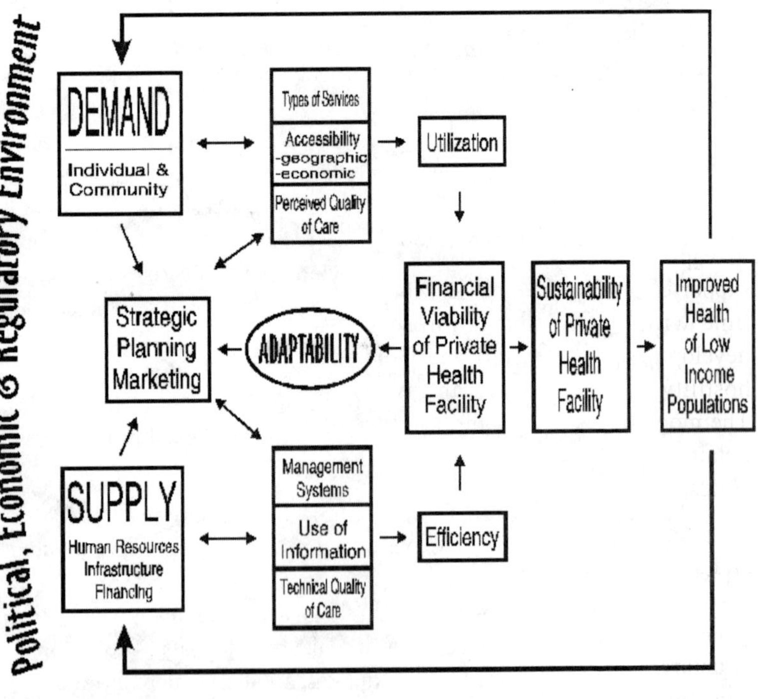

Exhibit 1: Client (NGO/Community) Driven Strategy on Sustainability

Exhibit 1: presents a sketch on client-driven model of sustainability. Within the constraints posed by it's political, economic, and regulatory environment, the organization processes as inputs both demands by individuals and communities for services, and the human, material, and financial resources it will need to satisfy those demands. The organization's strategic planning and marketing capacity determines the extent to which these inputs contribute to the utilization of the services provided, as well as to the efficiency of its operations, and ultimately the cost of its services to the intended clients. Service utilization and operational efficiency, in turn, determines the immediate financial viability of the organization. The organization's ability to monitor this performance and to feed it back into its strategic planning and marketing processes — its adaptability — has obvious implications for the organization's long-term sustainability (Ibid).

Contextual Hostility

It is no more possible to separate health system development from its context than farming from the weather (Scott C, 1994).

> *Interestingly, we have come full circle in our thinking about development theory and practice by re-establishing the role of national and international policy and political factors in development. However, this is done within a holistic framework for development which recognizes the interdependencies between community, national and international variables (Ickis J, de Jesus E and Maru R, 1986).*

The environment, which surrounds a health system, creates opportunities and poses threats that influence significantly its basic operations and its capacity to grow and develop. External conditions range from the supportive to the antagonistic. Moreover, these conditions can change over time with sudden and unforeseen consequences for health system development. Brinkerhoff and Goldsmith report that an environmental hostility appears to have an inverse relationship with sustainability. The more hostile the conditions, the more difficult it is for a system 'to obtain and process the inputs it need for maintenance' (Brinkerhoff D and Goldsmith A, 1992).

Despite these admonishments, there is a tendency for governments and donor agencies to ignore the importance of external conditions when approaching the health sector in developing countries. The operational level grabs all the attention while the main players focus exclusively on the structure and function of the different parts of the health system. The common pattern of pre-investment activity among donors and governments is as follows: the first step is to identify specific operational constraints within the existing health system. This is followed by an analysis of technical and managerial shortcomings related to these constraints. Finally comes the design of appropriate corrective interventions. Aside from the World Bank reviews, which do at least consider the implications of economic conditions for the health sector, few analyses examine the links between operational weaknesses and the wider context of sustainability.

In order to study the sustainability of NGO managed health care initiatives and its effectiveness in hastening social sector development activities the study focuses on the following context in the next chapter.

NGOs and Sustainability of Their Health Programmes

'Sustainability as a process' and sustainability is a complex issue - is commonly understood and interpreted in development literature in different ways, but most frequently because of the emphasis given to various debate on development goals making it often confused (Riddel, 1995). Sustainability of NGO managed development projects is defined as a 'different approach' – which has a range of more practical implications for NGO evaluations – to concentrate less on whether a particular intervention has become 'self sustaining' and to focus on broader issues. One of these broader issues would involve the examination of the ways in which the individual or groups of people, or specific organisations involved in the project or program have the capacity to take over successfully the distinct project or activity when the sponsoring NGO withdraws. Broader still would be an examination of the way in which the project has enabled not so much the project but beneficiary themselves to be or become more able to survive without external inputs within this context it is useful to make a distinction between financial sustainability, and institutional sustainability for the purpose of the present study (Riddel et al, 1995.)

Financial sustainability - this is achieved to the extent that those other than external agents are able to provide the financial input and run the project. Thus, the beneficiaries themselves could be paying for a greater share of the costs; the host government takes over the financial burden of the donor; or again, the form of the project could be changed in order to create more, or even new, internally generated revenue raising opportunities. Yet it should be easier to indicate whether there are visible signs of improvement towards greater financial sustainability including the possibility of prospects for achieving sustainability in the near future. Two following problems can be discussed in this context –

- Difficulties often arise between managing achievements of financial sustainability and that of quality of care.

- Whenever, the focus is more on financial sustainability at the cost of introducing paying for quality care and user fees, the long term sustainability is further questioned.

Therefore, the popular notion of donors on financial sustainability is to make a community self-reliant, not necessarily self-sufficient in a selected sector specific developmental activity. At the same time the donors consider the primary responsibility of the program sustainability is that of the concerned NGO or the- community the NGO serves. However, it is achievable with desired donor support. In most cases the continuous effort to meet the local needs further necessitate the continuity of donor support.

Institutional sustainability – in the present discussion of sustainability of NGO-led development projects, institutional sustainability and managerial capacity building play a significant role. Institutional sustainability is an issue of assessment of the extent, to which discrete interventions have, or have not, enhanced the capability of the beneficiaries, especially their capability to carry forward their own development themselves. It concerns participation, ownership issues and human resource development.

These dimensions of sustainability, commonly involves the imparting of managerial capacity and more generally, the building, sustenance and strengthening of local capacity and often local institutions. It involves the growth and development of different capacities, e.g., the capacity to identify and resolve problems; the capacity to negotiate; the capacity to manage and administer; the capacity to strengthen the power of poor groups, and to utilise that power to draw resources to the poor. When this notion is focussed explicitly on beneficiaries, it involves the building of nurturing of skills, ideas, networks, contacts, enthusiasm and vision among those whose participation the particular activity funded. It is the creation and enduring aspects of building peoples' capabilities which is most often of greater value and importance than either the financial sustainability of discrete projects, or the ability of local organisations to continue running these particular projects.

From the above discussions, it becomes obvious that sustainability in NGO – led development projects needs to be understood in terms of their financial components, their institutional components, their human resource components and their community management component, without exclusive focus on any single element. It is important to judge NGO projects within the context of their ability to stand on their management capacity in terms of program sustainability.

But sustainability also needs to be seen beyond the narrow confines of the discrete projects and program support management. It must also include the notion of enhancing both the capacity of the executing NGO and ultimately, the capacity of direct beneficiaries to take more control of their own lives and their development. Thus, by referring to all these, tend to define sustainability in NGO programs as follows:

> *'All NGO projects and programmes need to be implemented with a view to furthering the ability of the beneficiaries to take more control over their lives. This will mean from the outset (pre-project assessment stage) that the funding / external organisation will need to review the steps required not only to encourage the executing NGO to become more direct owners of the project as soon as possible, but equally, to ensure that the focus of attention extends beyond the discrete projects funded to the primary beneficiaries'.*

Most immediately, all NGO projects need to be drawn up with a view to assessing the extent to which they should attach the final and institutional sustainability, wherever possible within an explicit time-table, and in relation to the direct and indirect impact they will have on the environment. This assessment will need to include reviewing the concrete steps and processes that need to be taken in order to increase the likelihood that an appropriate level of benefits will continue to be delivered for an extended period of time after major financial, managerial and technical assistance has been withdrawn.

Equally, however, the requirement to review all initiatives funded against the achievement of sustainability does not necessarily mean that the future financial or institutional sustainability should in all cases be a necessary requirement for funding discrete projects. In particular, NGO program sustainability need to be pursued only on condition that, specially for the poor and where basic needs or services are being provided, the quality of, and access to, the basic good or service provided will not be radically compromised. Where the good or service provided is considered essential to the basic well-being of the beneficiaries, and where alternative funding cannot be found, the inability to achieve either financial or institutional sustainability should not constitute an impediment to funding such NGO initiatives (Riddel et.al., 1995).

The above factors of sustainability are focusing only on the project level activities of the development intervention. Theoretical approaches to assessing sustainability could be improved by assessing the aspects of government policies and support (where the project is implemented), management capacity of the NGO, local participation, financial management, technical component, socio-cultural factors in a donor – recipient perspective (Hossain, 2000).

As the present research, is focused on the study of NGO programs in the Indian State of Rajasthan, the theoretical approach underlying the research aims at understanding the issues of sustainability by assessing the discussed review on NGO managed health care initiatives at the project level in the larger context of the:

- effectiveness of management capacity,
- role of democratic institutions (Panchayat Raj Institutions) vis-à-vis management of NGO services,
- commitment of government policies and donor support for program sustainability,
- and analysing the implications of NGO managed health care for National Health Policy reforms and government co-operation in promoting of sustainability.

With this backdrop, the ongoing literature review focuses on the socio-demographic profile of the targeted population of the state of Rajasthan, under the present study.

Chapter - IV

Profile of Health Care and NGO Programmes in Rajasthan

Background of Socio-Demographic and Health Profile of Rajasthan

Characteristics of the Target Population in the State

Three-quarters of the population of Rajasthan, live in rural areas. Rajasthan with a total population of 68 million spread over 33 districts, 248 blocks and 44795villages is the largest State (area-wise) in the country. Over the years IMR (79 per 1000 live births) and MMR, 670 per 100,000 in the State have not shown any declining trend and continue to remain much above the national average. The age distribution is typical of populations that have high fertility, with relatively high proportions in the younger age groups and low proportions in the older age groups. Family percent of the population is below age 15, and 5 percent is age 65 and above. The overall sex ratio is 926 females per 1, 000 males and child sex ratio is 883 per 1, 000 males. The sex ratio is 989 females for every 1,000 males in rural areas and 928 females for every 1,000 males in urban areas, suggesting that slightly more men than women have migrated to urban areas in Rajasthan (NFHS, 2015-16).

The State Directorate-lEe, Government of Rajasthan, including NFHS findings, provides a variety of demographic, health and socioeconomic background information. In the state as a whole, 89 percent of household heads are Hindu, 9 percent are Muslim, and 1 percent each are Jain and Sikh. Muslims and Jains, live disproportionately in urban areas, where they comprise 20 percent and 4 percent of- household heads, respectively. Twenty-three percent of household heads belong to other backward classes (OBCs), 19 percent belong to scheduled castes, and 12 percent belong to scheduled tribes. Forty-six percent of household heads do not belong to any of these groups. Questions about housing conditions and the standard of living of household members indicate some improvements, as per the NFHS-4, 91 percent of households in Rajasthan have electricity and 85.5 percent have piped drinking water in compare with 66.1 percent and 81.8 percent in NFHS-3, 2005-06. However, 45 percent of households use improved sanitation facility, According to 2015's NFHS-4 reports that indicate 55 percent of households in the state are deprived from the sanitation related facilities.

Three-quarters (85.4 percent) of males and more than two-third (56 percent) of females age 15six and above are literate, an slight increase of 12 percentage points in literacy rates since the time of NFHS-3. However, still literacy rate among rural women is 49.8 percent, which indicate the inequality in educational outcome. Seventy-six percent of children age 6-14 currently attend school, an increase from 59 percent in NFHS-1. The proportion of children attending school has increased for all age groups, particularly for rural girls, but girls still lag behind boys in school attendance. Moreover, the disparity in school attendance by sex grows with increasing age of children. At age 6-10, 88 percent of boys attend school, compared with 70 percent of girls. By age 15-17, 62 percent of boys attend school, compared with only 29 percent of girls.

Social Status of Women

Marriage practice in the state of Rajasthan is still matters. Women in Rajasthan tend to marry at an early age. For instance NHFS-4 indicates 35.4 of women get married before age of 18 years, which is 49.5 percent in rural Rajasthan, including 11 percent who are married but *gauna* has yet to be performed. The proportion of women age 15-49 who has been married is more than twice as high in rural areas (49 percent) as in urban areas (20.3). Older women are more likely than younger women to have married at an early age: 48 percent of women who are now age 45-49 married before: they were 15, compared with 19 percent of women age 15-49. Although this indicate the proportion of women marry young is declining rapidly, the majority of women in Rajasthan still marry before reaching the legal minimum age of 18 years. On average, women are fours younger than men they marry. As part of an increasing emphasis on gender issues in NFHS-4, the survey asked women about their participation in the household decision making. In Rajasthan, 81.7 percent of women are involved in decision making on at least one of four selected topics. A much proportion (41 percent) are involved in making decisions about their own health care. Forty-four percent of women do work other than housework. However, 25.1 percent of women experience spousal violence. Only one- third (18.6 percent) of these women work for cash. Forty-three percent of women who earn cash can decide independently how to spend the money that they earn. Fifty-seven percent of working women report that their earnings constitute at least half of total family earnings, including 30 percent who report that the family is entirely dependent on their earning.

Fertility and Family Planning

Fertility has remained fairly constant in Rajasthan. At current fertility levels, women will have an average of 2.4 children each throughout their childbearing years. The total fertility rate is one of the highest in India (higher than any other state except Uttar Pradesh and Meghalaya). This estimate is slightly higher than the estimate from NFHS-4 (2.4 children per woman). This decrease in fertility is likely due to better enumeration of births in NFHS-3 rather than to a real increase in fertility. In Rajasthan, rural women, illiterate women, Muslim women, scheduled-caste and scheduled-tribe women, and women from households with a low standard of living have much higher fertility than other women. Fertility rates are lower in the Southeastern and Southern Regions than in other regions. A more striking feature is the high level of childbearing among young women. Among women age 20-49, the median age at first childbirth is 20 years. Women age 15-19 account for 6.3 percent of total fertility. Studies in India and elsewhere have shown that health and mortality risks increase when women give birth at such young age-both for the women themselves and for their children. Family planning programmes focusing on women in this age group could make a significant impact on maternal and child health as well as reducing overall fertility in the state.

The appropriate design of family planning programmes depends, to a large extent, on women's fertility preferences. Women may have large families because they want many children, or they may prefer small families but, for a variety of reasons, may have more children than they actually want. For 8 percent of births over the three years preceding NFHS-2, mothers report that they did not want the pregnancy at all, and for another 8 percent of births, mothers say that they would have preferred to delay the pregnancy. When asked about their preferred family size, nearly one-third (29 percent) of women who already have three children and nearly one-fourth (22 percent) of women with four or more children respond that they consider the two- child family ideal. This gap between women's actual fertility experience and what they want or would consider ideal suggests a need for expanded or improved family welfare services to help women achieve their fertility goals. In Rajasthan, 96 percent of women want at least one son and 89 percent want at least one daughter. A preference for sons is indicated by the fact that almost one-half of women (48 percent) want more sons than daughters but only a negligible proportion wants more daughters than sons. If women in Rajasthan are not using family planning, it is not due to lack of knowledge. Knowledge of contraception is improving: 53.5 percent of women percent of currently married women age between 15-19 know at least one modern family planning method. Women are most familiar with female sterilization (40.7percent) followed by male sterilization (0.2 percent), the pill (79 percent), the condom (74percent), and the IUD (1.2 percent). Knowledge of modern spacing methods has increased by 23CE 37 percentage points since the time of NFHS-1; although use rates of these methods remain very low.

Almost sixty percent of currently married women age between 15-49 is use some method of contraception, an increase from 47 percent at the time of NFHS-3. Contraceptive prevalence is higher in urban areas (64.1 percent) than in rural areas (58.3 percent). Female sterilization is by far the most popular method: 31 percent of currently married women are sterilized, a moderate increase from 25 percent at the time of NFHS-1. By contrast, less than 2 percent of women report that their husbands are sterilized, a small decrease between NFHS-1 and NFHS-2. Overall, sterilization accounts for 80 percent of total contraceptive use. Use rates for the pill (2 percent), IUD (1 percent), and condom (3 percent) remain very low. Contraceptive prevalence in Rajasthan varies considerably among socio-economic groups.

Muslim women stand out as having a much lower contraceptive prevalence rate than women who belong to other religions. In NFHS-4 Rural women, scheduled-tribe and scheduled- caste women, and poor women are also less likely than other women to use contraception. Urban women, women who have at least completed high school education, women who are not Hindu, Muslim, or Jain, and women from households with a high standard of living are all more likely than other women to use the three modern spacing methods of pills, IUDs, and condoms. Given the emphasis on sterilization, women tend to adopt family planning only after they have achieved their desired family size. As a result, contraceptive use can be expected to rise steadily with age and with number of living children. In Rajasthan, contraceptive use does indeed go up with age, peaking at 64 percent for women age 40-44. Use also goes up with the number of children, peaking at 58 percent for women with three living children. Son preference appears to have a considerable effect on contraceptive use. Women who have one or more sons are much more likely to use contraception than are women who have the same number of children but have only daughters.

For example, among women who have 2-4 children, only 14-17 percent of women who have no sons are currently using contraception, compared with 39-44 percent of women who have no daughters. Nine percent of currently married women are not using contraception but say that they want to wait at least two years before having another child. Another 9 percent are not using contraception although they do not want any more children. These women are described as having an, 'unmet need' for family planning. The unmet need is highest for young women, who are particularly interested in spacing their births. The unmet need for contraception among women 30 years and above is almost exclusively for limiting births. These results underscore the need for strategies that provide spacing as well as terminal methods in order to meet the changing needs of women over their lifecycle.

For many years, the Government of India has been using electronic and other mass media to promote family planning. Exposure to mass media is low in Rajasthan. Among the different types of media, television has the broadest reach. Nevertheless, only 30 percent of ever-married women watch television at least once a week and only 17 percent are exposed to radio. Sixty-three percent of women are not regularly exposed to television, radio, or other types of mass media. Only 36 percent of women saw or heard a family planning message in the media during the few months preceding the survey. Exposure to family planning messages is particularly low among disadvantaged socioeconomic groups, such as women from households with a low standard of living (10 percent), scheduled-tribe women (14 percent), and illiterate women (22 percent). The majority (86 percent) of women who use modern contraception obtained their method from a government hospital or other source in the public sector. Only 7 percent obtained their method from the private medical sector. The private sector plays a larger role in urban areas (supplying 13 percent of users of modern methods) than in rural areas (supplying only 4 percent of users of modern methods).

An important indication of the quality of family planning services is the information that women receive when they obtain contraception and the extent to which they receive follow-up services after accepting contraception. NFHS-4 demonstrates, In Rajasthan, only 17.5 percent of users of modern contraceptives who were motivated by someone to use their method were told about any other method. Moreover, at the time of adopting the method, a health or family planning worker told only 43.5 percent about possible side effects of the method they adopted. Seventy percent of modern contraceptive users, however, have received follow-up services. From the information provided in NFHS—4, a picture emerges of women marrying early, having their first child at 19 years of age and having four children before ending their childbearing. However, 46 percent of women with four or more living children do not use any method of family planning, so the risk of pregnancy remains substantial even for that group.

Infant and Child Mortality

Basic information on infant and child mortality provides estimates of infant and child mortality and factors associated with the survival of young children. The infant mortality rate is 41 percent before the age of 1 year per 1,000 live births, which is down from the corresponding NFHS-3 corresponding rate of 65 and NFHS-2 estimate of 80. And The Under-five mortality rate (U5MR), 51 percent deaths at age 1-4 years per 1,000 children reaching age one, the infant deaths in NFHS-4. NFHS-3 indicates that 1 in 13 children die in the first year Observed increase between the two surveys is most likely due to better enumeration of life, and 1 in 9 die before reaching-age five. Child-survival programmes, might usefully focus on specific groups of children with particularly high infant and child mortality rates. Such as children who live in rural areas or in the Western Region. Children whose mothers are illiterate, children belonging to scheduled castes or scheduled tribes, and children from poor households. Notably, the infant mortality rate is 45 percent higher among children whose mothers did not receive any of the recommended types of maternity-related medical care than for children whose mothers received one or two types of maternity-related medical care. Along with the above groups, efforts to promote child survival need to concentrate on female children, mothers at the age extremes (below 20 years and above 30 years), first-order births and those of order four or above, and mothers whose children are closely spaced. Infant mortality is 36 percent higher among children born to mothers under age 20 than among children born to mothers age 20-29. Infant mortality is almost three times as high among children born less than 24 months after a previous birth as among children born after a gap of 48 months or more.

Health, Health Care and Nutrition

Promotion of maternal and child health has been one of the most important components of the Family Welfare Programme of the Government of India. One goal is for each pregnant woman to receive at least three antenatal check-ups plus two tetanus injections and a full course of iron and folic acid supplementation.

In Rajasthan, for children born in the three years preceding NFHS-4, 63 percent mothers, received antenatal check-up in the first trimester. And only 38 percent received four antenatal care visits. For 52 percent of these children, 89.7 percent mothers, whose last birth was protected against neonatal tetanus and for 17.3 of mothers received iron and folic acid supplementation for 100 days or more than they were pregnant. Coverage by all three interventions is lower for women living in rural areas or in the Western Region and for women in disadvantaged socioeconomic groups than for other women. Coverage is also low for older women and for women who already have four or more children. The Family Welfare Programme encourages women to deliver in a medical facility or, if at home, with assistance from a trained health professional and to receive at least three check-ups after delivery. During the three years preceding NFHS-4, eighty-four percent children of births in Rajasthan were delivered in a medical facility in the last five years. Among births delivered at home, 19 percent of births were assisted by a health professional and 52 percent by a traditional birth attendant. Only 6 percent of the births outside a medical facility were followed by a postpartum check-up within two months of delivery. Overall, these results show that coverage of maternity-related services is low in Rajasthan.

These services are reaching more women during pregnancy than during delivery or after childbirth. They also point to the important role of traditional birth attendants for the substantial proportion of births that occur at home. Government of India, recommends that breastfeeding should begin immediately after childbirth, and that infants should be exclusively breastfed for about the first four months of life. Although breastfeeding is nearly universal in Rajasthan, very few children begin breastfeeding, immediately after birth, only 5 percent in the first hour and 34 percent in the first day. NFHS-4 shows, only 58 percent of children under-six months of age are exclusively breastfed. The median duration of breastfeeding is 25.5 .months, or slightly over two years, and the median of exclusive breastfeeding is only 1.8 months. At age 6-8 months, all children should be receiving solid or mushy food in addition to breast milk. However, only 30.1percent of children age 6-8 months receive the recommended combination of breast milk and solid/mushy foods.

NFHS-4 uses WHO recognized standards to assess children's nutritional status, weight-for—age, height-for-age, and weight-for-height. Children who are more than two standard deviations below the median of an international reference population are considered underweight (measured in terms of weight-for-age), stunted (height-for-age), or wasted Stunting is a sign of chronic, long-term under nutrition, wasting is a sign of acute, short-term under nutrition, and underweight is a composite measure that takes into account both chronic and acute under-nutrition. Based on international standards, 36.7 percent of children under age of five years are underweight, thirty nine percent are stunted, and 23 percent are wasted along with almost 9 percent severely wasted. Although, Child nutritional status in Rajasthan has been bit increasing since the time of NHFS-1, NFHS-2, NFHS-3. Stunting rate among children declined from 44 percent to 39 percent in the 10 years between NFHS-3 and NFHS4, and the percentage of children who are underweight decreased from 40 percent to 37 percent. However, in the same period, wasting among children improved from 20 percent to 23 percent. However, despite these gains in stunting and underweight, child malnutrition is still a major problem in Rajasthan.

Under nutrition is higher in rural areas than in urban areas and is particularly high among children age 12-35 months and children from disadvantaged socioeconomic groups. The prevalence of under nutrition is somewhat higher for girls than for boys. 60.3 percent of children age 6-59 months is anemic, including a large majority of children in every subgroup of the population.

Child immunization is an important component of child-survival programmes in India, with efforts focusing on six serious but preventable disease-tuberculosis, diphtheria, pertussis, tetanus, polio, and measles. The objective of the Universal Immunization Programme (UIP), launched in 1985-86, was to extend immunization coverage against these diseases to at least 85 percent of infant by 1990. In Rajasthan, only 17 percent of children age 12-23 months are fully vaccinated, another 60 percent have received some but not all of the recommended vaccinations, and 23 percent have not been vaccinated at all.

The proportion of children who have received no vaccinations has fallen considerably between NFHS-3 (26.5 percent) and NFHS-4 (54.8 percent). However, there has been a decline in the proportion 'of children fully vaccinated between NFHS-1 to 17 percent in NFHS-4. This decline is due to decreases in measles and DPT3 coverage, which have offset gains in the coverage of BCG and polio vaccines during the period between the two surveys. The largest increases in vaccination coverage between NFHS-1 and NFHS-4 are for the first two doses of polio vaccine, undoubtedly because of the introduction of the Pulse Polio Immunization Campaign in 1995. Based upon NFHS-4, 54.8 percent of children age 12-23 moths fully immunized (BCG, measles and 3 doses each of polio and DPT). Eighty-eight percent of children age between 12-23 months receives BCG.

71.6 percent have received three doses of DPT vaccine, 65.4 percent have received three doses of polio vaccine, and 78 percent have been vaccinated against measles. Dropout rates for the series of DPT and polio vaccinations are a continuing problem. Forty-eight percent of children received the first DPT vaccination, but only 26 percent received all three doses; 76 percent received the first polio vaccination, but only 45 percent received all three doses of polio. National policy also recommends that children under age five years receive oral doses of vitamin A every six months starting at age nine months. However, 39.6 percent of children age 9-59 months, have received any vitamin A in the last six months. NFHS-4 collected information on the prevalence and treatment of three health problems that cause considerable mortality in young children, fever, acute respiratory infection (ARI), and diarrhoea.

In Rajasthan, 26 percent of children under age three were ill with fever during the two weeks preceding the survey, 22 percent were ill with ARI, and 20 percent had diarrhoea. Six out of 10 children who became ill with ARI or diarrhoea were taken to a health facility or health-care provider. Knowledge of the appropriate treatment of diarrhoea remains low. Fifty-six percent of children (under age 5 years) with diarrhea received oral rehydration salt (ORS) packets and 43 percent of mothers incorrectly believe that when children are sick with diarrhea, they should be given less to drink than usual. 56.2 percent of children with diarrhea received some form of oral rehydration therapy (ORT) 7 including 20 percent who received ORS. The percentage of children with diarrhea who received ORS has increased since NFHS-1, when it was only 12 percent. Based on a weight-for-height index (the body mass index), more than one -third (36 percent) of women in Rajasthan are undernourished. Nutritional deficiency is particularly serious for women age 20-29, Muslim women, women in rural areas and women in disadvantaged socioeconomic groups. Women who are undernourished themselves are also much more likely than other women to have children who are undernourished. Overall, one-half (46.8percent) of women in Rajasthan have some degree of anaemia, and 16 percent are moderately to severely anaemic.

Anemia is a serious problem among women in every population group, with prevalence rates ranging from 37 to 58 percent. Pregnant women are much more likely than non-pregnant women to be moderately anaemic. less than one-half (46 percent) of households use cooking salt that is iodized at the recommended level of 15 pa1is per million, suggesting that iodine deficiency disorders are likely to be a serious problem. Rural households and households with a low standard of living are much less likely than other households to be using adequately iodized cooking salt. Forty-three percent of currently married women in Rajasthan report some type of reproductive-health problems, including abnormal vaginal discharge, symptoms of urinary tract infections, and pain or bleeding associated with intercourse. Among these women, more than three-fourths (78 percent) have not sought any advice or treatment. These results suggest a need to expand reproductive-health services and information programmes that encourage women to discuss their problems with a health-care provider. In recent years, there has been growing concern about domestic violence in India.

NFHS-4 found that in Rajasthan, there is widespread acceptance among thirty-three percent women that they are beaten by their husband, is justified under some circumstances. Furthermore, 25 percent of women are most likely to believe that wife-beating us justified if a women shows disrespect for her in-laws. More than half (23 percent) of women accept at least one of six reasons as a justification for a husband beating his wife. All over, more than one-fifth (23%) of women experience physical or sexual violence. Among women, who face physical violence since age 15, 90 percent of husband is the most common perpetrator for ever-married women, 68 percent perpetrator is mother or step mother for never married women, 18 percent is teacher, 16 percent is step father and 15 percent is sister or brother physically mistreated by their husbands. Overall, only 12 percent of women received a home visit from a health or family planning worker during their pregnancy.

The survey collected information on the prevalence of tuberculosis, asthma, malaria, and jaundice among all household members. Disease prevalence based on reports from household heads must be interpreted with caution, however. Prevalence of all four conditions is higher in rural areas than in urban areas. Men are more likely than women to suffer from tuberculosis, asthma, and jaundice, but women are more likely to suffer from malaria. Most households in Rajasthan (63 percent) seek treatment from the public medical sector when a family member is ill. More than one-third (36 percent) normally use the private medical sector. Use of private-sector services is higher in urban areas than in rural areas, and it is also slightly higher among households with a high standard of living index than among other households. Most respondents are generally satisfied with the health care they receive. Respondents are more critical of staff attitudes and cleanliness in public-sector facilities than in private-sector facilities (NFHS-2). Median waiting time is longer in rural areas (10 minutes) than in urban areas (4 minutes). Overall, there is no difference between the public and private sectors in terms of the median waiting time (Annex- Status of health services during the study period in Rajasthan).

With the understanding of state situation concerning the information regarding the socio-demographic and health status, the review focuses on the role of Non-governmental organisations cooperating with government system in facilitating and contributing to primary health care initiatives in the state.

Non-governmental Health Care in Rajasthan

The role of NGOs in strengthening community participation in health initiative in the State of Rajasthan, is understood while analysing various government schemes that is operated at grassroots activities. NGO health activities include health care services viz. preventive, promotive, curative and rehabilitative including population programme management and intersectoral development mostly in rural areas.(GOR, Directorate-IEC)

Community participation and state-intervention for community action in health can be understood by the overview of several schemes as devised over a period in the state would give an idea as to what is happening in this area.

The performance of population programme management in its various incarnations, viz. Family Planing Programme, Family Welfare Programme, Maternal and Child Health, Safe Motherhood and Child Survival, in the past has not been particularly successful due to want of community orientation. Several well intended approaches to involve the communities in the process have failed due to various reasons, the chief among them being lack of efficient and effective management, though the schemes themselves have had sound conceptual framework. An overview of several schemes devised over a period would give an idea as to what is happening in this area.

Village Health Development Committee (VHDC)

The VHDCs would have representation from all the communities and be vested with the responsibility of looking after the health needs of the village communities. The members would attend all the meetings organised by the NGO, and assist the staff of the NGO in the programme implementation. They would also assist the CHWs, if provided in the village. Of course, the NGO assists the villagers in constituting the VHDC in the village, and orients them on various aspects of Primary Health Care. Subsequently, depending on the felt developmental needs of the village, the committee can take on other activities such as biogas, drinking water, education, smokeless *chulas*, agricultural cooperatives, and so on which are in the interest of the villagers.

The NGO thus acts as a catalyst and facilitator in the developmental process. For example, the village community feels that the pupils from the village, girls in particular, cannot easily access a school located at a distance of around three kilometers in inclement weather. A decision is made by the VHDC that the village should start a primary school of its own. The staff from the NGO would assist the village community in seeking necessary permission from the Government's Education Department, give ideas to the VHDC as to various options available for fund raising, and other such assistance in the efforts of the VHDC.

Mahila Mandals

Most NGOs use this strategy as part of community involvement as the programmes of both Government and bilateral agencies focuss on the girl child, or on women. With the initiation of intervention in the form of Reproductive Health programme in Rajasthan, the focus now is on women. This has been necessitated by the status of women being low in the state, and so needing special attention. The aim of the Mahila Mandals, be they has been in urban (including slums), rural, or tribal areas, is to end the exploitation of women. The NGO sector has been able to play a major role in mobilising women for their programme interventions, be they in health, education, employment, etc. This forum of women is particularly effective in the arena of health promotion, disease prevention and use of the indigenous systems of medicine. Since the mother is the custodian of health in the family, involving women is a must in the most effective strategy for community participation in the Population Programme, as well as in deciding the number of children they would like to have.

The Integrated Child Development Services (ICDS), scheme is used to increase its coverage manifold to make it effective by the use of members of '*Mahila Mandals*' to cover the target population including pregnant mothers and children below 6 years of age.

Youth Groups

The youth form an important and vibrant segment of the society. Discussion with youth groups brought to the fore that their full potential is still untapped, particularly for Population Programme Management. Noninvolvement of the youth is based on the assumption that it is too early to expose them to the topic of human sexuality as they have not yet entered the family building process. Hence, they have been kept out of the programme. Whatever has been attempted in the form of population education is based on halfhearted measures and appears to be an afterthought rather than a well thought out strategy. An appropriately designed family life education programme for both school/college going and out of school youth would not only make them aware about human sexuality and related issues but would have direct a impact on their reproductive behaviour as and when they become the target population for the programme.

The existing youth fora, such as National Cadet Corps (NCC), National Service Scheme (NSS), Scouts and Guides, Nehru Yuvak Kendras, Student Unions, Youth wings of various political parties, though meant basically for youth development, could be involved in population programme management. A majority of these fora are found in formal settings; the Nehru Yuvak Kendras are meant for the development of rural youth who may not be part of the formal system. The youth, when consulted, indicated that day by day they feel the pressure of overcrowding, particularly in the context of employment, where the opportunities are shrinking fast. The youth of today feel that the existing fora could be effectively used for spreading family life education right from the middle school level.

Community Based Depots

Following the decision of the Government of India, to implement target free approach to the family welfare programme from April 1996, the concept of Community Based Depots (CBDs) has come into existence. The CBDs are generally a petty shop or a grocery shop, where from eligible-couples, can collect their supply of contraceptives as and when they need. The rationale has been that the supply side has been weak and has largely been inaccessible.

Moreover, culturally, males are reluctant to approach health workers, who are generally females, to demand, for example, condoms for use. The National Family Health Survey has also brought out the fact that there exists an unmet need for family planning services to the extent of 20 percent in Rajasthan, which works out to 8.1 million. With the introduction of CBDs, one set of issues appear to have been solved, whereas another set of issues, such as social, psychological and technical barriers seem to have been left out. Since the concept of CBD is new, it may be too early to make judgments on its effectiveness.

Panchayati Raj system

The Panchayati Raj Bill, which became the Constitutional (Seventythird

Amendment) Act, 1992 (Institute of local self government-GOR), was to ensure decentralisation of management to the Gram Sabhas. This was based on the valid premise that the grassroots level institutions would be more sensitive to the needs of the community and must be involved in the "community management" of the programmes meant for them. Though, there has been a certain amount of clarity on the role of the elected representatives to the Panchayat Samitis, it is not backed by required financial allocation, leave alone autonomy. It was hoped that community participation could be elicited best through this strategy. A detailed account of the role of Panchayati Raj institutions and its cooperation with NGOs managing health and population programmes in the state is discussed in the study of NGOs in the present research.

It would be relevant to add here that the Gram Sabhas are indeed best suited for population programme management. Technically technically trained grassroots level staff could support the members of a well-oriented Health Committee from the village panchayat. In this way, the accountability of the staff delivering the services could be ensured through close monitoring and supervision of the staff. The Pinhead Samiti could become an "NGO" of sorts with the required autonomy to carry out the functions of village development, including population programme management. The Panchayat Samiti could be given the autonomy for even selecting a professional support service organisation for its training needs and other support that it may need. The community health "volunteers" could be identified and recruited by this Samiti, and would directly report to the Health Committee and not to the members of the health system of the Government, a mistake which caused a great deal of damage to the CHW scheme in the past (Directorate-IEC, GOR).

Panchayat Swasth Sewa Scheme

This scheme also aims at involving the Panchayati Raj institutions, but with a slight difference, and is expected to be implemented during the Ninth Plan Period. An expert committee that was set up met in August 1995 recommended the formulation of a new scheme giving sole responsibility to Panchayats, which is almost absent in the existing Village Health Guide scheme. It was recommended, that the scheme could be named as 'Panchayat Swasth Sewa' Scheme, and introduced with the following components:

1. Under the scheme it is envisaged that a motivated social worker from the village itself should be encouraged and assisted by the Government and the Panchayat so that he/she may become a

strong catalyst for health related activities; such a person may be named Panchayat Swasth Sahayak (PSS).

2. There should be one PSS for 1000 population in the plains areas and for around 700 population in hilly, tribal and/or difficult areas. It must be emphasised at all times that the PSS is a social worker who is being assisted by the Government in his efforts. He/she is NOT a Government employee in any sense of the term.
3. The Centre should provide financial support by paying an honorarium @ Rs 300/ per month and medicines worth Rs 100/ per month, along with a durable kit. The PSS would have to play the role of a guide, advisor, enabler and teacher of the community visavis health related issues, by identifying and treating common ailments and assisting the implementation of various national health diseases/control/eradication programme, etc.
4. Initially, the scheme will be launched on a pilot basis in two districts of each state, and one district of each Union Territory in the current plan. The entire country may be covered in a phased manner by the end of the 9th Five Year Plan, if such an experiment is successful.

Traditional Birth Attendants

One of the ageold institutions at the village level is that of 'Traditional Birth Attendant', who conducts deliveries. The Government system is not able to reach majority of these women in rural areas due to various reasons, particularly inaccessibility of government health facilities (IEC,GOR). A strategy was designed to train them in conducting safe deliveries. However, their role in promoting the use of contraception remains limited. The good rapport established by the TBA could be exploited by using "birth based approach" to family welfare programmes, as the women are most receptive at the time of delivery. The TBAs could be provided with effective communication skills.

Health Cooperatives

Joint action groups in the form of milk/weavers/agriculture cooperatives do exist in rural areas, though their numbers may be small at present. The well known experiment of Amul in Kheda district of Gujarat has shown that cooperatives can transform the face of the economic development of a district. Following on these lines, Uttar Rajasthan Milk Union Ltd (URMUL) was established in Bikaner District of Rajasthan with a view to duplicating the Amul model, and it has been fairly successful. Drawing lessons from these experiences, Health Cooperatives could be formed, or health could form a part of the existing activities with an appropriate number of health care workers working closely with the rural communities.

These workers could be made responsible for health and population programme management, and paid by the Cooperatives themselves.

Local Voluntary Groups (LVGs)

This category of volunteers, are largely made use of by the Family Planning Association of India (FPAI), which is operational in the city of Jaipur. The idea is to draw 56 volunteers from each slum pocket of the city, and train them in various aspects of population programme management to make them link persons between the community and the FPAI. Though the initiative is new, FPAI plans to continue and expand this programme, to more such areas where socioeconomically backward segments live.

Self help Groups

Some of the NGOs in Rajasthan, under the PVOHII Scheme funded by USAID, have initiated Selfhelp groups in their respective areas of operation, with a view to ensuring sustainability of health care activities after the funding is over. Since, these groups consist mostly of women from the village community, to support families in need, they could be mobilised for the purpose of involvement in the delivery of health and population programme as well.

Religious Institutions/bodies

There are several misconceptions, among people from various religious persuasions against the adoption of family planning methods, particularly use of contraception. This is mostly due to lack of support from religious leaders to the programme. The most striking reason for such a prejudiced approach is the excessive coercion that was exerted during the Emergency in the form of forced male sterilisations. Other reasons such as lack of awareness about the modern contraceptive technologies, no consultation with the religious leaders by the Programme managers, and so on also do have some influence. For true community participation, on the health and Family Welfare programme management, religious leaders, once convinced, could play an important role, given the highly religious tradition for which Rajasthani culture is well known (AKHS).

'Health &Family Welfare' NGOs in Rajasthan

As among other indicators of development, there appears to be paucity of

NGOs involved in action programmes for management of Health & Family Welfare Programs in the state. It is possible to count these NGOs in a single digit, unlike the others engaged in sectors such as education, rural development, tribal development, primary health care, agricultural development, etc. The prominent ones are Family Planning Association of India and the United Nations Fund for Population Activities UNFPA, an international NGO funding population programmes in the State of Rajasthan (Annex-II). There are several NGOs who combine the family welfare component as part of Primary Health Care. The number of such NGOs also fluctuates over a period depending on the funding cycle of government schemes or of donor agencies. There is no such thing as an NGO managed health facility, where the Family Welfare is a permanent feature.

NGOs Quantity vs Quality

According to the latest list, there are about 560 NGOs in the state of Rajasthan. Of these, 41 percent (N = 229) are located in the Jaipur and Udaipur belt alone. In Udaipur District also, the majority are located in Jadhol Block, which is a predominantly tribal block. Statewide distribution of the NGOs is represented in the Organogram (Annex-III). It is also true that though the number of NGOs runs into hundreds, those, which are really active, may not be much many. The issue of the quality of these NGOs is open to debate.

The existing data indicate that in more than half the number of districts (N=18) less than 10 NGOs supposedly exist and one really has no idea as to how many of them active, and out of them how many are engaged in population programmes management. Given the shifting nature of NGOs' priorities, depending on the availability of funding, most of the districts barring eight (viz. Ajmer, Bharatpur, Bikaner, Churu, Jaipur, Jodhpur, Kota, Sawai Madhaopur and Udaipur), where there is a substantial number of NGOs or the activities carried out are known, it will not be surprising if there is not even a single NGO working in the field of population programme management at all in the remaining districts.

It was also found that of the NGOs funded especially by international funding agencies such as UNFPA, SIDA and USAID. Six NGOs in the state, which are directly funded, by the USAID and MOHFW under PVOH-II programme as well. These NGOs in Rajasthan viz. Seva Mandir in Udaipur and Bal Rashmi Society in Jaipur and Social Work Research Centre (SWRC), Ajmer District, Bhoruka Charitable Trust, Churu district, Rural Health & Development Trust, Jaipur, Tarun Bharat Sangh, Alwar.

High concentration of NGOs in certain pockets in the state seems to have led to some joint action particularly in Udaipur region. 'Parivar and Saathi Manch' have come into existence with a number of NGOs operating in the region as its members. The main objective of such joint action is to divide the area of operation so as to avoid duplication. There appears to be some kind of political concerns as well, in the sense that combined action of these groups is aimed at fighting the monopoly of a few bigger NGOs located in the region (IDS, Jaipur).

Government schemes - for Community Participation and NGOs involvement in Health & Family Welfare

Government of Rajasthan, in the recent past has initiated several new innovative schemes with a view to increasing community participation and NGOs involvement in population programme management. Notable among them are: Jan Mangal, Rajlakshmi, Swathya Karmi and Vikalp. While these will be dealt in separate papers, a brief note about these schemes is given.

Jan Mangal Yojna

Under this scheme, it is envisaged that there would be a male female team, preferably husband and wife, who would act as volunteers for promoting the use of contraceptives among the eligible couples in the village. This scheme was introduced in the recent past and hence its effectiveness is yet to be gauged. The notable feature of the scheme is that incentives are linked to performance, not in terms of output indicators but of impact indicators which are normally measured at the end of the year, rather than immediately after the "target" has been achieved as was the case in the past.

Rajlakshmi Yojna

This scheme stipulates that parents having a female child and willing to adopt a terminal method will be eligible for this scheme. Under this scheme, UTI bonds will be issued in the name of the female child and she would receive a sum of Rs 20,000/ as and when she reaches 21 years of age. There are a few exceptions to the rule in case of death of the female child before attaining the stipulated age.

Swasthya Karmi Yojna

Yet another scheme initiated by the Government of Rajasthan was that of Swasthya Karmis, following the success of Shiksha Karmi Yojna (in the education sector) in rural Rajasthan. Since it is in the early stage of implementation, it may not be possible to ascertain its effectiveness.

However, the specific objectives are to provide/promote:

- Curative services for minor ailments to people in remote areas and difficult villages;
- Critical maternal and child health services to the vulnerable segment of the population i.e. mothers and children in these villages;
- Family welfare programme and higher coverage with spacing methods, especially among young couples, and their followup until adoption of terminal methods; and
- People's participation through involvement of NGOs to ensure sustainability of the efforts.

The highlights of the Swasthya Karmi Yojna:

- The NGOs will play a key role in implementing the scheme, including the selection of manpower needed, supply of medicines and other equipment, and monitoring, supervision and coordination with the health sector;
- The scheme will be implemented through people's participation in the form of Gram Swathya Samiti which would be responsible for guiding and supervising the Swasthya Karmis and participation of the people of the village;
- The Swasthya Karmi is the most peripheral health care provider and would provide an integrated package of MCH and health care services, including treatment of minor ailments at the village level; and
- The scheme has an inbuilt component of sustainability, in that a user fee would be charged for medicines, and this revenue would be used as a revolving fund for further purchase and dispensing.

VIKALP : A Case of Government-NGO Collaboration

One of the best illustrations of Government-NGO collaboration is that of a new initiative known as VIKALP started in 1995, a joint effort between the Government of Rajasthan and the Indian Institute of Health Management Research (IIHMR), Jaipur. The Vikalp model, an alternative approach to family welfare programme, was initiated a year before the much publicised and poorly implemented "targetfree" approach by the Government of India. The VIKALP model brought out the salient features 'Government - NGO' collaboration should have. Its most important aspect is that of 'innovativeness in the area of family planning' which is very sensitive. Other dimensions of this collaborative effort are:

- A formal MoU between the Govt. and IIHMR

- A clear role definition
- A feasible and innovative model
- A healthy relationship and mutual respect
- A constant interaction
- A harnessing of the internal capacity of both Government and IIHMR

It is now acknowledged that NGOs have played a significant role in the past, supported by several experiments such as CRHP in Jamkhed, Athoor Block Experiment by the Gandhigram Institute of Rural Health and Family Welfare, SEWA experience near Baruch in Gujarat and Mandwa experience by FRCH, which are but a few examples. Research has shown that NGOs are found to have the following major advantages:

- Flexible
- Known for involving communities
- Accountable
- Capable of evolving micro-plans and
- Having regard for client satisfaction.

Like the two sides of a coin, there is a down side as well. Due to the availability of large amounts of funds from donor agencies, there has been mushrooming of fly by night NGOs. Documentation shows, a majority of NGOs lack the spirit of volunteerism for which this sector is well known. Even if registered and endowed with the spirit of volunteerism, the control is with a handful of individuals who may not be fully capable. They lack skilled manpower, and if somehow skilled manpower is available, they have high turnover of staff as the staff are recruited on project by project basis. Discontent among the staff due to ad-hocism and lack of cohesive personnel policy, lack of career development opportunities, lack of transparency, misuse of funds, lack of a second line of leadership, and presence of godfathers generally leads to lethargy and lack of accountability, there is no strategic plan as the NGO sector lacks direction, and they keep shifting their focus depending on the availability of funds, political patronage and administrative red tapism, and so on. In spite of these shortcomings, the state policy is sensitive to the essential constraints and achievements of NGO co-operation in facilitating the constitutional mandate of 'Primary Health Care' for the mass population. In this direction, understanding of some of the key functions, in which the NGOs are particularly strong, like those of advocacy, awareness and demand generation and inter-sectoral issues in primary health care approach and social development the role of government is understood to be equally important to look into the policy implications on sustainability of NGO initiatives.

Contextual Review of Programme Sustainability: PVOH-II in India

In recent years the issue of sustainability has received significant attention from the development agencies. One of the main reasons is the failure of many projects to achieve an acceptable level of sustainability. An official investigation into the efficacy of donors' aid reflects this view by identifying sustainability as a particular concern: A subject requiring much more attention is the life of projects beyond the time of the donors' involvement. Perhaps, one question above all deserves asking more often about most aid: this will help in the long run to increase the recipients' self-reliance? (Cassen et al, 1986)

Unfortunately, the answer is no, especially in those situation where donors' involvement did not go beyond a typical one-time financial contribution to the voluntary organisations. As mentioned elsewhere in the review, 'If development were a one-time procedure like a vaccination with sustainability… But development is not such a procedure. Simple infusions of outside resources rarely generate self-sustaining improvements in productivity and quality of life (Honadle and Vansant, 1985:)'

Therefore the question is: what does and organisation, with outside resource 'infused' into the system, need to do to ensure 'self-sustaining improvements'?

The resolution of this problem is not possible unless one addresses a more fundamental issue: What is to be sustained? Sustainability of a health care project, from a donor's perspective, is traditionally defined as: Sustainability is the ability of a health project or programme to deliver health services or sustain benefits after major technical, managerial and financial support have ceased (Lafond, 1995)

Therefore, it is not projects per se which one wishes to sustain, they are merely means to an end. Rather, sustainability, according to the above definition, refers to the benefits (or, outcomes) arising from projects and the capacity to deliver activities, which result in these benefits. It is also important to note that the sustainability of the organisation, which initiated the benefits, is not a necessary condition for project sustainability- It is the system which should remain operational in the long run.

The traditional definition has several loopholes, especially when one looks at the issue from the viewpoint of a recipient organisation. Evidence suggests that the persistent demise of externally financed activities is just a symptom of a deeper sustainability dilemma facing voluntary health care system to throughout the developing world. The system, on the one hand, continues to suffer from miss-allocation of resources, inefficiency, inequity and exploding costs; on the other hand it is constrained by the relative poverty of the beneficiaries and low resource generation capacity. Sustainability of a particular project benefit does not mean much unless the whole system becomes sustainable through co-ordinated long-term investment to address the total system ailment.

From the viewpoint of a voluntary organisation of any developing country, the definition of sustainability should therefore include the issue of survival of the organisation itself. It is a dynamic process by which the organisation builds its capacity to act as a strong catalyst in the system, and contributes towards system sustainability. While the effectiveness of singular investments is important for health system development, sustainability will not result from a series of sustainable projects or interventions if the investments do not come together to help the organisation and ultimately, sustain the system.

The present study, however, follows the traditional definition and rephrases it in the following way: Sustainability is the ability of a private voluntary organisation to ensure the flow of an acceptable level of Mother and Child Health (MCH) benefits to the community, initiated under PVOH – II project, even without significant managerial, technical, and financial assistance from external sources.

The above definition has several dimensions:

- It encompasses only the PVOH-II related benefits;
- It considers only the acceptable level of benefits (subject to the development of a criterion of acceptability);
- It leaves scope for project sustainability even if the organisation decides to pull out from the project; and
- It is recognised that external support and sustainability are not always conflicting.

The traditional definition is followed for several reasons. First, the scope of the study is limited to exploring the sustainability issue in relation to a particular project (i.e., PVOH-II). Therefore, the wider issue implied in the alternative definition remains beyond our scope; second, sustainability, defined in the traditional way, is less difficult to measure; and third, the alternative definition risks transcendentality and thus gives a vague idea about the recipient organisation's responsibility and projected direction regarding the sustenance of benefits. The traditional definition, on the other hand, is able to concretely define the role of the organisation.

The level at which the PVOH-II related benefits ate to be sustained is another important issue. Each organisation got involved in the project with a specific set of goals or desired output. The mid-term evaluation, mentioned in section 1.5, clearly revealed that a large number of these organisations were lagging far behind the goals. The goal of sustaining the achieved benefits, for these low-performing organisations, would thus imply sustaining the poor health status of the community. Further, some of the goals fixed at the beginning of the project may seem irrelevant or unachievable after five years. The projected coverage and quality standard of health care may need refinement in the context of society's dynamic change. Therefore, it is extremely important that the issue of sustainability should be resolved on the basis of an assessment of the project's performance during the project period, and be associated with a 'correction plan' if it is below the accepted level.

The dilemma of sustainability

Can primary health care and family planning programme in a developing country improve the quality of services, expand coverage, and enhance the sustainability simultaneously, or; Are these mutually exclusive goals? If they are, what should be the priority? This is a matter of debate. Harvey (1991) pointed out the futility of planning sustainability of such programme by the following arguments

> *The quest for 'self-sufficiency 'in international assistance programming has become fashionable.... The idea that we can recover from the world's poorest people a substantial portion of the costs of their own health care-particularly preventive health care – is based not in sound reasoning but in wishful thinking. We need to stop wishing and face a few simple truths (Harvey, 1991).*

And, according to Harvey, the major truths are: self-sufficiency emphasises income- generation to the detriment of social objectives and reverses priorities to serve consumers within easy reach (i.e., those who can afford to pay) first; it encourages a belief in will-o'-the-wisps, substituting unsubstantiated hopes for reasonable expectations (cost-effectiveness, for example), resulting in distorted policies.

However, many authors with equally persuasive assertions have countered the above points. For example, the experience of many countries, including developing countries, tells us that free services are often 'freely unavailable'. In most developing countries, policies are already distorted in favor of well-off citizens: Health services are usually available in urban areas, whereas many poor and rural areas are not served at all. Cost-recovery can attempt to cross-subsidise these services (Ashford and Haws, 1992).

A number of other studies have argued that even the poorest citizens are willing to pay a small amount of services they value (Lande and Geller, 1991, Lewis, 1987)

The arguments presented above revolve around a single attribute of the issue: the financial sustainability of a programme – whether operating costs of a health programme can and should be recovered from the community living at a near-subsistence level. These do not even address to the other aspects of financial sustainability; for example, is it possible to control the operating costs through attaining higher efficiency? Should we put more emphasis on cost- effectiveness of an intervention for the sake of sustainability?

It is true that, from the viewpoint of a donor agency, the notion of financial sustainability is more relevant than other (broader) issues of sustainability. Strictly speaking, the agencies' major concern at this time is "finding ways to finance recurrent costs of primary health care programme" (Esselman, 1994), once the agency's fund ceases to flow. This viewpoint, once taken literally, immediately creates a dilemma. As explained by Gibson and Ferrand (1994):

> NGOs are required to say how the project will become sustainable by donors, interpret this as meaning self-financing or taken over by government (even though neither may be feasible) and concoct a project application which somehow promises that this can be deliver. This interpretation of sustainability thus encourages them to place completely unrealistic expectations on their key stakeholders: beneficiaries and government. In practice, many NGOs seek to solve their sustainability dilemma by simply looking for another donor at the end of the project period (Gibson and Ferrand1994)).

The dilemma thus lies in the interpretation of donors' expectation regarding sustainability and its apparent non-feasibility in the hard reality. One may also add that, by this interpretation, no project of any voluntary organisation in the developing world is sustainable. Even much vaunted development success, such as the Grameen bank in Bangladesh, rely on significant external support,— in their case, large amounts of money at very low interest rates (Costello et al, 1990).

The proper way to get out of the dilemma is to recognise that a strategy for sustainability, even by the donors' standard, does not necessarily imply a quick switch-over to self-financing, or, a sudden transfer of activities to the resource-starved government. It is rather an opportunity to build internal capacity of the system so that, over time, it becomes less and less vulnerable to hostile external shocks. This strategy must be an integral part of the overall project design so that, from the very beginning, the project helps an organisation build three types of capacities.

- The capacity to secure sufficient resources locally;
- The capacity to use resources effectively and efficiently to meet real health need; and
- The capacity to manipulate external favourable factors.

Obviously, sustainability, interpreted as above, requires that an NGO or an organisation do an introspective stock analysis of the following six elements:

- Commitment to address community's real health needs
- Vision about the future direction
- Community participation at every stage of the project
- Attention to consistent improvement in quality of services
- Efficient and effective resource management
- Resource generation from internal sources

The concern for sustainability is thus appropriate when one interprets it in such a wider perspective. The interpretation requires that 'sustainability becomes the core concern', of a project design originally – not just an afterthought' - quest for money. The organisation requires having a clear vision about its role in the community and a strong commitment to implement the role. It should concentrate on building rapport with the community to ensure the community's involvement in the project. This can be expected only when, in addition to the above elements, quality of services is regularly monitored. Next comes the question of management and generation of resources. The resources mobilised through donors' assistance need to be utilised efficiently and effectively so that the initial investment does not leave an unwarranted legacy of economic inefficiency or ineffectiveness to the next generation of stakeholders – to answer strategy to achieve financial sustainability. The question of financial sustainability or resource generation comes last; the need for exploring different options for community financing should be understood, planned, and experimented as a logical counterpart of the other five strategic goals.

PVOH-II Programmes in India -The study of NGOs in Rajasthan

The NGO sector is quite varied across the country. There are regions, which are conducive to the growth of 'social action groups' and regions, where it is difficult to come across even one functioning NGO. There have been period in our society when groups were encouraged and supported to initiate specific programmes and activities, plunge into primary health care, women's empowerment, economic development programmes, environmental protections and so on. Scanning the country as a whole one comes across a fascinating picture - areas where Gandhiji inspired many young people to initiate constructive work, when Jai Prakash Narayan called upon the youth to fight for the rights of the poor, projects like Jamkhed, which inspired the poor to take charge of their own health, trail blazing work of "Self Employed Women's Association" inspired which groups to work for economic empowerment of women, the pioneering work of Sundarlal Bahuguna which tugged the conscience of many socially concerned people to protect the environment, and most recently the right to information movement spearheaded by '*Mazdoor Kisan Shakti Sangathan*' in Rajasthan which has questioned the fundamental premise of development work. Such inspiring movements are few and far between, yet they have left a indelible mark on social action in India.

The growth of NGOs, is partly the result of enlightened national policies, programmes and the availability of development assistance from the Government and international donor agencies. It is now quite a well-accepted fact that in the early 1980s the Government of India and international agencies consciously promoted development of women and children through the initiatives in social services sector viz. Primary Health Care, Primary education, Safe drinking water and sanitation and various rural development measures. Social action groups, university colleges, research institutes, and autonomous bodies were actively encouraged to debate status of women and children, conduct research, initiate programmes and so on. The famous report of 1975 - "Towards Equality", kick-started work in the areas of women's issues in social development. Similarly in the late eighties, international attention on environmental issues made many groups sit up and think about ecological issues. In short, the donor community (both Government and International) played a significant role in shaping the programmatic content of the NGO sector.

Another aspect of the NGO sector, which is widely debated, revolves around existence of a nurturing environment. We are often tempted to label some regions as being more NGO friendly than others. For example, it is said that states like Gujarat, Maharashtra, Karnataka, Tamil Nadu, Rajasthan, etc. are more conducive to the survival and growth of NGOs. This does not imply that the other states are hostile but a commentary on the administrative, social and political culture of a state in comparison with others. For example, the Government of Rajasthan sponsored projects like Shiksha Karmi and Lok Jumbish consciously created an environment where small and large groups were not only encouraged to work on primary education, but were systematically helped to develop technical and managerial capabilities to do so. Similarly, with the launching of Women's Development Programmes (WDP) in 1984, a large number of women activists, teachers, administrators and researchers got involved. Over the years, many of them set up their own organisations or joined existing groups. WDP also sensitised many NGOs to gender issues by involving their staff (especially women) in training and capacity building activities. Similarly the SWACH programme provided a good forum to initiate debate on sanitation, water and health issues.

In the last twenty years, Rajasthan has seen many innovations in Government - NGO collaborations, which contributed to the growth of the NGO sector. While this is indeed a very positive trend, people associated with the NGOs have often lamented over the problem of initiating health care related work. Many groups work on health education, awareness building and even family welfare programmes - but the numbers of groups engaged in field based health-care service delivery are few and far between. With the exception of well established, organisations like SWRC, Tilonia and Seva Mandir, Udaipur- NGOs have found it very difficult to sustain their work in the health sector. Availability of medical and paramedical professionals, investment in infrastructure, accessibility of referral and back-up services, all these have contributed to the expansion of health programmes in the state of Rajasthan. Some NGOs started health programmes, but had to abandon them because they could not sustain it, but some other NGOs are trying to sustain the health activities in the unserved areas. In spite of their large number of growth, the absence of a vibrant NGO community working in health care in Rajasthan was quite apparent (Gulhati, 1994). While one can still find a few, organisations engaged in primary health care, women's health remains a weak spot. Existing women's organizations, which have done commendable work in women's empowerment, point out the indifference of health care service providers to women's perspectives, aspirations and needs. It has been one of the most neglected areas of social action in Rajasthan. These neglected aspects of women's health are addressed through community based MCH and Family Welfare activities sponsored by MOH& FW, Government of India and financially supported by USAID. This programme was operational in selected Indian states including the state of Rajasthan since the early

1980s, under the project names of 'Private Voluntary Organisations in Health' PVOH-I and PVOH-II.

Impact of NGO Initiatives in Partnership with USAID

USAID has played an active role in health and family planning activities, and has made clear contributions to the substantial drop in fertility and child mortality. The objectives of USAID's assistance is to reduce current high level of fertility and improve women's reproductive health by increasing access to, quality of, and demand for a broad range of reproductive health and family planning services and to address related fertility parameters, including the status of women, in India. However, because India has only made limited use of new technologies and service approaches, progress in recent years has been considerably slower than in many other countries. USAID is now playing a major role in introducing new service approaches and technologies, to improve quality of services and increase access. In the 1990s, USAID's program in India, successfully established grassroots support for improving Government services and has brought in the participation of a wide range of non-governmental agencies or Private Voluntary Organisations (PVOs) to complement and strengthen the overall family planning and reproductive health program. To increase access to quality services, USAID has supported training of PVOs' health officials and family planning providers throughout the states wherever its PVOs are operating; introduced new training methodologies to make the training programs more competency-based and client-oriented; trained midwives and other village-level private practitioners and traditional doctors; and provided more than 30 PVOs with a wide-range of health and family planning services, increasing service coverage thorough strengthening partnership with NGO or 'Private Voluntary Organisations in Health' (PVOH) programmes in India (MOH & FW, GOI).

Genesis of PVOH-II

In April 1996, Government of India abolished method specific targets in the Indian family welfare programme and declared the resolve of the Government to move away from vertical family planning, maternal health, child survival programmes to an integrated "Reproductive and Child Health" approach. Many donors and multilateral agencies and the World Bank expressed interest in supporting this initiative. In 1997 Government of India, announced that RCH, will be taken up as district based projects and different donor agencies were allocated districts. Prior to this effort, the Government's recognition for the growth and involvement of NGOs, led to financial support for 32 NGOs, by the 'MOH & FW' and the USAID launched

PVOH- I project in the beginning of eighties. The intention was to complement and share Government efforts through wider outreach to improve the health of mothers and children. PVOH-I was meant to increase the interaction between the public and private health sectors. PVOH-I identified and supported innovative projects to improve health care through community participation. The long term goal of PVOH-I was the reduction of infant mortality and fertility among the poor and disadvantaged section of society, by strengthening NGO sector so that it could expand and provide a basic package of 'Maternal and Child Health services', especially immunization, antenatal care, ORT, nutrition and family planning. PVOH-I demonstrated that NGOs had the capacity to deliver primary health care services to remote and under-served populations using flexible and innovative strategies (USAID). This encouraged the 'MOH and FW' and USAID to explore further cooperation with NGOs, through the PVOH-II project.

PVOH-II supported 131 small and large NGOs in thirteen states across the country, with a total poppulation coverage of about 2.5 million. The life of each project varies from three to five years and the size of grants ranges from Rs. 2,00,000 to Rs. 10, 000, 000. PVOH-II NGOs work in remote rural areas where Government infrastructure is minimal or non-existent. All projects focus on the needy, the poor and the disadvantaged. The NGOs supported by PVOH-II vary widely in the scope of their activities. Some of the NGOs who have already having a base in health activities, used the funds to expand the area of geographic coverage. Other NGOs, used PVOH-II funds to diversify into other development activities mainly for women, while a few NGOs that had multisectoral community based programmes used PVOH-II support to initiate health programmes. Although, the goals of PVOH-II were generally similar to those of PVOH-I the project objectives were more comprehensive. In contrast to PVOH-I where both integrated and vertical programmes for tuberculosis and blindness control were supported all PVOH-II projects were integrated primary health care projects with a focus on Maternal and Child Health. Recognizing that improved health care was dependent on more than just heath service delivery PVOH- II encouraged NGOs to integrate water and sanitation activities, income generation programmes ad literacy training, especially for women.

The PVOH-I experience had shown that the majority of NGOs, though committed to health outreach services lacked the technical capability to successfully implement Maternal and Child Health (MCH) programmes. PVOH-II addressed the issue of capacity building through provision of technical assistance, information exchange and networking through two distinct approaches. One approach was to fund a group of intermediary

NGOs called 'Support Service Organisations' (SSOs). The aim and objectives of SSOs were to provide technical assistance to community based NGOs to plan and implement 'MCH and FW' programmes and included training for these NGOs in technical and managerial issues. The other mechanism was to support the creation of Technical Assistance Unit to provide need based technical support to each of the implementing NGOs.

These NGOs are known as Private Voluntary Organisations (PVOs) under PVOH-II scheme. Technical assistance input was not limited to the "medical or health" interventions. Assistance was provided to the NGOs on a variety of needs that they determined, to design health information systems; conduct quantitative and qualitative surveys, training of community based health workers, development of sustainability plans and building capacity for operations research. The technical assistance took the form of work-shos, field visits, special training programmes tailored to suit the needs of various cadres, exposure visit to model NGO sites, and in implementing action research projects.

Government of India's 'MOH&FW' and USAID's Joint effort for the period of 15 years experience with NGOs through PVOH-I and PVOH-II challenges some basic assumptions about the role of NGOs in health projects, also provides some indication of what future NGO initiatives should encompass, of what NGOs can reasonably be expected to achieve in primary health care and of the type of support they require in order to succeed. This can be understood from the following features of NGOs activities under PVOH-II.

PVOH-II NGOs typically cover populations ranging from 45,000 to 1,00,000 spread over two to three blocks. The grant supported operating costs as well as certain items of infrastructure such as the construction of health posts and clinics, mobile vans for outreach services and equipment for Information, Education and Communication. The NGOs contributed to 25% of project costs of drugs and pharmaceuticals. NGOs focused on improving access to an essential package of preventive and curative services and on promoting health education for behaviour change. All NGOs used the three-tier service delivery strategy with varying degrees of success. However, there was a uniform emphasis on providing services at community/village level through community health workers. A team of paramedics invariably composed of a nurse midwife, health educators and social workers supported these workers. The tertiary level consisted of the medical officer and a project manager (Table I describes the function of each cadre).

Very often, NGO workers were the only providers of health care and all NGOs have provided substantial training input to their community level health workers. These workers are most often local married women recruited from the villages and are paid very small honoraria. In almost all projects, community health workers were selected from the community and were the crucial link between the NGO programme and the community. Curative care was the strategy used by the NGOs to gain access to the community.

Curative services have a high visibility, serve an immediate need, and are much easier to deliver than preventive services. However, the curative services that were designed, to be used as an entry point to the community remained an important component of the NGO services and in some cases overshadowed the preventive aspect as per the project design.

The major preventive health interventions that PVOH-II NGOs undertook were family planning, immunisation, ANC services, Safe delivery. Several projects emphasised care at delivery. The majority of projects trained traditional birth attendants and provided pregnant mothers with safe delivery kits. Little attention was paid to new-borne care although there is one outstanding example of a project that successfully trained TBAs in neonatal - resuscitation. While several projects trained, made a systematic effort at educating communities on the high-risk signs and planning for alarm and transport in case of emergencies. Regarding immunization and family planning, most facilitated government services by providing transport to the ANM, mobilising target groups, and maintaining record. Some NGOs provided services directly.

Community Participation in PVOH-II

Sustained improvements in health status can be achieved only when communities take responsibility to promote and maintain good health. One of the key assumptions of the PVOH-II project was that NGOs represented the communities, in which they worked and would naturally involve communities in project activities. The idea was that this concern and commitment of the NGOs for the communities would translate into their involving the community in planning, implementing, monitoring and finally perhaps taking on the ownership of the health programme. Several NGOs articulated this in their project proposals, some actually attempted to introduce elements of community participation in their programme, very few pursued this with commitment, and still fewer actually were able to transfer the responsibility into the community's hands. Community participation strategies in the majority of the projects were limited to forming or strengthening village level groups and training local community members as grassroots health workers. The use of these strategies differed between NGOs.

A few NGOs spent considerable effort on forming and strengthening village level self help groups, limited mainly to women. Women's participation in PVOH-II is substantial for several reasons. Women were an important target group and they were seen as primary providers of health care for children. Not unsurprisingly, they were the target of health education and health services. Because of relatively long duration of the project, several NGOs succeeded in establishing 'Mahila Mandals' which have initiated savings and credit schemes. Project did attempt to involve 'Mahila Mandals' in income generation activities, but this strategy succeeded only in very few projects. In one case, women health workers participated and were elected to power in local 'village –panchayats'.

In case of purely 'health' NGOs, such as hospital based NGOs, whose only programmes was the provision of health care, community groups were seen merely as an audience for targeting health messages and very often even a trained health worker's task was to round up the community groups for an immunisation session or a health education session. The inability to evoke community participation in these projects could have been due to a lack of understanding of people's real capability to contribute to the programmes. NGO personnel needed skills in facilitating and maintaining constructive dialogue with communities on their health related needs and priorities. These are as important as medical skills, but were not recognised as such in this category of projects. Thus, in quite a few NGO projects, community participation was seen as an instrument to provide health services to communities, rather than as a mechanism to empower communities to take charge of their own health. The NGO thus became the giver and the community remained a passive recipient.

Table: 1-Levels of Service Delivery under PVOH-II

Types of Providers	*Range of Services*
Community Level	Motivation for ANC, Immunisation, Family Planning by home visit, Maintenance of Village Health Record, Provide basic first aid and curative services (scabies, worms, ORS) Organisation of Mahila Mandals and Village Health Committees, Assisting labour and delivery disposable kit, Referral services, Income generation activities, Growth monitoring/nutrition Programmes
Sub-centre Level	Record keeping of services provided ANC services Immunizations Curative services (ARI, ORS)Motivation and home visits, Growth monitoring and development, Attending Deliveries, Supervise community level workers, Community awareness (IEC), Referral services

(*Contd...*)

First Referral level (Static Center/ Mobile Units), Doctors	Curative services and Referral, Some preventive services e.g. ANS, Family Planning, School health examinations, Supervision of lower level frontline workers

Private Voluntary Health Organisations in India-The Challenge of Sustainability

The NGO sector in India is at a threshold. The 1970's model of ideology-driven, individual-based, single-focussed (Comprehensive Rural Development) NGO scenario is fast being replaced by an alternative paradigm of donor-dependent, organisation-based, service-oriented NGOs. The structural change in the sector has gained momentum from the increasing attention and influx of funds from international donor agencies. The limited success of the public health care system to provide minimum health care to the poor and underserved has also helped trigger the entry of NGOs in to the public health care market.

A phenomenon gradually emerging out of this new paradigm of donor-NGO relationship is 'projectisation' of development. The NGOs receive funds on the basis of a well-defined project. The projects are finite (with a beginning and an end), have clear goals and objectives to overcome specified problems, are based around defined sets of activities and have measurable outputs. Development, in this new paradigm, is largely packaged into bundles of activities, typically three and seldom more than five - years in duration (Gibson and Ferrand, 1994). The project framework, first introduced into official aid projects, is now the dominant planning framework for NGOs.

Sustainability has assumed a new and indispensable dimension in this projectization process. On the one hand, the NGOs are required to package their inputs to deliver services through a professional time-bound mechanism; on the other hand, they cannot but see the futility of the process, if the services stop flowing (and thus the benefits of services) after a given period. Th community may not be ready to share the expenses, workers may refuse to work without compensation; buildings, vehicles, and other capital items would require recurring maintenance; and so on. The donors' funds, which come to help jump-start the development process, thus bring forth a potential opportunity to come, and threat to other, about extending the boundary of organisational role in social development.

The NGOs, which received donor's funds in the PVOH-II project, are not homogeneous with respect to their understanding of the imporatnce of sustainability and capacity to deal with the issue. There is significant variation (across the PVOs) in resource base, managerial commitment, and vision.

Although all of them were required to include a sustainability plan in their project proposal, it could hardly be expected that the issue was taken with equal seriousness by all of them. The interpretation of sustainability given in the previous section makes it clear that failure to address the issue would ultimately lead to a self-defeating path of organisational as well as system's development.

Chapter - V

Designing and Planning of Present Research

The Problem

The present study is an attempt to focus on the emerging issues regarding the sustainability of health care benefits initiated by the NGO sector. The increasing donor dependence of the NGOs in the developing countries has been inciting the researcher to raise these issues of sustainability and to explore different ways of dealing with uncertainty associated with such dependence. The present research examines some of these issues on the basis of the Government of India and USAID supported MCH & Family Welfare programmes under PVOH-II (Private Voluntary Organizations in Health-II) scheme, as was implemented by NGOs/PVOs (Private Voluntary Organizations) in the state of Rajasthan.

It is evident from the review of literature that there is a need to look into the theoretical and operational dimensions of 'sustainability of non-governmental health care'. The present study would attempt to resolve some of the following problems viz:

1. Does investment act as a catalyst to sustainability, or as a deterrent?
2. Are the NGOs responsible for investing in health and are their methods suited to sustainable health system development?
3. Has increased NGO-government cooperation resulted in greater effectiveness leading to programme sustainability?

RESEARCH DESIGN

Broad Objectives of the Study

The broad objective of this study is to understand the sustainability of non-governmental health care through a set of case studies of NGOs in Rajasthan.

This study is designed basically to understand 'the operational strategies followed by the NGOs to achieve sustainability of Mother and Child Health (MCH) care benefits', initiated through a USAID-GOI supported project (PVOH-II).

Specific Objectives

The present study is descriptive in nature, based on multiple case studies using qualitative data. Hence, no hypothesis is desired for testing. The study has the following specific objectives:

- To understand, and assess qualitatively the present sustainability position of each of the organisation with respect to the system instruments and determinant factors,
- To identify, major issues of NGO strategy on the basis of observed strength and weaknesses during the implementation process,
- To look-into, the ongoing operational NGO strategies linking democratic institutions, PRIs and Government Co-operation and its implications on NGO initiatives to sustain the impact of PVOH-II project activities,
- To understand, possible areas of NGO-Government cooperation for promoting national strategy of HFA through strengthening Govt.-NGO partnership in health development i,e, Key Policy Implications for future support in sustaining Non-governmental health care in the state.

Conceptual Framework

The proposed study of 'sustainability of non-governmental health care' is placed within the conceptual framework of investment practices involved in the service delivery system catering to the development needs of local conditions and the institutional needs of donor-government relations. The development of a sustainable health system depends on a fundamental change in political and institutional relationships, which govern the use of resources in the health sector.

The analytical framework proposed for this study categorises the determinants of health care sustainability as contextual and investment-related. Contextual factors denote the political, economic and organisational structures, and other players that influence the health systems. Investment relates to all activities that determine the use of resources for health system development. For the purpose of the present research, sustainability is defined as 'the capacity of the health system (non-governmental health care) to function effectively over time, with a minimum of external support.

The study attempts to understand a conceptual framework for discussing sustainability issues and to build the analytical blocks on that basis. The conceptual framework is presented in Fig 1. As shown in this framework, the issue of sustainability is seen as a dynamic process. The process starts when a NGO resumes its operation in a certain community base and continues till it achieves a self-sustained steady growth path.

The framework is based on several assumptions:

- The representative NGO has a well-defined mission to serve the community without profit motive;
- There is a huge unmet but perceptible need in the community for minimum preventive and curative health care;
- The community does not have sufficient organisational capacity and skill to create an atmosphere where these needs can be addressed.

What should be the role of a voluntary organisation in this scenario? The answer is not so simple because the role of a PVO, in a specific situation, depends on the social chemistry of PVO-community relationship (in that particular situation). However, given the assumption that community's need is the principal justification behind the PVO's emergence and existence, one can trace out an optimum transition path of a NGO and the corresponding process of sustaining benefits of health care initiated by it.

The basic understanding is based on the premise that the benefits accrued from a project generate, a transformation process – transformation of NGO community relationship over time. The benefits are less likely to be sustained if the project fails to initiate this process. Sustainability is thus, considered as a natural product of this transformation process.

In the initial stage of a project, the NGO directly provides the services to address the immediate need of people; it assumes the role of a feeder or a provider. Fixed and/or outreach clinics are set up; health workers start delivering services; physical capital (building, vehicle, etc.) is built up to facilitate the provision of services. Almost the whole of the operating costs is covered by the project fund. The community, at this stage, is best described as an absolute receiver of benefits; the needs are partially met without claiming any reciprocal responsibility.

In the second stage, the NGO would engage in mobilisation of internal resources and manipulation of favourable but dormant factors of sustainability. It would not stop favouring free (or heavily subsidised) services; but may scale it down. At the same time, the organisation would put its efforts more in the direction of mobilisation of resources – both internally and externally. It would involve the community in sharing the responsibilities, especially in filling up the gap of physical and human resources. For example, some of the clinical services (consultation, drugs, etc. may now come with a price tag.) Or, the community may be urged to contribute space, volunteer, or other supports. Simultaneously, the organisation would look for additional external supports from donor agencies, or the government. It would try to manipulate the potential funding sources to fill up the increasing resource gap. The community, at this stage, would partially respond to the PVO's deal; the response may manifest in dissatisfaction, negotiation, or, agreement to share the burden.

The third stage comes when the NGO is ready to act as a facilitator and the community is found to be totally concerned about the continuity of the project benefits. In other words, a health care system is built up and the NGO intensifies its rapport with the community through more comprehensive approaches, such as, generating need based income-generating projects. Quality issues take a front seat since people start translating their need into demand and respond with willingness to pay for care. The community, in such a scenario, may thus be denoted as responder. The PVO, on the other hand, squeezes the extent of direct loan and subsidy to the community and invests on improving the quality aspects of services. For example, the staff associated with direct service delivery may receive higher level of training in the health care of women and children; more sophisticated equipment for preventive and curative care are purchased, and so on. The major transition, however, is experienced in the internal management of the organisation; the efficiency in the internal management of the organisation; the efficiency in allocation and utilisation if resources (human and non-human) receives greater attention. The PVO, with a broadened infra-structural base, more efficient management, and costs shared by the community, makes headway towards financial sustainability.

In the final stage, the NGO emerges as a successful organiser of the community so that the local community is prepared to provide time, resources, and political support to sustain the programme benefits for the achievement of longer-term outcomes even without any direct involvement of the PVO. In other words, the community assumes the role of an actual participant in the development process. The PVO, on the other hand, outlines a new and extended shape to its interface with the community. More emphasis is placed ion addressing the people's need for technical assistance in their income generating efforts and creating and appropriate atmosphere for applying modern technology of production.

Parameters of Sustainability

The conceptual framework, explained above may be denoted as a general pathway to sustainability. It has three distinct characteristics:

- Sustainability, of the benefits of a programme is modelled as a product of dynamic interaction of the NGO and the community; in other words, community's participation is an in-built ingredient in this framework;
- It is built on the proposition that in developing countries, sustainability of benefits is closely linked, and sometimes synonymous to the sustainability of the catalyst organisation (i.e, NGO);
- Financial sustainability cannot be meaningfully addressed unless the dynamic relation between NGO and the community reaches a certain stage of development; and it is not a self-propelling process.

The progress along the pathway needs a vision and consistent effort to break the barriers on the way. Specifically, sustainability requires that the NGO would have to attempt to move away from its original role of a provider towards a role which is more facilitative, institution-based, strategically broader, and longer-term in time horizon (Gibson and Ferrand 1994). The next section discusses this, how it can be done.

Instruments of Sustainability

The main argument of this section is that a transition of a NGO from one stage to the next one, as shown if fig 4.1, becomes feasible only if it develops as several social instruments. The instruments may be broadly categorised as:

- Need-based projects
- Organisational units at the community level
- Service quality
- Accumulated Assets
- Resource generator
- Resource manager

Each of the above categories is described below

Need-based Project: For sustainability it is absolutely necessary that the NGO gets involved in those services which are priority needs of the community. For example, PVOs working with sex workers must address the needs for STD control and treatment since this is the major health problem among them. A SSO which provides technical assistance to PVOs, must identify their real training needs and meet those needs. A deviation from the community's perceived need, which is not so rare in the present Indian context, creates conflict and generated indifference among those for whom the services are meant. These benefits are hardly sustainable. The most rational way to address community's real need and to ensure its effective solution is to avoid a top-down strategy and involve the community from the inception (or, planning) of the project through its implementation.

Organisational Units at the community levels: There is hardly any disagreement over the view that community's participation in the development process, which is the most important ingredient for sustained flow of a project benefit, cannot be ensured without organising it in some way or another. The task becomes easier for a PVO, when it commits itself to a certain ideology and keeps it as guiding force for any kind of community service. A more common way is to set up small organisational units, such as Youth Club, Women's group (Mahila Mandal), Self-help groups, etc., and gradually empower them to take over a part of PVO-initiated services. Alternatively, the NGO can utilise the existing local dectralised organisational resources (such as Panchayati Raj Institutions) to share some of its activities. Failure to establish new or utilise existing organisational units often implies the failure of a NGO to penetrate into the community and be acceptable to them.

Service Quality: At the initial stage of development, the quantities get better scores in the assessment of project performance. Quality aspects, especially providers' competence, accessibility, and acceptability – the three major quality attributes of a health care programme – are often neglected at this stage. A programme without sufficient quality assurance is bound to be self-defeating in the long run. For example, it is common experience that a significant proportion of women who accept certain contraceptive through a birth control programme discontinue the use due to health problems and method failure. Most of these dropout cases could be avoided if sufficient attention is given on 'how', but not, 'how many', contraceptives are disturbed. The fall-out of the neglect of quality aspects is plummeting rate of utilisation in the long - run.

Accumulated Assets – The pathway to sustainability is a long-term process. It is expected that a NGO would accumulate physical and human assets during the process and create a strong infra-structural base. The physical assets may include building, modes of modern communication, transport, service equipment, etc. On the other hand, the human assets would consist of skills manpower at service delivery points, trained management staff, good working condition, etc. A NGO with strong asset base is less vulnerable to adverse external shocks and thus is more prepared to switch from one role to another.

Resource Generator: Sustainability requires a phased-down withdrawal of external support to its minimum. In other words, it is extremely important that the NGO identifies a range of alternative, reliable local sources of fund (both governmental and private) and starts trapping these sources. Although it is hardly possible to achieve 100 percent cost recovery through this process, especially for primary health care projects, the potential contribution of local community should not be undermined. The success in resource generation substantially depends on the PVO's success in improving community's economic well-being through income-generating projects and people's willingness to pay. Together they define a process of resource generation and one can not expect gliding up along the pathway to sustainability without consistent effort to keep the process alive.

Resource Manager: Resource generation is self-abortive if it is not associated with an effective and efficient resource management process. Inefficient management of resources ultimately takes its toll in terms of spiraling recurrent cost increasing tension. Without an effective instrument of resource management the NGO is likely to be caught in a low-level equilibrium trap.

The argument presented in the above section is that in order to achieve sustainability, a NGO must develop the given instruments to their optimum level. The question is: How can the managers of donor-supported health projects do this? The question is vital for designing the methodology of the present study.

Following Brinkerhoff (1991), one can suggest the following three kinds of perspectives for a programme manager: looking out, looking in and looking ahead. Looking out, means relating with the context or external environment surrounding the project functioning. Project managers should identify the critical contextual factors, government policies, local institutional structure, and all other relevant factors beyond the control of the NGO may utilise the opportunity of favourable patronage of a local municipality and piggyback on it for future expansion of project activities.

Looking in, means making the project functional and maintaining its internal organisation, operational as far as possible. Typically it includes all operational factors, such as, management of inputs, process, information, their relation to project output. The project managers should diagnose the ailments in the present input-output relationship and solve them systematically. For example, a serious lapse in quality of service could be solved through continuing training of health workers. Adequate and regular supply of drugs and contraceptives should be ensured to fill in the input gap The external and internal information system should be strengthened to facilitate monitoring, evaluation, and self-improvement. All these and other "internal fix-it" activities are important to develop the instruments mentioned above.

Looking ahead involves working to achieve the project's long-term goals. This would mean developing leadership factors including vision, mission, and commitment to the community. Simply speaking, the NGO leadership without a clear vision and commitment is likely to get stuck in the primary stage of the pathway. A successful metamorphosis requires looking much ahead of its regular operational management.

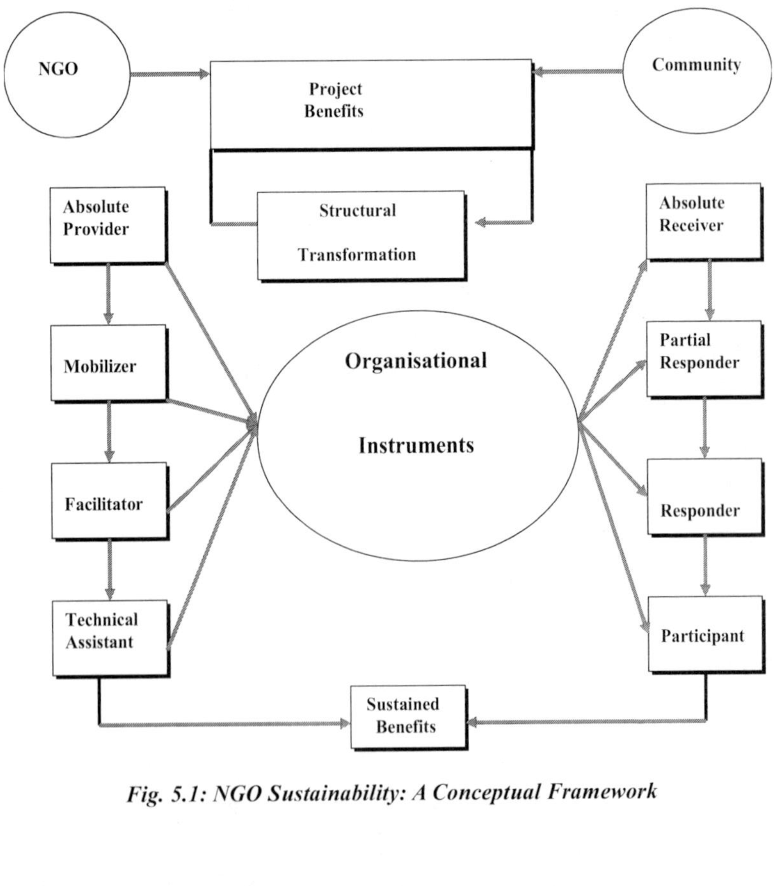

Fig. 5.1: NGO Sustainability: A Conceptual Framework

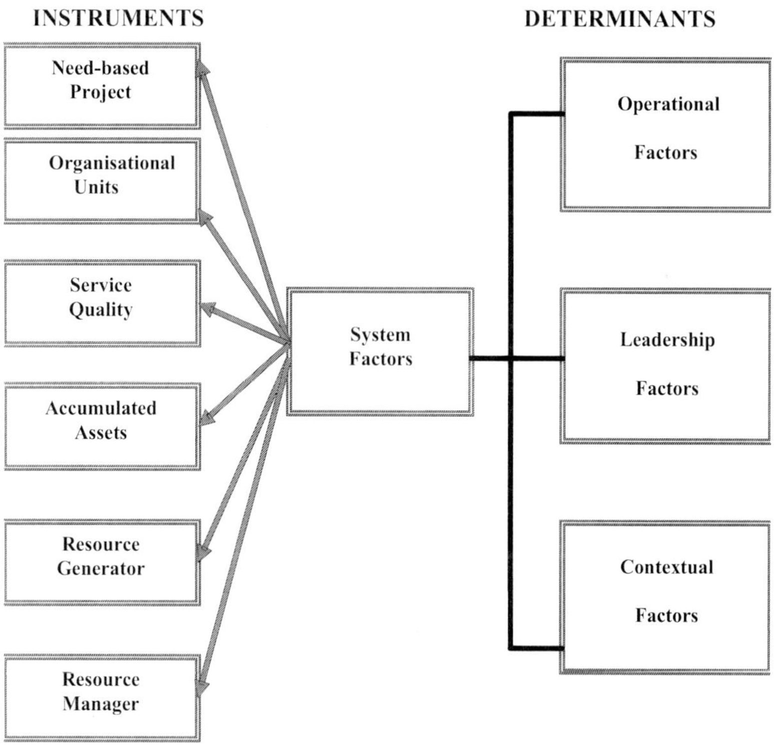

Fig. 5.2: Instruments for Sustainability

The functional relationship between instruments and the determinant factors contextual, operational and leadership) is given in fig 5.2. Combined with Fig 5.1, it gives a one-way relationship between the determinants and the instruments, and between the instruments and different stages of sustainability. Therefore, to assess sustainability, one needs to see the present status of the instruments and diagnose their deficiencies through a systematic assessment of the determinant factors.

As argued earlier, the sustainability issue is yet to get an appropriate attention from the donor-aided voluntary agencies in India. Therefore, any formal problem-solving study on this aspect requires a great deal of sensitisation over this issue. This is a typical case where a client's (i.e., the organisation's or the NGO's) active participation and interest are absolutely necessary to draw up a solution to answer sustainability. Hence sensitisation and advocacy for sustainability plan was taken as methodological part of the study. This process was carried out through series of dialogues with the top and mid-level management staff, and the grassroots-level workers, review of records, findings from the evaluation and visit report from the project area villages by the NGO, by the consultants and by the team members from the NGO. In addition, reports from several workshops were also consulted to understand the effectiveness of the program management and preparation for sustainability.

Research Methodology

The present study has three parts: project introduction and diagnosis for strengths and weaknesses, strategy for sustainability, and achievements and lessons for future plan on sustainability. The methodological procedure for the diagnosis part is based on the conceptual framework presented earlier. Specifically, the procedure involves assessment of the following three important aspects:

1. Qualitative Assessment of NGO strategy on sustainability,
2. Strengths and weaknesses in the contextual, operational, and leadership factors,
3. Location of the NGO in the pathway to sustainability in the future context, i.e. what stage the NGO belongs to the determinant factors, which were first classified into following groups:

   Contextual Factors: Population characteristics, political support, public health care/support service system, other non-government providers, and donor support.

   Operational Factors: Project inputs, information system, and process factors (such as, monitor and evaluation, mobilisation of resources, etc.)

   Leadership Factors: Vision, mission, commitment, and development of leadership.

Then each NGO was assesses and scored (on a 1-5 scale) with respect to its capacity to influence the six system instruments.

In the second stage, the instruments were assessed with respect to their maturity. In other words, a short-list of the determining factors was derived on the basis of the severity of impacts of the selected factors on the instruments. Finally, based on the average score of the instruments, the sustainability potential of the project was evaluated and marked in the pathway to sustainability.

The data for the analysis may be classified as follows:

- Published and unpublished project documents, such as, project proposals, income-expenditure statement, reports prepared by external consultants, review of mid-term and 'End of Project' (EOP) evaluation reports etc.

- Interview with the project staff and project managers, co-ordinatos.
- Findings derived from project related workshops and training programmes.
- Personal observations and interaction with local community beneficiaries
- Reports (survey, evaluation, etc.) of other studies

Research Process

Preparatory and Consultation Phase

(i) Demographic Profile - District offices consulted are, Rajasthan State Statistical Office, Department of Medical and Health, State Census Office, NFHS.

(ii) All the Blocks coming under NGO managed health programmes, are covered under discussion, and under each block two to three villages are visited.

(iii) Number of beneficiaries interviewed was decided within these villages after consultation with the NGO members, at their office and in their field areas.

Pilot Phase

One of the project villages under each of the three NGO managed health programmes was visited to have a preliminary understanding of the NGO activities.

Discussion Phase

The detailed field work data collection process followed the under mentioned stages:

(a) By interviewing and discussing with NGO project staff and volunteers. This helped to know the history, environment of the project area, and the involvement of local community in the project including their participation perspective and understanding to explain the success and failure of project strategies.

(b) Through a cordial focus group discussion, the perspective of local community about the quality of NGO managed health care and related missing factors in these process was understood.

(c) Independent project beneficiary interaction as well as group-dialogue with target population enabled to understand the villagers' health care facility conditions prior to the project as well as the changes brought about by the project's intervention, respectively in three different villages under concerned NGOs.

(d) Apart of these three types of interviews and dialogues in a mutually responsive atmosphere, there was some informal gatherings with NGO-members, local community, members from the Panchayat Institutions and related government officials in each of the project blocks, and this supported to understand the nature of Govt.-NGO relations in the present project. The conversations and data recorded in a notebook.

Report Writing Phase

Study Objectives in the Visit of Project Area:

The primary objective of this field based NGOs study is to provide in-depth understanding of socio-economic status and issues of women's health (MCH and Family Welfare) and reproductive rights of women in three different districts in Rajasthan. The data on health, education, working status, prenatal, natal and postnatal care, role of women in decision making processes over fertility and contraception, social and economic decisions within and outside the household, etc. are crucial features of the project. The analytical frameworks of the study purports to highlight the determinants of Sustainability viz. the key social instruments such as socio-economic and reproductive rights of women, status of girl child within households in study areas of NGO projects, community management structures strengthening local resources generation potentials, NGO's interaction and co-operation with PRIs and available benefits from the Panchayat system during project implementation, NGOs innovative schemes, range of community financing techniques, NGO management strategy, NGO and government health facility cooperation, Donor agency - NGO relations in the project under study.

Selection of NGOs for the Study

With this backdrop the present research focuses on the Sustainability of PVOH-II programmes as managed by the PVOs/NGOs in the state of Rajasthan. Six different NGOs/PVOs spread over the state in different geographical conditions implemented this scheme. These NGOs are;

1. Seva Mandir (SM) in Udaipur

2. Social Work Research Centre (SWRC) in Tilonia
3. Tarun Bharat Sangh (TBS) in Alwar
4. Bhoruka Charitable Trust (BCT) in Churu
5. Bal Rashmi Society (BRS) in Jaipur
6. Jaipur Rural Health Development Trust (JRHDT) in Jaipur

The NGOs selected for the purpose of this research is based on the following criteria:

1. They should be implementing MCH/Family Welfare programmes;
2. They should be funded by a common bilateral agency;
3. They should have a specific operational period;
4. They should be operating in the State of Rajasthan.
5. They should be focusing on Women's Health and social action.

Sampling Technique

The NGOs meeting the above criteria constitute 50 percent of the total number of NGOs involved in the state of Rajasthan viz:

(i) Bal Rashmi Society (BRS), Jaipur;
(ii) Bhorukha Charitable Trust (BCT), Churu;
(iii) Seva Mandir (SM), Udaipur.

The rationale behind the selection of NGO can be described as follows;

They are of different types of origin based on the following types;

- Type of Management System (Private/Corporate/Voluntary)
- Type of Programmes *(Intersectoral Linkages with Primary Education and Livelihood and Primary Health Care, Women Empowerment and Women's Health)*
- Type of target groups (Tribal, Rural or Urban Slums)

Moreover, out of these six NGOs supported under PVOH-II programme the above mentioned three NGOs were selected for study, which are of different programmatic bases of operation and different approaches of Management systems as identified under the present study.

1. Seva Mandir (SM) in Udaipur

- *Health care is approached as intersectoral social action linked with integrated tribal development programmes having target population as Tribal community*
- *Community Empowerment based on integrated tribal development and women's health*
- *Management system fuctions as Voluntary organisation*

2. Bhoruka Charitable Trust (BCT) in Churu
    - *Health care services is integrated with rural development activities having target population as Rural Community in the desert district addressing women's health issues*
    - *Management system functions as Corporate Social Responsibility organisation*
3. Bal Rashmi Society (BRS) in Jaipur
    - *Health Care services is integrated with Child focused and Child development having target population as rural community including childrens from Urban Slums*
    - *Rights based approach, advocating rights perspective of child development and women's health*
    - *Management system functions as Private organisation*

Constraints and Limitations

It can be linked to Policy implications from the programmatic understanding of the entire process in which health programmes are planned, implemented, monitored and evaluated by the NGOs with the support from various sources. It is basically focusing on the processes of programme management and its strategies related to sustainability. The divergence approaches involved in the programme can be studied in keeping in view of the factors of sustainability within the broad framework of contextual hostility.

Since the data were not collected through a structured survey method, but through an open ended qualitative questionnaire, the study heavily depends upon the personal observation and judgement of the researcher. This was unavoidable since the project data often reveals very little about the quality of an organisation's performance. However, the NGO assessment was always done on the basis of understanding processes and review of the 'participatory evaluation reports of the project', interaction with project workers and managers, were elicited through a series of workshops and interactive meetings at the project site. The details of the outcome of workshops are discussed in the respective case study. The interactions with the beneficiaries during field visits elaborate the NGO's experiences of linking program effectiveness with the existing local system of health services delivery to ensure sustainability. The project study was followed by the pilot-study to understand the description of the location and situation in which the project area is covered under PVOH-II project, as managed by the NGOs and their organisational development strategies and decentralised planning.

Chapter - VI

Case Study of NGO Programmes in Health

The present chapter undertakes the case studies of the three selected NGOs under PVOH-II project in the state of Rajasthan based at three different geographical locations in different districts. The case study of each of the NGOs begins with general introduction to the organisation, the area situation and community profile, background of NGO activities, and rationale for the PVOH-II project. This is followed by NGO management structure, strategy used for project implementation, achievements and constraints observed, community perception about the health care services, NGO- Government co-operation and cost effective mechanism, and issues on sustainability followed by future plans and key programmatic recommendations. The following are the names of three NGOs selected for the case study:

- SEVA MANDIR (SM)-UDAIPUR
- BHORUKA CHARITABLE TRUST (BCT)-CHURU
- BAL RASHMI SOCIETY- (BRS)-JAIPUR

SEVA MANDIR-Udaipur (Annex-VI)

Udaipur has many NGOs that are engaged in helping the rural people around the district in uplifting themselves and Seva Mandir is one of the most important ones in this category. A great educationist, administrator, diplomat and social worker of Udaipur - 'Late Dr. Mohan Singh Mehta', established this NGO. While the foundation stone for the main building of this institution was laid in 1931, its actual working started in 1967.

In the beginning, Seva Mandir had only two activities:

- A Citizens Forum (of some responsible and enlightened citizens of Udaipur)
- An Adult Literacy Project (for some villages near Udaipur)

But gradually, the work has grown in many dimensions of rural development and its area of work has also expanded to a great extent. Now Seva Mandir is working in nearly 400 villages around Udaipur and its staff consists of about 200 full time & 800 part time workers.

While, in general, Seva Mandir is working for an all-round upliftment of the rural people, the main aspects of its work are:

- Adult and non-formal education,
- Health-improvement and maternity services,
- Improving agriculture and cattle rearing,
- Development of water resources and water-conservation,
- Forest Development,
- Training in (Local self governance) Panchayati Raj and autonomous rural development,
- Preservation of folk-culture and its development,
- Increasing and improving rural employment, especially for utilising the leisure time of rural or urban women.

Seva Mandir has a very well-equipped library library-cum-reading room at its Udaipur Headquarters and its Training centre at '*Kaaya*' (16 kms. in the south of Udaipur) a marvellous place for training and improvement of Seva Mandir workers.

On the whole, this voluntary agency in Udaipur, is a really doing very important work in the rural hinterlands of Udaipur and many volunteers from other agencies from other parts of the country or even from abroad come here to study its unique functioning.

The Seva Mandir, Udaipur, a registered (1969) NGO is working in the area of rural development in the 4 blocks of Udaipur district, of Rajasthan. A board of trustees and the Chief Executive governs the NGO and General Secretary is Mr.Ajay S.Mehta B.A. (Hons), and M.Phil. who looks after the overall administration and is the key person. The NGO is a well acclaimed institution with funding from USAID, Canadian Indian Village Association [CIVA], Interchurch organisation for development Co-operation [ICCO], Netherlands and Protestant Association for co-operation in Development [EZE], Germany, for its various health activities.

Vision & Mission of Seva Mandir

Late Dr. Mohan Singh Mehta, the founder of Seva Mandir, dreamt of a socially just society. His ideology was framed around his vision of Seva Mandir (SM) as an instrument of empowering the under privileged so that they would be able to assert their rights and at the same time re-establish faith in their traditional beliefs and institutions. In his words, "Seva Mandir" represents a purposeful effort as a citizen's obligation to address the deepest problem of society. The present Chief Executive, Mr.Ajay Mehta, echoed this during interaction.

The mission of Seva Mandir initially focussed on promoting literacy, through which the literate masses would demand their rightful share from the society. However, it subsequently diversified with broader emphasis on development activities, which aimed at improving socio-economic upliftment and self-reliance of the community. Thus, health figured as one of the components of development initiatives of SM and consequently, was not a priority issue for the NGO and it certainly matched and was in tandem with the community expressed by the key NGO staff and also informed that this was objected to by the previous teams which monitored/ evaluated "health activities" of the NGO.

About Seva Mandir

In an attempt to address injustices of the social reality, the late Dr.Mohan Singh Mehta envisioned an institution and founded 'SEVA MANDIR' (SM) in 1969, an NGO to empower the underprivileged to enable them to assert their rights and participate in managing their own affairs. A board of trustees and the Chief Executive presently governs this 26 years old NGO, a registered trust.

The NGO is presently actively working in the 4 blocks of Udaipur district and the chief areas of its activities include:

- Education, including adult & non-formal education
- Water, watershed and wasteland development
- Agriculture
- Forestry development
- Health and Sanitation
- Women's development

Seva Mandir is supported, financially, by the Indian and the Rajasthan Governments, as well as by some rich foreign donor-agencies. Some rich individuals also support its work financially.

In 1985, the NGO launched its "Primary health care and Health Education" Scheme with funding from another donor agency covering 152 villages from 4 rural blocks of Udaipur district. However, after its completion in 1990, from March, 1991, through Ministry of Health &

Family Welfare, Government of India, with financial assistance from USAID, the NGO continued the earlier project and extended to cover 200 villages. The total project cost is Rs.28.04 lakhs [grant-in-aid (GIA)] and is extended upto March, 1996. However, the NGO had received only Rs 10.8 lakhs GIA till date and the delayed and part receipt of GIA had greatly affected the morale and enthusiasm of the NGO.

The Scheme provides MCH & FW & curative services through well trained cadre of primary health care workers viz. 100 Village Health Volunteers, 65 Home remedy Workers, 11 Community Health workers and 175 TBAs. The second tier consists of 2-referral health centres [RHCs] manned by 1 Ayurvedic MO, 1 Nurse, and 2 paraprofessional assistants at each of these centres. The referrals from the community/referral health centres are made to the Medical College hospital, Udaipur and this line up is fairly satisfactory. However, there is an urgent need for strengthening and developing these RHCs as 'base hospitals' with transport (ambulance/ Jeep) for mobility of MOs & transfer of difficult case to Udaipur.

The project management calls for improving the health managerial skills of MOs and developing a curriculum [based on CSSM programme of GOI] for continued training of field health staff. There is vast scope for strengthening MIS, self-monitoring, quality checklists, cost accounting, etc. Consequently, the training needs and professional inputs desired in this regard have been spelt out.

Lastly, the NGO in view of its credibility with funding agencies had a full confidence to sustain the health coverage, personnel and benefits at the same level through "alternative donor agency", user fees for services (selectively), Medical Insurance Scheme and community resources mobilisation initiatives.

The Private Voluntary Organisations in Health (PVOH)-II Project is implemented from August 1987 to August 1997 with financial assistance GIA from USAID and Government of India [GOI]. The main objective of the project is to work for the health, family planning and nutrition services for the poor by utilising and strengthening, the private and voluntary sector. The goal of the project is to reduce morbidity, mortality and fertility among the rural poor, particularly the morbidity and mortality of under-five children.

About PVOH-II Scheme (Annex-IV: Map of Project Area)

Project Title- Health Education and Primary Health Care

The MOH&FW, GOI/USAID funded project entitled "Health Education and Primary Health Care" was sanctioned initially from March, 91 to

September, 95 with a grant-in-aid (GIA) of Rs 28.04 lakhs and further extended upto March, 96 with additional GIA of Rs 7.19 lakhs. The project in Udaipur district covers 4 rural blocks/ 20 zones /200 villages /10,000 families /50,000 population approximately. The NGO primarily serves the Bhil tribals and other rural communities, which are greatly underprivileged socio-economically with poor literacy, health & communications and with strong traditional beliefs and faiths.

Objectives

- *To increase the capacity of village people under the project area*
- *Promotion of healthy behavioural change in the community*
- *Improve their situations by mobilising their own resources*

Strategy adopted in the Project Management

- Provide treatment for the minor ailments "at the doorstep" by training one of their own village persons
- Immunise the children and pregnant mothers against communicable diseases
- Educate the village people as regards proper diet of infant, children, and pregnant and lactating women
- Make efforts towards Income Generation Activities through integrated interaction in their professional activities.
- Educate people how to avail of and utilise the existing governmental and non-governmental health agencies functioning in the area
- Reduce IMR through provision of TBAs

From 1985 the NGO was carrying out 'Health Education & Primary Health Care' activities in 152 villages through village level health workers under funding from another donor agency. However, with the advent of PVOH-II scheme in 1991 the NGO besides sustaining those health activities/ personnel/benefits further expanded to cover in all 200 villages, thus adding 48 new villages to the earlier ones and the old funding ceased consequently.

Community Profile, Health problems

The project covers a vast area 6565 sq.kms approx. from 4 rural blocks of southern Udaipur district covering 50,000-population/10,000 families/ from 200 villages divided into 20 zones. The area is rugged terrain, hilly, with poor transport and communications. The PVOH-II project is limited to four blocks in Udaipur district. These are: Kherwara block- 85 km, Jhadol block-50km, Badgaon block-3km and Girwar block-50km distances from the NGO office at Udaipur.

The average family size is 5.33, about 40 % are in the 0-14 years age group, 3.22% above 60 years age group, 83 % belonging to SC/ST group, 77% illiterate, 93% engaged in agricultural work, 77% boys got married before 21 years of age and 42 % females before 18 years of age. A sample survey in 1993 revealed 30 % of eligible couples using FP methods. "Untrained persons" conducted 54% of deliveries and crude estimate of infant mortality was 90 per 1000 births.

The most common morbidity was infectious diseases viz. GIT, Skin, Eye, ARI, Malaria and Malnutrition. The community and the NGO perceived TB as Public health problem. Surprisingly very low vaccination coverage was observed that is 15% unvaccinated and 85% partially/fully vaccinated. The main objective of PVOH-II project is already enumerated in the introduction. They are in tandem with community health needs. However, they were not quantified and operational targets not fixed thus resulting in laxity in monitoring and project implementation.

Project coverage and Project Management design

The area of coverage is too large as detailed above and in the course of discussions the Project Director mentioned that project benefits resulted in 'qualitative' deficiencies generally expressed it. However, it was observed that a three-tier system was developed and it was as follows:

1st Tier: Village level workers viz. Home Remedy workers (65), village health workers (100), Community Health Worker (Promoted from village health worker on better work performance) (11) and Trained TBAs (175). The interviews with these workers, perusal of their kits/ records and opinion survey of community members revealed that this "front line indigenous trained" village level health workers formed a credible and committed primary health care personnel.

2nd Tier: The Referral health centres (2) one at Saru (Girwa block) and another at Khojawada (Kherwada block) each has one MO (Ayurvedic), one nurse, one VHW and one part-time worker. They approximately cover 10,000 population each and at present are run in rented buildings. However, they have inadequate infra-structural facilities and are able to treat only common morbidity referred by village level workers and all difficult/serious cases are referred to nearest Govt. C.H.C. or Udaipur hospital. The two referral health centres are being built with funds from another agency and this again was a 'point of conflict' between the NGO and monitoring Evaluation team interacted with. Besides the 4 Health Educators provided supervision and monitoring to the village level workers.

3rd Tier: The CHC and Udaipur medical college hospital provided the referral back up for the difficult cases. The village level workers are provided with "NGO identity card with photograph" and the PHC worker invariably accompanied the patients and arranged for their care at these bigger institutions. The district health authorities circular (from CMHO) according recognition and weightage to PHC workers of NGO with photo identity card and the generally well acclaimed status of the NGO in the district ensured quick service at these centres. The community members to the interacted during the focus interviews corroborated this.

Project Management Structure

Central Level	**Board of Trustees** (President, CEO and Executive Council) In-charge of various units, Health Educator, Lady Medical Officers
Block Level	**Block Co-ordinator** Health Educator, Forestry In charge, Lok-sanskriti Programme
Zone Level	**Zone Workers** Medical Officer (Two Zones), Lady Health Assistant
Village Level	**Community Health Worker** TBAs, Home remedy workers, Parivar Sathi as motivators

Project Management

The NGO has a well-defined organisational structure for implementation of 'health' as a component of its development activities viz. Multi-sectoral approach. Because of this, at the zone level and at block level the 'non health/medical' personnel viz. Zone workers/block secretaries were overall in-charge of health activities. An interview of these personnel revealed that they were not too familiar with the details of health work/activities but only knew broad areas of activity/work of the health personnel. This approach coupled with large area of coverage and lack of transport (vehicles for travel) has led to deficiencies in the 2nd level (2nd tier) of health care delivery. Thus, there has been no monitoring, supportive supervision, quality checklist, & high-risk approach in health care delivery.

As PVOH-II funding was not regular, (viz. 1991-Rs 4.87 lakhs+Rs 0.5 lakhs; 1994 –Rs 4.5 lakhs approx. grant-in-aid received), the initial NIHFW monitoring report was not favourable the key SM & PVOH-II staff were not enthusiastic about the "scheme *per se*". Hence, the health work which also receives funds from other donor agencies viz. Canadian Indian Village Association [CIVA], Inter-church organisation for development Co-operation [ICCO], Netherlands and Protestant Association for co-operation in Development [EZE], Germany viz, Rs 9.8 lakhs was perceived as one activity of 'NGO' and the details viz objectives of different schemes etc. was perceived only by the chief Executive, SM and project Director, PVOH-II. Even the 2 other medical officers of health unit expressed their ignorance about PVOH-II scheme/objectives and other health schemes/funding agencies, etc.

The management style, of functioning was 'centralised' and the inter-personnel rapport and co-ordination was satisfactory. However, there was no free flow of desired information even at the HQ health unit level and this to a great extent had resulted in implementation of activities in the routine way. The key functionaries of the health unit perceived their roles and responsibilities in a general way and functioned as per the directions and guidelines issued periodically by the health unit chief. However, specific job responsibilities, tasks, vis-à-vis the various health schemes were not known to them with the result the task of accomplishment of objectives were not possible.

The selection of staff was through the local newspaper advertisements and subsequent interview and appointment on 'contract' basis. The staff utilisation was optimal at head quarter level, those of health educators and Referral health centres were sub-optimal. The mobility was a restricting factor due to adequate transport and logistics. The training needs of village level workers were fairly well organised. But the training need of middle level managers was not given much importance.

Service Delivery

The NGO is a provider of safer water supply, sanitary disposal of excreta through construction of sanitary latrines, sludge disposal through promotion of kitchen gardens, MCH & FP services, curative services, arranging for TB services through DTC (District TB Center) under NTCP (National TB Control Programme) and health education with more emphasis on "AIDS awareness" in recent times. Besides other development activities the NGO was also strong in income generation activities through apple-craft, garments, etc.

Trained 'Home remedy workers' (HRW) who are mostly illiterate/ semiliterate and provide mostly simple traditionally supported 'Ayurvedic' medicines for common ailments provide the curative services. However, their popularity and acceptance of services depended on host of factors and were definitely of help to those in remote/interior/difficult villages with poor communications. The "village health worker" who is a literate person is provided with more inputs in terms of training and supplies and good VHWs are identified and rewarded with a better status as " Community Health Worker" to cover more than 1-2 villages. These workers provide primary health care and receive a nominal honorarium from the NGO for their services.

- The TBAs provide mostly ANC & NC services and is supervised by Lady Health Assistants (LHA), a female intermediary functionary who in-turn is supervised by LMO and by MOs of RHCs and Block secretaries and zone workers.
- The health Educators through VHWs organise village level 'health education programmes' through folk methods and a demonstration of these was made which were found to be very effective.
- There is a clear and smooth functional referral services/system from village level (HRW/VHW/TBA) to RHC of SM to CHC of Govt. Medical College hospital at Udaipur

The NGO linkage with State Govt. agency viz. PHC/CHC/Dist. hospital was good mostly due to the personal efforts/influence and past positions in the State government health services of Dr. G.C.Lodha & Dr. C.S. Paliwal.

Besides the reputation and image of NGO as a provider of social welfare services including health in the region played a great role. There was adequate supplies of condoms ORS, Vitamin A, IFA tabs, TB drugs, IEC material, etc from state health services to the NGO.

MCH Services- ANC, PNC, Immunisation, nutritional awareness are carried out by the grassroots level workers. In case of risk, seriousness, they are referred to Referral Health Centres. During ANC visits by the health workers, following four messages are conveyed usually; Early registration and its importance, TT immunisation, Nutrition advice and importance of Family Planning.

Family Planning Services- in collaboration with govt. schemes, Seva Mandir uses different approaches to motivate the couple to adopt birth spacing methods. For example; in the promotion of girl child scheme, the Govt. of Rajasthan offers Rs.1000/- for a girl child, which is payable at her 21 years of age, provided the couple does not have more than two children.

Substitute a son with a trees scheme, to encourage people to plant a tree in place of a son. According to the message, a tree yields material benefits and support like a son. Dai training for conducting safe delivery is a regular feature of the NGO.

Strengths and Weaknesses of the NGO

Community Participation, capacity building of community organisations, promotion of self-reliance, health services provision involving traditional system of medicine, staff competency and integrity to work as a team, high level of government co-operation are some of the essential strengths with the NGO supporting management of project activity as well as sustainability.

Lack of infrastructure, for field level staff including their housing arrangements is not considered an important issue by the management leading to staff dissatisfaction, Wastage of resources is observed in case of Lady MO she being not attending the field areas nor she is taking proper care for any of the risk cases in those villages, there is a sense of bureaucratic pressure at the top-management down the line on to the field level staff supervision, inadequate information management system mostly limited to the purpose of solving the reporting requirement of the activities performed.

Achievements and Best Practices

The health unit tries to approach curative aspect from all angles so that the community stands gained in all respects. Also people have a choice in the type of medicines they wish to have. No where is any drug or treatment imposed on them. The paramedical-workers provide the first source of treatment and also send for referrals. The referral in case of normal conditions generally is – Sub-center to PHC to District Hospital. In case of emergencies referral is directly to the Specialists.

Achievements of the PVOH-II project of Seva Mandir

Coverage of villages increased to 200, 48 added as a result of PVOH-II project. TBA programme grew in strength. ANC, INC, PNC, birth spacing, supplementary feed for pregnant and lactating mothers were focussed upon.

- RHCs were created to strengthen the curative, promotive and preventive aspects;
- Schools health programme was started to inculcate the habit of healthy living, from childhood and provide timely guidance to protect children against diseases;

- Women's health and IDS awareness program was initiated;
- The post of LHAs was created to supervise the work of TBAs

Also during the same period:

- Network of village workers expanded
- TBAs assisted births increased
- School health program started
- Inter-sectoral linkages strengthened
- Efforts to integrate IGA with health started
- RHCs of health education and health care made as focal point
- Organising treatment of TB patients started

As of today, the health education component remains the most important one, 60% of minor ailments are cured in the village itself. The TBA programme has grown in stature and now the primary area of focus remains AIDS awareness and prevention.

A good network of LHAs, TBA, AWW, ANM seems to be high point of ANC activities of Seva Mandir. However, the number of TBAs vis-a-vis the ANM, is not enough. TBA alone and her interaction with the community probably need more focus. The process already has been initiated but there is room for intensification, given the difficult area, illiteracy of women and lack of interest in health programmes of the people.

Also the competence level of the staff is fairly good, efforts are needed to further hone their skills. The area of focus is the first dimension – will. It is not that the people are not gaining, they are, but then again the curative side needs a little more focussing. Promotional actvities through health education remains the mainstay. No doubt, it is important, but a combination of tangible benefits is, what is required.

It is not imperative that Seva Mandir itself should provide; it can interact with the government to intensify their services so that people at large stand benefited. Also gramkosh being the foundation of sustainability in the years to come, needs to have a more permanent source of income in the form of an IGA which is commonly viable to the whole area, increase savings and revolution of the money in the gramkosh.

The two Rural Health Centers (RHCs) are really a big asset to the people, not only in terms of the treatment given but also the calm and soothing disposition of the doctors and staff of RHCs. These RHCs provide the basic treatment. Efforts are on to upgrade the facilities in the service in the same in terms of increasing the bed capacity. The RHCs have also become the focal point of the health education and cure in the areas they cater to. To support and strengthen the health component, the Health Unit has made available to the people with some very simple indigenous and low cost technologies. The focus of this aspect is to provide solutions with in the existing village resources. These in addition to promoting healthy living, also provide a source of income. Some of the technologies introduced include construction of sanitary latrines, digging compost-pits, making smokeless furnace and soap, and developing kitchen gardens.

Major Constraints of the Project

Girwa, Badgaon, Jhadol and Kherwada blocks of Udaipur district are fairly large and are characterized by undulating topography and remoteness of many villages. The community is mostly tribal and settlement is scattered or dispersed. Agriculture is the mainstay of people, supported by labor works. The literacy level is low and so is due to intermixing of castes as well as import of culture other than tribal. Today, the scenario is more or less similar to the general status of women in India. It is against this background that Seva Mandir's health interventions need to be understood.

The cultural taboos are strong enough to make a sustainable impact difficult. Especially the taboos related to eating practices during pregnancy. Usually the women avoid consuming milk and milk products, foods like '*bhindee*', '*arbi*', '*ghee*' etc. as it seems to affect the baby. Efforts are constantly being made to explain that the uterus and digestive tract do not overlap; therefore, foods as mentioned above do not harm the baby.

This combined with promotion of kitchen gardens has set the trend for increased awareness about the importance of a healthy diet and its effect on the baby. Practice of the same by pregnant women, however, needs more attention. The provision of supplementary feed that consists of groundnut, jugglery and soybean flour contributed to improving the nutritional status.

When talking of the women groups, the familiarity and practice related to TT seemed to be maximum. The ANC check-ups were not really higher up. This reflects the constraint faced by the health workers in terms of illiteracy of women, remoteness of villages and absence of ANM in some areas.

However, it cannot be generalized that community is not aware universally. The villages that are well connected, nearer to roads, sub-center is in working order, the ANM is regular and devoted, have higher knowledge levels, relative to the interior and remote areas. Also, the interventions seemed to suffer due to paucity of fund.

Community Participation

Community is involved to implement the activities in Seva Mandir to catalyze and sustain community participation in health. At the village level there exists the Gram Samooh, the *Mahila Bachat Samiti*, *Purush Samiti,* village health committies and the para-medical workers in the form of VHW/ HRW/CHW/TBA.

Community based structures & their functioning

The idea behind forming a village group (*Grama Samooh*) was to organise people around a common platform, to build leadership resources at the local level, to create a forum which can demand accountability and transparency from other groups' government etc. and to create resources, which can be encased to sustain activities organisation withdraws.

The Gram Samooh usually with 25-30 members, are mixed groups, where both men and women participate. There is a President or the *Adhyaksh,* the Secretary and the Treasurer. It meets once a month, the members on joining, pay a membership fee Rs 11/- The bank account is opened in the name of the group in the nearest bank. And the joint signature of President, secretary and Zonal worker of Seva Mandir operates the account. The main sources of fund for gramkosh of Gram Samooh are:

- Labor contribution for e.g. the villagers when they engage in labor activities like building and anicut, contribute 20% of the labor to the Kosh; penalty on disputes etc; and sometimes savings.
- Attendance, contribution, minutes of meeting, bank account pass-books are some of the records that are maintained by the *Gram Samooh*. From within the *Gram Samooh* are formed three member committees for different programmes like watershed, forestry, health etc. The President co-ordinates the meeting, secretary maintains the records and prepare minutes of the meetings, treasurer collects money. The Zonal worker of the concerned zone also attends the meeting. It is through this group, that all programmes start.
- There are several *Mahila Bachat Samitis* existing in the block. These are co-ordinates by the *Mahila Vikas Unit*. There are 20-30 women in these groups. There is a president, treasurer and *Mantri*. The savings rate is Rs 5/- per month. Meetings are held once a month, differential savings do not exits, however, some groups save up to Rs.10/- as well. They maintain attendance, saving, loan, interest and expense registers. Loans are usually of

small amount and given for consumption purposes – treatment of illness, getting school uniform made, paying off loans etc. 24% rate of interest per annum and a fine of Rs. 5/- per month on late repayment or for not attending meetings is practiced.

- Some groups are very old and some are new. Also in some, after about Rs 5000/- has got accumulated they distribute amongst themselves and then start savings afresh. Usually 75% of the money is in circulation and 25% is kept in the funs. Amongst other things, health related issues and problems are incorporated here to increase the income and control of the same with women.
- *Purush Samitis* are few and found in some villages only. One such example is a Samiti which was initiated looking after the RHC at Khojawada. There are usually 30 members in this. The savings rate is much higher about Rs 5 per month. The loans taken are also for big purposes – starting a shop, bulk cattle fee purchase, construction of house etc. They are not very common. The idea of forming these Mahila and *Purush Samitis* is to meet the every day or frequent loan requirements while the Gramkosh or the corpus of Gram Samooh is for long term sustainability.

Since the pattern of settlement in these tribal dominated blocks of the Udaipur district is sometimes dispersed and sometimes clustered, therefore, the health intervention in a dispersed and scattered village starts with 60 households and in a closely clustered village with 120 households respectively. The 'Village Health Committees' that are formed in a village are proportioned such that every 20 families there is one male, one female and one youth i.e. the membership ranges from 9 to 12-15 depending upon the type of these villages. At present, this is the most important forum of addressing health issues. The ANM also attend these meetings. It is envisaged to diversify and broaden the scope of these committees.

Type & Extent of Community Participation

Some of the villages are so remote, where even ANM does not reach, but it is the omnipresent 'Dai' who is a great boon to women. Even in complicated deliveries she is the first contact for treatment (if possible) or referral. Considering her importance and stature among people she is promoted with time to '*Dai-Maa*' and '*Moti-Dai-Maa*' or the one who is experienced.

Seva Mandir has cashed on their acceptance with the community their experience of conducting deliveries and their interest in health, to promote safe deliveries. The training given to Dai was most effective, combined with the provision of the Kit enhanced her role. Having talked to cross section of women, who had delivered a child within the past three months of PFE, and also the older generation of women, revealed the increased importance and faith on trained TBAs to conduct safe deliveries. Sometimes training of local men and women generates awareness, enhances and sustains participation, This reason behind Seva Mandir creating a strong line of para-medical workers, at the village level was threefold – create a resources base in the village itself, easy acceptance by the community and their sustained presence in the villages. The VHW/HRW/CHW/TBAs are truly an asset to the villages in which they work.

In addition, collective forums provide support to increase participation. This has implication at the policy level and programme planning and implementation level. Seva Mandir's health interventions make room for the heterogeneity of the community, the different health practices they have been following, and their specific cultural requirement. The policy framework including the interaction with the government provides room for resources and time i.e. needed accountability of staff and involvement of women in the programme.

Relevance and effectiveness of these Community Based structures

The health unit feels that, for health interventions to be successful, people's capabilities and motivation needs to be built, so that they understand their own problems, prioritise their needs and arrive solutions. This approach

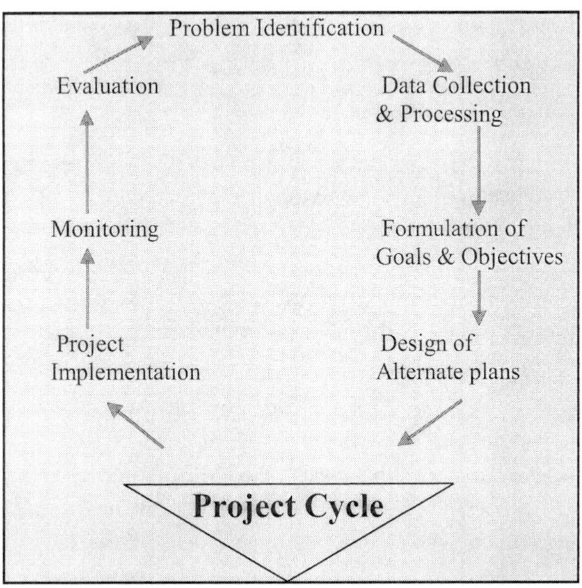

stressed an intensive health education, establishment of a network of village health workers and improved domestic and environmental hygiene.

At the base of the Health interventions lies promotive and preventive services and health education is the single most important component. The entire gamut of health interventions form the subject matter of health education which is imparted through 40 easy ways to follow demonstrations, folk media and local culture is also used to spread and impart these messages.

Seva Mandir's health programme can be said to be a movement towards community managed programme. Slowly planning, evaluation, decision making is moving from outside the community to inside. The process of demand generation by the Gram Samooh initiates the process of community participation. It is a process that envisages movement from passive to active, individual to group, knowledge to action, external to internal and dependence to independence. As of today, participation has become a key to programs developmental interventions. Participation implies the involvement of the people in their right from the stage of conceptualization to that of final evaluation.

The intervening organisation like Seva Mandir remains, but its input declines as community's empowerment increases. Here the idea behind formation of the Gram Samooh is the reflection of the above ideology. Specifically in terms of their health project the already existing Gram Samooh and other programmes like water shed management, forestry, literacy were used as entry point, also village health committees created to make the health interventions more intensive. To involve people, usually an existing structure or intervention is used; or new structures are created or specific programme committees formed. This initial step making an entry has already been made.

In case of Seva Mandir, it holds true of PVOH-II project interventions as well, all programmes are need based. It is people who through the *Gram Samooh* send in their demand or needs and based on that the interventions are planned and implemented. Even to monitor interventions, from within, the *Gram Samooh* are formed committees that ensure proper functioning of programmes. Specifically in terms of health, participation in such programmes manifested itself as:

> *Consultation with members of the community about their health needs; revealed about the fact that, it is people who analyse their health situation, the underlying structural causes of continued ill health or poor health care delivery system. After understanding the problems and deciding the course of action this participation in decision making*

and choosing strategies empowers them, it inculcates in them a new feeling of involvement, responsibility and ownership. This empowerment stage leads to the stage where community holds the providers accountable.

The thrust now is on community preparation and sustained education work with it. The health service delivery staff now is accountable to the community. The most advanced stage of community participation is one where the community is able to create, sustain, nurture and promote health care services and activities in a manner i.e. self reliant. The community at this stage acquires skills, infrastructure and resources leading to self - management.

Several factors have helped Seva Mandir reach its present stage of participation as shown in the following diagram:

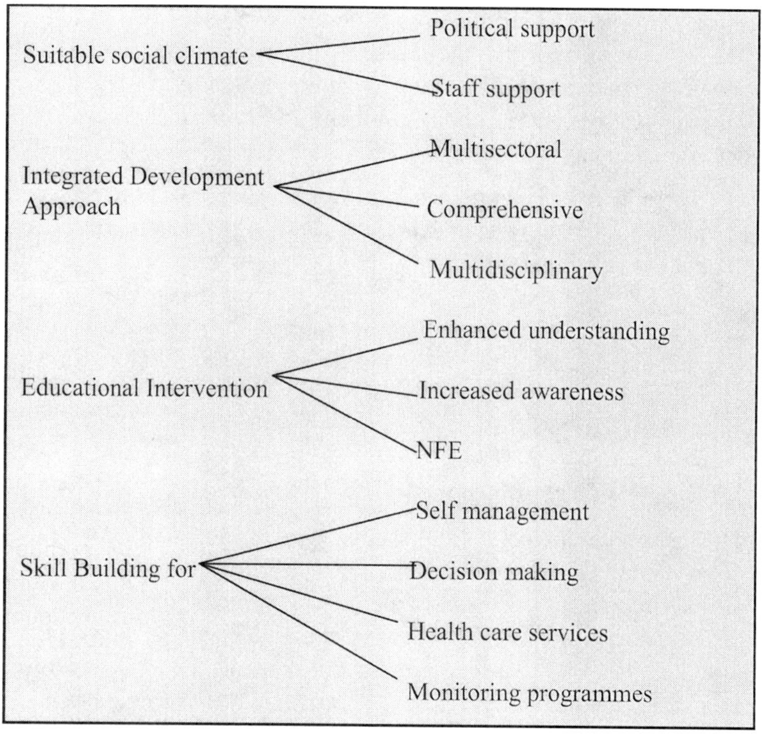

In addition, collective forums provide support to increasing participation. This has implication at the policy level and programme planning and implementation level. Seva Mandir's health interventions make room for the heterogeneity of community, the different health practices they have been following, and their specific cultural requirements. The policy framework including the interaction with the Government provides room for resources and time that is needed, accountability of staff and involvement of women in the programme. The community in their project area is an active stakeholder. They contribute in form of user fee for medicines received, insurance cover for health check-ups, contribution on no-profit no-loss basis for all low cost technologies – smokeless *chulhas*, kitchen garden, sanitary latrines, It is important here to understand that the purpose is not to fleece the people but to inculcate in them a habit of contribution so that they feel involved and tomorrow when Seva Mandir withdraws they will not feel the pinch.

The development of Gramkosh as the corpus for the village is an important step towards achieving sustainability. In some cases of these funds, the amount of money is quite large. Here again the labor cost and contribution are a major source of income of the Kosh. The possibilities of linking these with panchayats are also a step towards sustainability through community participation. All along the approach of the organisation towards community is empowering. The community is already expressing its needs and sometimes even offering solutions for the same.

The important point here is that the process of involving people on a sustainable basis is well underway, but the structure on which this is dependent needs strengthening. It is important to understand what circumstances prevented the opportunity from maturing. The question is what forces people to remain the way they are. Every society has its own way of thinking and acknowledging this difference is the beginning of participation. Several factors helped Seva Mandir reach its present stage of participation.

Multiplier Effect of Groups for diversification

The health interventions have been closely interwoven with other programmes of the organization. Sanitary latrines were an integral part to strengthen the education component on sanitation and hygiene but getting these made, would not have been possible without the support and technical expertise of the engineering unit. Not only that, it is very difficult to involve people around a health programme however, the presence of already existing programmes like watershed management, non-formal education centers etc., atleast provided a platform through which people could be addresses. The presence of Gram Samoa at the village level also provided the community with a forum to air their requirements related to health and issues of women's health.

The support and interaction with other units of the organization is also worthy of mention. An area of strengthening emerged – Health Unit's with the *Mahila Vikas* Unit and vice-versa. This unit had an immense role to play specifically, in addressing MCH issues and also duplicity of the efforts can be avoided in the same if both the units could identify common areas and work on them together. Overall the organization seemed well equipped to implement the PVOH-II project.

Project Management Structure and Capacities

The health program of Seva Mandir is spread in four blocks of Jhadol, Badgaon, Girwa, and Kherwada of Udaipur district. For purpose of close monitoring and efficient services these blocks have been further divided into zones viz.,

Jhadol	*Badgaon*	*Girwa*	*Kherwada*
-Gorana -Magwas -Oughna -Oda -Bichiwada -Falasia -Madri	-Madar -Kadia -Bagrunda -Delwara -Godach	-Suron Ka ghoda -Patia -Godgia -Prasad -Alsigarh	-Kojawada -Nayagaon -Kalyanpur -Bhomta vada -Juthri

Seva Mandir is a huge organisation and is also working in a large are, therefore each unit in itself a miniature version of the same; further the integrated approach melts the barrier between the various units from block downwards.

The Project Director heads the PVOH-II and the Health Unit who is over all in charge of all the different programmes. The MOs have been given areas to look after, like the Lady Medical Officer looks after MCH, FP, TBA, Reproductive health and STDs programmes. In executing the programme she is supported by 2 LHE who look after two blocks each and at the same time are responsible for documentation of activities, compiling the data from the field, planning for the monthly activities and bringing to the notice of the LMO issues of concern. All programmes are planned, designed, executed and monitored after consultation with each other.

Similarly, the school health programme, AIDS programme, insurance scheme of RCHs, coordination with the Government are looked after by the MO. Two Health Educationists (HE), who are looking after 2 blocks each, supported him. Also there exists a Co-ordinator who basically coordinates the working of the entire HEs present in the office. It has been planned very meticulously considering the vast area of operation and the size of the organisation. Moreover, Seva Mandir lays emphasis on integrated approach to development wherein they synchronize all the activities at the grassroots level.

In each block there is a block office, which is administered by the Block Secretary, he is overall in-charge of the block and all decisions pertaining to his block irrespective of whether it is a health program or a watershed development programme or any other, it is he who take decisions. The Block Co-ordinator supports him, and together they supervise the working of different program supervisors.

These program supervisors monitor the working of the zonal level staff and they in turn are directly in touch with the community and para-workers at the village level. At the zonal level, the zonal worker functions along with the LHA supervisors the health activities. The LHA or Lady Health Assistant primarily looks after MCH and the family activities and supervises the working TBA.

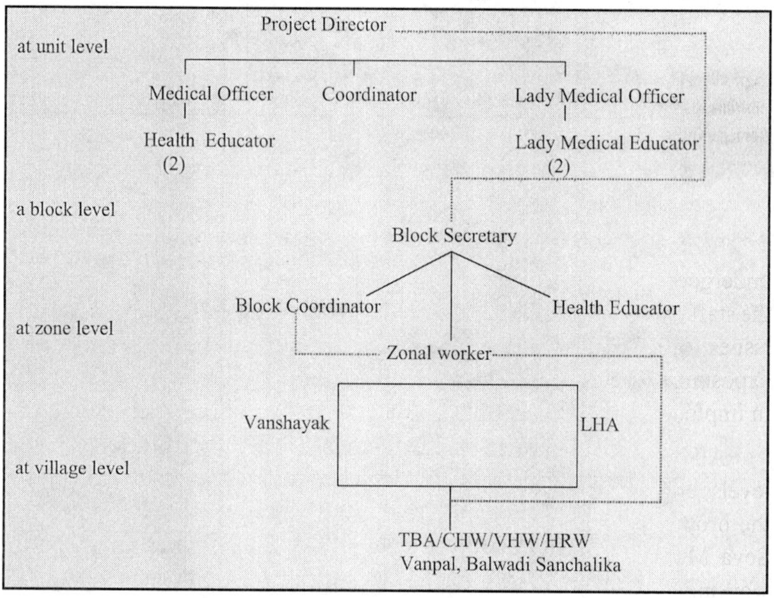

5.1.12 Health intervention operating channel

As the part of the health unit there are six health educators at the block level whom together with the zonal workers monitor the working of LHAs and CHW/VHW/HRW. The staff when recruited has a meeting with the

Unit head, the Block Secretary the zonal worker. Their possible areas of work are discussed on only after both are satisfied, the job chart is drawn out.

Health Management in a Multisectoral Approach

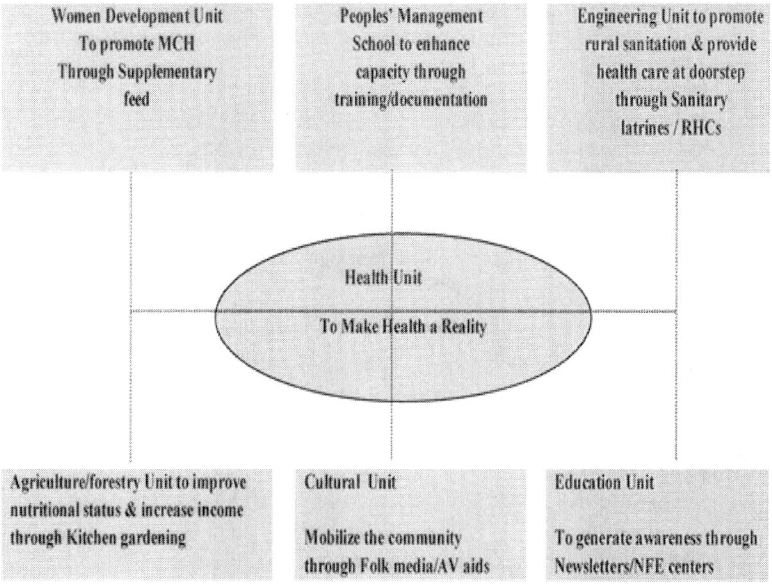

Each job chart is reviewed from time to time. The staff once recruited undergoes training. The idea behind training is three-fold, firstly to bring the staff on a common platform in terms of their understanding about health issues, secondly to upgrade their capacities and skills, and thirdly for exposure, so that in addition to learning there is also scope for innovation in implementing the programs.

All decisions are made in consensus. Any proposal passes through all levels, unit, block and zone, only after everyone has given comments does the proposal or the idea gets discussed. The decision-makers may be in Seva Mandir's headquarters but is endorsed by all. Also the units are working hand-in-hand. Seva Mandir is a unique effort of unity in diversity. All units are different and yet all work hand-hand to realize the purpose of Seva Mandir.

Staff Competencies

Village Health Workers are generally 5th-8th pass, local residents of the village, interested in health activities, and are acceptable to the community. On recruitment they undergo eight days orientation training, in which they are told about 12 points of health interventions, record keeping, and using the medicine kit. Every six months they undergo two days refresher training.

The purpose of this refresher training is to assess the level of knowledge of the VHWs from time to time, reinforce the components which need focus and also update on the new areas of health that have emerged.

The Home Remedy Workers are usually those who have, for generations been practicing traditional system of medicine (TSM). Proposal for their recruitment is submitted through the Gram Samooh. It passes from the village through the Zone and the block to the headquarters and after approval five-day orientation training and six monthly two days refreshers are organized.

The *Balwadi Sanchalika*, though a part of the women development Unit, is also trained by the Health Unit to use certain bio-chemis medicines for children. These medicines are mild and have no side effects. Since she is illiterate, therefore she has been provided with a guidebook with colored illustrations so as to identify which medicine need to be given and for which ailment. Most *Balwadi Sanchalikas* feels confident of using these medicines.

The community Health Worker is promoted to Village Health Worker/ Home Remedy Worker. It is usually because of their good performance that they are promoted. On becoming CHWs they look after five villages including their own.

The Traditional Birth Attendant (TBA) has been in existence for a very long time, and in their own way have been helping the community get access to basic services. They became an integral part of the Seva Mandir's health interventions in 1989. These TBAs or Dais is the ones who are highly respected by the people and the community has a lot of faith in them. Usually a TBA belongs to the village where the ANM does not work. The reason behind this is that together they are able to cover a larger area and each complements the other. The five-day's orientation training that the Dai undergo is a comprehensive package covering the gamut of MCH services.

The TBA is also introduced to the various records that she maintains with the help of VHWs. They also undergo refresher training and on the basis of their performance they are promoted as Dai Maa, *Moti* (Senior) *Dai Maa*, signifying their experience and seniority. LHA is usually 8th pass and on selection undergoes an orientation training of 5-7 days and bi-annual refreshers.

The Health Educators are a group with diverse qualifications and experiences; these range from being Post-graduates in Humanities to having as Sanitary Inspectors elsewhere. In addition to supervising health activities at Unit, Block, Zone and village levels, they are also involved in other programmes of Seva Mandir. Their job-responsibilities include co-ordination with the government at local level, visiting schools for health education and assisting MOs in school health check-ups, organizing and participating in block meetings etc.

The MOs supervising the health interventions based at Unit level are highly qualified health experts having vast experience of working with the government. Their sound technical knowledge and good rapport with the government has greatly helped the organization and the government to work in partnership. They ensure effective implementation of the programs along with the able guidance and support from Project Director, the Chief Executive and the Board members.

Training happens as regular activity, as part of campaigns, meeting, as workshops, for preparation of education material, to disseminate and share knowledge, and establish linkages. Capacity building is an ongoing activity, every forum is used to re-inforce the fundamentals, identify the problems, provide solutions to the same.

The organization has good linkages with CHETNA (Ahmedabad), RVHA, SORT, VHAI, IIHMR, CICO-DICON, RNT Medical College, and Udaipur, to name a few. The staff got opportunity to attend training and workshops organized by IIHMR and USAID during the project period. Also they visited Sevadham Trust, Pune to learn from their experiences related to PVOH projects. The staff of the Health Unit has had a lot of exposure and undergone many training. Some of the agencies with which they collaborate are shown in the tabular form as follows:

Partner Organisations Contacted	***Areas of Partnership***
VHAI, RVHA, Govt. of India	- Family planning, training etc.
CHETNA, RVHA	- Reproductive Health
IIHMR	- Strategic Management and family planning programme
CICODICON-Chakshu Jaipur and Boroda	- Eye camp training
FPAI	- Training on FP and TBAs
Indian Network of NGO's	- AIDS
PRIA	- Participatory Evaluation training
Center for Research in Rural & Industrial development	- Gender training

Besides these examples, there are other training that were undergone and imparted, and training institutes, medical colleges, etc. with which they collaborate. There Dai training component has a field experience part if which is done in *Zanana* Hospital, also renowned doctors of the city participate as resource persons in these programmes. Plans are on the anvil to impart such training that can bring the staff on a common platform of understanding.

The Project Director and the two MOs are the medical personnel of caliber. As expressed by other staff, their guidance and direction has greatly added in streamlining the interventions. Also, they truly reflected the ethos of Seva Mandir- that of integrated development. It was encouraging to see a medical person so well versed in other aspects of development scenario.

The health educators form the first line of the implementing team. Both the female and male health educators are well versed in their jobs, however, there is a lot of variation in their background which also brings to the forefront their felt need that at least educators should have a common and uniform understanding of health issues. A dilemma exits regarding the block health educators reporting. They are administratively reporting to the Block Secretary and technically to the Health Unit. This sometimes affects their working and outputs. However, this is more of a systematic problem, which can be addressed only by the management.

The pattern of recruitment and functioning of LHAs appeared satisfactory but the main strength lies in the capability of paramedical-workers - the VHW, CHW, HRW and TBA. The training imparted is intensive and course content exhaustive, constant re-enforcement makes retention powerful.

However, the number of training and refreshers including meetings seem to take a lot of staff's time from field visits and monitoring. Probably, this is the reason combined with difficult terrain, low literacy level, poor conditions and cultural background of the people that in-spite of the well-versed and knowledgeable staff that the impact on the community could have been more. A huge reservoir of information exists with the unit, obtained from the villages.

Management Information System

An efficient Management Information System (MIS) is the key to effective implementation of all programmes. As of known, there exists a four-tier structure within the organization – Unit, Block, Zone and Village. The records maintained at the unit level include personnel file, visits reports –

daily visit report and inspection report, tour plans, and advance request forms. Expenses - settlement report, internal monitoring formats, QPRs, QES etc.

The correspondence file, leave adjustment, medicine supply file etc. are maintained for monitoring the working of the RHCs. For monitoring health activities several formats are used at all levels like, registration of pregnant women (ANC, INC, PNC), supplementary feed form, hamlet level family health survey form etc.

In addition to having a well laid MIS, regular meetings are also held usually on a monthly basis at all levels. The dates and venues of all meetings are fixed. The agenda is not prepared formally but usually the meetings begin with the presentation of progress reports, the difficulties encountered, the inputs expected and planning future course of action.

These meetings also provide a forum for reinforcing health messages and skill building. The environment is conducive to learning, sharing of ideas and problem solving. Other programme staff represents these meetings also, which help in updating and incorporating inputs to strengthen the programmatic interventions. The staff however, felt that streamlining of the same is required for effectiveness of these meetings.

Issues on Sustainability

As known from the discussion and the review of records, the NGO attended the countrywide 'Sustainability Workshop' held in August, 95 at Bangalore at the national level. The project team on the 2nd day of their visit introduced the concept and approaches of sustainability of PVOH activities/benefits. During the visit the details of sustainability was discussed with the project Director and the gist of it is as follows:

- As the NGO is providing Primary Health Care and Health Education in the 4 blocks since 1985 (unto 1991 under different donor agency) it intends to continue the same at the existing level viz. service coverage, health programme and personnel.
- The details of the cost estimates was calculated and submitted to alternative donor agency and in view of the credibility of NGO it is confident of obtaining funds from another donor agency.
- Besides, the present practice of collection of 'user fees' for services will be continued.
- The NGO recently has introduced 'Medical Insurance Scheme' for 132 families at Saru Referral Health Centre at a cost of Rs. 18/-

per family per annum. Based on its success it intends to extend and expand the same in a phased manner.

In conclusion, as the present scheme of PVOH-II is an extension of health activities of the NGO under PVOH-I during 1985-1991, the organisation is trying to initiate measures to sustain the benefits of on-going activities in the project area.

Sustainability Perception & Withdrawal Strategy

Since 1984, the focus at Seva Mandir has been on training local men and women, so that resources are created in them to feed the village system. Also, use of traditional knowledge system in the health programme was given weightage, as it was locally available, low cost and easily acceptable to the community.

The thrust was to build people's capabilities and motivation so that they would understand their own health problems. The aim was to sustain an attitudinal change towards health and to promote community involvement and self-reliance in planning and implementation of health schemes and treatment of minor ailments. The objectives defined, aimed to establish a process of continental health education, establish a network of village level workers who are reservoirs of knowledge and act as a village doctors when the need arose, to improve domestic and environmental sanitation and thus reduce the incidence of diseases.

At present there are 92 VHW, 58 HRW, 21 CHW and 86 TBAs. The thrust has been to provide treatment through ISM, homeopathy and allopathy as well. Intensive health campaigns are also organized to create awareness, voice problems, address the same and to evolve the future course of action. During these campaigns, trainings are imparted, audio visual aids are used, and local folk media is used to spread messages.

The formulation of Village health Committees further strengthened the health interventions. Moreover, the constitution of these committees in terms of representation by men, women and youth gave an opportunity to take into account the insight and perception of these three major sections of the society, which made on the programme more broad based and holistic.

In addition condom dispenses have been provided in villages and roadside *dhabas* to promote spacing and prevent AIDS, also efforts are on to strengthen the Government centers, so that they are able to tackle some of the emergencies. BP instruments, laboratory reagents will also be provided to health sub-centres in the area served by Seva Mandir. Also, the ides of *Parivar Sathis* has been mooted.

The idea is to build local resources person who can train further and ultimately the village itself becomes self reliant in terms of imparting training. An important feature of sustainability that is being focussed upon is that organization intends to make the community self-reliant. It has envisaged a withdrawal strategy spread in 4 stages. The thrust of this intervention is that moving from stage one to four, Seva Mandir's contribution will lessen and the communities will increase, till a point is reached when people say "we can manage".

It is a process that envisages movement from passive to active, individual to group knowledge to action, external to internal, learner to teacher, dependence to independence. Community participation along with financial sharing and effective networking is essential ingredients of achieving sustainability.

Social or community sustainability has a number of dimensions, of which the first one is will. Practically, those benefited by the project derive enough gains from the project to have the will to continue. Various interest groups will incur varying gains and costs and even one disgruntled important group may be able to block the continuation of the innovation introduced in the project.

The second dimension is skill. Do the participants have the needed skill – both, technical, managerial and leadership kills to maintain the project. And finally if the groups affected have both the will, their needs to be organization or structures through which the will and skill can be exercised.

These may be existing structures, user groups, village development committees' etc. These organisations must enable those groups affected by the project (Government, Men, Women, Minority, Ethnic Groups) to negotiate effectively about the distribution of the gains and costs and to solve problems. Considering these aspects from the point of view of sustainability of the health intervention of Seva Mandir, the organisation certainly is very well equipped to exercise the skill and will.

It is a name to reckon with, as a well evolved long term strategic plan, has a comprehensive funding base which maintains projects inspite of paucity of funds, has good relations with the Govt. right from the medical services Directorate to the ANM at the Sub-Center level.

Although the competence level of the staff is fairly food, efforts are needed to further boost their skills. The area of focus is the first dimension– will. It is not that the people are not gaining, they are, but then again the curative side needs a little more focussing. Promotive services through health education remains the mainstay. No doubt it is important, but a combination of tangible benefits is what is required. It is not imperative that Seva Mandir itself should provide; it can interact with the Govt. to intensify their services so that people at large stand benefited. Also *gramkosh* being the foundation if sustainability in the years to come, needs to have a more permanent source of income in the form of IGA which is commonly viable to the whole area, increase savings and revolvement of the money in the *gramkosh*.

Sustainability is not so much problem as to increase the coverage of people under health intervention. Efforts are already underway to increase the touch with the community, and it is hoped that very soon there will be marked improvement in the indicator rate as expressed by Dr. Lodha, head of Health Unit while discussing about the perception of Sustainability under PVOH-II.

Coordination with Government Health Programme

The very fact that Seva Mandir has never thought of setting up a parallel health structure to the government's and their understanding that both are complementary has paved way for good relationship between the two. This relation manifests itself at all levels from the policy making to the sub-centre level. The CMHO, Udaipur Dr. K.L.Kumath was quite supportive of the Seva Mandir's health interventions. He stressed the fact, that very often NGOs are able to get a health project sanctioned, but the expertise t o carry out the same is not up to the mark. However, he acknowledged Seva Mandir's efforts and also encouraged their supportive approach, through which it has now become easier to identify the target group, say for immunization.

Even at the block level the Medical officer of PHC at Badgaon block felt that the combination of Govt. infrastructure and the presence of Seva Mandir with the community made everyday working easier, and also during epidemics; "we realize how much we need for each other".

The ANM of Gorana Zone in Jhadol block also accepted the fact that it is not easy for her to identify patients in her own area all by herself, the presence of TBA has helped her in identifying villages where focus is required and also, she says, as a result of working together the immunization coverage has gone up. Also the TBA at times gives much required technical assistance. Not only this, the ANM also attends the village health committee meetings. TBA and ANM work together for immunization – TBA motivates and identifies mothers and children and ANM administers the vaccine.

Also the health educators participate in the PHC meetings. There is also a proposition that the LHAs will also attend Zonal level PHC meetings.

Also during the discussions with Deputy CMHO (immunization), It became apparent that government has well-classified machinery, but under staffing at PHC and sub-centre level posed problems for them in terms of increasing immunization coverage. He was of the opinion that atleast in the areas where Seva Mandir is working and knowing the organization's contact with the community, it was important that a more complementary system emerges wherein the Seva Mandir staff motivates for immunization, shortlist children every week/fortnight and the ANM goes to administer the vaccine.

It is true that this complementary relationship exists, but it is not a common feature in every village or block. What is required is the intensification of efforts and both Govt. and the organisation come forward to work in hand. In fact in village Rama in Badgaon block, the ANC, INC, PNC immunisation coverage were quite good and incidentally the Govt. machinery and the Seva Mandir workers do compliment each other in increasing the reach of health services.

The coordination with the Govt. is good in this area whether it is the supply of ORS packet or timely treatment. Problem is the remoteness of villages and lack of transportation, which sometimes impede timely help.

Cost sharing Efforts

Efforts made towards financial sustainability translate themselves in the form of user fees, insurance cover, cost sharing, introduction of low cost technology with a twin purpose of satisfying the 12 point health programme and providing for an income generation activity.

The medicine kits that have been provided to the health workers contain many medicines that are bought and items like IFA, ORS etc. Which are obtained free from the government. The health workers charge a minimum price on no-profit no-loss basis for those drugs, which are bought, rate list is available in the kit and the health workers charge as per the prescribed rate. Each kit is able to provide during the orientation training, each kit is able to generate enough money to replenish the kit contents again. The community also does not feel the pressure, as the charges are bare minimum.

The community in its project area is an active stakeholder. It contributes in the form of user fees for medicines received, insurance cover for health check-ups, contribution on no-profit no loss basis for all low cost technologies – smoke less *chulhas,* kitchen garden, sanitary latrines. It is important here to understand that the purpose is not to fleece the people but to inculcate in them a habit of contribution, so that they feel involved and tomorrow when Seva Mandir withdraws they will not feel the pinch.

In the two RHCs at Kojawada in block Kherwada and at Saru in Girwa block, medical insurance schemes are in operation Rs 18/- per family per year is charged from the patients, all treatments are given free. In both the centres this scheme is operational, however, the hospital staff feels that this amount is too small to sustain activities for a long time. Efforts are on to explore the viability affordability and possibility of increasing the amount for insurance cover.

Low cost technology has been introduced in the village as a part of promotive and preventive services, and also to provide economic support in the form of kitchen garden, cheaper soap making, composite pit, teeth cleaning material, sanitary latrines, smokeless *chulhas* etc. The community either contributes in cash or in kind, thereby was sharing the cost producing these technologies. Sometimes, the contribution is only in terms of labor, but then accumulated to, it adds up to quite a substantial amount.

In some villages, community centers have also been created with the contribution from the community. The thrust everywhere, is on fact that the community must pay for the services, contribute in cash or kind. The purpose is to involve community. To further the twelve point health programme and meet the objectives of improved nutritional status, increased income, family welfare and planning, and sanitation, different activities were envisaged – composite pit for sewage disposal and increasing fertility of soil and cleanliness, soap making and sanitary latrines for cleanliness, kitchen gardens for increased income and nutrition, supplementary feed for pregnant and lactating mothers, the VHJW,HRW and Dai Kits, the medicines with Balwadi Sanchalika.

For all these services the community either contributes in case or kind. For example, in making supplementary feed.

Coconut, jaggery, groundnut, soyabean	-	Provided by Seva Mandir
Flour and oil	-	The community contributes

In case of sanitary latrines,

WC, vent pipe, door and cement	-	Provided by Seva Mandir
Labor and bricks	-	The community contributes

The very first-kits (VHW, HRW, Dai, Balwadi Sanchalika)etc. are provided by the organization during the first orientation training, the kits contain usual medicines as well as Govt. supplies like IFA, Condoms etc.

The health workers charge the communities on no-profit no loss basis. The Govt. supplies are given free of cost.

Therefore, each kit is able to generate money for every new kit. There is contribution and sharing with the community for all services delivered. Several of these structures are being utilized to promote IGAs. Soap making, kitchen gardening etc. are some common activities which relate directly to health interventions.

Responsibility Sharing with Local groups

The VHW, HRW and CHW are given a fixed honorarium and the TBA is rapid on task basis. The *Gram Samooh* now gives a portion of this. In some villages, like Talai in Jhadol block, the *Gram Samooh* pays Rs 25/- to the VHW. Similarly, in several other villages, the *Gram Samooh* has started paying part of the amount, but it is not fixed and also it is not a regular practice.

In case of Seva Mandir, it holds true of PVOH-II project interventions as well, all programmes are need based. It is people who through the *Gram Samooh* send in their demand or needs and based on that interventions are planned and implemented. Even to monitor interventions, from within the *Gram Samooh* are formed committees that ensure proper functioning of programmes.

The development of *Gramkosh* as the corpus for the village is an important step towards achieving sustainability. In some of these funds, the amount of money is quite large. Here again the labor cost and contribution are a major source of income of the kosh. The possibility of linking these with panchayats is also a step towards sustainability through community participation. All along the approach of the organisation towards community is empowering. The community is already expressing its needs and sometimes even offering solutions for the same.

The Purush Samitis that are operational look after the maintenance and management of the Khojawada RHC. The *Mahila Bachat Samitis* are also taking over the responsibility of proposing and selecting the TBA from amongst themselves. The scope of work of the Village Health Committees has also broadened over the years in terms of the representation of members, initiating new programs in health care and taking up matters with the relevant government counterparts.

Use of Project Experience

For past thirty years Seva Mandir has been working in Udaipur district. Ever-since, programmes have covered all possible sectors in development–

literacy, forestry, watershed etc. Also it has worked closely with Government, therefore basically with the advent of PVOH-II project, Maternal and the Child Health care became important, also AIDS programme got strengthened.

The TBA programme, an important component of the PVOH-II project activities, has attracted many NGOs both within and outside the State for getting their TBAs trained. CHETNA, Ahmedabad, had organised a TOT in reproductive health, it also provided training materials. Kalyani and many other NGOs also send their TBAs for training to Seva Mandir's TBA training programmes. Also there is collaboration with the RNT Medical College, Ayurvedic Medical College, Govt. Hospital for exposure of health workers or referrals.

The Identity Cards given to the health workers are recognised by the government and they attend to patients referred by Seva Mandir' health workers.

Experience with GOI (MOHFW), USAID and TAU

USAID, Government of India (MOHFW) and NIHFW provided coordinated technical assistance through financial resources, training, monitoring and technical support. Various meetings and workshops were very useful, especially in terms of developing deeper understanding about MCH and FP interventions.

Through PVOH-II project interventions, the efficacy of collaborative effort of the public and private health departments became apparent. Project staff at Seva Mandir also felt that Participatory evaluation was direction giving, positive in approach, and felt that a new genre of Participatory ideology had arrived.

Technical Support from Technical Assistance Unit (TAU)

The organization benefited through the training and inputs provided by USAID, TAU, and IIHMR whether it was related to sustainability or technical aspects. However it was felt that some material during the training could have been in Hindi or in local state languages.

The Technical Needs Assessment of the project was done in 1995. The purpose of the visit was threefold, to assess the health needs of the people vis-a-vis the effectiveness of service delivery component, understand the management system and draw out a sustainability plan. The organization found this visit useful in terms of the issues it raised, however it was felt that more intensive input related to the same would have been useful.

Future Plans

There is an ever increasing demand from people and the government that *Seva Mandir* must branch into health interventions and increase the coverage for the same. The organisation, however feels that time has now come when they would like people to learn and develop on their own. There is a wish that people must become self -reliant. Needless to say that *Seva Mandir* shall always be with them, but the community's role will be more. Following are some of the plans that the organization has envisaged related to health interventions.

- Strengthen the sub-centre in collaboration with the Govt. for ANC and PNC, ten sub-centres in four blocks have already been taken up.
- *Parivar Sathi Yojna* has been launched wherein the CHWs will train the VHWs thereby reducing dependence on Seva Mandir.
- Intensive health campaigns are being planned for all your blocks for integrated development and total upliftment
- Rehabilitation programme for invalid and the aged through Income Generation Activities
- AIDS awareness programme to be promoted by involving adolescents and through NCC
- Mobile clinic comprising two people on foot is being envisaged
- Training to bring health educators on common platform are being planned with All India Institute of Hygiene and Public Health, Calcutta.

Programmatic Suggestions

The emphasis on benefits of breastfeeding may be highlighted through the following message:

1. Breastfeed as soon as possible after birth,
2. Care for her breasts/nipples – Women's Health issues
3. Exclusively breastfeed for the first four months of life,
4. Reinforcement of the messages related to continued feeding, giving more fluids and dehydration being the most important danger sign during a child's diarrhea need to be emphasized, for mothers through VHWs and TBAs
5. Through the staff at all levels was technically competent but there is scope for management, Training of Trainers, Fields workers

training to enhance their over all perspective of the development scenario.

6. Documentation of the qualitative process and efforts of the organization can strengthen their information base.
7. As the training imparted are many including the refreshers and monthly meetings, it was felt that to improve the presence of the health workers in the field, on the job training may prove more useful.
8. Computerization of the data has begun, a computer within the health unit may be useful.
9. The concept of the Gramkosh is very sound; however it is possible to think in terms of diversifying its sources of income and revolving the fund for more productive use.
10. *Mahila Bachat Samitis* of Mahila Vikas Unit represent a good combination of SHGs and IGAs; the Health Unit may think of utilizing this forum more effectively, specially in relation to strengthening MCH and FP activities.
11. Both the government and organization accept the complementarily, however there is scope for strengthening the co-ordination between the two at the block level
12. Functional literacy component may help the paramedical workers socially the TBAs in performing their jobs effectively

As on the period of field visit, Seva Mandir is on the threshold of completing a full circle- it initiated a process of empowering people through health awareness and literacy and as on date it is initiating programmes that are a result of people's participation and increased conscious of their struggle for a process of sustainable health development.

Bhoruka Charitable Trust (BCT) (Annex-VII)

Late Prabhu Dayal Agarwal, a great philanthropist, and the founder Chairman of Transport Corporation of India (TCI) –Bhoruka Group of Companies, founded the Bhoruka charitable Trust (BCT) in 1963. BCT is actively involved in "Integrated Rural Development" in the villages of Rajgarh Block, District Churu, in the state of Rajasthan since 1973. BCT began various developmental activities including establishing of charitable dispensaries on different parts of India. In 1975, the trust took up a major development project in Rajgarh. The trust, with emphasis on economic and social development of the villages in district Churu has strived towards a more integrated and contiguous approach to development.

Since 1984, the trust has expanded its area of operation to almost all the villages of Rajgarh block. More developmental projects have been undertaken involving professional staff from the fields of medicine, social work, rural development and agriculture etc.

Organisational Vision:

Providing integrated approach to Rural Development

Mission

Dedicated to socio-economic transformation of Rural and remote areas of India, especially the weaker and socially underprivileged groups, through physical, social, cultural and economic development of rural people, groups and institutions.

Brief Profile of BCT's Development Project

As stated the Trust with emphasis laid on a more contiguous and integrated approach to development has undertaken a number of projects with a focus on the overall development of the area. The projects include:

- Non formal education for girls and women development
- Drinking water
- Low cost sanitation
- Comprehensive rural health development project
- Afforestation and waste land development
- Agriculture development
- Low cost housing
- Integrated child development services
- Promotion of grass root level development agencies
- Mahila Shiksha Karmi Yojana

Socio-Economic Context of The Region And Project Area

The project area falls under the *Thar Desert* and it's characterized by extreme climatic conditions. During the summer month temperature touch nearly 50o C. while the cold seasons takes a dip to temperatures as low as –5o C. Lack of proper roads, public transport and communication facilities and more important a severe shortage of drinking water contributes it to being on of the mots backward and undeveloped areas in the state of Rajasthan. All this despite, there is a thriving city of Haryana state, which is just 50 km from the project headquarter.

An estimate population (1991), of about 43,000 people are spread over 40 villages in the health project area. None of these villages have a government health facility/institution; villages are separated from the neighboring ones by 4-5 kms. of sandy track, and high elevations of sand dunes. Lack of roads and communication facilities, each of basic and amenities like drinking water, electricity and extreme weather conditions have an adverse influence towards the health situation in this area.

Rationale of PVOH-II Project

The present study has been conducted in the Rajgarh block of Churu, a desert district in Rajasthan, situated west of India. It has attempted to involve the Bhoruka Charitable Trust (BCT), an influential NGO in the study area, in an experimental effort on improving the quality and the effectiveness of the child health care services, provided by the untrained/semi-trained and also unlicensed village health providers (VHP) including both the rural medical practitioners (RMP) and the health workers). These providers, particularly the medical practitioners, are popular to the qualified medical community as quack, but they only are the doctors who are available at door-steps all the time in the villages and provide health services to the rural communities predominantly. The patients are normally brought for care to the qualified practitioners only when the situation becomes critical and the village health providers fail to manage the cases. Majority of these practitioners are either untrained or semi-trained and therefore, mostly unlicensed. This consultation pattern of the patients is unlikely to be different for the other common ailments. This was the background of the health services in the project area.

The Health Programme of BCT

Since 1992 a 'Comprehensive Rural Health Development Project' funded by the Ministry of Health and Family Welfare GOI/USAID under the PVOH-II scheme had been implemented by the trust to improve the general health of the trust with a target population of 50,000 spread over 40 villages in Rajgarh block.

With the experience gained over for more than the last 2 decades, the trust submitted a proposal seeking grant-in-aid under PVOH-II to cover a population of 50,000 spread over 41 villages in Rajgarh block.

A joint appraisal team from NIHFW, New Delhi reviewed the proposal and recommended the project for funding. A special Grants Committee (SGC) of MOHEW, New Delhi, concluded that PVOH-II scheme by GOI approved the project in 1992 and activities got underway.

The primary health centers and sub-centers are virtually not serving the target population in these villages. The plain and single reason is the harsh conditions, which deters any employee from working in these areas. The 40 project villages come under the beat area of PHC, Sarkhoo that is situated at a distance of 60 kilometers from Bhorugram. A 20 beded Community Health Centre (CHC) at Rajgaon is about 40 kilometers from Bhorugram, the head office of the project. Besides this of the 35 sub-centres in Rajgarh tehsil, only 2 sub-centres are situated in the project villages. These are very poorly staffed and the village community prefers to visit other areas, through at a distance for treatment on an average people have had to travel 30-4 kilometer by camel or bus to visit the nearest health centers situated at Rajgarh town or Hissar in Haryana.

Consideration of the Area and the Population

Rajgarh block, where the BCT is functioning, is a desert area and, a mid very extreme weather conditions, it has hardly any natural resources for human prosperity. The people, about 65% of which belong to higher castes, about 22% schedule caste and about 13% backward classes (as estimated through the base-line survey, conducted prior to starting the PVOH-II project, ref. To (Government of Rajasthan [GOR, 1992]), depend mostly on agriculture and animal husbandry for their sustenance. Under-ground water being saline, there is acute shortage of water. The people use mostly the stored rainwater for drinking purpose. The socio-economic and health status of the people is poor, coupled with low literacy rate (64.1%), particularly among the females (30.2%), as quoted in the base-line survey report of the PVOH-II project.

As per the base-line survey, by the NGO, the crude birth rate (CBR) in the project area was 31 per thousand and the general marital fertility rate (GMFR) was about 196. The total marital fertility rate (TMFR) was about 5. The average size of the household was rather high, between 6 and 7 and the sex ratio has been 844, lower than even the district estimate of 947. About 77% currently married women started cohabiting with their husbands in between 14 and 18 years of ages. About 60% of these women delivered their first children between 16 and 20 years of ages. The infant mortality rate (IMR), as estimated through the same base-line survey, was 98.5. Against the backdrop of these socio-economic and demographic characteristics of the population the Comprehensive Rural Health Development Project under the PVOH-II scheme was launched in 40 out of a total of 210 villages in 1992.

Two major objectives of the project were:

(1) Supporting and testing innovative approaches to community-based health care, family planning, womens health and nutrition

(2) Supporting dissemination and utilization of the most effective treatment methods, such as oral dehydration for diarrhea.

Study Coverage

The project covers 40 villages in Rajgarh tehsil. The estimated population is about 43,000 (1991) spread over the 40 villages in the project area. Under the PVOH-II scheme, the health services to 40 villages were provided at three levels. At village level, the key persons of the project were the female health volunteers (FHV) who were basically a group of literate village women, mostly class VIII pass, groomed to function as health educators, catalysts, guides and coordinators. They were identifying the cases requiring family planing, immunization, mother and child health care. Also, they were expected to provide curative services for primary ailments. To provide health services to the inaccessible PVOH villages, two Mobile Medical Units (MMU) were deployed at the intermediate level between the villages and the central health service facility of the BCT at Bhorugram. Each MMU (Emergency Medical Unit) team was constituted of a doctor, a nurse/ANM, a male health worker and a driver.

The central health service facility at Bhorugram was a 10-bedded maternal and child health centre, well-equipped with X-ray and operation theatre (OT) facilities and also ante-natal, natal and post-natal service facilities. It was also functioning as a referral center. The functioning of the project staffs at all levels were being coordinated by the PVOH-II coordinator and the coordinator was accountable to the Project Director of BCT. The key persons who formed the core group in implementing the current operations in the project area included the Project Director and the PVOH-II coordinator, the Community Organizer and the central health facility in-charge. In other-words, the 'comprehensive rural health development project' was created to address the above issues of health services system in the project area.

Project Activities - Broad Objectives

To provide Primary Health Care facility to proposed villages in the desert area by strengthening he existing infrastructure for the expansion of the community based outreach services, especially in the areas of Family Planning, Maternal and Child Health, Immunization Nutrition and Women's health, Environmental education to the project population with the special focus on women, young girls and children aged 5 years and below.

Specific Objectives

- To train and educate young village women, teachers, Dai etc., in Primary Health Care and utilize them for providing health care services at grass roots level.
- To improve the health of children and young married women through regular immunization and nutritional support.
- To reduce the IMR, MMR, CISR and CPIC in the target villages by providing a package of preventive, promotive and curative health care services.
- To improve the level of environmental sanitation, personal hygiene, chlorinating of water resources.
- To educate young married women between the age 15-44 years for adoption of family planning methods using spacing methods.
- To support the dissemination and utilization of most effective treatment, methods such as oral dehydration for diarrhea.

Key Interventions

The project in its functioning has a three-tier approach:

- Services at village level by Female Health Volunteer (FHV) – Tier 1
- Two mobile teams at the intermediate level – Tier 2
- MCH Center at village Bhorugram as a referral level – Tier 3

Community Level

Female health volunteers (FHVs) have been identified in consultation with local community. Many of the FHV's are Non Formal Education teachers or traditional birth attendants or young married women who could read and write and who the community felt is interested in service to the community. Special attention has been taken by the trust to involve needy women including disabled women in the programme.

The activities which the female health volunteers performs include

- Registration of pregnant mothers for ANC
- Motivating mothers for immunization
- Promoting breast feeding especially at early stage

- Maintaining birth/death and eligible couple records
- Motivating couples to use FP methods
- Identifying and motivating mothers for TT immunization
- Awareness creation regarding chlorinating of drinking water
- Distribution of safe delivery kit to pregnant mothers

At the beginning of the project an initial training was undertaken in 2 batches. At the start of the project one-month training was undertaken. The FHVs are paid an honorarium of Rs.300 per month for their services.

Mobile Medical Unit (MMU)

In order to improve the out-reach services in the project area, two mobile units have been established. This tier 2 comprises each of one medical Officer (MO), one Auxiliary Nurse Midwife (ANM) and one driver each mobile teams conduct out-reach services in two zones demarcated in the project area. A detailed action plan for mobile team visits is fixed every month. Each of the project villages has clear dates painted on the walls in the villages. The visits are divided in two sections. The first 15 days of the month cover for general health care services while the latter halves of the month are utilized for immunization activities. Further as there are only 2 doctors (MOs) present on these days when the ANM posted at MCH Center joins the mobile team the other MO looks after the OPD services at the MCH center. The community organizer also accompanies the mobile team at regular duration to conduct health education activities in the villages visited by the mobile team. Prior to the visit the FHV informs the community identifying concerned cases and motivating people to visit the medical team.

Some of the activities carried out by the mobile team include:

- Antenatal care
- Immunization
- Curative services
- Referral
- Community Awareness

Referral level

The MCH center at Bhorugram, provides in-patient as well as out-patient visits to services referred from the MMUs in the villages as also general cases. The referral centre situated at Bhorugram consists of 10 bedded hospital, basic laboratory services, X-ray, labour room, operation theatre for minor surgical interventions. The MCH is staffed with one MO, one compounder, two nurse/ANMs, one laboratory / X-ray technician and two ward attendants.

Health Awareness of Health Services Delivery

The tentative specific MCH indicators, which were proposed to be achieved by the end of the project period, along with the MCH baseline indicators and the achievements made under the project have been given and interpreted briefly as per the findings of the KPC study and Evaluation report (Annex-V), which are mentioned as follows. The KPC survey as well as the Participatory Evaluation reflected a number of important findings vis-a-vis health care delivery and health awareness.

Age Distribution- 4% of the mothers survey were aged 35 years or over and only 10.7% were below 20 years of age. BCT will target program interventions to enhance child and maternal survival by addressing the fertility behavior of rural dwellers through education of Female Health Volunteers (FHVs), Medical Mobile unit staff and also through the activities of staff of *Lok Jumbish* (statewide district primary education programme), ICDS and non-formal educators.

Over 56.3% of the children (169) in the survey were under 12 months of age. One possible explanation for the large number of infants less than 12 months of age is that many mothers are spacing births less than two years apart. If this is the case, then a bias in the methodology is presented because interviewers were trained to ask mothers questions about the youngest child if she had more than one child under the age of 24 months.

In summary, BCT emphasized on the birth spacing with intervals of two years apart and the risk of child bearing below the age 18 years and above the age of 35 years in its implementation.

Education/Occupation- 78% of the mother (244) surveyed cannot read. For those mothers that can read, which is small number BCT will develop simple written health messages, which can be used by FHVs. For those mothers that cannot read, BCT must train FHVs and involve other project staff in non- written health education techniques which could be used for groups and families. This could include demonstrations, role-plays, pictorial presentations and group discussions.

Breast feeding/ Nutrition- Universally used breast feeding messages state that, mothers should exclusively breast feed during the first four to six months of age, that infants should start to breast feed as soon as possible after birth and that breast feeding should continue well into the second year of a child's life and for a longer possible period.

91.7% of the children in the 0, 1, 2, and 3 month age group in the survey were being exclusively breast fed. 35.7% of the 42 children in the 6,7,8 and 9 month age group had been given solid or semisolid food. About 50.7% of mothers, when asked, did not know that children should be introduced to foods other than breast milk between four and six months of age. 6% indicated an age for food introduction earlier than 4 months.

The biggest problem regarding breast-feeding practices, therefore, is the need for early introduction of food and fluids other than breast milk in the project area. BCT emphasized the benefits of exclusive breast feeding during the first four to six moths and weaning thereafter by targeting mothers, FHVs, TBAs during its project implementation.

Only 40.1% of mothers' breast-fed their child within the first eight hours after birth. B.C.T will continue emphasis on benefits of early initiation of breast-feeding after delivery during the training of TBAs, FHVs and other project workers.

All of the children except one in the survey had been breast-fed at some time however; at the time of the survey 93.3% were still being breast-fed. Mothers will be encouraged to continue breast feeding up to the child's 24 months of age B.C.T. will reinforce the benefits of breast feeding for the first two years of a child's life, as also on the other important messages regarding breast feeding.

Growth Monitoring- only 15% of the mothers in the survey reported that their children had a growth monitoring contact in the three months preceding the survey.

This represents a stronger need, for a co-operative effort between the various project staff of B.C.T., as in this case, the ICDS scheme in the area is being run by B.C.T. itself. B.C.T will provide education on the positive aspects of growth monitoring and efforts will be made to enhance the coverage of children under the scheme. FHVs and Anganwadi workers need to be trained to co-ordinate their activities to ensure that children are weighed and those weights are recorded. This probably represents an area where the various project units and the health unit of BCT can collaborate.

Diarrhoeal Diseases-The Government of India, Child Survival and Safe Motherhood (CSSM) programme, diarrhea messages stress the importance of giving extra fluids and continued feeding during the diarrhoea episode, and providing extra foods when the child is recovering from diarrhoea.

Approximately, 84.8% of the children in the survey were given the same or more breast milk than usual during the diarrhea. 59.6% of children were given more or the same amount of foods as usual during diarrhea.

BCT will provide messages through FHVs for mothers in the project areas that stress the importance of giving more fluids and continued feeding during a child's diarrhea- suggestion made in the evaluation recommendations.

One of the project objectives outlined in the proposal is that mothers will use ORT to treat their children's diarrhoea cases. The CSSM programme also stresses the dangers of using medicines to treat diarrhoea. Approximately 22.2% of the mothers in the survey were giving ORT to their children at home during diarrhea. 47.2 % of the mothers also were giving their child medicine for the diarrhea. 65.3% of the mothers reported giving their child a local home remedy.

Respiratory Tract Infection- 130(43.4%) among children has symptoms of Lower Respiratory Tract Infection (LRTI) during the 2 weeks preceding the survey. An important health messages in this regard is prepared for mothers to recognize danger signs in their children having LRTI and to take them to the nearest source of medical care for prompt management with approximate antibodies.

82% of mothers knew that fast and difficult in breathing is a danger sign in LRTI while 59.3% of mothers cited chest in drawing sketch. Of the 108 children who experienced fast and difficult breathing 86.1 % received some form of medical treatment. BCT emphasized on messages relating to recognition of danger signs and regarding the importance of prompt referral. Also, health workers are trained on the principles of case management in LRTI. The CSSM programme modules available with the government should be used to help the beneficiaries in this direction.

Immunizations- about 57.7% of 300 mothers stated that their child has received some form of immunization while 33.3% stated that they had their child's card had never been made for their child. Antigen - specific immunization coverage rates for 12-23 month age group is BCG 62.6%, OPV123 74%, DTP123 63.4% and measles 55.7%. These percentages represent population based coverage rates for the surveyed on the immunization card or as reported by the mother. Health workers were trained on interview techniques to elicit information regarding immunization.

The rate of children fully immunized (BCG+OPV123+DPT123+ Measles) in the project evaluation is lower than the national EPI coverage estimate of around 60% but higher than the state figure which is around 16%.

In the surveyed population, the difference between the first and the third OPV is about 21.8% and between the 1st and third DPT is approximately 20.2%, probably a reflection of the impact that Pulse Polio Immunization has had on the population in the project area.

As per the report of final evaluation, comparisons with baseline data and with the State data obtained from the NFHS-I show that BCT's performance has improved and is higher than the average reported for the State in most of the cases.

The percentage of mothers (57.7%) who stated that their child had received immunization contrasts with the low coverage rates (47.3%) found in the KPC survey. This fact suggested that vaccinations given during immunization campaign are not reaching children the number of times required to fully immunize in the first year of life. For this fact, BCT emphasized on training FHV/TBAs to counsel mother and reinforce the messages on the importance of completion of the EPI schedule during a child's first year of life.

Maternal care- over 51% mothers felt that ANC services should commence in the first or second trimesters. While only 31% reported having visited a health site during their antenatal period, only 32.3% of them had three contacts, which is the recommendation under CSSM programme. This indicated about the intensive efforts that were aimed at the provision of ANC services by the NGO.

Over 54.7% mothers reported having received adequate protection against Tetanus during their pregnancy by receiving 2 or more doses of tetanus toxoid vaccine. Protection against tetanus is only one component of the ANC services and there may be tendency to equate ANC with protection against tetanus. Only 13.3% mothers said that they had taken 3 packets or more of Iron supplement tablets (3 packets = 100 tablets), another indication that the emphasis on ANC is largely on Tetanus toxoid administration. For this fact, BCT has emphasized on working out a system within its health infrastructure to ensure a schedule of composite ANC services starting by the first trimester.

About 47.3% mothers expressed that they ate more or it as usual in the period of pregnancy, while 34.7% stated that they ate less. Cultural beliefs among some mothers hold that eating more during pregnancy will result in a large body and consequently a difficult for delivery. BCT's emphasis on maternal nutrition to provide supplementation is part of its comprehensive health care development package.

51% of deliveries were attended by a health professional including trained TBAs, up from 9.1% at the time of baseline survey. This is an achievement considering the terrain, transport and infrastructure facility in the area. BCT has an ongoing programme of training TBAs' to conduct deliveries in the area served by it.

An important aspect of health care delivery system at BCT is the continued and regular supply of essential drugs through the referral center as well as the MMU. In additions, the FHV also keep a set of essential drugs that are checked by the ANM for expired dates if any etc.

Community Perception about the Health Services System

Discussion with women members revealed that women gave much value to the need for immunization although they were not able to explain various types of immunization given to their children. Most of them knew about the constituents of a balanced diet, even the types of diet required to prevent night blindness. Deliveries by trained personnel, health services at the center level, regular participation in the meetings of women groups are some of the essential features of community perception in favor of community based health services of BCT.

Main Observations

- Discussions with women groups about issues of health showed that women gave much value to the need for immunization although most of them were not able to explain the various types of immunization given to their children. Majority of them knew about what constitutes a balanced diet although as the KPC data reflects, mothers had little knowledge about what diet is required to prevent night blindness.
- A good number of pregnant women were registered for ANC. It was observed that awareness levels of women were better off than those places, which had posted with an FHV. Further most FHVs had a fair knowledge about key health issues such as criteria for identifying high-risk cases among pregnant women.
- A major area of concern was the lack of involvement and participation of male in the village based community health activities. A typical village scene in this area would show male members passing their time while women do most of the household activities. A PRA exercise with the women group showed that against 26 numbers of activities that perform during a day only 6 activities were performed by men out of which playing cards, drinking and quarreling with their wives are the major ones.
- Discussions with male members reflected that they do not see issues of health as priority, even the activities in the project area are basically women specific, which need not require their participation. For example while discussing about issues of family

planning, men of the village did not see it as their area of concern and failed 'operation' (Tubectomy of women) as the main solution to FP. The KPC data also reflects that the community least utilized spacing methods, more out of not seeing the value of spacing methods, rather than ignorance. It is thus important that awareness programme directed to men including their household would be more beneficial to the target population availing services. Even many villages' women complained about their mother-in-laws refusal to use oral pills for spacing.

- Given the backwardness of Churu district as well as the villages with difficult terrain such as Lilki and Kusumbi, there was hardly any communication links that exists with either the block or district administration including health facilities. The absence of roads and lack of electricity makes the area more worst. In such a situation BCT's activity has brought about appreciable changes in providing some health delivery services with the involvement of local community. According to assistant chief Medical officer, there are no NGOs working in this area other than BCT.
- In the selection of FHV the marginalised section of the community were taken care to cover their population as the target group in the project. A visit to the village of one FHV who is illiterate reflected that she was known in the village for her good work where as her records were maintained by her school going daughter.
- A positive trend in the organization's effort to involve community was reflected by the willingness of villagers to provide temporary space for the mobile unit in their villages. This mobile unit which undertakes to each of the project village every month (be it regular medical check-up or a immunization day) holds the said clinics at the village centered, usually a place where everybody agrees to come.
- Active *mahila mandal* supported the project implementation and regular meetings organised by FHVs were the key to community participation.
- A number of members from the *mahila mandal* were not clear about their roles even the objective of respective organizations. This shows *mahila mandals* are formed merely to fulfill the activities under project. No proper strategy is designed to answer the genesis of these *mandals*, their roles and responsibilities, monitoring of their activities and the sustainability of their functions.

- Lack of initiatives to involve male members of the village community in project activity limited the projects reach to the targeted population rather than to the households in the respective villages. For this reason project activities remained as a matter of concern for the female members rather than those of male members from the community.

Best practices story from the Field Study

Kamla, a resident of village Sadpura, which was a PVOH-II project area, she was working as a FHV for the PVOH-II project activities. She has been working in her village as a FHV for the past four and half years. Kamla suffers from polio, but was keen to work for the project. Said Kamla, *"I like my work, it gives me a feeling that I am doing something for my village people who live there."*

Kamla's personal life was one filled with a lot of struggle. "The fact that I was disabled, my parents found it difficult to get me married. When they could not find a suitable groom for me, I was given away to my sister's husband". One year later Kamla was sent to her mother's place. "I was seen as a burden and of no use", she says. For the past 12 years Kamla has been living at her parents home, with her young son. On being asked how she joined the Trust activities, Kamla replied, "I used to see the doctor and nurse coming to my village. One day they held a meeting in the village asking whether the village people could nominate a lady who help them with their activities in the village. I was surprised to know that the village members had nominated my name for the work. I was always eager to do such work and it was God's wish that I got into the work."

Kamla, thus began working for the trust. Describing her work activities she stated, " My area of work is the whole village. I undertake meetings in the village for village women where I tell them all about good health and all the suggestion that I was taught at the training programme in Bhorugram. " I also keep some medicines which I give to people as and when required. But my main activities involve pregnant women and children. Before the immunization day, I tell mothers to take their children for immunization and also see to it that all immunizations have been received". I also conduct meetings of the *Mahila Mandals* and discuss similar issues with them. As Kamla finds it difficult to go to the Trust at Bhorugram every month, because of her disability, she has been given permission to attend meetings every quarter. The ANM or the Group organizer collects all her filled formats.

On being asked what she did with the money that she receives, Kamla shyly said, "I saved all the money in the bank and shall use it for my son's education, when he is a little older". Kamla however felt that the money that the FHVs receive is very little. "We work very hard and there is so much to do. I am not asking for too much but the present amount just too little". "Moreover", she added, "I have heard that the project will come to an end very soon. What will happen to us?", Kamla wonders!

Organizational Capacities and Gender Concerns

Infrastructure- the PVOH-II project is well equipped with the necessary infrastructure. The referral center has all the necessary equipment required for day to day treatment as also emergencies. The field consists of good number of vehicles, although requiring repairs and overhauling.

At the field level, the *Prabhu-Kutirs*, which are structures constructed by the Trust for various project activities have not been utilized for the various activities. At present there are about 14-15 such *Prabhu-Kutirs*. Besides building more such structures preferably with some contributions from the community, the *Kutirs* should be put into more effective use by the various projects. Such *Kutirs* would help in sustaining the various project activities. This shows an example of community involvement in local development initiatives with the NGO.

Organizational Structure - The PVOH-II organizational set-up can be divided into the programme staff and administrative staff. Both, the programme unit as well as the administrative unit are under the responsibility of the project coordinator, who co-ordinates all the projects managed by the NGO, all the activities of the Trust come under the overall responsibility of the Project Director.

The pogramme unit consists of doctors (2), community organizer (1), compounder (1), ANM (3). In addition there is an X-Ray and lab technician and 3 attendants posted at the referral center at Bhorugram. The administrative unit consists of computer programmer (1), accountant (1), store-keeper and typist (1) and drivers (2).

One of the major problems was the frequent breakdown of the electricity in the area. The project including the living staff quarters in the whole complex depends on the generator backup. The PVOH-II team was a group of very hard working and devoted paid workers. A highlighting point was that the team especially at the field level all belongs to the area. The Group Organizer, who plans all activities of the PVOH-II project, hails from that very area. This has helped the organization to undertake activities more intensively because of a good understanding of the socio-political environment.

The management efforts in the selection of the field workers / FHVs are indeed appreciable. Having taken the consensus of the village community in the selection process has led to a high acceptance of the health workers in the area.

An area of concern however was the absence of women staff at the supervisory levels of the project. The fact, that many issues in the project activities were sensitive, viz. Family planning etc. It was important that there could be one woman at the supervisory level who could plan various activities along with the male group Organizer. It was also observed that the present Group Organizer is heavily loaded with a number of activities along with the male group-Organizer. It was also observed that the present Group Organizer is heavily loaded with a number of activities which he may find difficult to handle. It is important that the management addressed this issue and created space for women at the supervisory/middle management level.

Another problem expressed by the organization has been the high turnover of doctors. Given the harsh work and living condition of the area, this was not surprising. It was also observed that a communication gap existed between one of the doctors with the management. In this regard it is crucial that the management take notice of these problems which could otherwise escalate into more serious conflicts between staff leading to a drop in work efficiency as also creating an unhealthy work environment.

Given the importance of creating awareness in the community about health issues, it was observed that many FHVs did not have clear information about certain issues viz. chlorinating of water. It was important that technical training be given to the health workers by staff possess the technical skill. Further many FHVs were still not adept in identifying cases independently especially certain common diseases like TB and respiratory diseases.

Finally, a conscious effort was required to create opportunities for the staff of various projects to share their project experiences on various issues, such as community participation, gender issues, sustainability etc. This exercise would help in creating a more learning experience, build a healthier working environment between staff as well as generate new ideas in programme implementation. This culture was lacking in the working environment of the organization.

Networking with other Agencies

The Bhoruka Charitable Trust in its PVOH-II programme was working closely with the Block and District Administration in areas of family planning and control of TB as well as cataract operations. Discussions with doctors at the District and Tehsil hospital reflect that during cataract, and family planning camps, all services/facilities are provided for by the NGO, to the doctors on visit. Patients were picked and dropped during these operations. Food was also provided in these camps.

Many of the doctors were of the opinion stated that although BCT is undertaking remarkable work in health care, the stress should be more on prevention rather than curative aspects of health issues.

BCT's links with other agencies was also appreciable, during the project period BCT supported some 35 small village based organizations and clubs, helping them financially by providing Rs. 500 per month for various small village activities. It also conducted training and orientation programmes for the members of these organizations. Regular meetings were held at the BCT office at Rajgarh tehsil of these organizations. As the Bhoruka Charitable Trust is part of the Transport Corporation of India (TCI) group which also holds the IIHMR in its purview, there is a continuous interaction with the IIHMR which supports the NGO activities, providing suggestions, technical training, research in various fields of Community Health in partnership with BASICS, USAID.

Issues on Sustainability /Replicability

The fact that the PVOH-II project had to close in June 1997, much concern has been expressed by the organisation as to the continuity of the various services provided for, after project withdrawal. One of the advantages that BCT enjoys was that it gets much support from its mother organisation, the TCI group. However, this support also had its limitations, which will be discussed later in this section.

A very positive trend towards sustaining the project services has been the communities' acceptance to pay for health delivery services, both at the referral center and also at the MMU visits. Although being a very nominal amount, it has infused the community with a sense of responsibility as well as ownership to various programmes. Further, in programmes such as construction of household sanitary latrines (funded by CAPART), the community has participated in sharing the cost towards the construction.

However as stated above, the support that BCT receives from the TCI group has its problems too namely:

- The community identifies BCT as a provider, which it has been doing since its establishment. At the beginning many development work such as construction of wells, ponds, roads, schools etc. were undertaken by the BCT family. This was reflected in the communities identification that, "the owner (BCT) would help us whenever we need anything". Further, none in the community were aware that the PVOH-II project would be discontinued in June 1997. During a discussion with community elders, it was gauged that the community felt about the fact that the trust had been helping them out by doing various development activities free of cost, the Trust would continue to do so in the years to come. Such a perception of the community is a matter of concern. BCT required to workout on strategy to change its image from 'working for people' to 'working with people'.

- Within the three-tier system in the PVOH-II project, there have been some attempts to create continuity in services, although there were various areas of concern too, both of which have been highlighted below:

Referral Centre

The referral center at Bhorugram had achieved a lot by ensuring that people pay for the services provided for at the center. However, a specific area of concern has been the high turnover of doctors and the absence of a lady doctor. Since the last one year a number of doctors have left the organization. This was despite the fact that BCT pays a much higher salary than the given PVOH-II structure. This was an important area of concern and will have to be addressed by the NGO to sustain the activity.

Mobile Unit

One of the highlighting features of the PVOH-II activities in BCT has been the successful undertaking of the MMU services. During the discussion, the community responded very positively to the services of the mobile unit for its regular health service, which includes diagnosis, immunizations as well as prescribing medicines. The management of the BCT is very interested to continue the services of this activity. It hoped to continue it in three ways,

(a) regular financial support from the TCI group,

(b) increase in cost of health delivery service, and

(c) Exploring avenues for further funding.

Health Posts

According to the management as well as staff of the PVOH-II, the major component of this project was at the level of the village with the work of the FHVs. Much concern was expressed at the continuation of the services of these FHVs. The management agrees that the FHVs were the backbone to the whole project and require to be sustained. Discussions with the community about what they felt about continuation of the FHVs services and their contribution towards the same, met with mixed response. While women members said that the work of an FHV should continue, the men did not feel the same. Most did not consider the importance of health services in their area. One reason was that while women in the community felt the need for such services, they do not have the power to make a decision as to what they could do, or how they could participate. The men members from the community on the other hand, because of not being involved in the activities, do not see a need or do not see health as a priority in the area. And as decisions fall in their jurisdiction, they reject the idea of continuing the services of health workers. The problems of directing ones activities in a single direction have been discussed earlier. The issue discussed above was a good example that reflected the need to involve the whole community with more focus on women's issues affecting health services delivery rather than only focussing on women as frontline workers as undertaken in this project of BCT.

Health Service Delivery and Health Awareness

The discussion with core team members at the NGO, the interaction with key functionaries and suggestions in the reports from the Mid-term and Final Evaluation reflected some important area that BCT required to address to concentrate on the effectiveness of Health Service Delivery in the project area. These areas are mentioned as follows:

Breast Feeding -There was a need for more focus on making mothers aware about the benefits of early breast-feeding. As resistance usually stems from the household, it was important that IEC to popularise this practice be directed towards the household rather than mothers only.

Growth Monitoring- Stress needed to be laid on making mothers aware about the importance of growth monitoring. This needs to be taken up during meetings and various other health education awareness processes.

Co-ordination- with other project activities such as ICDS should be undertaken and linking FHVs and Anganwadi workers in the orientation of various aspects of child survival and safe motherhood including the aspects of growth monitoring.

Diarrhoea diseases-awareness levels of mothers as regards of the issues of dehydration need, to be emphasised upon. The Health Education package required to be creatively designed to attract the community to participate in these awareness creation activities. The awareness packages should have addressed the problems of high dependency of mothers on medicines for diarrhoea. Effective IEC packages directed to this issue need to be stressed upon in the long run.

Organising training - for local healers as well as health workers to lay emphasis on the use of ORS with home based preparation to treat dehydration during diarrhea.

Respiratory Tract Infection - Health awareness messages should have stressed in addressing the high incidence of lower respiratory tract infections (LRTI). An attempt should be made to orient mothers to recognise danger signs in children and importance of prompt referral.

More important, FHVs and other workers such as anganwadi workers as also *Mahila Mandals* needed to be trained in recognising signs of respiratory tract infection and providing prompt referral.

Immunizations - Stress needed to be laid on overall awareness building of mothers on timing and purpose of immunization. Special focus was to reduce dropout rate in OPVB and DPT immunization.

Maternal care - BCT required to increase its services to a large proportion of the community in ANC activities.

- Stress on increasing awareness on consumption of iron supplements tablets.
- Training/refresher programmes for FHVs of the component of ANC and PNC.
- Health Education activities must include provision to counsel mothers on the need to eat more during pregnancy

Family Welfare - Improved levels of awareness about birth spacing through mobilisation of women, men and more necessary, the household. Meetings with household at regular intervals would help in this regard. The reason for involving men in family planning is because, invariable and in most matters it is the men who are decision-makers. It is also important thus to mobilise the household in these matters.

Innovations in Sustainability - Information Sharing through Networking

It was understood both from the experience of NGO, the review of reports and evaluation findings that both the mothers and the VHPs were only partially aware of the right way of managing the focussed diseases at home and at the health service facilities outside. On the other hand, the qualified practitioners having recognised medical qualifications at the BCT hospital, at the government hospitals and the primary healths centres and at the private health clinics and the nursing homes in the Rajgarh block were already aware of it. The other stakeholders like the panchayat committees, the small NGOs, the formal and the non-formal educators, the youth clubs and so on were not unaware about the problems in availing quality child health care services, but it did not emerge as a priority to them in comparison to other important socio-economic and logistic problems. In this situation, benefiting the organisation in the form of motivating and providing technical assistance to the BCT was important. So that it could play a leading role in bringing all the stakeholders together through a planned process and facilitate sharing of information, useful for better management of the child health problems. It was understood in this approach that the demand for quality service would generate through more and more awareness generation through information sharing. The information referred to here, be particularly the lines related to the treatment procedures at home and outside and also the treatment outcome. Besides these, the strategies encouraging community initiative toward solving such public health problems were also categorised as information.

Thus, an information-sharing model shown in the Diagram-1, with the arrows indicating the direction of information flow was though appropriate in the context of the present study. In the diagram, the lines with arrows at both the ends means basically both way sharing of information – one might be the flow of advocacy/know-how and the other might be the flow of feedback information. Things seems to have not been viewed in this fashion before, but to empower the VHPs technically and motivate them to provide effective and quality services, keeping consistency with the scientific procedures of the qualified practitioners, information sharing through such networking seems quite a realistic proposition.

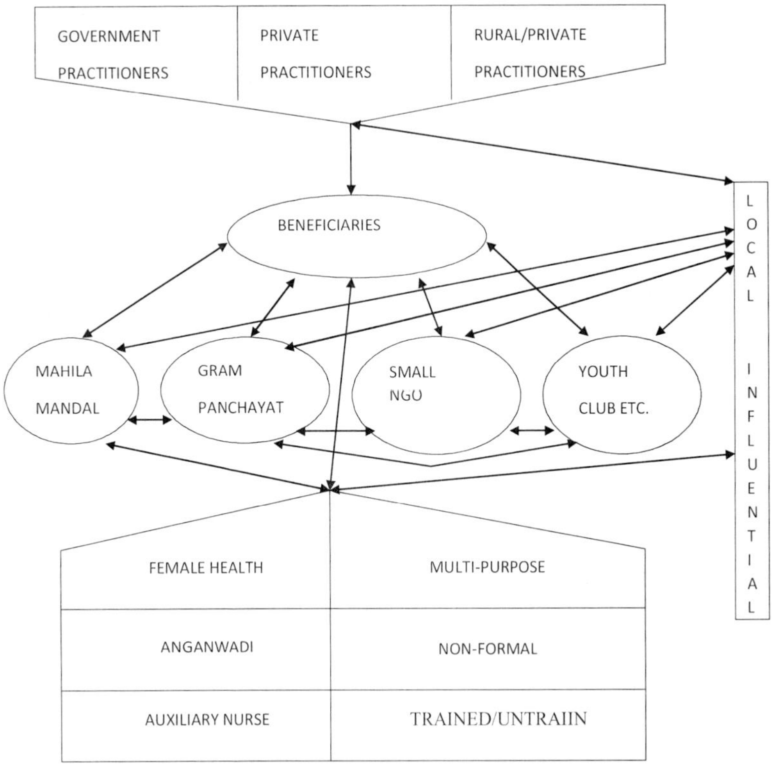

Diagram 1: A Model of Networking among the Stakeholders in a Health Service Delivery System

Basically, the networking was necessary to make the qualified practitioners, the VHPs and the health workers function as a team with the BCT, functioning as:

(1) a coordinator cum catalyst in building up the team concept, and

(2) A facilitator in the process of sharing of information/know how as also feedback from the receivers of information and services.

Thus, it was necessary for the BCT to take the initiative of networking not only with various health provider groups but also with different community groups, namely the *mahila mandals*, the panchayat committees, the small NGOs, the youth clubs and so on. Also, it needed to establish both the inter and the intra network links for various health provider groups and different community groups. The task, however, was realized as complex in view of:

(1) Unorganized functioning of the RMPs,

(2) 'Panchayat committees' minimal involvement in health development programmes,

(3) Difficulties in running the *Mahila Mandal* activities in the project area due to lack of interest of the local community (women and men),

(4) Disinterest of the local NGOs in becoming some sort of partners to the incentive-less networking effort.

Under given time and financial constraints of the study, it was thought to be wise to involve only the VHPs, the qualified practitioners, and, of course, the core project team of BCT. The methodology that was developed for sharing information through networking was not the commonly used one-way training approach. It involved, basically, the following steps;

(1) Target setting: decide first the information state that is to be achieved within the given time frame.

(2) Current status assessment: find out the current state of information and the gap between this state and the state to be achieved.

(3) Interactive Information sharing: fill-up the information gap through an interactive process, involving dialogue and / or discussion among the stakeholders, facilitated by a resource person, having equal respect for all the involved stakeholders.

(4) Behavioural contracting: ensure that all the stakeholders sign on a social contract form which describes the minimum attainable behavioral changes that all the stakeholders commit to achieve within the given time frame against the backdrop of the upgraded information state.

(5) Monitoring and feedback: ensure continuous monitoring of the behavioral changes of all the signatories to the social contract by a method acceptable to them and give continuous feedback to them to facilitate behavioral change as per the contract.

This methodology was referred in the abbreviated form as SEASHCOMOF, indicating the five steps – target setting, situation assessment, information sharing, behavioral contracting, monitoring & feedback (BASICS, USAID).

It was decided that the local qualified medical practitioners would be utilized as the resource persons. The reason was that they had the best knowledge about the local epidemiological characteristics (including the socio-economic and cultural ones) and the practicing pattern of the VHPs. However, before involving them in sharing information, the intervention objectives were, first of all, made known to them. It was informed that the VHPs had two segments to work with:

(a) the RMPs and

(b) the health workers.

The former group was providing the clinical services and the latter group was providing mostly the preventive services (included in the latter group, the FHVs, the ICDS workers and the NFE workers). The latter group was supposed to help the mothers in diagnosing the focussed diseases, educate the mothers on the scientific home management procedures of the focussed diseases and advise them on the situation when they should consult the RMPs or the qualified practitioners for availing curative or preventive health services. Also, they were supposed to educate the mothers on the essentials of quality services that they should look for from the practitioners.

Rather, it was an information sharing process through mutual interactions with the resource person playing both the roles of a facilitator and a medical expert. Group exercises/discussions were also a part of the information sharing process. This innovation of 'Networking' was designed and practiced to promote Sustainability.

Programmatic Suggestions

- Given the social setup and the family system it would be more advantages to perform awareness generation activities towards the household so that a family is involved rather than an individual is targeted.
- Awareness generation in health issues required a clear understanding of the technical areas such as chlorinating of water, identifying various illness need to be included in the plan of activities of FHV to reach the health education messages to maximum population.
- Overall the awareness programme should be directed towards the household so that the health programme is seen as household specific with focus on women.
- There felt an immediate need to restart use of audio-visual aids as also fold art in HE activities. This was especially important as the KPC survey reflects that a large percentage of mothers cannot read.
- Some initiatives should have been taken to involve schooled children in HE activities. The issue of health can be taken up in the form of games, quizzes, painting, plays etc.

- An intensive effort must be laid on improving the levels of literacy of the community especially women. Collaborative efforts with other projects such as NFE, *Lok Jumbish* etc. should be undertaken.
- An attempt to define and build strategies to involve womens groups such as the *Mahila Mandal* should be taken up. *Mahila Mandals* can be used effectively to generate awareness as also to act as pressure groups within an area. Their potential needs to be explored.
- There was a need to build a communication team that can work on awareness themes for all the projects being undertaken by the trust. In this regard, the various organizations that were at present linked with BCT can be effectively utilized for this purpose.
- BCT required focusing more on activities of health prevention rather than the curative aspects of health.
- It was important that ANMs/FHVs needed to be motivated to undertake follow-up activities for TB patients to ensure regular treatment.

Community Participation

- Establish clear objectives roles and responsibilities of *Mahila Mandals*
- Meetings of *Mahila Mandals* need to be undertaken around issues such as methods of Health Education, a specific health issue, income generation activities etc.
- Develop strategy to start self-help groups and credit groups
- BCT must take special efforts to motivate men of the community to participate in project activities. Further, the problem of drugs and alcohol addiction must be addressed. In this regard youth groups can be formed which can pursue in such activities. Such groups may work in issues and activities that they were interested in with regular inputs on health, education etc.
- Stress should be laid on creating regular opportunities for community to put forward their suggestions as also plan future activities. *Mahila Mandals* can play a very important role in planning and implementing the various activities.

Organisational Management

- There was a need for women to be appointed at supervisory levels in the project activities.

- The issues, of high turnover of doctors need to be addresses at the management level. It is recommended that doctors with a MBBS would be suitable, rather than specialists who in many cases are not required in these areas. Further soon after appointment, the medical personnel need to be oriented to village life as also to the specific development issues.
- Training activities in health should be the prerogative of the medical personnel. Doctors should be involved in building appropriate training designs as also conduct the various programmes which requires technical input.
- There was a need for more involvement of ANMs in the project activities especially at the field level. Besides monitoring of the activities of the FHV, ANMs can play an important role in helping FHVs to plan future activities as also meetings with *Mahila Mandals* on various health issues. ANMs can closely support the ICDS worker in her activities.
- The administrative staff should be oriented to the activities that are undertaken at the field. Periodic field visits of the administrative staff could be undertaken.
- The BCT management must consider promoting some of the staff. The computer in the PVOH-II has a strong field inclination and can effectively undertake field-based activities. This step could prove to be an incentive for the other staff in the various programmmes.
- It is important that the management take note of all grievances of staff in a serious and sympathetic manner. Regular meetings of staff both group (project and other projects) as well as individual meetings should be held to discuss problems and other grievances. This would help in building a healthy work environment in the organization.

MIS and Documentation

- The PVOH-II programme needed to stress on documenting qualitative aspects of project activities.
- To systematize daily work activities, it was necessary that daily task planning were built. Both the office as well as field staff should undertake this exercise.
- To strengthen the monitoring activities, a clear set of indicators must be developed as also redefine the existing monitoring formats.

Networking with Other Agencies

- In the various support activities with small organizations, BCT must develop a clear cur strategy plan to define the collaborative areas in this support. For example the various organizations can take an initiative to build a team for various awareness generation activities in the area.
- Common working areas in all the projects being undertaken, need to be identified and defined. This effort would help BCT to push towards a more integrated approach towards development.
- Best practices in the various projects should be replicated in the health project.

Sustainability

- Linking economic benefits from the existing and ongoing schemes of the government and Non-government programmes to the members from the Mahila Mandals, Communmity groups and VHPs should be the part of management strategy in the project area.
- Involvement and interaction with members of Panchayat for ensuring popular participation of community development activities should be the plan for project management to incorporate the ongoing benefits of *'Panchayat Swasthya Scheme'* in the project area.
- Inter-sectoral coordination through linking non-health benefits to the family members of the target group through involvement in different community development programmes of the NGO should be an essential strategy for planning sustainability of ongoing health initiatives.

Bal Rashmi Society (BRS) (Annex-VIII)

Bal Rashmi Society, Jaipur was founded on the 14th. Nov. 1972, - The Children's Day, with the motto of ***"Save Children, Save Generation"***. Initially four children of the deprived community of scavengers were provided a 'home' with complete care including the care of their emotions and psychological needs. This home of *Bal Rashmi* has gradually flourished by having four to twenty, twenty to hundred and then to one hundred and then to one hundred eighty three poor, destitute, downtrodden and orphan children without any discrimination of caste and creed. The initial focus of the society was child welfare from the weaker section. As part of these efforts BRS built up a residential school for the destitute and a residential home for orphaned children in Khedi village of Jaipur district.

In 1981, floods affected the area surrounding Jaipur and BRS worked for the relief of the victims. This was among their first exposure to health related work and proved to be a significant occurrence in the organisation's history in the state of Rajasthan.

BRS has latter realised that welfare of children was not possible in true sense unless integrated welfare of the family and the community as a whole was undertaken. The dimensions of BRS were, therefore enlarged so as to cover a variety of programmes for overall development of the family and the community as would be stated in the following discussion.

The Society

BRS is a heterogeneous body of people from different castes, creeds and ideologies having diverse legal, sauce-cultural, and economic status. According to the secretary of BRS, "those who happen to be the 'have not' are oppressed, exploited and marginalised having some sort of dependence upon the 'halves'. Under the set up it is our organisational strategy to work for their self-reliance and political empowerment to bring them into the mainstream of the society. These 'have not', whether educated or not are full of enthusiasm and dreams. If given a chance and a supportive hand these people have immense potential to achieve community solidarity and become self-reliant. Especially the rural women are very enthusiastic in taking active part in our health awareness and income generation programmes".

The Philosophy

Based on their convictions and experiences it is clear and is important is to listen to people instead of informing them what is good or bad for them. The Society believes in doing things under the prevailing circumstances without spending resources for an opportunity.

The Mission

The mission of the organisation is to work towards the socio-economic development of women and children particularly the children in rural and urban areas of Jaipur district.

The Approach

The Society operates for the benefits of deprived sections, socio-economically backward people, scheduled castes and scheduled tribes, other backward communities like *Sansis* etc. An integrated approach is adopted while taking social development programmes viz. child development, health, water and sanitation, awareness creation for social, economic and political rights, women empowerment, legal aid etc through the involvement of local community.

Operational Area

BRS operates in five districts of Rajasthan viz. Jaipur, Dausa, Tonk, Bhilwara and Sawaimadhopur covering both rural and urban areas. The Resource-cun-Training centre in the Society caters to the training needs of small and upcoming NGOs in Rajasthan. Seminars and workshops were also organised at the regional level for networking, exchange of information and experience with other NGOs from several States of India.

Organisational Resources

'Children Homes' and 'Bhavishya Nirman Kendra' - a vocational training centre- at village Bhavsar Issarwala, Khedi; two primary and two middle schools at Jaipur; a Primary School at Bassi; a 15-beded hospital at Lalgarh; a one bed hospital at Mansar Khedi, and five medical subcentres are spread over the above area duly equiped with requisite facilities. Mobile vans and vehicles including ambulance are available for fieldwork.

Financial Resources of the NGO

- Grants in aid from Govt. of India
- Grants in aid from Govt. of Rajasthan
- Aids and contribution from foreign organisations
- Donations from institutions, trusts and individuals
- Membership fees
- Agricultural receipts
- Miscellaneous receipts

Welfare Programmes in Project Area

BRS is running several welfare programmes in the rural areas as well as in urban areas. Mostly these programmes support income-generation activities to enable the local community and the beneficiaries, self-reliant and sustainable.

Homes for the Children

BRS is running well-maintained 'Children Homes' providing shelter, food, clothing and education under one roof. Psychological needs of the children are also taken care of and each child is paid special attention by the housemothers and brought up in a healthy home like atmosphere. Since abandoned children, children from broken families and those suffering from abject poverty or living in humiliating conditions are admitted in these Homes, where every care is taken to ensure that they grow as normal healthy citizens.

KILKARI, a fondling home for the new borne abandoned mostly by unmarried mothers due to social taboo has a capacity of 30 children. It is one of the four recognised institutions by the Govt. of Rajasthan of this kind. The abandoned children are brought here through the court, the police, the State Social Welfare Department, hospitals and nursing homes and from the roadside when people call upon the Society after finding deserted little one. The children in the age group of zero to five years are brought up with care and affection in groups of five each with a house mother. The playrooms of KILKARI are enviable due to availability of variety of entertaining and educate toys and games. The infants living at KILKARI are given in foster care and adoption to childless couples of Indian nationality after following the prescribed process of law and getting permission from the family court. This is done to provide a family life to them right from their infancy and a secure future. So far 10 boys and 15 girls have been given on adoption. Despite a strong gender bias in the society it is creditable that the NGO have been able to give so many girls in adoption to doting couple.

Schedules for Addressing the Area Problem

Four Schedules were canvassed to collect the necessary data on risk factors operating at community, health worker, and household and mother and child levels.

Schedule -I: In respect of the community was designed to collect data about the availability of health, education and infrastructure facilities and access to them.

Schedule -II: In respect of the health workers was designed to collect data about personal and social background, education and training, service experience and job satisfaction, tasks performed and training received, correctness of knowledge about risk factors and interventions to deal with them in different situation.

Schedule -III: In respect of the households was designed to collect information about the target group mothers. This was about age at marriage and consummation, children born alive, surviving or dead in the last two years.

Schedule -IV: In respect of the mothers who had had a live-birth in the last two years and was designed to collect information about age, marital status, education, religion, caste, occupation, income, expenditure, family assets, drinking water, sanitation, hygiene, social participation, mass media contacts etc. Similarly it was designed to elicit information about socio-economic, cultural, environmental and biological risk factors operating before, during and after pregnancy, for about one year.

Introduction to PVOH-II Project

The first attempt at a health care programme was started with 14 villages in Bassi *tehsil*. This was followed by PVOH-I scheme under which BRS was a grantee supported by MOH&FW and USAID. This covered 85 villages in Bassi tehsil. A rural health centre (RHC) was constructed at Lalgarh with x-Ray, pathology and in-patient care facilities as part of this project. The focus of services included immunisation and basic maternal health care in addition to curative health care provision at the centre. PVOH- I was operational from 1987-1990. Following this, the referral health centre (RHC) at Lalgarh continues to function. A part of the existing area covered has been included along with an additional area from the neighbouring tehsil- Jamua Ramgarh to constitute the operational area under PVOH-II project.

BRS, Jaipur took up a project under PVOH-II scheme named by **'Gramin Swasthya Sewa'** with the assistance of USAID and MOH&FW, Government of India. The project was implemented in 107 villages from Jamwa Ramgarh Tehsil and 42 villages from Bassi Tehsil with a total population of about 92 thousand. The project was for the duration of three and a half years with effect from January 1992 to June 1995.

Objectives of 'Gramin Swasthya Sewa'

The NGO aimed to provide a package of MCH & Family Welfare, Immunisation, nutrition awareness and health education services and to reduce birth rate and IMR.

Specific Objectives

- Provide primary health care services including nutritional rehabilitation to malnourished children less than 6 years of age
- Provide immunisation services and curative care
- Train Dais and village health volunteers in primary health care activities
- Involve Mahila mandals as part of community participation

Service Provision

- Health Care Services (Immunisation, ANC, Cataract operations)
- Provision of training on preventive and promotive health care aspects
- Supply of Family planning methods
- Nutrition rehabilitation
- Income generation activities through *Mahila Vikas Kendra*
- Health Education and awareness activities
- Support services to other NGOs

Project Management Design

For providing the above services the project management design involved a three-tier approach backed by services of mobile teams.

- Female Health Volunteers (FHVs) were proposed to provide services in the villages with an average of one FHV per village.
- Establishment of 3 Health Posts, each to be manned by an ANM and a manned by an ANM and a trained dai for provision of health and family welfare services. Two helath posts, were to be located in Ramgarh tehsil and one at Khedi in Bassi tehsil.
- Setting up of one MCH-cum-nutrition rehabilitation centre at Khedi. The centre was supposed to perform a dual role of functioning as a referral centre as well as a project co-ordination centre.
- Two mobile teams were envisaged to provide health care services in the outreach areas. Income generation activities through 9 units by involving *Mahila Mandals* were other sources of linking community development.

Project Management Structure

The human resource for providing services at each level was:

(a) Project co-ordination office

Administrative officer	1
Asst. Accounts officer	1
Office assist/typist	1
Attendant	1

(b) MCH-cum-Nutrition Rehabilitation centre

(i) SMO/Project Co-ordinator(Paediatrician)	1

	(ii) Ophthalmic assistant	1
	(iii) Nurse/ANM	1
	(iv) Health extension educator	1
	(v) Supervisor for income generating schemes	1
	(vi) Lab.technician	1
(c)	Mobile team	
	(i) Medical officers	2
	(ii) ANM/Nurse	2
	(iii) Attendant	2
	(iv) Driver-cum-projectionist	2
(d)	Health post	
	(i) ANM	2
	(ii) Trained dai	2
(e)	Female Volunteers	150

Project Management Strategy

Co-ordination and linkages

The project co-ordination (management) office is located in Jaipur. Project co-ordinator with the help of supporting staff performs the overall administrative function of the project. Apart from this a co-ordination committee was set-up comprised of officials from the government health department from the block level and community level health system, Project co-ordinator, secretary-BRS, 2-4 community leaders, women volunteers to establish linkages with other government and non-government organisations functioning in the project area. This committee was envisaged to provide strategic direction to the project management team periodically in an advisory capacity.

Monitoring and Supervision

Project management team including the functionaries are guided and supervised by their respective supervisors. At the grassroots level female health volunteers are supervised and guided by Health educator. Mobile team functionaries are guided by the two MOs responsible for Mobile health care. Project Co-ordinator -cum-Senior MO looks after the overall implementation responsibility and motoring of monthly activity.

Relevance of the NGO Activity

BRS has defined its total project area and has a list of villages in the area and this information is updated every year, in the month of June. Also available is a list of the target population for service delivery and an area map.

Specific Problems

The baseline-survey completed in 1992 cited the following factors as being the major problems in the project area. Illiteracy, high number of currently married women needing reproductive health services, high number of children under 3 years of age needing immunisation and other child health services, Tuberculosis treatment and cataract surgical services needed as number of patients with these diseases is high.

Through interviews with project staff and community, the major health problems seem to be Pneumonia, diarrhoea disease, Malnutrition, Measles among children and Obstetric Labour, Gynae problems among mothers.

MCH services are delivered to the door-steps in the form of TT & distribution of IFA tablets for mothers and immunisation for children. Family planning acceptance of spacing methods is yet very low as is expected in a population of this nature. Undernutrition among children is detected as part of growth monitoring. Tackling this problem by admitting the children into the IP ward at Khedi centre and treating them there has not found popularity among the people.

The project objectives target Tuberculosis and blindness as additional areas for intervention, in addition to Maternal & Child Health. With an ophthalmologist as a medical officer and three doctors on the rolls, BRS should be in a position to handle these diseases as well.

From this, and our observations on the field we feel that the project objectives are relevant to the needs of the area. The NGO has been active in this area since 1972 and has a good understanding of the community and its needs.

Strengths and weaknesses of the Project Management

The following factors have been identified as strengths and weaknesses of the NGO during visit and interaction with the team and VHWs and members from the *Mahila Mandals* and special interaction with government health officials from the project area.

Strengths

- The organisation has a sound -base in the project area, in the form of its long-standing presence & physical infrastructure including the Orphanage, Hostel and Hospital at *Khedi* village. This fact increases the acceptability of interventions.

- Leadership at the top is very experienced and strong. Ms. Alice Garg, the Secretary of BRS is a good leader, capable of leading her team.
- The staff turnover at the middle level (Medical Officers, Health Educators) is low. This is a good sign and can be advantage when implementing a sustainability plan.
- Human Resources at the top and middle levels are good. Dr. Ghiya is a seasoned hand at family welfare activities and Mr. Mathur has had a 30-year experience in the PHC set up. They are also potential training resources for the project.
- The Management Information System (MIS) framework is good with an excellent tool in the form of the consolidated village register but utilisation can be improved upon.
- Non-health sector activities like *Mahila Mandal* organisation and Income Generation activities are already in operation. This could be a major step towards sustainability.
- Supervision is a systematic process with Mr. Mathur, who is having a specific supervisory visiting schedule and list of activities at each visit.
- The organisation has past experience with PVOH-I, following which some infrastructure still stands like the centre at Lalgarh. This has given it a distinct edge in dealing with another Maternal & Child health project.

Weaknesses

- Leadership is strongly vested in the hands of Mrs. Garg, secretary, BRS. Second line leadership can be built up, since this would be a strong point towards sustainability of health benefits.
- Interaction with govt. functionaries is low, even partly because of low intensity of governmental efforts in the area. But from a sustainability point of view, the organisation needs to build up more Govt. support in the area.
- There has been progress in *Mahila Mandal* organisational activity. But the institution of the Community Health Volunteer is somewhat weak at the moment, with even the existing CHVs being mainly curative in function. The CHV is a major link person between

organisation and community, hence this institution needs to be strengthened.

- Though the infrastructure for an efficient MIS is available, the Information System is directed mostly towards generating Quarterly reports in the format prescribed by NIHFW. A more locally useful means of handling information needs to be identified and developed.
- Networking with other NGOs/Organisations working in the area has been mentioned as a general objective, but has not received the attention that it could warrant. This would enable sustainability by co-operating with a group of "other" providers.
- Lack of timely availability of financial support from the MOH&FW and the lack of sensitivity on the part of the ministry to respond the delay is considered as a major hindrance to effective implementation. This remained as a weakness in the system of Government-NGO co-operation. Even salary of the project functionaries was not paid for a period for more than six months resulted in loss of morale and this in turn affected the quality of implementation.
- The project area with difficult terrain mostly cut off in rainy season from the reach of the project team even for the local community. This fact caused the recommendation of the 'Project Appraisal Team' to reduce the project area to 149 villages. This diverted the attention of local CHVs, Mahila Mandals and community villagers and created inconvenient for availing the health care facility under the project. This remained as a problem with the 'Project conceptualisation during the time of its feasibility' leading to loss of potential resources.
- The reporting format in use is itself a constraint since the NGO was more involved in collecting information and formatting them for reporting rather than concentrating on qualitative outcome of the services covered. This remained a technical problem and became necessary for the establishment of community based health information management system throughout the project period.

Issues on Sustainability

The project has drawn some lessons from its experience with PVOH-I, which was also based in *Bassi* tehsil. A curative centre was built up as part of this project, at Lalgarh. This centre continues to function. The field activity however is much scaled down.

A discussion was held with Ms. Garg regarding the sustainability of PVOH-I. From this the following points became clear:

- BRS had prepared a "Follow up programme" with regard to PVOH-I. This was a basis for receiving a grant of funds ("sustainability grant") following PVOH-I. This grant helped in carrying out the infrastructure built during PVOH-I.
- The project leadership, Ms. Garg and Mrs. Mishra could not attend the National workshop on sustainability, as part of the initiative of Donor strategy to focus on 'Sustainability Planning', at Bangalore in August 1995. Therefore, a plan for sustainability has not been prepared by the organisation as yet as expressed during this visit.
- The project area visit has resulted in a thought out process regarding sustainability and a plan was in the process of being prepared by the organisation. A discussion was held on the basis for sustainability of PVOH-II. It was clear that sustainability would depend on processes initiated by the organisation right through the project management.
- The processes involved in managing project implementation that were to form the basis for achieving sustainability of ongoing activities are discussed under the following discussed headings.

Building a High Level of Community Awareness

The Project Administrator, Mr. Mathur, has a Health Education background with 30 years of service in the PHC sector. Health Education at an individual and family level is given alongside mobile services. The organisation also has some unique features like a mobile library on a camel cart, organising "corner meetings" etc. Women awareness camps of 3-5 days duration are also held.

Also, the organisation has an activist overtone in its functioning. Making people aware of their rights and making them demand their due was also an organisational thrust area. BRS has a 'legal aid cell' which regularly helps in this area.

Creating Community Based Institutions

The organisation proposed the creation / strengthening of community based institutions like *Mahila Mandals*, *Trained Dais* and Community Health Volunteers.

There are Mahila Mandals in 38 villages currently and the organisation hopes to facilitate the formation of more Mahila Mandals during the visit. The institution of the Community Health Volunteer has not yet been fully developed. The ideal envisaged was a first contact person who will be able to cure simple ailments. Though some initial training has been done, progress in this area has been limited. Training of Dais has also been organised but there was still some progress that were needed and yet to be made.

Promotion of Income Generation Activities

The organisation has, as part of its possession, a tract of land yielding fruit and vegetable produce. This has been used for the destitute children in its school and hostel.

Activities envisaged as part of project

Pottery units, where women groups were organised into different self help groups. BRS given designs and know how, local women create multiple units and BRS arranges for marketing. This group was met and some samples were shown from the - Chalk making and pickle making units in the NGO.

Fee for Medicine

This policy was in operation currently at all the health posts. BRS proposes to expand on it to include fee for services as well. Even with all these projections, the organisation was likely to encounter problems with sustainability.

NGO Co-operation with Government

The Govt. presence in this area was low. The PHC visited under study lacked even electricity and a water connection. Therefore, co-operation with the Govt. was at low ebb and this was not a factor, which could be depended upon in the sustainability process. The people used mobile and static health care facilities of BRS for all purposes of their health seeking treatment.

Networking with Other Health Service Providers

One of the objectives of the PVOH-II project was to network and facilitate the work of other health providers in the area. This was an aspect, which needed to be strengthened, if any role has to be played by other providers like other NGOs or private practitioners. Probably, a directory of such providers could be generated which will help in building links with local providers.

Monitoring and MIS

The data management process of the organisation was as follows. Information was collected and generated at the field level by project health workers. This was entered into a village level Register, which was a composite collection of all data pertaining to a village. From there, extracts are prepared on a standard format – used for monitoring of field activities.

The format lacks population figures, which could facilitate decision making at a field level. The information system as a whole appears to be geared to filling the NIHFW prescribed 'Quarterly Progress Report' (QPR) formats, rather than a self-monitoring process. This format was sent to the health post, where all the village formats are put together into a consolidated sheet and were sent to the project office.

Here all the data was put together into the QPR format as required by NIHFW. Generally, the formats do not use denominators and therefore yield only numbers and not percentages.

Supervision seemed to be systematised, with the Administrative Officer following a fixed schedule of visiting the health posts and checking on information collected and done at each post.

The supervision system could be taken advantage of initiating a more meaningful MIS where the information gathered as was discussed at each level and conclusions drawn in a participatory fashion before putting it in formats. Communication system was good in the project between field staff and supervisors. There was a job chart for every worker and they work on a fixed day/place schedule.

Outstanding Features of the Project

Following mentioned two features that struck us as being innovative in the project area:

Mobile Library - The organisation had a mobile library on a camel cart, which went into the villages and functioned as a lending library. There was not much of a problem with book loss, according to the driver/manager and the concept has been accepted in the rural community. This concept was definitely a useful one for organisations involved in education and literacy programmes.

Village level register- this NGO has developed a register for each village which was maintained by the health worker for that village. The uniqueness of the register was in the fact that it contained listings and information pertaining to all the groups within the village in one single book. This replaced the large number of registers that one usually encounters at the village level. The process of putting information into and compiling extracts from this register could be easier than with separate registers. The size of the BRS composite register as it was existed is large but the organisation planned to cut the size when it printed the next lot.

Key Observations in the Project Management

The project was implemented in January 1992 and all its units started functioning within the first year of the project as envisaged. The income generation work was taken up more than a year later i.e. by May-June, 1993. Implementation process- during implementation period, the project activities of the organisation faced some problems in covering the inaccessible villages by van, for carrying out their nutritional rehabilitation activities and for pursuing income generation work. The organisation adopted some appropriate and need based steps wherein in some of the inaccessible villages were addressed through motorcycles, income generation work related to making of chalks and pickles were replaced by animal husbandry and the children identified for nutritional rehabilitation were given food in the project villages itself.

Achievements of the operational targets for project

Having a comparative view of the MCH indicators made an assessment of the achievements under the project. The tentative specific MCH indicators, which were proposed to be achieved by the end of the project period, alongwith the MCH baseline indicators and the achievements made under the project have been given and interpreted briefly as per the findings of the KPC study and Evaluation report (Annex-V), which are mentioned as follows:

Child Care- there is an overall improvement in the child health care practices. The coverage under immunisation increased by 25% in case of BCG, DPT and 29% in case of Polio and 13% for measles immunisation from the baseline levels.

Maternal Care- the coverage under ANC care increased substantially. ANC check-up (at least three times) were carried out for over half (51%) of the pregnant mothers and 73% of them were TT immunisation (complete doses) against the base line level of 7% and 19% respectively. Consumption of IFA tablets were reported to be 67% by the end of evaluation period compared to the baseline level of 16%.

53% mothers had the knowledge of ANC services before 3rd trimester. About one-fourth of pregnant women consumed more food during pregnancy. This is partly due to lack of awareness and partly due to lack of ability to afford. A bulk of 51% of pregnant women consumed less food during pregnancy. Most of them revealed about their feeling that eating more food during pregnancy would lead to bigger size of the baby and consequently, a difficult delivery.

Report shows up to 31% of the deliveries in the project villages were conducted by untrained hands involving relatives, friends' etc. 42% through traditional birth attendants and 27% through professionals' conduct.

Regarding initiation of breast-feeding, a majority of (70%) stated it after 8 hours of child birth, while remaining 30% mentioned it within 8 hours. Similarly working mothers 32% agreed for feeding within 8 hours compared to non-working 28% mothers. Ninety-nine % of mothers exclusively breast fed their child up to 4 months. The continuation of breast-feeding along with the food supplementation is 81%.

During diarrhoea 99% of the mothers continued breast feeding and giving fluids to their children and 76% continued with food supplementation. ORT is given by 33% of mothers and treatment sought for diarrhoea is reported to be 64%.

86% of the children (12-23months) have received some immunisation, with 44% of them received BCG, 31% DPT (3 doses) and 38% polio drops (3 doses). 31% children received measles immunisation. The highest coverage in polio with one dose (86%) which can mainly attributed to Government's Pulse Polio programme. The irregularity in logistics and supply was accounted for low coverage in immunisation in the project area.

The proportion of family planning acceptors declined marginally (1%) instead of increasing by end of the project period compared to the baseline level. This low level of acceptance of FP methods could be due to coverage of young mothers with child under 24 months of age in the sample compared to coverage of all eligible women (15 – 45 years) in the baseline survey and the mid-term evaluation.

Safe deliveries practices have improved to 27 percent compared to the baseline level of 11 percent. The coverage under different immunization improved from the baseline level. The maximum increase in coverage was for polio (27%) followed by BCG (25%), DPT (22 %) and measles (13%).

All knowledge and practice MCH indicators show better performance in case of literate mothers compared to the illiterate ones.

Community perception

Majority of the village community was satisfied with the services provided by the NGO. But the reason for dissatisfaction as mentioned was, irregular visits of the mobile team, no peripheral level working, poor infrastructure including bad roads etc. The frontline functionaries of the project team was having the opinion about the coverage of vast area instead of concentration in specific villages within the reach – inaccessible villages, emphasise on curative aspect was more than the preventive and promotive aspects, irregular supply of medicines, vaccines and contraceptives are other constraints.

NGO had put its genuine, sincere and best efforts to cater to community needs as planned. Organisation's main objectives had been fulfilled through awareness generation and provision of services in the outreach population. Effective strategy was maintained in raising the level of community awareness. For example, the occurrence of no polio drop-out case in the community during the project period, couples undergoing sterilisation after two children, organisation of village-women through *Mahila Mandals,* coverage of one half to over two-thirds of the women under the ambit of MCH care was a remarkable effort in the inaccessible, socio-economically backward community etc, paved the way for long term strategies in achieving sustainability.

Appropriateness of Project to the Community Needs

The appropriateness and relevance of any programme undertaken was assessed based on the target population it intends to serve and the surroundings in which they were living. Based on the field visits to the area and after having discussed with the beneficiaries and the service providers it was found that the entire area was not conveniently reachable considering the location and spread of the villages. One had to cover a distance of 50-60 kms. to reach out to the farthest village of the project. Again, the area was devoid of proper roads, was sandy with open and wide stretches of dunes bushes, rocks and ditches.

Primary Health Center, *Bhanpurkallan*, which is the Block PHC with 27 sub-centers under it, provided some medical facilities in about 105 villages. The PHC has no indoor facilities; no 'operation theatre' and majority of the sanctioned positions remained vacant. Similar was the situation in most of the sub-centers.

Lack of proper transport in the desert area made it all the more difficult for the villagers to reach health care delivery outlets. Low female literacy, poverty, ignorance were some of the other important features of the area. Therefore, this project was needed; it was catering to unsaved/ undeserved areas.

The common ailments experienced by children were diarrhoeal diseases, respiratory infections, measles, polio, skin infection, malnourishment etc. Women suffer from reproductive tract infections (RTI), anemia and other problems arising out of lack of antenatal, natal and post-natal care. Incidence of blindness was very high in the area.

In the absence of adequate and proper medical aid, even the minor health problem turned into major health issues. The major brunt of inadequate medical facilities was borne by the women and the children.

The organization's effort was likely to provide MCH care services through interventions of health facilities, both curative and preventive, focussed on women and children. The interventions made have been towards creating awareness, changing health-seeking behavior, improving MCH and family planning coverage. Poverty being the mother of all problems, the project also helped the people in poverty alleviation by doing some income generating activities.

The strategy of implementation of the project through a three-tier approach backed by mobile services and with a special provision for nutritional rehabilitation of the malnourished children was some of the important and appropriate features of the project. Income generation work was also managed in helping to them to have some supplementary income.

Thus components, dimensions and strategy of project implementation are considered to have addressed the community needs at the macro level.

Selection of Project Area

The project had an ambitious target of covering as many as 149 widely scattered villages spread over two tehsils. While implementing the project, the organisation had problems in covering all the villages, whether it was provision of services through MCH – cum – Nutrition Rehabilitation Center, or through Health posts or visits of the mobile team. Though the mobile team tried to cover the scattered area yet a compact area could have been served better.

Nutrition Rehabilitation Programme

The Nutrition Rehabilitation Programme for children was based on the concept that the child would stay in the center as an inpatient for rehabilitation. The programme was not very successful. The main reason was that in most of the cases the young age of the child necessitated the mother's stay along with the child, while very few mothers were willing to leave their family responsibilities and stay with the child. Consequently the number of children hospitalized was less than expected. This was an innovative approach and the organization applied corrective measures.

Services through Mobile Team

Two mobile teams were supposed to provide services in the out reach villages through 50-55 proximal locations in such a way, that each location was to be visited at least twice a month.

Actually, in some villages the services have been provided once in a month, while in others once in two months time, and there were still other villages where the mobile van could not reach. This showed that despite the fact that the organization had put in their best and sincere efforts to provide outreach services, some villages could not be adequately covered due to accessibility problems.

Coverage of these remotely located villages for MCH care was in itself a positive achievement. However, a separate implementation process could have been a possibility.

Income Generation Activity

The income generation activities of the organization, though of secondary importance, next only to MCH care, were less successful than expected.

The organization planned to open 9 units (4 chalk making + 3 pickle + 2 Dehydration of vegetables) for income generation work and was to operate them by involving *mahila mandals* under the overall charge of a supervisor. The programme made less achievement than expected due to marketing problems. Moreover, one supervisor found it difficult to mange all the units, which were located at different places. Lack of transport facilities was the other constraint.

Thus, the IGA activities suffered due to marketing problems. Realizing this the organization shifted its focus from making of chalks and pickles to animal, husbandry activities which goes more with the villagers way of living.

The organisation wanted to give their best activities by making changes in some of the major activities, as follows:

- Supplementary food was provided to the identified malnourished children in the villages itself.

- Part of the area, which was inaccessible by van, was covered through motorcycles.
- Loans were given to some 200 beneficiaries from 9 villages for animal husbandry activities.

Opinion of Project Functionaries

The project functionaries always felt that their main objectives have been fulfilled through provision of services, though some of them may not have been provided on regular basis. The staff had put in their sincere and best efforts to cater to community needs. However, the main gap remained in organizing Income Generation works. The staffs further felt that had they put in all their genuine efforts in a compact area, the achievement would have been very good.

The main reasons for any of the shortfalls were the cast spread of the area. The staff asking for more salaries, need for more vehicles, irregular supply of medicines, vaccines and contraceptives were the other constraints.

The organization had been able to generate enough awareness in the community. In some of the villages the community was actively involved on the delivery of MCH services, while in some of the remote and inaccessible villages the awareness was less than expected.Due to the organisation's eye care services particularly organisation of eye camps, the NGO had build a good rapport in the area. In future the organization would provide MCH services by having a good support from the community. During the last 2 years no case of polio has occurred in the project area, which is perceived as a very big achievement as recorded during this visit.The numbers of cases accepting sterilization after 2 children have increased substantially. Many couples have received the benefit of *Raj Lakshmi Scheme* of the Government of Rajasthan, which were given to couples who undergo sterilization after 2 children.

Due to organization of *mahila mandals*, bringing them on a common platform has strengthened women. They have started coming forward for all developmental activities of the village. The Project co-ordinator strongly felt that the organisation could continue to provide services in the area by filling up gaps and lacunae observed in implementation of the programme.

All the above findings and observations revealed that the project had been successful in achieving its objectives. The main reasons for all the shortfalls were mainly the vast spread of the area coupled with limited resources, organization not having a proper appraisal of the situation before launching the programme and very little coordination and linkages with Government and other NGOs.

Perception of Village opinion leaders

Eighty percent of the leaders were satisfies with the services provided by the organization while 20 percent were dissatisfied. Reasons for dissatisfaction reported were "irregular visits of mobile team", no peripheral level working, bad roads, no transport facility etc. All leaders reported IEC activities having been carried out by the organization during the last 6 months.

Strategies on Sustainability

Sustainability of project activities after the expiry of the project period was one of the prerequisites of grant given NGOs under the PVOH-II scheme. The salient features of the sustainability plan as given by Bal Rashmi Society are discussed under the following points.

- The MCH center – cum hospital was planned to be run by the organisation mainly through the funds of the Society. However, some nominal charges would be taken for medicines, hospitalization etc.
- A separate laboratory has been set up which has been visualized as a source of income. There were no laboratory facilities in the area within accessible limits where patients could go for investigations so this laboratory could cater to clinical investigations need of the area and generate some money for other activities.
- The organisation had planned to raise their fresh team of grass-roots level workers and equip them to provide basic services.
- The society had planned to provide outreach services through the existing van and two motorcycles.
- Community involvement had been envisaged through motivation of committed grass-roots level workers. Community is expected to provide all round help, especially during organization of camps as observed.

Key Constraints Observed

- Absence of a planned strategy for the NGO to cover all the remote and inaccessible villages,

- Identifying marketing outlets for linking women groups to the benefits of income generation activities,
- Appropriate Management Information System for better assessment of programmatic coverage and related feedback,
- Participatory community based IEC strategy with the mentioning of issues of Maternal and Child Health care to address practical problems,

Taking note of issues involved in carrying out nutritional rehabilitation of children, Sustainability plan to have been based on gradual withdrawal of the organisation, designing of project management strategy to organise regular meetings with staff, replenishment of the health-kit, effective co-operation with government agencies for regular supply of logistics, essential medicines, and referrals in emergency.

Suggestions

The sustainability plan of the NGO seems to be quite realistic, but keeping in view the spread of the area with some villages being really inaccessible, it seemd the organisation had really to put in more number of persons and other resources to cater to the needs of the community.

There existed a need for more coordination of activities especially immunization, safe delivery, family planning and income generating activities.

The coordination with Health Department could enable the NGO to procure vaccines and contraceptives and thus improved the coverage. Only basic medicines should be procured and some arrangement should have been made to meet needs in emergency. This could be done through regular contact with the government Health department.

Similarly safe delivery practices could be promoted through more interaction with the Government network especially by involving peripheral level health workers. For income generating activities more liaisons could be maintained with Government Rural Development department.

Government had been running many programmes for the rural population for up-gradation of their skills and for carrying on income generation activities. The NGOs interaction and coordination with project officers of these programmes could help solve some of the problems faced in income generation works.

Programmatic suggestions-

- Provision of health education and awareness to mothers about nutritional value of locally available different types of foods and introduction of nutritious foods in child's diet,

- Information for pregnant mothers about the importance of different immunizations so that they take necessary effort to complete immunization,
- Upgraded skill and knowledge sharing the advantages of home based management of ARI and Diarrhea,
- Improving, encouraging and ensuring 'safe-delivery' and its practice by trained personnel at home, and periodic organization of Dai training in collaboration with government,
- Popularizing temporary/spacing methods of family planning by promoting the use of IUD, oral pills and condom

Lessons Learned

This section is utilized to informally discuss the project in its total perspective i.e. right from the time of preparation of community need based proposal, its objectives, and implementation, reporting procedure to sustainability of activities.

An attempt has been made to critically relate the findings of the project achievement with the planned coverage, resources available and socioeconomic and other cultural influences. The following findings emerge:

- The NGO has put up their genuine, sincere and best efforts to cater to community needs as planned. Their main objectives have been fulfilled through awareness generation and provision of services in the project area.
- The NGO has been able to generate enough awareness in the community, which is the first step for any programme to be successful. Occurrence of no polio case in the community during last 2 years, couples undergoing sterilization after 2 children, organization of women through *mahila mandals* etc. paves the way for long-term sustainable achievements.
- Coverage of one-half to over two-thirds of the women under the ambit of MCH care is no less an achievement for the different areas and the socio-economically backward community.
- However during implementation of the project activities the organization faced some problems in covering the inaccessible villages, for carrying out their nutritional rehabilitation activities and income generation works.

- The organization adopted some appropriate and need based steps wherein some of the villages, outreach services in accessible by van were provided through the motor bikes, Income generation work related to chalks and pickles were replaced by animal husbandry activities which is more close to villagers way of life and the children identified for nutritional rehabilitation were given foods in the villages itself.

Despite the above achievements the following issues need to be spelt out

- The project had an ambitious target of covering 149 widely scattered villages with limited manpower and other resources. Some of these villages were very remote and inaccessible by van.
- It would have been better had the organization worked either in a compact area or had a separate set up for the remote villages.
- The Nutrition Rehabilitation programme was based on the concept that the child would stay at the center alongwith his/her mother for a couple of days' time. Keeping in view the number of children in the family, the other responsibilities of the mother and the ignorance in the community the number of children hospitalized were less than expected.
- The nutrition rehabilitation of children was a comparatively innovative approach and the organization supplied supplementary food to the identified malnourished children in the villages. The modified implementation process quite appropriate.
- The three health posts under the project were supposed to cover 10-11 villages each. In actual practice, each Health post extensively covered 2 to 3 villages and provided few services in the remaining allocated villages.
- This modified approach is considered as need based. Position of one health educator and one supervisor for the IGAs for the entire project area seems to be inadequate. Moreover, they were not provided with any independent transport to carry out their responsibilities of the IGA and IEC activities were less than expected.

In depth appraisal of the situation could have been of some help before launching the programme along the following lines:

- Proper plans for covering remote and inaccessible villages and other villages.

- Operational indicators based on Baseline survey.
- Proper Management Information system for better control and feedback.
- Taking note of practical problems in organising IEC activities.

Sustainability plan has been based on gradual withdrawal strategy of the organization.

- Most of the female volunteers showed unwillingness to work in the area or cooperate with the mobile team or even attend monthly meetings organized by the project coordinator on the pretext that the salary of Rs/-. 100 per month are low and no travelogue allowance (TA) is paid for attending monthly meetings. Keeping in view the part time nature of job, the salary cannot be considered very low.
- Regular meetings with the staff and some travelling allowance (TA) in the initial stages of the project could have been solved.
- Proper marketing outlets were not there for selling the produce of income generation work, resultantly the programme did not move as expected. Marketing strategy for the products should have been developed and followed for IGAs.
- The vaccines and medicines received by the organization from the Government sources were not always sufficient and at time were used to be nearing to expiry date.
- There should have been better contact with the Government Health Department for obtaining supply of contraceptives and vaccines.
- Only basic medicines should have been procured with better rapport, some provision should have been made to meet the needs in emergency health care services.
- Some of the project staff showed dissatisfaction with the salary structure as they always compared their remuneration with that of Government local employees. This at times led to lesser coordination of activities in the villages.
- While selecting the workers care should have been taken to induct those workers who have some voluntary spirit of working.
- There was no provision for replenishing the kit given to the village level workers. And the replenishment of the kit should have been taken up on regular basis.

The organization has been involved in a big way in eye operations, organization of 3-5 eye camps in a year and post-operative care activities. Since the focus of PVOH-II project as per the project proposal was on child survival and safe motherhood (CSSM) organizations eye care activities, though good, were viewed as of lesser importance. However due to constant interaction with the NGO the organization developed a good rapport.

Other Programmatic suggestions

- There is a need for proper feeding practices of the children. Mothers should be educated about nutrition value of different locally available foods and introducing nutritious foods in child's diet.
- Mothers need to be educated about the importance of different immunizations so that they make it a point to get them immunized from one source or the other.
- More knowledge and skill need to be imparted to mothers for home management of ARI and diarrhea, as these are the two major diseases.
- There is a need for improving, encouraging and enduring "safe delivery" and its proper practice by trained persons at home.
- There exists a need to popularize temporary/spacing methods of family planning viz. IUD, Oral Pills and Condom.

To conclude, the project was rightly addressed to the community needs. However, when coming to implementation of planned activities, performance under some of the components of the project was less than the expectations. A few changes were made by the organisation in the implementation process. Overall, the achievement of the project is very good, and the changes made were appropriate and need based. Sustainability planning was not incorporated in the organisational design of project management initially even in the end of project period. Managerial effectiveness to sustain the benefits of the project in the long run to achieve sustainability remains a distant logic for the NGO. Community participation in the form of strengthening of *Mahila Mandals*, CHVs and provision of training of Dais, remained limited to the project activities instead of linking economic benefit of the government programmes available for the project area. Involving village-panchayat in participating in NGO activities in the form of representation and mass mobilisation was not a focus of the project management. This widens the gap between the 'Panchayati Raj Institutions' responsiveness and NGO priority for the local community in the project area. Linking with economic benefit programmes became difficult for the NGO in absence of a clear-cut strategy for addressing local community need throughout the period of project implementation. Project specific initiatives in isolation of the responsibility of the existing democratic institutions and absence of a supportive co-operation within the village based social dynamics are the key environmental factors very much operating as a hindrance to sustainability.

Chapter - VII

Analysis & Discussion on Sustainability of Health Care

Present chapter analyses the factors of sustainability of the NGOs as discussed in the case studies in previous chapter. This analysis is based on the discussion of the capacity of NGO effectiveness followed by qualitative assessment of NGOs based on the observations on the social instruments of sustainability, as was discussed in the methodology. This is followed by a note on the NGO capacity in the form of its strengths, weaknesses and related management strategy needed to focus on sustainability.

SEVA MANDIR

Capacity of NGO Effectiveness

Health services of Seva Mandir started in 1984 in ten villages of Kherwada block. From the very beginning the thrust was on the curative and promotive services. It was felt that to make health a reality, people must be aware of the common causes of ill health and how to prevent it from illness. It was felt that people needed some curative services for treatment of minor ailments because of the remoteness of the villages from the nearest centre of cure. Therefore health education along with basic curative services began.

The health intervention were based on 12 point health programme, which was elaborated under PVOH-II project to cover 20 points in all which are included in the following list:

- Ladle with handle
- Kitchen garden
- Smokeless furnace
- Soak pits
- Sanitary latrines
- Water filter with double layered cloth
- Dustbins
- Compost pits
- Children inoculated with 1,2 and 3 doses
- Children provided with booster

- Pregnant women inoculated with 1,2 and 3 doses
- Houses with windows and Houses with separate cattle shade
- Family planning
- Covering faces with soil and washing hands

Four pillars of health i.e., nutrition, increased income, family welfare and planning and cleanliness support this programme. Envisaging the health interventions to promote healthy living and at the some time providing treatment for minor ailments at the doorstep, require well-trained and equipped VHWs. These para-medical workers were thus imparted comprehensive training and refreshers to help them understand the entire gamut of health care interventions related to MCH and family welfare, sanitation and hygiene and referral services.

Also considering the fact that, area of operations were remote, where in some cases, even basic medicines were not available. Therefore it was decided by the NGO to provide the health workers with medicine kit. The VHWs who are literate were given a health kit consisting of 21 items including paracetamol, stemctil, interquinol, baralgan, dispirin etc. Government sponsored items like IFA, ORS, condoms etc scissors, soap, pen, records, health education book – the 'Arogya Darshika', *Choti-choti bimariyon ke gharelu ilaaz,* Flip books for health education. The idea is that people must have excess to at least some common drugs, which sometimes also help save time in case of emergencies.

The home remedy workers are healers who have practising ISM for generations, sometimes they are illiterate. However, acknowledging their vast experience and knowledge and easy acceptance by the community, they also have been provided with a kit, which has about 20 traditional herbal combinations, the usual government supplied drugs and the health education material.

TBA or Dai is a major resource as far as women and children related health issues are concerned. Seva Mandir has strengthened Dai's skill and has provided her with a kit that greatly helps her in conducting aseptic deliveries, tackling anaemia in women among other things. There is yet another person who has been strengthening considering her contact with the mots vulnerable group – the small children, she is the Balwadi Sanchalika. Medicines for common ailments like cold, cough, stomach-ache, diarrhoea, skin disease, fever, tooth ailments ate given by the Sanchalika. The Sanchalika's are illiterate, therefore the bottles and caps are very colourful and corresponding to the colour of bottle, the cap, the prescription of medicine for a specific disease, a guide book has been given to them including a kit with bio-chemic medicines.

The health unit has tried to approach the curative aspects from all angles, so that the community stands gain in all respects. All community has a choice in the type of medicines they wish to have. The para-medical workers provide the first source of treatment and also send for referrals. The referral in case of normal conditions generally is – sub-centre to PHC to district hospital. In case of emergencies referral is directly to the specialists.

An interesting fact noticed during the interaction about the community perception of availability of services from different sources and their preference for the same. It seems that people had evolved their own referral services: however, they did acknowledge the timely help that health team provides and also their credibility in the government hospitals. The two rural health centres are rally a big asset to the people, not only in terms of the treatment given but also the calm and soothing disposition of the doctors and staff of RHCs. These RHCs provide the basic treatment; efforts are on to upgrade the facilities on the service by increasing the bed capacity. The RHCs have also become the local centre for the health education and cure in the areas they cater to. To support and strengthen the health component, the health team has made available to the community some very simple indigenous and low cost technologies. The focus of this aspect is to provide solutions with the existing village resources. This in addition to promoting healthy living also provides a sense of income for the NGO. Some of the technologies introduced include construction of sanitary latrines, digging compost pits, making smokeless furnace, soap and developing kitchen gardens.

The PVOH-II project portrays the real emphasis of Seva Mandir's health intervention i.e., health education. The thrust is to make healthy living a habit and for that, different tools and techniques are used. The health educators, LHAs the para-medical workers all are well versed to spread these messages. Sometimes specifically demonstrations are offered, sometimes they happen on the job.

Intensive health campaigns are also organised. The thrust is again on promoting the 12 point health programmes and integrated development inclusive of all sectoral interventions. It is usually in four phases of six months each. Women's health awareness camps are organised twice a year. Also door to door contact wherein about 5 VHWs get together and they take five-village cluster at a time for 5 days. There are meetings, role-plays, movie shows etc along with meeting community individually.

Everywhere the ideas is to make people aware and well versed in all aspects of health education and then constantly reinforce the same so that a habit can be promoted. From time to time the messages are reinforced through folk media.

Girwa, Badgaon, Jhadol and Khedwara block of Udaipur district are fairly large and characterised by undulating topography and remoteness of many villages. The community is mostly tribal and settlement is scattered or disbursed. Agriculture is the mainstay of the people, supported by labour works. The literacy level is low and so is the per capita income. The supposed better status of women among tribal seems top have diluted due to intermixing of castes as well as importation of non-tribal cultures. Today the scenario is more or less similar to the general status of women in India. It is against this background that Seva Mandir's health intervention need to be understood. Broadly, the health programme of the NGO can be categorised into three phases 1994 -1986 was essentially on eof learning, assimilation and percolation of future strategies. The health unit had by now understood that, for health interventions to be successful, people's capabilities and motivation needs to be built, so that they understand on problem, prioritise their needs and arrive at solutions. This approach stressed an intensive health education, establishment of network of VHWs and improved domestic and environmental hygiene. At the end of this phase, following are the outcomes as noticed:

- 85 VHWs are trained
- Health campaigns are carried out to develop model health villages
- Health programme diversification started
- Village health committees are formed
- 959 patients benefited from the referral facilities

During the second phase from 1986-1989 earlier aims and objectives gained and new ideas emerged, the concept of rural health centres and TBA programme was mooted, and low cost technologies were introduced. The TBA programmes were launched with the view to focus on MCH and family welfare activities, reducing IMR and MMR and create yet another resource base in the village for a self-reliant health unit. Also during this period the intersectoral approach was envisaged to make health interventions more holistic with the following outcomes:

- 35% increase in the number of VHWs from 1986-1989
- TBA added to network of VHWs
- 235 mass media events held by health unit in 1989 Immediately following this was the third phase from 1989-till date.

This period was also the one, when PVOH-II project was launched. During this period following are the changes noticed at Seva Mandir:

- Coverage of villages increased to 200 with the addition of 48 villages
- TBA programme grew in strength with the provision of ANC, INC, PNC birth spacing, supplementary feeding for pregnant and lactating mothers
- RHCs were created to strengthen the promotive, curative and preventive aspects
- School health programmes was started to inculcate the habit of healthy living from childhood and provide timely guidance to protect children against diseases
- The post of LHAs was created to supervise the work of TBAs

This phase saw the following achievements:

- Expansion in the work of village health workers
- TBAs assisted births increased school health programme started, AIDS awareness programme started
- Inter-sectoral linkages strengthened
- Efforts began to integrate income generation activities with health
- RHCs have become focal point of health education and health care
- Organising treatment of TB patients

As of today, the health education component remains the most important tool with 60% of minor ailments are cured in the village itself. The TBA programme has grown up remarkably (Annex-V: on KPC and Final Evaluation Report).

Strategies on Sustainability

The very fact that Seva Mandir has never thought of setting up a parallel health structure to that of the government and their understanding both are complimentary which has paved the way for good relationship between the two. This relation manifests itself at all levels from the NGO programme execution to that of implementation at the village level. The CMHO, Udaipur, Dr.K.L.Kummat was quite supportive of NGOs health intervention. He acknowledged the good work of Seva Mandir for which it has become easier to identify the target group for immunisation.

Even at the block level the medical officer of PHC at Badgaon block felt that the combination of government system and the presence of Seva Mandir with the community made everyday working easier and also during epidemics 'we realise how much we need each other'. One ANM from Jhadol block accepted the fact that it is becoming easier in the presence of TBAs who helped her in identifying villages where focus is required to work for immunisation coverage. TBAs and ANM work together for immunisation, TBA motivates and identifies mothers and children and ANM administers the vaccine. Also the health educators participate in the PHC meetings. There is also a proposition that the LHAs will also attend zone level PHC meetings.

In the two RHCs at Khojwada in Kherwada block and the other at Saru at Girwa block, Medical insurance schemes are in operation. Rs.18 per year are charged from the patients. All treatments are given free. In both the centres this scheme is operational, however the hospital staff feels that this amount is too small to sustain activities for a long time. Efforts are on to explore the viability, affordability and possibility of increasing the amount for insurance cover.

Community organisation building, mobilisation of the community linking health programme with income generation activities, community financing mechanism such as user fees, health insurance, revolving fund through self-help group formulation and cost sharing are some of the steps organised by the NGO to achieve sustainability. Networking linkages for sharing the best practices and the achievements with Government and the other NGOs is very useful in advocating sustainability of NGO programmes in health.

Contextual Factors

The major contextual factors affecting the sustainability of the PVOH- II project is discussed according to their impact on NGO management strategy.

Favourable factors

Community Need

The organisation is increasingly realised the need for some structured means to encourage and motivate the villagers, especially the women community to train and involve them and the members of the village groups. The NGO has been successful to a large extent in raising awareness among the women community in the project area. It established the *Lok sanskriti vikas ikai*-the cultural unit and a small training centre at Kaya, a village in the tribal area. This is very much used for the exchange of IEC activities for health and social mobilisation messages in the project area through cultural practices.

Seva Mandir's involvement with community development had identified with local need in the form of its change in focus from literacy programmes to a wider concern for the well-being and development of tribes, led it in 1984 to decide to work in the areas of health care.

Initially, Seva Mandir decided to invite villagers, if they wish to avail health care facility at the village level, to nominate one of their family members for training as a village health worker. In later part these health workers serve the community as Home Remedy Workers (HRWs), to administer indigenous herbs and plants for the treatment of minor ailments and TBAs to provide aseptic delivery and family planning services including supplementary nutrition.

Seva Mandir believes, that the encouragement of the revival of traditional cures is worthwhile, since they are safe and inexpensive, and also because they can be made available locally. They also encourage the maintenance of biodiversity. The NGO has promoted a network of model health villages to provide examples for the remainder. The real struggle is reflected in working with local community for realising people's health in people's hand in meeting effective demand for health care.

Community Response

The NGO effort in mobilising community response received remarkable support in the form of popular participation in health and community development programmes. Community awareness is created through a series of meetings with *mahila mandals*. As a result of which health network of model health villages are created with the involvement of women groups and village health team to serve as the link between the community and the rural referral hospital of the organisation in project villages. The organisation also receives substantial response from different social action groups in terms of donation to their corpus fund.

Other supporting projects

The major strength of the organisation lies on its focus and approaches to integrated action on health and social development. From a modest beginning more than two decades ago- not only in terms of size but also in terms of its understanding of how to be relevant for the poor- Seva Mandir has reached a stage where it can claim to have activated the potential grassroots development work at various levels, that is at the level of the poor, the government system and the voluntary sector.

With adult education as the entry point, Seva Mandir has to date expanded its activities to include wasteland and watershed management, water resource management, women's development, health and sanitation, social forestry and to mention only a few.

Unfavourable factors

Cessation of PVOH-II grant

The MOHFW and USAID support almost 75% of the total project outlay. This cost takes care of total non-recurring and recurring cost of the project. This was a sizeable support, which once stopped, could pose substantial threat to sustainability.

Poor paying capacity of the Community

Resource mobilisation through increased user fee or any other direct mechanism is difficult due to two basic reasons; the target population is extremely poor, and a sudden increase in existing or application of new charges would generate some sort of resistance among the community.

Decrease in focus on MCH due to flow of other Projects

Seva Mandir is always overburdened with a variety of social development projects due to its good name and credibility for its commitment to social need. There is a danger for excessive attention of health team towards the provision of curative health care for effective cost-recovery, which can divert the prime focus of MCH care at the end of the project period. Health care at the community level is taken care by a cadre of village health workers, but strategic direction and supportive supervision are the key to assess and upgrade the quality of services periodically as rendered to the local community.

Operational Factors

Favourable Operational factors

- The VHWs are found to be the real strength of the project. They are the link between target population in the community and the health services of the NGO. With low salary they are serving the organisation for the benefit of local community in the respective villages.
- Over the project period, there has been a significant achievement in skill building and expertise among the managerial team in creating a critical mass of skilled human resources. In general both

members from a family is provided the opportunity to work in the organisation at the field level to ensure effective monitoring, regularity of services, recognition in the village community and contributing to family income of the couple.

- Two hospital buildings of the NGO serve as referral centres, Rural Resource centre and a centre for training for health education resources with having out-door and in-door facility for the clinical care. The building and other assets in the hospital determine the NGO's confidence and commitment to continue its activities.
- Training modules and instruments constitute an integral part of the input strength of the project. Village health committee, linking with government health programmes, Referral heath centres, government -collaboration are some of the effective operational strategies favourable in the direction of sustainability.

Major unfavourable aspects associated with the operational factors

- The programme focused only on preventive and promotive aspects of MCH care and motivation for family planning services. Demand for continuity of good quality of care has been raising as a consequence of the increased awareness, but SM is not sufficiently ready to deal with the rising demand to continue its activities in the absence of regular availability of lady doctor in the hospital, as seen in the case of project period.
- The major potentials of resource generation were remaining largely untapped. The *Mahila Mandals, Basic Health Workers, Home Remedy Workers and Village Health Committees* were yet to receive a definite direction and guidance for owning the project. Different village based project units of the organisation could be used in linking health care with income generation activities, economic benefit programmes of the government and the NGO etc. while approaching community development activities. All these projects are conceptually and theoretically integrated at top-management level but hardly integrated programmatically at the field level. There is a long way to go to achieve measurable results in this direction.
- Integration of health care activities required to be addressed within the opportunity of existing framework of community welfare activities of the NGO. Various community projects diverted the organisational attention to focus in an integrated manner resulting in missing the synergistic effect and deviating from ensuring higher cost-effectiveness for the MCH activities.

- The strategy on project management training was ad hoc, and to some extent, biased. While the top managerial staff (Project Co-ordinator, Secretary, MOs) having similar capacity of responsibility attended almost all the project related training programmes, exposure to other NGO experiences. But the supervisory staff and village based health workers received hardly any external training and exposure input.

Leadership Factors

Major favourable aspects with respect to the leadership factors

- Interest to sustain the most essential and primary ingredient for sustainability. The interaction with Programme Co-ordinator and Medical officers of the NGO, reflected the willingness of the organisation to sustain the health care benefits to the project area community.
- Programme Co-ordinator involved in the management other community development projects of the NGO such as; Social forestry, care and welfare of the women and children, women empowerment, community advocacy, non-formal education, networking and co-ordination of social action involving community participation. Organisation's President is the guiding force for promoting sustainability.

Major unfavorable factors are

- Seva Mandir is a big organisation working in the grassroots set up. But planning and formulation of key policy decisions are taken unilaterally at the top-management level. Lack of decentralised planning in decision making, disparities among head quarter and field staff facilities affect the implementation process in most cases. Personnel management policies favouring contractual offering and uncertainty in the involvement at the period specific field based project put the functionaries in difficult situation. High turnover of profession staff due to the existing working situation affects the quality of project management and so thus limiting the opportunity for sustainability.
- There is evidential support for the lack of long-term vision and planning about resource mobilisation and utilisation of community support for sustaining the benefits of the project activities. Unilateral directions are always provided with a top-down control mechanism. Though the leadership quality is dynamic, it needs

encouraging coherence, participatory planning and decentralised decision making for effective management strategies.

- The organisation needs to have more effective participation of women in the leadership at all levels of functionaries instead of projecting women members as frontline health workers at the grassroots level.
- Networking and co-ordination of activities are limited to the exchange of experience sharing with government and other NGOs in the state and participation in national and internal conferences and seminars, and state level consortium on social forum for advocating gender equality in development etc. But it has hardly made any effort to link institutions of Panchayats at the village, block or at the district levels. This suffered an adequate value addition to the component of decentralised planning, and linking co-ordination of organisational decisions involving health care decentralisation. Sustainability of health care benefits is the equal responsibility and concern of all the actors of development in the context of health care decentralisation. This fact was highly neglected by the NGO management during its project period.

These favourable and unfavourable factors taken together create a sustainability profile of the NGO. These also help to identify the status of the social instruments discussed in the literature review on 'Instruments of Sustainability'. The following table shows a relative scoring of each of the relevant instruments with respect to the responsible factors discussed above.

SEVA MANDIR

Qualitative Assessment of Sustainability

[On the basis of positive and negative Factors observed on a Five point scale]

(1-5 scale: 1=very poor, 5=very strong)

Instrument	*Scoring*	*Positive Factors*	*Negative Factors*
Need-based Project	4	Targeted poorer women and children for comprehensive tribal development projects on adult education, school health education, environment al protection, social forestry, alternative systems of health care with suitability of community need assessment	Need for curative, preventive and promotive services to provide holistic health care is not effectively addressed. This is evident in the absence of preparation for an integrated nutrition and health package

(Contd...)

Quality of service	3	Preventive, promotive and curative intervention with committed group of village level health workers involving traditional healers, RMPs and ISM practitioners are well integrated	Insufficient training and exposure to the health workers, specialised training on quality of care needs improvement
Community Organizations	3	Focus on formation of *Mahila Mandals* and self-help groups, home remedy workers and network of health villages. Attempt to utilise these groups in generating internal resources. Good experience in working with the community	Not clear direction to the *Mahila Mandals, grassroots workers* in planning resources. The health units have long way to go to act independently in health care activities. No co-ordination established with panchayat system through these community organisations
Accumulated Assets	4	Completed the main project hospital building by own initiative. The hospital land was added to total asset of the organisation, well equipped training centres	Some systematic plan to recover the maintenance of assets. This asset still remains untapped for generating resources for health care in the absence of professional staff
Resource Manager	3	Dynamic project leadership. Clarity of organisational vision and mission strategy. Good number of exposure to training workshops and sharing events. Significant interest in sustainability	Centralised decision-making process. Management decisions are mostly ad hoc and individual-based. Needs consciousness about cost effectiveness. Potential linkages with other projects is up-to some extent tapped
Resource Generator	4	Substantial effort in income generating activities and linking it with self-help initiatives. User fee charged for ambulatory and curative care. Great potential in utilising land assets to subsidise health care activities	Recovery of operating cost through user fee and other means is still a distant goal. Interest from corpus fund is insufficient for meeting staff salary. Some specific direction towards utilising land assets for cross-subsidisation of health care. NGO introduces new projects for sustainability

The above analysis of the qualitative assessment of sustainability on the basis of positive and negative factors observed on a Five- point scale reveals the following. The average score is 4.25, which is sufficiently higher than overall average of 3.0. This implies that the organisation is located somewhat above the middle of pathway to sustainability and needs to concentrate its strategies on the development of some of the instruments vigorously.

Strategisation

The above assessment can be strategised by the following SWOT matrix, which can be used to devise the optimum management strategy. The present report contains only the most relevant components of the matrix.

The analysis shows about the fact that there is sufficient strength in the organisation to achieve sustainability. The optimum strategy should be one, which extracts maximum opportunities on the basis of the strengths and minimises the threats. In this situation, the optimum strategy should be focusing in the direction of extracting opportunities on the basis of these strengths and minimising the threats to continue the NGO health programmes.

Strengths	**Weaknesses**
• Physical infrastructure (Hospital building, land assets, vehicle etc.) • Dynamic project management team and NGO leadership • Experience in working with community (especially women groups) for social action and holistic development of the tribes • Dedicated group of Village level health workers and health services promoters • Strong interest in sustaining health care benefits • Established two hospitals in remote and populated villages	• Drive to mobilise internal resources needs more emphasis • Operational management decision is mostly centralised and ad hoc • Too much emphasis on preventive and promotive aspect but lack emphasis on linking health care benefits with other community programmes of the government and of the NGO • Technical training is very much a need for grassroots health workers with emphasis on curative health care for emergency and at risk cases
Opportunities	**Threats**
• Huge unmet need for MCH care • Leadership role in networking with other NGOs in the region and co-ordination with Panchayat raj institutions (PRIs) • Strong ongoing projects on variety of community projects in social development • Potential recognition in the state • Significant progress in knowledge and awareness among women creating potential demand for services • Interest of donor agencies in 'health and family welfare sector reform , HIV/AIDS awareness projects, women empowerment for reproductive health care in the state • Accumulated knowledge and skills gained from the technical assistance under PVOH-II project • Good community response to SM drive towards sustainability • Scaling up of activities makes the NGO initiatives provide better management in a more challenging manner	• Disadvantaged social condition and poor compensation threatening low retention of village level health workers and professional staff • No possibility of extension of PVOH-II grants • Compensation of private health care providers • Community's poor paying capacity on health care • Overloaded with external funding projects for social development dilutes purpose of attention for MCH care for the poor and needy • No linkages established with PRIs and other NGOs to avail external co-operation for organisational co-ordination

BHORUKA CHARITABLE TRUST (BCT)

Under the PVOH-II project in the name of 'Comprehensive Rural Health Development' project BCT covers 40 villages having the target population of 50,000. Female Health Volunteers (FHV), Mobile Medical Units (MMU), Health Posts, Hospital building for curative, referral and emergency clinical services, institutional networking are some of the key strategies adopted by the NGO to provide community health activities during the project life.

BCT is a corporate NGO backed by Bhoruka Group of companies, a sister concern of Transport Corporation of India (TCI). Provision of curative health care facilities is the key objective of the health team of BCT. Financial backing in the form of charity is the key source of corpus for the organisation. However, project implementation strategies incorporate community participation as the key to achieve programmatic achievement in the present project.

Strategies on Sustainability

Involvement of women community in the process of organisation of *Mahila Mandals* for health education awareness, income generation, and women empowerment to develop leadership quality among them is the key community mobilisation strategies adopted by the society. This sort of awareness generation integrated with income generation and women empowerment related mass mobilisation is considered to be a designed approach of the organisation to achieve sustainability.

Quality health care at the doorstep of the community is a surer test for increasing the demand at the grassroots set up is adequately met by the NGO during the life of the project. For sustaining benefits of project activities and health services delivery the organisational strategic focus was limited to the delivery of project specific health care services through the organisation's well-constructed Rural Hospital, Mobile Medical Unit and Rural Health posts. The cost recovery mechanism would be introduced through the introduction of user fee, community financing and community contribution mechanisms.

The government health infrastructure is situated at far distance from the project area. This is the reason for which, after the project period the linking with of the existing government system is not the priority of the NGO, but looking for more projects to continue the ongoing activities under a different name is the classical understanding of looking into the issue of sustainability. The community dependency on NGO system is no way different from that of depending on the government system other than the delivery of quality care at the doorstep. This is probably the spirit of voluntary action, which can be sustainable for creating community involvement in health development.

Accordingly, it was decided that all health related activities under the existing PVOH-II project would continue through the MMUs visit to project villages and at the referral health posts with the introduction of user fee accepted to the local community. Apparently this seems to be a prudent step because with a delayed approach to sustainability drive the NGO should be very cautious about the constraints before defining its future strategies.

During the life of the project implementation, BCT never considered sustainability as an issue that would affect the programmatic benefits to the local community. Probably, therefore the organisational strategic focus was limited to the delivery of project specific health care services through the organisation's well-constructed Rural Hospital and Referral Health posts.

All the agenda of community participation, women empowerment, capacity building of *Mahila Mandals* remained limited to project specific strategies for the effective management of project to deliver quality health care. But not leading to the strengthening or operationalisation of linkages with existing government system in the project area. Co-ordination with government system is limited to the frontline workers for completing the targets of immunisation coverage, distribution of family planning aids, IFA tablets etc.

Another strategy for sustainability adopted by BCT is to train the RMPs in the area of operation. Even training of TBAs is designed into the project operations for the expansion of outreach coverage and benefiting the targeted population within the project period. After which the role of NGO is completely unaware of the area situation unless and until it gets another project these activities can never been addressed or even been discussed. This is explaining the lack of vision of the NGO leader in fulfilling its social commitment instead of concentrating on its business commitment to the donor. This is opposed to the NGO effectiveness in achieving health care sustainability.

The commonly accepted fact for the local community at the project villages is that BCT is providing free and charity health care services out of the support it receives from its parent organisation- TCI. This is reflected in the community's identification that, '*The Seth- the owner would help us in our difficult time even after the closure of project life*'. Further no one in the community is aware that the project will be ended by the year 1997. Therefore, the provision of continuity of health care services at the free of cost would continue even after this period. Such a perception of community is a matter of concern, which clarifies further that charity driven social action is hardly having any possibility for sustainability. Unless the NGO modifies its strategy to address these issues it is premature to discuss its potential position on the road to sustain the benefits of health care to the local population.

Within the three-tier system of PVOH-II project, there have been some attempts to create continuity in services although there are various concern areas too, both of which are discussed under the heading of following instruments of assessing sustainability.

Contextual Factors

The major contextual factors affecting the sustainability of the PVOH-II project is discussed according to their impact on NGO management strategies.

The favourable factors are

Community Need

The NGO has been successful to a large extent in raising awareness among the women community in the project area. However, effective awareness also generates effective demand for health care. The health status of women and children of the poorer section is still remarkably low and miserable and the fact remains valid that community care in public health delivery system is still far from being able to address the raising demand on its own.

Community Response

The NGO effort in mobilising community response received remarkable support in the form of its involvement in awareness creation through a series of meetings with *mahila mandals*. As a result of which health posts were created by the women groups to function as a referral link between the community and the rural hospital of the organisation. The organisation also receives substantial response from different community groups in terms of association of local community development activities.

Other supporting projects

The major strength of the organisation lies on its focus and approaches on social welfare activities through the rural development. Community development projects relating to the improvement of social-economic situation, primary education, extension of non-formal education to girl children, management of natural resources, soil and water conservation, and water supply encourages the project team to exchange respective experiences and co-ordinate implementation problems for effective implementation in the project villages. A tremendous scope for inter-sectoral action through the convergence of inter-project co-operation is very much evident.

Major unfavourable factors

Cessation of PVOH-II grant

The MOHFW and USAID support almost 75% of the total project outlay. This cost takes care of total non-recurring and recurring cost of the project. This was a sizeable support, which once stopped, could pose substantial threat to sustainability.

Poor paying capacity of the Community

Resource mobilisation through increased user fee or any other direct mechanism is difficult due to three basic reasons; the target population is extremely poor, and a sudden increase in existing or application of new charges would generate some sort of resistance among the community, and the community perception for the acceptance of availing free services by the charitable trust. These facts make it more difficult to ensure sustainability.

Irregularities of Female health Volunteers

FHVs remain absence at the time of agricultural cultivation in which period the activity gets affected in the respective villages. In case of unmarried members the possibility of drop out is maximum due to their marriage or for having alternate opportunity. Even the threat of the closure of project support brings more uncertainty to the life security for these FHVs, discourages them to concentrate their activities in the usual spirit.

Referral Centre

A specific area of concern has been the high turnover of doctors and the absence of a lady doctor. Since for the last consecutive years, a number of doctors have left the organisation despite of the provision for a higher salary than the PVOH-II project offers.

Mobile Unit

The management of BCT is very much interested in supporting the ongoing MMUs provided it gets adequate assistance in the form of regular financial support from the TCI group, increase in cost of health delivery services and exploring avenue for further funding through new projects. This understanding and approach may be a possible threat to the sustainability.

Health Posts

Lack of male involvement in the PVOH-II activities at the grassroots level ignored the male members' possibility of consideration for support to the continuity of 'Health Posts' in the respective villages. Even though the women community expressed the relevance of continuity of these health posts, but due to lack of decision making power, their voice have hardly any say in the continuity of these 'Health Posts'. Management strategy at the BCT is very much concerned about this issue.

Operational Factors

Favourable Operational Factors

- The FHVs are found to be the real strength of the project. They are the link between target population in the community and the health services of the NGO. With low salary they are serving the organisation for the benefit of local community in the respective villages.
- Over the project period, there has been a significant achievement in skill building and expertise among the managerial team in creating a critical mass of skilled human resources. In general female members from a village is provided the opportunity to work in the organisation at the field level to ensure effective monitoring, regularity of health services concerning women and children, recognition in the village community and contributing to family income.
- The hospital building of the NGO serves as a referral centre, Rural resource centre and a centre for health education resources with having out-door and in-door facility for the clinical care. The building and other assets in the hospital determine the NGO's confidence to continue its activities.
- The decision for continuing the health services was a necessary step to maintain the availability of quality health care to the village community after the closure of project period, is a strategy in support of approaching sustainability.

Major unfavourable aspects associated with the operational factors

- The programme focused mostly on promotive and curative care. The demand for continuity of good quality of care has been raising as a consequence of increased awareness, but BCT is not sufficiently ready to deal with the rising demand to continue its activities as it was providing during the project period.
- The major potentials of resource generation were remaining largely untapped. The *Mahila Mandals*, and FHVs was yet to

receive a definite direction and guidance for owning the project. Different village based project units of the organisation could be used in linking health care with income generation activities, economic benefit programmes of the government etc. There is a long way to go to achieve perceptible results in this direction.

- Integration of health care activities required to be addressed with the existing facilities of rural development activities of the NGO. Management strategy for focusing on the requirement of multi - sectoral projects diverted the organisational attention in supporting an integrated manner of programme implementation, which resulted in the missing link of the synergistic effect for continuity of health services.
- The strategy on training was ad hoc, and to some extent, biased. While the top managerial staff (Project Director, Co-ordinator, MOs) attended almost all the project related training programmes, and exposure to other NGO experiences. But the supervisory staff and FHVs received hardly any training and exposure input.
- The role of Traditional Birth Attendants (TBA) is extremely important to sustain the activities and its impact. It was surprising to see that this potential instrument of self-sufficiency was never explored effectively e.g. in the form of sharing of responsibilities and organisation and training of new TBAs etc. Also the training of RMPs within the project life could not created much impact other than referring a few cases of emergency for curative care.

Leadership Factors

Major favourable aspects with respect to the leadership factors

- Interest to sustain the most essential and primary ingredient for sustainability. The interaction with Project Director, Project Co-ordinator and Medical officer of the NGO, reflected the willingness of the organisation to sustain the health care with the introduction of necessary community financing mechanism.
- Project Director manages other community development projects of the NGO such as; water sanitation, primary education, water supply and environment protection, rural development activities and networking and co-ordination with other NGOs in the state. Organisation's secretary is the guiding motivation for promoting sustainability.

Major unfavourable factors are

- There is evidential support for the lack of long-term vision and planning about resource mobilisation and utilisation of community support for sustaining the benefits of the project activities.
- The organisation needs to have more effective participation of women in the leadership at all levels of functionaries instead of utilising them at the grassroots level health activities.
- Networking and co-ordination of activities are limited to the exchange of experience sharing and participation in national and internal conferences and seminars and state level consortium on social action forum for promoting corporate social responsibility in community development. But it has hardly made any effort to link institutions of Panchayats at the village, block or at the district levels. This suffered an adequate value addition to the component of decentralised planning and decision making involving health care decentralisation. Sustainability of health care benefits is supposed to be the outcome of equal responsibility in the form of people's participation and contribution of all the actors of social development. This fact was highly neglected by the NGO management during its project period.

These favourable and unfavourable factors taken together create a sustainability profile of the organisation. These also help to identify the status of the social instruments discussed in literature review on 'Instruments of Sustainability'. The following table shows a relative scoring of each of the relevant instruments with respect to the responsible factors discussed above.

BHORUKA CHARITABLE TRUST

Qualitative Assessment of Sustainability

[On the basis of positive and negative Factors observed on a Five point scale]

(1-5 scale: 1=very poor, 5=very strong)

Instrument	*Scoring*	*Positive Factors*	*Negative Factors*
Need-based Project	3	Targeted poorer women and children for comprehensive rural health development project on primary education, school health education, curative health care with suitability of community need assessment	Need for curative, preventive and promotive services to provide holistic health care is not effectively addresses through establishing linkage with other projects

(*Contd...*)

Quality of service	2	Medico dominated, curative intervention with committed group of village level health workers	Insufficient training and exposure to the health workers, specialised training on quality of care needs improvement
Community Organizations	3	Focus on formation of *Mahila Mandals* and self-help groups. Attempt to utilise these groups in generating internal resources. Good experience in working with the community	Not clear direction to the *Mahila Mandals* in planning resources. The units have long way to go to act independently in health care activities. No co-ordination established with panchayat system through these community organisations
Accumulated Assets	3	Completed the main project hospital building by own initiative. The hospital land was added to total asset	No systematic plan to recover the maintenance of assets. This asset still remains untapped for generating resources for health care
Resource Manager	3	Dynamic project leadership. Clarity of organisational mission. Good number of exposure to training workshops and sharing events. Significant interest in sustainability	Centralised decision-making process. Management decisions are mostly ad hoc and individual-based. Needs consciousness about cost effectiveness. Potential linkages with other projects is largely untapped
Resource Generator	1	Substantial effort in income generating activities and linking it with self-help initiatives. User fee charged for ambulatory and curative care. Great potential in utilising land assets to subsidise health care activities	Recovery of operating cost through user fee and other means is still a distant goal. Interest from corpus fund is insufficient for meeting staff salary. No specific direction towards utilising land assets for cross-subsidisation of health care

The above analysis of the qualitative assessment of sustainability on the basis of positive and negative factors observed on a Five- point scale reveals the following. The average score observed is 2.0, which is less than overall average of 3.0. This may be attributed to the fact that some of the major instruments are still not developed. This implies that the organisation is located somewhat in the lower level of pathway to sustainability and needs to concentrate on the development of some of the instruments vigorously.

Strategisation

The above assessment can be strategised by the following SWOT matrix, which can be used to devise the optimum management strategy. The present report contains only the most relevant components of the matrix.

Strengths	**Weaknesses**
• Physical infrastructure (Hospital building, land assets, vehicle etc.) • Dynamic project leadership • Experience in working with community (especially women groups) for social action • Dedicated group of female health volunteers	• Drive to mobilise internal resources needs more emphasis • Operational management decision is mostly centralised and ad hoc, and top-down • Too much emphasis on curative aspect but lack emphasis on linking benefits from other

(Contd...)

• Strong interest in sustaining benefits • Established fully equipped hospital in outreach populated village • Requisite emphasise on curative health intervention through provision of quality health care services	community programmes of the government and of the NGO • Technical training is very much a need for grassroots health workers • Absence of Women leadership in organisation • Too much of community dependency on charity driven project management strategy
Opportunities • Huge unmet need for MCH care • Leadership role in networking with other NGOs in the region, women organisations and co-ordination with Panchayat raj institutions (PRIs) • Strong ongoing project activities on community development • Potential recognition in the corporate social responsibility forum in the state • Significant progress in knowledge and awareness among women creating potential demand for services • Interest of donor agencies support and capacity in receiving more projects in health & family welfare sector • Accumulated knowledge and skills gained from the technical assistance under PVOH-II project • Corporate backing makes the NGO initiatives provide better management of health care	**Threats** • Social condition and poor compensation threatening low retention of village level health workers and high turnover of professional staff • No possibility of extension of PVOH-II grants • Compensation of private health care providers • Community's poor paying capacity on health care • No anticipated external fund for this purpose • No linkages established with PRIs and other NGOs to avail external co-operation for organisational co-ordination • Poor community response to BCT drive towards sustainability • No possible cooperation for continuity of health posts

The optimum strategy should be one, which extracts maximum opportunities on the basis of the strengths and minimises the threats. The strategy for BCT is understood to be based on its drive towards sustainability, a part of which was discussed before this analysis. The analysis found that the effort for sustainability comes out of genuine interest of the top management in the form of reactive and competitive instead of a clear cut strategic planning and designing from the day one of the project implementation.

Bal Rashmi Society

BRS is having a team of well-trained, experienced and devoted workers who function at the grassroots level for child development, rehabilitation, education and health care activities. The NGO is one of the 32 projects funded under PVOH-I scheme in January, 1987 which ended in September 1990. The findings of the PVOH-I experiences showed that this NGO had implemented the project successfully in the rural outreach areas of Bassi *tehsil* in Jaipur district.

Visit to the rural health centre located in a remote village in Lalgarh, which was established under PVOH-I revealed the following observations:

- The local health care is addressed through this health centre with the attendance of 50-60% patients per day.
- The local community apprised the services rendered by the society as per the need and emergence of the area situation.
- Infect the organisation has been able to retain all the staff meeting within the expenses from the resources mobilised from various sources including local donations and to some extent through volunteered services.

Under the present project the NGO has covered a total of 149 villages covering a population of 91609 (as per 1981 census) where in SC/ST population was reported to be 50%. Project villages of Jamwa Ramgarh *tehsil* of Jaipur district, which is 28 kms away from Jaipur district and about 30 kms from the nearest PHC Banpurkalan, where one of the government health care units functioning in the area. The entire area is not conveniently approachable considering the location and the scatteredness of the villages. One has to cover a distance about 50-60 kms to reach the farthest village of the project area. Keeping in view the distance, scattered locations of villages in Jamwa Ramgarh *tehsil* and other problems relating to the implementation of the project, it was decided with the consent of the Chief Medical Officer to cover only 107 villages from Jamwa Ramgarh *tehsil* and 42 villages from Bassi *tehsil* near Khedi. This was the origin of government-NGO co-operation since the beginning of PVOH-II project of the society.

Capacity of NGO Effectiveness

In the year 1983, BRS stepped into the field of health for the needy rural community. In the beginning 14 villages were taken up on the strong demand of local people where medical and health care facilities were not available. The programme was carried out in collaboration with GOI under PVOH-I scheme covering a population of 40,000 in 83 villages of Bassi *tehsil* in Jaipur district. One MCH hospital and five sub-centres were built up at Lalgarh and in the adjoining area. People had low mortality and means of communication and transport were very limited. Lalgarh hospital, is the rural research centre, which is equipped with 15 beds with modern diagnostic facilities like x-ray, Pathological laboratory and qualified doctors and paramedical staff.

Under the PVOH-II project, a massive health programme was undertaken by the society in the name of '*Gramin Swasthya Sewa*' in April 1992. The programme through two sub-centres, two mobile units and one nutrition centre for malnourished children covers 91,000 population. Working in the mids of filth and squalor of slums and in rural areas among people belonging to neglected sections of the community, BRS is confronted with problem of ill health, malnutrition and death at every step. The programme has four major aspects such as;

- Health education, preventive and curative measures
- Hospital and health sub-centres and training of VLHWs (Village Level Health Workers)

The society provided package of MCH and family welfare services, immunisation to pregnant mothers and children, nutritional support to malnourished children of less than 6 years of age, preventive and curative health services at the centre and at the doorsteps of the people. In order to ensure sustainability the awareness camps, meetings, films shows and puppet shows were organised in the project area to educate people about personal health and hygiene, home and environment sanitation, immunisation, safe drinking water, prevention and cure of common diseases. Mahila Vikas Mandals have also been an effective medium for organising such health programmes.

Mobile Services

In remote villages of Jamwa Ramgarh and Bassi Tehsils where communication was difficult and people were unable to get medical facilities; Bal Rashmi regularly sends two mobile vans with doctors and pra-medical staff to cover six to eight villages every day on a weekly basis. Our mobile units covered 86 villages and provided treatment at the doorsteps to pregnant women, children, TB patients, eye care-patients as reported by BRS.

Maternal and Child Health Services

Registration of pregnancy cases through VHWs and mutil-purpose (Females), pre-natal care, immuniztion of pregnant women, iron and folic acid prophylactics against nutritional anaemia in mothers and children, post-natal care of women and child through trained MPW (F) and Dais, obstetric services by doctors at the health centre and, if necessary, at the doorstep, growth monitoring and immunisation of children etc. were provided. Nutritional aid was provided to poor families in the form of bulgur and oil on a regular basis. Training of Rural Health workers and Rural Sanitary workers is also organised.

Family Planning

Poor rural people, especially SCs and STs and other backward communities in the project area have large families, which is one of the main reasons for their poverty. Bal Rashmi through its field staff, doctors and extension education team motivates and mobilises eligible couples to adopt temporary family planning methods, for birth spacing between children and also permanent measures when necessary. Condoms, oral pills etc. are supplied to the eligible couple on a regular basis. The society workers accompany and assist the motivated women for sterilisation to urban hospitals in mobile vans.

The medical and health department of Government of Rajasthan has been extremely helpful in collaborating with the NGO in family planning and health related activities by ensuring regular supply of medicines, condoms and other family planning aids and providing sterilisation services to women motivated by the organisation.

Eye Care - In addition to the regular health programme the organisation was also conducting eye camps in the project villages at periodic intervals. To provide an example regarding the total number of patients served under 40 eye camps in which 15364 persons were treated for eye ailments and 1226 for cataract, glaucoma etc.

Health Education programme – Keeping in view of the organisations capacity in the field of family welfare the society has undertaken a population education programme in Bassi and Jamwa Ramgarh *tehsil* of Jaipur district. The activities covered under this programme were to educate adolescent girls about physiology, menstruation, pregnancy, reproductive health, contraceptive choice etc to educate pregnant women about pre-natal and post-natal care, STD/HIV reproductive morbidity, abortion and contraceptive choice for spacing and permanent birth control.

Strategies on Sustainability

Organisation of *Mahila Mandals* for income generation, women empowerment and to develop leadership quality among them is the key community mobilisation strategies adopted by the society. This sort of awareness generation integrated with income generation and women empowerment strategy is considered to be a permanent resource for the organisation to promote sustainability.

Another strategy for sustainability adopted by BRS is to cut the size of the area of operation. Accordingly, it was decided that all health related activities under the existing PVOH-II project would continue only in the two villages where the NGO is having a very good set-up of health infrastructure. Whereas the remaining of the project area would receive some sort of support services such as; health awareness, co-ordination with government functionaries after the closure of the external support to the project. Apparently this seems to be a prudent step because with a delayed approach to sustainability drive the NGO should be very cautious about the constraints before defining its future strategies.

During the life of the project implementation, BRS never considered sustainability as an issue that would affect the programmatic benefits to the local community. Probably, therefore the organisational strategic focus was limited to the delivery of project specific health care services through the organisation's well-constructed Rural Hospitals and Rural Health Centres. These hospitals are situated within the proximity, next to the government sub-centre. BRS has not initiated any co-ordination measure to link with the functioning of government sub-centres instead of concentrated on the delivery of health services. This is the reason after the tenure of project period functioning of the existing system is not the priority of the NGO but looking for more projects to continue the ongoing activities under a different project with a new name. The community dependency on NGO system is no way different from that of depending on the government system other than the delivery of quality care at the doorstep. This is not the spirit of voluntary action, which can be sustainable for creating community involvement in health development.

All the agenda of community participation, women empowerment, capacity building of *Mahila Mandals* remained limited to project specific strategies for the effective management of project to deliver quality health care. But not leading to the strengthening or operationalisation of existing government system in the project area. Co-ordination with government system is limited to the frontline workers for completing the targets of immunisation coverage, distribution of family planning aids, IFA tablets etc. Even training of TBAs is designed into the project operations for the expansion of outreach coverage and benefiting the targeted population within the project period. After which the role of NGO is completely unaware of the area situation unless and until it gets another project these activities can never been addressed or even been discussed. This is explaining the lack of vision of the NGO leader in fulfilling its social commitment instead of concentrating on its business commitment to the donor. This is opposed to the NGO effectiveness in achieving health care sustainability.

Contextual Factors

The major contextual factors affecting the sustainability of the PVOH-II project is discussed according to their impact on NGO management.

The favourable factors are

Community Need

The NGO has been successful to a large extent in raising awareness among the women community in the project area. However, effective awareness also generates effective demand for health care. The health status of women and children of the poorer section is still remarkably low and the fact remains valid that community care in public health delivery system is still far from being able to address the raising demand on its own.

Community Response

The NGO effort in mobilising community response received remarkable support from the area. Community awareness is created through a series of meetings with *mahila mandals*. As a result of which health posts were created by the women groups to function as a link between the community and the Rural hospital of the organisation. The organisation also receives substantial response from different community groups in terms of donation to their corpus fund.

Other supporting projects

The major strength of the organisation lies on its focus and approaches on child welfare activities through its Children's Homes. The village health workers and mahila mandals function as a great support for spreading messages of health awareness among children and the community.

Major unfavourable factors

Cessation of PVOH-II grant

The MOHFW and USAID support almost 75% of the total project outlay. This cost takes care of total non-recurring and recurring cost of the project. This was a sizeable support, which once stopped, could pose substantial threat to sustainability.

Poor paying capacity of the Community

Resource mobilisation through increased user fee or any other direct mechanism is difficult due to two basic reasons; the target population is extremely poor, and a sudden increase in existing or application of new charges would generate some sort of resistance among the community.

Irregularities of Village level health workers

VLHWs remain absence at the time of agricultural cultivation in which period the activity gets affected in the respective villages. In case of unmarried members the possibility of drop out is maximum due to their marriage or for having alternate opportunity.

Operational Factors

- The VLHWs are found to be the real strength of the project. They are the link between target population in the community and the health services of the NGO. With low salary they are serving the organisation for the benefit of local community in the respective villages.
- Over the project period, there has been a significant achievement in skill building and expertise among the managerial team in creating a critical mass of skilled human resources. In general both members from a family is provided the opportunity to work in the organisation at the field level to ensure effective monitoring, regularity of services, recognition in the village community and contributing to family income of the couple.
- Two hospital buildings of the NGO serves as a referral centre, Rural research centre and a centre for health education resource with having out-door and in-door facility for the clinical care. The building and other assets in the hospital determine the NGO's confidence to continue its activities.
- The decision for scaling down of activities was a necessary step to maintain the quality of programme in continuing the hospital-based activities after the closure of project period.

Major unfavourable aspects associated with the operational factors

- The programme focused only on promotive and curative care. The demand for continuity of good quality of care has been raising as a consequence of increased awareness, but BRS is not sufficiently ready to deal with the rising demand to continue its activities as in the case of project period.
- The major potentials of resource generation were remaining largely untapped. The *Mahila Mandals* was yet to receive a definite direction and guidance for owning the project. Different village based units of the organisation could be used in linking health care with income generation activities, economic benefit programmes

of the government etc. There is a long way to go to achieve perceptible results in this direction.

- Integration of health care activities required to be addressed with the existing facilities of rural development activities of the NGO. Management strategy for focusing on the requirement of multi - sectoral projects diverted the organisational attention in supporting an integrated manner of programme implementation, which resulted in the missing link of the synergistic effect for continuity of health services.
- The strategy on training was ad hoc, and to some extent, biased. While the top managerial staff (Project Director, Co-ordinator, MOs) attended almost all the project related training programmes, and exposure to other NGO experiences. But the supervisory staff and FHVs received hardly any training and exposure input.
- The role of Traditional Birth Attendants (TBA) is extremely important to sustain the activities and its impact. It was surprising to see that this potential instrument of self-sufficiency was never explored effectively e.g. in the form of sharing of responsibilities and organisation and training of new TBAs etc. Also the training of RMPs within the project life could not created much impact other than referring a few cases of emergency for curative care.

Leadership Factors

Favourable factors

- Interest to sustain the most essential and primary ingredient for sustainability. The interaction with Programme Co-ordinator and Medical officer of the NGO, reflected the willingness of the organisation to sustain the health care benefits to the project area community.
- Programme Co-ordinator manages other community development projects of the NGO such as; Rehabilitation, care and welfare of the children, women empowerment, community advocacy, networking and co-ordination of social action involving community action. Organisation's secretary is the guiding force for promoting sustainability.

Unfavourable factors

- There is evidential support for the lack of long-term vision and planning about resource mobilisation and utilisation of community support for sustaining the benefits of the project activities.

Unilateral decisions are always taken with a top-down control mechanism. Though the leadership quality is dynamic, it needs encouraging coherence, participatory planning and decentralised decision making for effective management strategies.

- The organisation needs to have more effective participation of women in the leadership at all levels of functionaries.
- Networking and co-ordination of activities are limited to the exchange of experience sharing and participation in national and internal conferences and seminars and state level consortium on social action forum for advocating gender equality in development etc. But it has hardly made any effort to link institutions of Panchayats at the village, block or at the district levels. This suffered an adequate value addition to the component of decentralised planning and decision making involving health care decentralisation. Sustainability of health care benefits is the equal responsibility and concern of all the actors of development in democratic decentralisation. This fact was highly neglected by the NGO management during its project period.

These favourable and unfavourable factors taken together create a sustainability profile of the NGO. These also help to identify the status of the social instruments discussed in literature review on 'Instruments of Sustainability'. The following table shows a relative scoring of each of the relevant instruments with respect to the responsible factors discussed above.

BAL RASHMI SOCIETY

Qualitative Assessment of Sustainability

[On the basis of positive and negative Factors observed on a Five point scale]

(1-5 scale: 1=very poor, 5=very strong)

Instrument	*Scoring*	*Positive Factors*	*Negative Factors*
Need-based Project	4	Targeted poorer women and children for comprehensive child development projects on school health education, curative health care with suitability of community need assessment	Need for curative, preventive and promotive services to provide holistic health care is not effectively addresses
Quality of service	2	Medico dominated, curative intervention with committed group of village level health workers	Insufficient training and exposure to the health workers, specialised training on quality of care needs improvement

(Contd...)

Community Organizations	3	Focus on formation of *Mahila Mandals* and self-help groups. Attempt to utilise these groups in generating internal resources. Good experience in working with the community	Not clear direction to the *Mahila Mandals* in planning resources. The units have long way to go to act independently in health care activities. No co-ordination established with panchayat system through these community organisations
Accumulated Assets	4	Completed the main project hospital building by own initiative. The hospital land was added to total asset	No systematic plan to recover the maintenance of assets. This asset still remains untapped for generating resources for health care
Resource Manager	3	Dynamic project leadership. Clarity of organisational mission. Good number of exposure to training workshops and sharing events. Significant interest in sustainability	Centralised decision-making process. Management decisions are mostly ad hoc and individual-based. Needs consciousness about cost effectiveness. Potential linkages with other projects is largely untapped
Resource Generator	3	Substantial effort in income generating activities and linking it with self-help initiatives. User fee charged for ambulatory and curative care. Great potential in utilising land assets to subsidise health care activities	Recovery of operating cost through user fee and other means is still a distant goal. Interest from corpus fund is insufficient for meeting staff salary. No specific direction towards utilising land assets for cross-subsidisation of health care

The above analysis of the qualitative assessment of sustainability on the basis of positive and negative factors observed on a Five- point scale reveals the following. The average score observed is 3.1, which is slightly higher than overall average of 3.0. This implies that the organisation is located somewhat in the middle of pathway to sustainability and needs to concentrate on the development of some of the instruments vigorously.

Strategisation

The above assessment can be strategized by the following SWOT matrix, which can be used to devise the optimum management strategy. The present report contains only the most relevant components of the matrix.

Strengths	**Weaknesses**
• Physical infrastructure (Hospital building, land assets, vehicle etc.) • Dynamic project leadership • Experience in working with community (especially women groups) for social action • Dedicated group of Village level health workers • Strong interest in sustaining benefits • Established two hospitals in outreach populated villages	• Drive to mobilise internal resources needs more emphasis • Operational management decision is mostly centralised and ad hoc • Too much emphasis on curative aspect but lack emphasis on linking benefits from other community programmes of the government and of the NGO • Technical training is very much a need for grassroots health workers

(Contd...)

Opportunities	**Threats**
• Huge unmet need for MCH care • Leadership role in networking with other NGOs in the region and co-ordination with Panchayat raj institutions (PRIs) • Strong ongoing project on child welfare • Potential recognition in the state • Significant progress in knowledge and awareness among women creating potential demand for services • Interest of donor agencies in 'health and family welfare sector reform in the state • Accumulated knowledge and skills gained from the technical assistance under PVOH-II project • Good community response to BRS drive towards sustainability • Scaling down of activities makes the NGO initiatives provide better management more feasible	• Social condition and poor compensation threatening low retention of village level health workers • No possibility of extension of PVOH-II grants • Compensation of private health care providers • Community's poor paying capacity on health care • No anticipated external fund for this purpose • No linkages established with PRIs and other NGOs to avail external co-operation for organisational coordination

The optimum strategy should be one, which extracts maximum opportunities on the basis of the strengths and minimises the threats. The strategy for Bal Rashmi Society is understood to be based on its drive towards sustainability a part of which was discussed before this analysis. The analysis found that the effort for sustainability comes out of genuine interest of the top management in the form of reactive and competitive instead of a clear cut strategic planning and designing from the day one of the project implementation.

Discussion on Sustainability

The overall project management strategy of the NGOs should have extended to avail the maximum of Government co-operation to attain and sustain the basic continuity of health care benefits to the local community by effective linkages with the institutions of village-panchayts, creating awareness about various government and non-government schemes aiming at the economic benefits of the local community, linking health activities to the formulation of women self-help groups through initiating micro-credit for the rural poor. These benefits make the local community more responsive and responsible to concern the sustainability of the health care benefits to them, which was introduced through the project for a limited period.

But the NGO initiative, in general is limited to the delivery of health care with the involvement of its village based health team, even the staff salary is a big question before the management after the completion of the project period. Big infrastructure in the village was not the priority but the operationalisation of health services is the need for the local community. This was the proposition of sustainability by the donor. Role of NGOs seems to be limited to function as a service delivery contractor instead of emerging out as an agent of social change to empower community to have the ownership in their health and development activity.

The analysis also identified several factors, which impede sustainability. They are discussed as follows:

- weak strategic planning which often only focused on a specific project supported by the organisation rather than linking the overall NGO support,
- management systems which were stronger at the field project level than for the NGO itself,
- information collected was not used for planning and monitoring,
- no formal social marketing function and even resource mobilisation opportunities was present in the project management system i.e. linking the beneficiaries to the ongoing economic benefit programmes in the project area is very much absent,
- NGO leadership at the field level are either changed frequently or transferred in most cases affects the project team to mingle with new style of leadership,
- few of the NGOs had a business orientation,
- many NGOs relied on village based volunteers to both lead and manage the day-to-day operations of the organisation,
- program costs were rarely compared with the anticipated surplus of a planned income generating activity (IGA); therefore it was not possible to determine, in advance, whether the IGA would be able to subsidise the intended program,
- fees for services typically covered the operating costs of a NGO, but were not enough to cover routine maintenance and capital improvements
- NGOs rarely calculated inflation into the price of the family planning commodities or drugs they sold,
- none of the NGOs had any reserves, nor were they generating any surplus which could be used to develop reserves necessary to support such organisations in an unstable economy,

- local resource mobilisation efforts were not successful at generating significant income,
- absence of appropriate government co-ordination at the field level, absence of linkage with the existing government system and the lack of involvement of PRIs in the local level are key weaknesses observed in the strategies common to all these NGO project management.

In view of these general findings, the following measures are necessary for sustaining programmatic effectiveness:

- Develop the NGOs' strategic planning capabilities including linking planned activities with their associated costs provide training on how to use information, especially financial and linking the marketing information, for planning and monitoring to develop the resource mobilisation capabilities of the NGOs including collecting and analysing resources mobilisation data and developing strategic plans adapt and expand project management and financial systems to serve the entire organisation.
- Identify approaches to lower program costs and deliver the services more efficiently provide leadership training for all levels of the organisation determine which revenue generating activities are appropriate for each NGO, including fees, local and international fundraising, government or community contributions, investments, and income generating activities.
- Provide technical assistance which is tailored to the specific revenue generating activities of each NGO including: developing fundraising approaches, pricing of services, and conducting feasibility studies link the information collected in this study with more complete service and management information to form a more comprehensive picture of NGO sustainability withdraw financial support slowly over the life of the donor supported project.
- Linking with local community organisations and institutions of panchayat system to avail maximum co-operation from the PRIs and ensure the involvement of local community in their benefits of health development activities. Handing over the responsibility of the functioning and management of local health problems to the local institutions through effective capacity building is the key to enhance sustainability.

This discussion leads to the lessons learned and strategic implications of the present study in understanding the key issues of sustainability, as emerged from three case-studies under the PVOH-II project in brief and their programmatic and policy implications for the major stakeholders and partners in health and social sector development. This is followed in the next chapter.

Chapter - VIII

Lessons Learned and Policy Implications

In this concluding chapter, an attempt is made to describe in nutshell the PVOH-II project and its various aspects, the key issues of sustainability as they emerged from three case-studies with lessons learned in brief and their programmatic and policy implications for NGOs, and the Panchayats as well as for the state and the central government within the context of International Donors.

Reflection on various factors affecting sustainability of non-governmental health care initiatives identified the following issues in the form of opportunities and challenges for further understanding of the practical situation in the state of Rajasthan. These issues, as identified from the findings of the case studies of three NGOs under PVOH-II project, further provided insight into the reflection are as follows. The strategic issues of government-NGOs co-operation under PVOH-II, state of GO-NGOs cooperation in Rajasthan, role of NGOs in decentralized health sector planning and status of non-governmental health care and health systems in the state of Rajasthan. The understanding of the processes involved in looking into the NGO strategies which was supported to address the issues of sustainability during the entire life of project management is the basis of the present discussion.

Present chapter further discusses the strategic implications for sustainability of non-governmental health care in the state of Rajasthan with specific reference to GO-NGO Collaboration in Health, NGO-Government Co-operation in Rajasthan, NGO Initiatives in Strengthening Issues of Women's Health in Rajasthan and GO-NGO Partnership in Health. In the end of the discussion, the study concludes with the policy implications for the Government of Rajasthan.

Overview of the Study Finding

The purpose of PVOH-II project intervention was to expand and improve basic and preventive health, family planning and nutrition services for the poor, by utilising and strengthening the private and voluntary sector. The three distinct components include a package of basic curative services and a package of preventive health services targeted at the poor and marginalised, and to strengthen NGO capacity for doing so. Little attention had been paid to the commercial sector, the focus being on the private and voluntary sector.

The foundation of PVOH-II falls into four major sections:

- Increase community action for health
- Improve community access to quality health care
- Promote self-sustaining outreach activities
- Build capacity of NGOs

The history of NGO experiences about PVOH-II revealed about the fact that this project supported 40 large NGOs and 91 small grants across the country. Even more NGOs had been selected from the states with an active and dynamic voluntary sector. The selection was done through advertisements in leading English newspapers and by word of mouth. The key criteria for selection was the ability to put up the mandatory 25% match, ability to include innovative strategies such as women's participation and show linkages with other development activities, indications of complementarily with GOI programmes, evidence of how the NGOs would sustain activities beyond the life of PVOH-II, and their working in remote, rural areas. Many of them were located in the backward districts.

On the subject of grants, two types of grants were supported in the PVOH-II. The first were outreach and these were NGOs with differing orientation, capability, competence and integrity. They were hospital-based NGOs, which had experience with service delivery but not outreach work, organisations having experience with integrated development programmes, but not experienced in health, and schools of social work. The emphasis of these grants was on training grassroots level workers to improve health education and community organisations, which was the fundamental basis of PVOH-II design, and improving the health status of mothers and children. The second set of grants were the Support Service grants, which were nine in all, these operated either within a state, or state-wide, or even in multi-state, as for example, Indian Institute of Health Management Research. One of the conditions was that they should have experience of working with NGOs, organisations with not only technical and managerial competence but also credibility of working with NGOs. This was an important factor in selecting these organisations. The purpose of this grant was to nurture small grassroots NGOs. There was variation in the kind of organisations that were supported – large federations of membership organisations, academic, research and training organisations, and management support organisations.

The Funding Profile of the project was as follows

Total Project Funding	:	$ 13.4 million
USAID Contribution	:	$ 10 million
GOI Contribution	:	$ 0.5 million
NGO Contribution	:	$ 2.9 million

The NGOs' cash contribution was $2.9 million, but the in-kind contribution had not been valued since it varied from one NGO to the other. The outreach grants size ranged from 5 lakh to 50 lakhs. The smaller and grassroots NGOs were supported for 2 to 3 years but the larger NGOs received support for 5 years. One of the lessons learned from this experience was that the life of a grant has to be long enough, as it is an important factor in developing NGO capacity. The support was for construction, vehicles, staff salaries, training of staff and providing health education material. The present research involves the study of the larger grassroots NGOs in the state of Rajasthan.

As per the profile of the grassroots NGOs, the project design emphasised innovativeness in proposals, somehow along the line, all projects were straight – jacketed into a three - tier service delivery system that followed the government system – grassroots workers, supported by middle level paramedical and then a medical or programme officer/ Co-ordinator at the head. Regardless of their orientation, NGOs had to follow this three-tier service delivery model, though they used their innovativeness to tackle some of the hurdles of this model.

The geographic focus of NGOs was enlarged regardless of their capability i.e., more villages were added to their intervention areas. Regarding interventions, NGOs used a mix of preventive and curative interventions, though not always a judicious mix. The curative interventions were visible and served as an immediate need, but they mostly overshadowed the preventive health aspects.

These strategies used by NGOs to increase community actions for health involved individuals, mostly women member from the community. Village level workers formed the crucial link between the community and the NGO. Their tasks varied from health education and motivation to community organisation. These cadres received substantial training inputs. However, the concept of training for grassroots workers in PVOH-II had some limitations – the training focussed on technical interventions, but their tasks involved communication, supporting and organising *mahila mandals* and talking to mothers, but they did not have the skills to serve them. That is why this component did not take off. These women continued to work as change agents within the community. The involvement of 2500 village level workers trained by NGOs as part of the PVOH-II project is a distinctive feature across the country. This accounted for approximately 500 village level health workers in the state of Rajasthan.

The second important strategy was ensuring the ability of NGOs to involve the community in the programmes – a key assumption of PVOH-II. There was wide variation in the kinds of NGOs that PVOH-II supported. Community participation requires more than goodwill. However, not all NGOs were able to achieve this successfully, as only one third of them were able to do so. Community participation was limited to working with groups, which were inactive, selection of village level workers (VLWs) in a majority of the NGOs.

A third strategy employed was to respond flexibly to community needs and priorities. PVOH-II supported more than just health, and this was its major strength. It was more in keeping with community priorities than preventive health care. Some NGOs had the skills to assess and address these priorities. There was a greater impact observed where this was done and certainly a promise of sustainability that interlined health with other community development programmes.

Finally, the strategy of leveraging for complimentary input to existed activities of the government. Large NGOs, that commanded diverse funding resources at the village level, creatively involved multi-sectoral programmes for communities. The other leveraging that the NGOs did was to withdraw on other Government of India supported schemes like DWACRA (Development of Women and Children in Rural Areas) and *Anganwadi*. PVOH-II did not support supplementary nutrition, but it was an important part of the programme. It was the fact for all NGOs that wherever they worked they met sure that the women and children of their communities got supplementary nutrition at the *Anganwadi* centres.

On the second major objective was to improve access to services, the NGOs should enabled to integrate traditional systems with western system of medicine but this did not happen, except for training TBAs in conducting safe deliveries. Training community volunteers as grassroots workers- this happened only where the NGOs did health education. Facilitating referral linkages for secondary and tertiary care was done with district hospitals.

All this helped to increase the geographical access to services. Thus PVOH-II harnessed the voluntary co-operation into a focussed MCH programme.

PVOH-II Organisational Structure/Fund Flow

Approval of Grants & Policy guidance

Monitoring Project Implementation

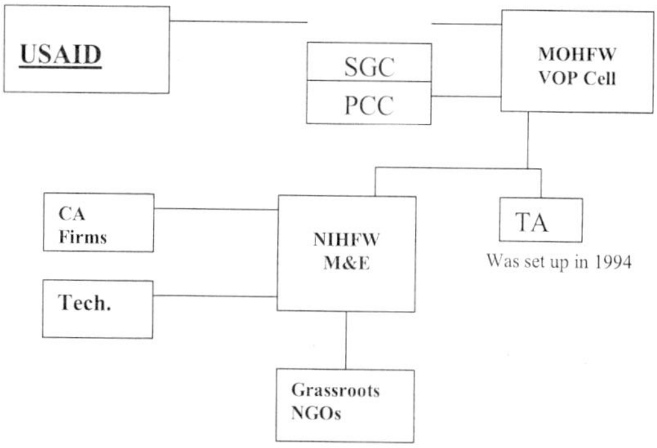

The organisational structure and fund-flow is discussed with the help of the above diagram. USAID and MOH&FW jointly implemented the project at the formulation level. Within MOH, an administrative cell called VOP (Voluntary Organisation Private) cell was supported by the technical arm called NIHFW (National Institute of Health & Family Welfare). There were two committees within the Ministry – the Special Grants Committee (SGC), chaired by the Joint Secretary was responsible for approval of grants and policy guidance to the project, and the Project Co-ordination Cell (PCC), which looked after the issue of monitoring and project implementation. The role of NIHFW was to provide monitoring and evaluation support to the grassroots NGOs. Financial monitoring of PVOH-II NGOs was taken care by a group of CA (Chartered Accountants) firms, which NIHFW contracted with. For technical assistance to the NGO project, initially, NIHFW was to contract organisations, but somehow this did not happen during the life of PVOH-II project. The monitoring support provided by NIHFW was not supportive, it was policing and not problem solving. In other words it was top-down rather than participatory. Fund releases to the NGOs depended on the recommendations of NIHFW and they were largely hampered sometimes because of real problems, and sometimes due to trivialities. In 1994 the Ministry and the USAID took the decision that the role of NIHFW would be terminated. They jointly set up the technical assistance unit (TAU) at Indian Institute of Health Management Research

(IIHMR)-Jaipur. The consultants, payment norms and scope of work were jointly co-ordinated by the ministry and USAID. The money released from VOP cell originally was on the basis of recommendation from NIHFW to the grassroots NGOs. After NIHFW's role was terminated, essentially there was no monitoring done. Therefore the NGOs feel this need of monitoring, is equally necessary as a part of technical assistance. Otherwise, PVOH-II did not have a chance to put it in place originally.

As part of the policy guidance, sustainability of NGO programmes remained as a major concern for USAID, the NGOs and the government at the time of recommendation of mid-term evaluation. However, working through the NGOs has itself been a learning experience and there is perceptible difference in dealing with NGOs now than before at the time of conceptualization of PVOH-II project, regarding the attitudinal change affecting government-NGO relationship and donor co-operation.

Strategic Implications from the Present Research

- Sustainability assumes a low priority, 'after thought' position in the NGOs project design and implementation process. Since the PVOH-II project was in its final stage when the present research began, this understanding is expected to provide less effect than the desired result. This fact strengthened the conviction that to have meaningful achievement in sustainability the NGO strategy has to become core concern since the designing of the project.
- However, the study has been successful in identifying the contextual factors behind sustainability. The most important factor regarding sustainability is the lack of long-run strategic vision among the project leaders. For example a significant bias in developing physical infrastructure (hospital building, vehicles, construction of health centers) without the provision for generating resources to maintain them clearly reflects the lack of expertise in the NGO's vision.
- Two other important aspects emerged to be very important in determining sustainability in the present context. The first is cost effectiveness, and the second is resource mobilization. The benefits which the project aims to sustain are those which come out of optimum utilization of resources. Sustaining present benefits and associated activities is meaningless if they are far less than what was desired. The practice of following project management benefits apparently attractive but less cost effective approaches has made the project fall flat after the donors pull out from the scene.

- The major problem facing the NGOs is how to pay the health workers after the project periods, who were exclusively appointed for PVOH-II project. To most of the workers, sustainability is directly related to their survival. The problem is more aggravated for those NGOs who hired a new set of huge number of workers at the beginning of the project. Some NGOs have tried to raise a corpus fund to finance the recurring expenditure; the attempt is partially successful for at least a few NGOs. Some others are trying to keep a manageable skeleton staff and transferring them to other projects with a natural adverse effect on the sustainability of health care. Some NGOs have just closed the chapter and are withdrawing from the project area without making alternative arrangements. The last option is observed for those NGOs who evidently do not have any commitment to the communities benefit from the health care sustainability.
- Financial sustainability of the project benefits requires mobilization of resources from different sources. The study finds an interesting scenario where the NGOs have been able to create a minimum mass of health awareness and some changes in attitude towards preventive health care among the community. But the curative needs for modern treatment, arising from the increased awareness, are still unaddressed by the NGOs to a large extent. The possibility of even partial cost - recovery through user –fees remains remote unless they redesign their programme with a well-defined goal to address the changing pattern of health care needs. The experience reveals that even with strategic shift towards curative care, the cost – recovery is significantly low. The NGOs practically do not have much option in this direction.
- A feasible alternative is suggested to concentrate on the following means of mobilizing resources and availing community participation to achieve sustainability:
  (i) Linking the health care components with other projects especially with the emphasis on community development with a vigorous stress on cost - effectiveness
  (ii) Building or mobilizing small institutions within the community towards the strategic fulfillment of need assessment, income/ savings generation, monitoring the curative care provided by the private health care practitioners, linking institutions promoting decentralized health care initiatives viz. *Gram Panchayats, Panchayat Samitis and members of PRIs*, and

developing manpower to take part in the health promotional activities of the NGO.

Lessons learned from PVOH-II experience

PVOH-II set out to expand and improve basic preventive health, family planning and nutrition services for the poor by utilising and strengthening the voluntary sector and the private sector. The private sector activities never really took off, and so there have not been any lessons learned from them, but very meaningful lessons have been derived from the NGO sector (NGOs).

Following mentioned are some of the basic assumptions derived from the experiences of PVOH-II NGOs on sustainability:

- NGOs can be an alternative delivery mechanism for integrated primary health care in the existing scenario.
- NGOs can ensure community participation and people's involvement and can extend their capability to transfer skills to the community in creating community self – reliance.
- NGOs can manage to reach the poor, the marginalised and the unreached population.
- NGO initiatives can be sustainable over the long run.

However, there are some critical issues, which need to be addressed while discussing the validity of the above lessons learned from the NGO experiences in the present context.

- It has been learnt that those NGOs, which are strong in service delivery, can be an alternative system even in their limited area but the number and range of these NGOs are limited. However, they did manage to a great -extent effectively compliments and supplements the work of the government system in place.
- NGOs do not always represent the communities that they work with and work for. However, if the NGOs had the orientation, skills, tools and approaches that were needed, then they could affect community participation. In reality, where the NGOs are strong in service delivery, there was weak community orientation. This is a set of knowledge in social sciences which is ignored by medical sciences and until it is acknowledge and brought into the mainstream of health and inter-sectoral action in development, the orientation of community participation and community involvement in health will not be possible.

- From the PVOH-II project experience, NGOs with community participation expertise do better than service delivery NGOs. The weak belief of clinical, medical, curative health care NGOs in the capability of community action makes them adopt approaches and strategies, which prevents self-reliance from developing further.
- In PVOH-II project experience shows that women groups and members benefited and were enveloped and included by NGOs as workers at the community level. But the truly marginalised were difficult to reach even for the NGOs. A lot had to do with the pure settings and the existing social structure and social system. NGOs having village level workers tended to appoint women from middle and upper classes and these women had no access to marginalised population. On the other hand, if a woman from the marginalised group had been chosen then she would not have been accepted by the upper castes. This is the ground reality, where a clear-cut strategy has to be devised by the NGOs to overcome and address. An NGO involved in community development will not ensure that the poor, the marginalised and the unreached will be reached – is a matter of great concern.
- When PVOH-II project was designed sustainability had been defined as financial sustainability-which NGO projects would continue project funded activities even after the funding ceased. If this is to happen, then there is a need for clear strategy planning and economic analysis right at the outset, even before the project is designed. Because, economically sustainable, low investment, incremental funding models are needed. A high cost system cannot be first initiated and then NGOs are asked to find a way to sustain it for the community they serve. NGOs found it difficult to grapple with the reality of financial sustainability because issues were not addressed when the projects were designed originally. The hypothesis was that if NGOs could contribute 25% in cash or in kind to the value of the project: that indicated sustainability (USAID). Unfortunately it did not happen in the real situation.
- However, the other aspects of sustainability that the NGOs did manage to accomplish. Sustained health benefits to the community have been made with community education – creating demand for services and utilisation, the linkages of NGOs established between the communities and the government system, empowering

communities to demand and access services, transfer of skills to community level providers, and incorporation of traditional providers into programmes. There were changes in health status and these changes can be really well sustained at low cost. Interestingly, NGOs are a diverse group of organisations in their orientation, commitment, capability, identity, integrity and their capable of delivering measurable results in health and non-health related areas.

The Critical Challenges of Sustainability

On the front of NGO strategy to optimise their involvement in sustaining the benefits of 'health action for social development', the above lessons learned further reflect on the critical challenges, which are discussed as follows:

- Identifying and selecting NGOs with adequate capability and commitment. Rigorous selection systems with selectors who have the appropriate experience, attitude and skills should be adopted. Clear selection criteria should be laid down to understand the reflection of programme priorities and the NGO should be located in the intervention area for all practical purposes.
- Designing realistic programmes built around NGO core values and competence. NGOs should be allowed to stick to their own 'knitting'. There is no point in developing straightjacket programmes, rather customised programmes specific to area of concerned NGO should be formulated. Every NGO has its own mandate, vision, and values and it should be allowed to select activities, which fit its values and capability. For administrative regions over-large project areas should be avoided even though they may be needy. When funds are provided the issues of priority to communities must be addressed otherwise it is very difficult for NGOs to get any credibility with the community. The programme has to be entered through a high priority area of the community. Also realistic time frames have to be in place as programmes take a while to start up.
- In case of building competence through technical assistance and training, the required fund allocation must address organisational development, systems management, development assistance and financial training. There is tremendous need to assist NGOs to diagnose technical assistance need and to help them to source high quality technical assistance. This facility for technical

assistance should be in place before the grants are made but not as it was in PVOH-II, when it came in very late in the life of the project. Skills and competence based training need emphasis on NGO capability. Demonstrative training techniques are more powerful and classroom training is no substitute for on-sight guidance as in case of PVOH-II capacity building training initiatives.

- Building competence through monitoring did not mean building accountability through monitoring. Monitoring itself is a powerful capacity building tool, provided it is done in a sensitive fashion. Effective monitoring is the same as the supportive supervision, and it is a function of the attitudes, orientation and skills of the monitoring agent. Unless there is clear and timely feedback, there is no use of monitoring.
- Providing and enabling environment, supportive systems and structures within which NGOs can operate are essential to achieve sustainability. Since NGOs are no different from other organisations, there is a need to ensure the conditions under which they work. For this, the orientation, experience, attitudes and values of the implementing NGOs are central. There is a need to be responsive to NGOs requests for information and guidance. There is a need to consult NGOs, as they know the field situation best. There has to be a timely and continuous release of funds, and flexibility in programme planning and implementation.
- Three types of infrastructure are important which need to be in place before any grants are made available for NGO initiatives; organisational, systems and strategic planning. In other words, once NGO programmes get underway, the pressures demand rapid disbursement of funds and rapid grant making but it will be a fatal flaw if the infrastructure is not in place before giving funds for activities. These involve the importance of strategic planning in NGO management.
- Finally, NGO programmes are management intensive, with no shortcuts and based on the priorities of social communication in development.

Issues of Government-NGO Co-operation under PVOH-II

Following critical issues are emerged as an outcome of NGO experiences, interaction with government counterparts in the state of Rajasthan and co-ordination with donor agencies and collaboration with social action groups under PVOH-II project, which needs further probing in the form of answering these questions.

- Can NGOs be viewed as mere contractors of government, or donor agencies, or activists, which can socially change to achieve sustainability?
- Can NGOs be entrusted to serve maximum population to work in the weaker and remote areas to promote sustainability?
- What should be the relationship between NGOs, government and donor agencies and between donor agencies and government to address the issues of sustainability?

In the context of PVOH-II project, there is a need to look into the lessons provided through the process of NGO experiences rather than a critique of the process itself. Also, the process of networking and partnership should be seen as one of equality between NGOs, government and donor agencies. The example of ICPD conference at Cairo and the power of NGO sector in articulating what has now been incorporated into a comprehensive reproductive health policy. Looking ahead on the nature of future direction and policy recommendations to involve NGOs to address the complexity of the problems of sustainability with the RCH programme, the present need is to draw lessons from the experience of PVOH-II and the working of NGOs in health sector, and to see greater role of NGOs as a part of civil society in the given conditions of pluralism and diversity in India.

In the case of PVOH-II, NGOs are seen in performing two roles- service deliveries and as support organisation to avail government co-operation. But the role of monitoring in ensuring accountability and of being conscience keepers was not considered. Certain changes in policy for family welfare programmes will smoothen relations between government and the NGO sector. Secondly, there must be decentralisation in decision making. NGOs are a solution, but a lot of debate and discussion is needed on how to use their potentiality for effective decentralisation of decision making. Related role of government and donor agencies is important in strengthening the realisation of NGO potentiality. There is a need to help NGO's access to funds other than those already available. There has to be a balance between careful and totally untrusting relationships. In the PVOH-II project, the precedent was to use funds for programmes other than those specified in the objectives to fulfil the needs of the community. Funding agencies should not think sectorially to become hindrance to achieve programme sustainability.

Considering the achievements of experiences of PVOH-II NGOs, there has to be a considerable emphasis on NGOs, as a blueprint to demonstrate the feasibility of the Reproductive health approach in the areas of education and mobilisation of community. It is important for the NGOs to work in partnership with government to approach the realistic perspective to achieve sustainability. There is a need to maximise the NGOs contribution for a sustainable health system to work for the disadvantaged population. In the present scenario of the NGO sector, NGOs are quite confused of their differential role towards different funding agencies focusing either on donor centred approach or on community centred approach to sustainability. The donor agencies and the government should be able to develop some sort of common code of conduct to identify and to work with NGOs with integrity. The role and method of co-operation between government, donor agencies and NGOs is important in this context to address thc issues of sustainability.

NGO-Government Co-operation in Rajasthan

The NGOs must adopt 'improving the effectiveness of the existing health and development departments' as one of their major agenda. This offers them a chance to have impact on a large scale in the state they are working with. This involves the NGOs' strategies for sharing of successful experiences, networking, advocacy, empowerment, co-ordination and partnership with their government counterparts for reaching out to the unreached mass in the state.

The government is the largest development agency and likely to remain so in the near future. Any improvement in the functioning of the government departments is bound to have a multiplier effect. The experience of institutional collaborations in Rajasthan shows that collaborations can be an effective means of improving the efficiency of the government system. However, the study also shows that system reform is not on the agenda of NGOs. Even in the cases mentioned above, NGOs can hardly be considered to be playing any major role to involve Panchayati Raj Institutions in which case there is limited scope for state involvement since the conceptualization of PVOH-II does not incorporate effective role of state government in the present project. However, there is a direct communication from the MOH&FW to the respective district authorities to share the information of sanctioning of the NGO project in the concerned district. This created further hindrance to the NGO-Government relation in the state. As, after having informed about the centrally sanctioned NGO project without a clearly defined state role brings the district functionaries into a more difficult situation to cooperate with NGO effectively. This aspect of NGO-Government relationship is not addressed through the existing collaborative effort of PVOH-II project. Role of NGOs is limited and even silence to this situation of Center-State administrative relations. This is leading to affect sustainability.

NGOs are mostly known for their grass root work. They are active in far-flung areas amongst the most marginal communities. In a society as hierarchical and stratified as ours, the importance of their work cannot be emphasized. At the same time it would be a naïve to say that grassroots action by itself is enough. It may turn into another type of relief. NGOs are aware of this.

System reform is considered to be the domain of social action groups. The development-NGOs we are concerned with in this study do not bother themselves with it. However, these groups are mostly concerned with policy level changes. Changes in policy even when they take place have to be delivered through the existing bureaucracy. If the bureaucracy remains unresponsive, the changes are rendered ineffective. This is best illustrated in the case of *Lok-Jumbis* programme for primary education. Sustained pressure on education issues has led to a major change in the policy. However the existing development NGOs are not able to follow up the changes with the sector specific department, in the government, which is refusing to give ground.

Adopting "system reform" as a major agenda by the NGOs will require some significant changes to work for the benefits of effective decentralization involving Government-NGO cooperation in health development. These are:

- ***Networking with other NGOs to seek changes-*** It is just not possible for a single NGO to be able to effect changes. As pointed out before, in the institutional collaboration issues in the state, NGOs are not able to play a very decisive role. One of the reasons is that they have no forum to raise a collective voice. Even in case of PVOH-II, delay in release of grants put the NGOs in a fix. They could not initiate any concretized action to initiate the process to get the funds in time, which badly affected their implementation. Here is the importance of the role the state to support the desired institutional networking of NGOs to address the issues, which are beyond the scope of individual NGOs.
- ***Preparedness to enter into a more open relationship with the government system***- Institutional collaborations subject both the partners to a continuous monitoring of each other's performance. NGOs do not have a tendency to cry foul at the slightest encroachment of what they consider their territory.

- ***Improve financial remuneration in their own organizations***- Most NGOs continue to operate on a very low salary structure. This is manageable as long as they remain isolated. But entry into an institutional collaboration opens them up. Resentment in the staff builds up. This measure is necessary for the long-term viability of the sector and sustainability of the programme as well. In case of PVOH-II experience, the staff turnover was found to be maximum. This led to the loss of resources utilized for the staff capacity building, and for a new staff the repetition of the same training would be costly. Thus affecting the programme implementation. Staff retention is the key to the achievement in the effective performance of a project.
- ***Must develop an essential competence in the task they undertake***- NGOs consider their rapport with the rural poor as their main strength. Their emphasis on the delivery of the service is muted. They are generally low on the skills. As for the salaries, on the question of performance too their performance comes under a greater scrutiny.
- ***Give sufficient priority to the collaboration effect***- It is often complained that NGOs do not give sufficient priority to the government work they undertake. This is natural to some extent, as the financial stakes are much lower. However, often the collaboration efforts address a very vital development issue. They do call for greater effort.

Reflection on Non-governmental Health Care in Rajasthan

Present research on sustainability of non-governmental health care is conducted with NGOs in the state of Rajasthan under PVOH-II project in India. This brings the practical understanding of the factors of sustainability in the context of the NGO effectiveness in terms of management strategy, Government-NGO co-operation and status of health systems development in the state of Rajasthan. Discussion on the reflection of non-governmental health care can highlight some of these issues in the present situation in Rajasthan.

In the state of Rajasthan many social action groups work on health education, awareness building and even family planning – but the number of groups engaged in field based health service delivery are few and far between. With the exception of well-organised established organisations like Social Work Research Centre (Tilonia) and Seva Mandir (Udaipur) – NGOs have found it very difficult to sustain work in the health sector. Availability of medical and para-medical professionals, investment in infrastructure, accessibility of referral and backup services, all these have contributed to the weak state of affairs for the health programme in the NGO sector. Some NGOs started health initiatives, but had to abandon them because they could not sustain it for a longer period.

The absence of a vibrant NGO community working in health sector development in Rajasthan was quite apparent. While one can still find a few organisations engaged in primary health care initiatives with women's health still remains a weak agenda. Existing NGOs working for women empowerment which have done commendable work in advocating gender issues in social development seems to be very much concern about the indifference of health care service providers to women's issues especially the need and aspirations of women in disadvantaged situation. This has been one of the most neglected areas of social action involving non- governmental health care in the state. Importance of National policy directions, state co-operation and International donor agencies priority are key to promote the agenda of Non-governmental health initiative in the state. Other than USAID there are three key donors operating in the state are SIDA, UNFPA and World Bank working for reforming health and family welfare sector in Rajasthan.

Since more than forty odd years the government has had an ambiguous relationship with NGOs especially working in the health sector. The government looks upon field based NGOs as sub-contractors who can implement specific programme in a most cost effective manner, assist the government in fulfilling targets and reach out to those areas, where the government has not been able to reach. With the exception of few influential NGO leaders, the government does not seen NGOs as partners in development. During crisis like drought or floods, the government invites NGOs to participate in emergency and humanitarian action in the form of relief and rehabilitation. However, the initiative to involve the NGOs invariably rests with the decision of the government. A large number of NGOs also see themselves as sub-contractors, willing to take on implementation of specific health programmes of government. Many of them came up as a response to grant-in-aid programmes of the government. It is popularly believed (in the absence of reliable data) that a significant number of NGOs come under this category of sub-contractors with no specific agenda of social transformation. Therefore, the organisations that do not see themselves as sub-contractors but partners in nation building are not very popular with most government officials as well as government agencies. With the establishment of well-established groups with political and social credibility, NGOs with an agenda of social transformation are often pitted against the government in struggles for local development.

Given this scenario, it was observed that the process of involving social action groups, NGOs, community based organisations incorporates building the capabilities of field based NGOs would hopefully impact the mainstream objectives of health sector reform through the implementation of Reproductive and Child Health program of the government. This will create an environment where close linkages will be possible between government, NGOs and donor agencies in realising the agenda of RCH programme in the state. The challenge is quite apparent about the fact of hastening the difficult agenda before health sector reform strategies bear the fruits of action. The close partnership forged in the early years of women's development programme and *Shiksha Karmi* Projects, *Lok Jumbish* for non-formal education and the experiences of NGO involvement under PVOH- II project in the state of Rajasthan would further strengthen the agenda of community action in health development.

Reflection on NGO initiative in Decentralized Planning

The involvement of NGOs with the grass-roots democracy arises out of their activities in the following areas-

- Organisation of the disadvantaged sections of rural society - e.g. the minorities, landless, SC/STs, agricultural/plantation labour, labour of the unorganised sector etc. It is these sections that have been provided a 'space' in the PRIs under the reservation policy.
- In addition to organising, most NGOs run training programmes - leadership development, capacity building, group dynamics and management and so on. Some of the NGOs have organised training specifically for PRI members (e.g.- SEARCH, Maharashtra & UMA in Karnataka, FRCH in Maharashtra, CINI in West Bengal, YIP in Andhra Pradesh...to name a few).
- The most valuable area of contribution of NGOs to engendering the PRIs has been in the organising of women (whatever sector the NGO works with - health, IGPs, SHGs, housing, water & sanitation, education, watershed...). The opportunities provided in small groups dealing with the above issues have been a kind of 'testing ground' for women to enter a larger arena, having been empowered in the smaller arena. Further, it has also been reported that women in PRIs who have been supported and nurtured by NGOs and those who have been involved in larger people's movements have gained a more 'assertive' stance which gives them an edge over other women in the PRI process. The best examples of this can be seen the 'Right to Information' movement in Rajasthan and the Anti-Arrack movement in Andhra Pradesh.

Inspite of these very positive aspects, many NGOs seem vary of getting directly or closely involved with the PRIs. An often heard comment is 'we are working in development; politics is not our cup of tea'! But, if PRIs, especially GPs, are the forum where development and politics has to be wedded, it is difficult to see how NGOs can keep non-aligned in the process. Perhaps some of them are bound by donor conditionality or wise enough to avoid working against the 'establishment'... But, sooner or later NGOs will get entangled in the politics of power transfer in the PRIs; the clearer their perspective on gender issues in health, the greater will be their contribution to the process of sustainability.

There is a strong emphasis on the decentralization of the whole system of health care, that is, decision making and financial resources will be transferred to the district level and below for planning, implementation and monitoring of health care services. Women's health needs and a gender sensitive approach will be integrated in all aspects of the programme.

Crucial elements in the reform of Decentralized Health Care

- Community participation: the linkages and relation between panchayati raj institutions (village, block and district) and corresponding health care institutions (Sub Centers, PHCs and FRUs). Community participation also means relating to relevant forms of local organization for improvement in reproductive and child health.
- Training according to identified needs of health personnel, administrators, and for panchayat members of health committees.
- District action plans, elaborated in line with the objective of shift of emphasis to the client-based approach and quality of service.
- Management of personnel, resources, equipment and supplies for the most cost-effective essential health system.
- Establishment of new indicators for community auditing and monitoring of system reform and implementation of regular supervision of the quality of services.
- Operational research, surveys and trials to determine best practice models.

Increased decentralization and community participation are supposed to significantly contribute to a solution of a number of deficiencies in the prevailing family welfare and primary health care system. Besides the negative effects of a target driven approach to family planning, the most important shortcoming of the current system is the poor performance of public health institutions at the lower levels, such as Community Health Centers, Primary Health Centers, and Sub Centers in the villages. Despite an impressive build up and staffing of these institutions, they are far from being fully utilized by the general public. Highly centralized, hierarchical and organizational complex administration with slow implementation is part of the problem. Lack of motivation of staff is another serious problem. Other problems are vacancies in key positions (anesthetists, lady gynecologists, etc.), lack of money for running expenses, and lack of drugs and other equipment. Vertical programmes of disease prevention and control are working side by side without any integration or coordination. Add to this frequent absence of staff, frequent transfers of the health workers, and one has a fairly complete diagnosis of the maladies of the present system of public health care. The effect is, among others, that higher well-staffed and equipped institutions, such as district hospitals, are over crowded with patients, often seeking rather elementary care, which could have been provided at a lower level. Little wonder that today private health care caters to about 3/4 of all curative services demanded, and that preventive activities/ services are grossly inadequate.

Diagram 7.1: ***Guiding Principles of reproductive health and linkages***

Panchayat members, teachers, NGOs, social action groups, private medical practitioners (allopathic as well as indigenous), women's organizations, youth associations, and other concerned members of the community are supposed to participate in the planning and implementation of RCH frame work with the objective of meeting the unmet needs in RCH care services (Diagram 7.1 – Guiding Principles of reproductive health and linkages), ICPD, POA, 1994.

Decentralized Planning

It means a bottom-up approach within the primary health care system, from the ANM via the MO at PHC to the Block and District levels. The local Sub Center's work plan should be based on an assessment of actual felt needs in the community. The Panchayat (Local govt.), its health committee, and suitable community representatives should be counseled before making the local needs plan. The ambition in the long run is that with quality of service and IEC work, sensitise the population to sound demands for primary health care and bring their felt needs in accordance with the former. The decentralisation of health plan, however, should be based on the felt needs of the deprived majority. Role of NGOs is important in the execution of this plan (Diagram 7.2 – Implementation of the RCH programme), ICPD, Programme Implementation, 1994.

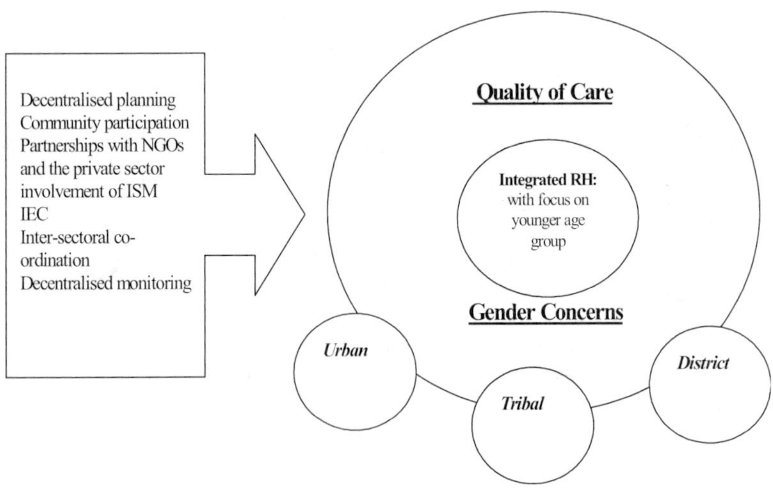

Diagram 7.2 - Implementation of the RCH Programme

So this is how Panchayati Raj (local government) and community participation is to be interpreted within the framework of bottom-up planning in the primary health care system with emphasis on RCH. These issues are addressed in the following recommendations for sustaining NGO action in health development in the state of Rajasthan.

Strategic Implications for Sustaining NGO Action in Health

GO-NGO Collaboration in Health and Social Sector Development

- NGOs are better equipped to participate in environment building, micro-planning and health-mapping, awareness generation, education and health of adolescent girls and boys, training of TBA, gender sensitisation of health service providers, creating village and sub-centre based forum for community involvement, support orientation and sensitisation of local medical practitioners (traditional healers, RMP and unregistered practitioners) etc. The government could hand over these activities to NGOs where feasible.
- NGOs can participate in the year long decentralised planning exercise, monthly meetings at the sub-centre, PHC and at the district level. In this process they can become the link between the government and the people. In particular, ANMs can benefit a great deal, their concern about security and outreach can be addressed.
- Given the proliferation of village committees for health, education, water, forest protection, common property resources, child nutrition and so on; it would be valuable to support NGOs to create a broad spectrum of common forum in the village with different 'experts' for different issues.
- NGOs can be involved in health education and preventive activities. While recognising the fact that the dividing line between preventive and curative services is rather thin, it would still be valuable to involve local groups in preventive work, unlike the case of PVOH-II NGOs.
- NGOs can play a crucial role in expanding the pool of people who have a holistic view of reproductive health and reproductive rights. Involving appropriate organisations in training, communication and advocacy will be valuable. In this context NGO involvement in campaigns and health *Melas,* especially in mass mobilisation against teenage pregnancy and safe abortion etc. are important steps.

- NGOs can conduct qualitative and quantitative surveys or studies on the prevalence of reproductive health problems, people's ability to cope with them and the availability of resources and services to approach these problems.
- NGOs can take over and manage a few health centres, especially in the areas where the government has not been able to provide services. Deputation of government workers to NGOs at all levels of health services system should be explored in the state.

NGO Initiatives in Strengthening Issues of Women's Health in Rajasthan

- Need for systematic orientation and training workshops to develop conceptual understanding of reproductive health and reproductive rights in the overall framework of primary health care and gender justice. Such district based initiatives could provide and opportunity for NGOs to come together and share ideas and experiences. Inviting pioneers in the fields of neighboring states of Gujarat and Maharashtra would be a great morale for the NGOs in Rajasthan to develop a shared understanding towards meaningful action.
- The above step can be followed up with training support for capacity building in project planning, implementation, on-going training of grassroots workers, management and monitoring of health activities. It is important to give adequate time for creating a team to support the process that help NGOs build their capacities and grow gradually. Providing space for reflection, on-going training and expose visits to other NGOs is important.
- Reproductive health is closely linked to women's social, psychological, and physical well being. NGOs can be encouraged to make health care as a base for empowerment of women.
- NGOs can develop a glossary of terms used for common reproductive health practices. This is necessary to forge better communication between health care providers and the community. Creation of informal forums on women's health and empowerment is essential to involve social action groups, health activists, teachers, trainers and health managers to share their experiences and strengthening mutual capacity.

Government – NGO partnership in Health

- The government in the state is mandated to provide basic health care services, and NGOs at best play a supportive role. NGOs cannot replace the government nor they can take over the health care services. Their involvement in service delivery is at best complimentary while serving the areas where government has not been able to reach. In order to do this, NGOs need the active support and co-operation of the government. There has to be an understanding between the government and the NGOs and in the absence of mutually acceptable trust, confidence a mandate for partnership will not be possible to create a common ground for collaboration.

- Transferring the initiative to the people through systematic devolution of decision-making powers can create a positive climate for people's involvement and participation. Therefore health care should be a priority area at the Panchayat level. This can create an environment where people can have say in how the services are managed and monitored. The present situation makes service providers accountable to their supervisors who monitor their activities on the basis of centrally administered targets and goals. It is not easy to create common ground when service providers do not see themselves as community based workers appointed to serve the community. This is evident from the experience of PVOH-II project.
- Grassroots social action groups have been working among the people for many years and have established a working relationship of trust with people in their respective area. Many of them have participated in people's struggle for survival and life of dignity and own their confidence. An opportunity for close GO-NGO collaboration in health initiatives is essential to forge a mutually respectful working relationship with government functionaries and NGO service providers.
- Creating an environment of trust and mutual respect is necessary pre-condition for supporting a common ground for collaborating work. This is possible only if a serious effort is made from the policy level to treat NGO and community with respect and dignity. The ongoing attitude of health administrators and service providers is the greatest barrier to the sustainability of health care.
- Lack of ownership among the people in government health programmes is a major constraint. The lessons learnt from the experiences of NGOs under PVOH-II project, women's development programme, *Shiksha Karmi* programme in the state of Rajasthan show that working towards a nurturing sense of

ownership among key opinion leaders in the community pays reach dividend in a people's centred programme. This helps in creating a common ground at the village level. The major challenge therefore is to make primary health care movement as a people's struggle for health.

- There are different types of NGOs operating in health development in Rajasthan; struggle oriented grassroots groups, service and welfare organisations, sub-contractors gearing to implementing government programmes, private medical practitioners seeking a tax umbrella and corporate social responsibility NGOs and so on. One of the challenging tasks is to distinguish between different categories of organisations, assess their commitment, accountability systems and capability in an objective and unprejudiced manner to create common ground for NGO action for promoting partnership in health.

Policy Implications for Government

Open new sectors for collaboration- Collaboration as a development strategy has proved its effectiveness. However collaboration efforts continue to be limited to the traditional areas of education and health. Of late, there has been movement in the land resource management sector also. Still vast areas remain untapped. All those programmes, which require intensive participation by people or monitoring of processes in remote areas, should be considered for collaboration. The most obvious areas are common property management, lift irrigation schemes, public health engineering (maintenance of hand pumps), livelihood sustainability, community action for health and primary education. Inter-sectoral action in development is possible in promoting the partnership among new sectors of collaboration.

Undertake more institutional collaboration arrangements- Government should realize the potential of 'institutional arrangements' to improve the effectiveness of its own staff. So far such arrangements have been more common in the field of primary health care and education. Now that the effectiveness of the model has been proven, it should be ready to undertake more such experiments in a wide variety of sectors. Such arrangements can be taken up at the district level too on an experimental basis, as is the case with *Lok Jumbis* programme for Primary Education in the state and 'Panchayat Swasthya Scheme' to empower panchayat members in the field of Primary Health Care.

Look upon NGOs as partners not mere contractors for service delivery-Government should look upon NGOs as partners in development.

The implication of this approach is that it should actively help in capacity building of the NGOs. So far this remains an exclusive domain of foreign donors. It should increase its budget allocation to the NGO activities by incorporating the necessary overheads. Even, in case of PVOH-II, the state government was not aware of the administrative difficulties and operational constraints of implementing NGOs in the state. The government in the state remained silent throughout the life of the project whereas these NGOs have achieved the credibility for they're good work as government partners in the past and even now.

Set up institutions geared to meeting the organisational needs of the small NGOs- While the larger NGOs have sufficient infrastructure, the small NGOs have few means to build their capacity. It is the small NGOs, which actively come forward to take up the government schemes. Large NGOs have their own agenda. Successes of schemes like 'self-help group', 'Panchayat Swasthya Scheme'; 'Women Empowerment for Rural Health' is based on the efforts of small NGOs. Government should help them build their capacity. Experiences and expertise of big NGOs, like those of PVOH-II can be involved to help government in strengthening the institutional capacity of smaller NGOs.

Establish and Operationalise Committees on Voluntary Action - centrally sponsored schemes (like PVOH-II project) which is backed by vertical structure became hindrance for NGO-government cooperation in the state, where the project operates. There was no scope for state involvement in project implementation at any stage in the life of PVOH-II project. Constitutionally, Health being a state subject, its involvement in programme management is important to implement and sustain the activities successfully. Therefore, NGOs effort remained limited to project implementation but not extended to government collaboration in the state in which these NGOs operate. This was the hindrance for replicability of the project benefits in the process of scaling-up to a larger population considering the limited scope for state cooperation. Establishment and operationalisation of 'State committees on voluntary action' would ensure the feasibility, operational strategy, and the nature of NGO-government cooperation, involvement of democratic institutions like the PRIs and the nature of operational dynamics as per the suitability of the state situation. This would ensure further support to the effective management of NGO programmes to sustain the benefits of community action in the long run.

Having a strong patriarchal feudal structure and related bureaucratic attitude of the state health system and its functioning of governance, the voluntary initiative in the state of Rajasthan faces the greatest challenge in transforming concerned social action in mainstreaming institutions, programmes and processes in NGOs action for reaching community health programmes to the outreach and disadvantaged population. The struggle for sustainability of Non-governmental Health initiative lies in realising these challenges through the institutionalisation of GO-NGO partnerships in health development as essential principle for the foundation of decentralised planning and management of health care and health systems for the rural India.

Chapter - IX

Way Forward

"Health for all" means that health is to be brought within reach of everyone in a given country, an accepted policy expectation nationally and community based reality locally. And by "health" is meant a personal state of well-being, not just the availability of health services—a state of health that enables a person to lead a socially and economically productive life. "Health for all" for Universal Health Coverage (UHC) implies the removal of the obstacles or hardship to achieve health—that is to say, the elimination of malnutrition, ignorance, contaminated drinking-water, and unhygienic housing—quite as much as it does the solution of purely medical problems such as a lack of doctors, hospital beds, drugs and vaccines. "Health for all" is thus a holistic concept calling for efforts in involvement of non-health sectors and actors such as in agriculture, rural development, industry, education, housing, and social communications. Medical care and technology alone cannot bring health to hungry people living in hovels. Health for such people requires a whole new way of life and fresh opportunities to provide themselves with a higher standard of living. Universal health coverage (UHC) is increasingly seen by global civil society as a key component of the framework for sustainable development after the Millennium Development Goals (MDGs), and of shaping the kinds of health system that promotes equity, access, and human rights. Primary Health Care approaches for health systems strengthening using Community system strengthening and community mobilisation are crucial for ensuring that UHC works equally for the general population as well as for poor and marginalized groups with the involvement of NGOs.

The approach that is being adopted to attain 'health for all' is based on the fundamental understanding that it is there, where people live and work, that health is made or broken in their community setting. People must therefore understand what health is all about, and it is the duty of those who know to help others to understand. But to gain such an understanding a minimum level of achievement of health is essential. Health care and social awareness must go hand in hand, the one leading to the other and each progressively reinforcing the other. The process briefly described is known as community involvement, community participation and community empowerment in health, health care and health services. NGOs involvement in health care sustainability with having strong base in different community settings are studied in the context for better health outcomes in the context.

What will be the role of NGOs in health in the new millennium? There are two important perspectives: challenges in the health sector and how civil society includingNGOs may promote health more generally and in rural areas, particularly in India. The aim of current health-sector reforms is to increase effectiveness, minimize cost, and reduce the public role in service provision and achieve sustainability. At the same time, equity cannot be achieved if governments withdraw from health systems strengthening as a public responsibility. Some studies suggest that the role of NGOs in such a changing scenario is not to take over government responsibility, but to focus on equity, justice, and caring, by filling gaps in basic and essential care for those who remain under-served, and in ways that connect with community initiatives and ownership. Advocacy by NGOs for reorientation of services to ensure more equitable access is also needed.

Further challenges are to promote health and to prevent diseases. The causes of ill-health are related to gross social inequity and poverty, macroeconomic adjustments and extreme market orientation, corrupt and ineffective economies, armed conflicts and disproportionate public spending on arms, environmental degradation and pollution, and unhealthy lifestyles. Three arguments exist for why the Third Sector or NGOs may be a growing force in tackling these difficulties. First, the sense of a global environmental and impending social crisis, the acknowledgment of a shared future—may fuel the quest for change at local, national, and global levels. Second, the international network of concerned individuals in civil society is becoming more influential in addressing the causes of ill health owing to better access to media and digitalized communication. Third, the number of people worldwide who are well- informed about health issues is growing as a result of better education and awareness about health & health care issues and rights based approaches. Transformation of public policy has taken place during the past few decades, especially in the new millennium, a much greater number of social agents and NGOs are likely to be involved in this work, for example, through partnerships and networks in which members of civil society groups will again have an important role to play in the health care and health systems development of populations.

The study findings are discussed in the light of transformation of public health policies and challenges for health systems strengthening and universal health coverage using primary health care approaches involving NGOs and their approaches to achieve sustainability as follows.

- Locally based non-governmental organizations (NGOs), play an important role in providing health services to and representing the needs of poor and marginalized populations in rural health systems and services. Much of their growth is linked to their roles as partners and subcontractors for donor governments and international NGOs, disbursing health care and health services funded by foreign aid in coordination with government in the context.
- Donor-government cooperation need to focus on supporting the low-cost adaptations that NGOs have developed themselves, such as downsizing, increasing volunteer recruitment, developing local sources of accessing health care for the outreach and disadvantaged community. Such a strategy will enhance NGO sustainability, protect the civil society sector, and facilitate governance of health care sustainability for rural health.
- Donor-Government cooperative strategies can contribute to capacity-building efforts and accountability requirements can prompt NGOs to professionalize and expand in sustaining their impact in health care delivery in cooperation with the local government institutions in the state in the context, for effective governance and facilitation of government-NGOs cooperation in the state.
- Local actions in rural health care would privilege NGOs with stronger grassroots connections and popular support. The need for volunteers, donations, or clients for user-fee-based services could make NGOs more accountable to the local population, including the beneficiaries of their work. This can facilitate decentralized planning and management in partnerships with local government institutions or Panchayati Raj institutions locally for greater accountability and accessibility of health care services and health outcomes sustainability.
- Increased local involvement can have other benefits of innovations, accessibility and equity in partnerships with district health systems using health systems strengthening approaches. Volunteer-based organizations, even NGOs having strong base in community setting can generate social capital among their participants, which

can produce new opportunities, facilitate the sharing of resources, and even create better health outcomes and sustainability.

- Local involvement can also improve NGO legitimacy with the local community. If more foreign or government funding becomes available in the future, NGOs that are sustainable using local resources can be selective about which donor or government grants and contracts they take, choosing only those projects that reflect local needs and interests. It can be an opportunity to disrupt the current, donor-focused patterns of NGO dominance, renew NGO accountability to the local population, and improve NGO sustainability in rural health using health systems.
- Donors can facilitate this transition in coordination with government by engaging in better dialogue with local NGOs about donor-government transition plans in consultation with state governments in context and supporting local adaptations that allow NGOs to lower their costs and develop local funding streams for health care innovations and sustainability.
- Community systems strengthening and community empowerment are crucial for ensuring that sustainability of health care benefits for UHC works equally for the general population as well as for poor and marginalized groups. Government support for flexibility in NGOs operational guidelines and encouragement for appropriateness in government cooperation can achieve sustainability of health care using primary health care.
- There is greater potential for improving public health through systematic collaboration between governments and NGOs. This study is an attempt to summarize and provide an overview of the role of NGOs in strengthening health care sustainability. There is a urgent need to collect more systematic evidence on the role of NGOs in health, to improve our knowledge and to give visibility to good practice and to the contribution of NGOs in health and health care sustainability, in keeping view of the factors as described in this book, the community interfaces are complex and there are many aspects, risks and benefits to be taken into account in partnership and cooperation with the government in the state, wherever health programmes are implemented. As execution of health, health care and health services are state subject under the constitution in India and so their sustainability.
- The public health sector must understand NGOs and NGOs must better adapt to the needs of the health sector and better organize

themselves as a group or network. States need to work with civil society to organize the social dimensions of health actions, to build wider constituencies for health rights and goals, and to strengthen public accountability and responsiveness within health systems.

- All these features confirm about the overall impression on the benefits of collaboration for both the state and NGOs outweigh the risks of possible tensions in NGO-state interactions. The public health sector must understand NGOs and NGOs must better adapt to the needs of the health sector and better organize themselves as a group inclusiveness of their diversity of operations. States need to work with civil society or NGOs to organize the social dimensions of health actions, to build wider constituencies for health rights and goals, and to strengthen public accountability and responsiveness within health systems.
- NGOs capacity building in health sector needs to be addressed in order to maximize the benefits of the collaboration. Strategic partnerships between GO-NGOs can offer opportunities for enhancing the legitimacy of health policies and programmes, improving public outreach, advocacy of health goals, information communication exchange, increasing resource inputs to health programmes and help achieving their sustainability as seen in the case studies in this research.

The usefulness of the present study, in looking at India's current guidelines and procedures for NGOs, inhibits the government from regulating NGOs in an enabling and supportive manner and NGOs from ensuring compliance in a timely and cost-effective way. Further, procedural opacity and density of the grants-in-aid system prevents both the government and the NGO sector from channeling precious government resources towards addressing critical developmental problems as well as health care programmes. The piecemeal approach to consultative planning between the government and the NGO sector significantly impedes the transfer of learning and innovations from the NGO sector to government policy-making. The present research have many strengths, including, the clearly defined role of state governments in implementing regulations and managing grants to NGOs,concerns about participatory approaches to engaging NGOs in policy-making and implementation, and the allocated provisions of grants-in-aid across government welfare initiatives in health & social sectors involving states. However, these need to be realigned to the contemporary reality of the health sector which is growing in number of organisations, complexity of work, quantum and quality of funds reaching the sector and the capacity building of health care workers and health professionals. The recommendations and actions points detailed in this study are important suggestions for initiating strategic steps towards initiating health care sustainability using primary health care and health systems strengthening approaches. These study recommendations need to be implemented collectively and in a coordinated manner to achieve sustainability of NGOs involvement in health and social sector.

***Gathering strategic partners and stakeholders:**

Early identification of relevant stakeholders in the government and NGOs in terms of the relevant bodies and representatives to form the core group in implementing the action items is critical. This is to ensure the inclusion of varied perspectives and that due attention is provided to all proposed actions in the concerned states.

***Identifying a committee to lead the Implementation:**

A national-level advisory group consisting of the identified stakeholders within the policy planning advisory bodies like NITI Ayog or an empowered committee with their due representation and related inter-sectoral ministries should be set up to oversee and guide the implementation of the proposed actions with the involvement of State Planning Board in states, where the health programme is expected to be implemented and sustained.

***Developing an Implementation Framework:**

Each proposed recommendation and action plans should be analyzed and useful in developing an implementation framework consisting of the timelines and resources required to implement these in a cost-effective manner.

***Monitoring periodic progress & Implementation:**

In cases where large and complex changes are proposed, constant monitoring of their implementation with regular engagement of state governments should be undertaken for initiating corrective measures for achieving sustainability.

***Advocacy of Evidence based Research and Dissemination:**

As recommendations are action oriented, targeted dissemination of the key changes undertaken and their impact on the functioning and sustainability of impact involving NGOs will be critical for timely uptake and compliance.

These aspects will be lessons learning and exchange for wider understanding, dissemination and replicability, mostly useful in strengthening partnerships and advocating research findings.

*Stronger roles for NGOs in Primary Health Care:

NGOs can contribute to primary health care broadly through program implementation in strengthening community systems and decentralized health action while addressing following strategies as highlighted –

(a) *providing assistance to develop or strengthen local NGO capabilities and activities with particular attention to local community development groups;*

(b) *conducting reviews and assessment of existing health and development programs and assist communities in the exercise of their own role in such reviews; a greater emphasis on evaluative techniques will render all new programs more accountable to community needs;*

(c) *placing primary health care in the context of comprehensive human development and ensuring their existing programs and new initiatives in promoting full participation by individuals and communities in the planning, implementation and sustainable innovations;*

(d) *expanding their capacity building efforts to respond to the needs of primary health care programs e.g., training of health workers, supervisors, administrators, planners and various rural development workers; included would be training schemes which build on the skills of traditional healers and midwives;*

(e) *developing locally sustainable and appropriate health technologies and use of resources, contribute to the creation of new and effective methods of health education which enable both individuals and communities to assume greater responsibility for their own health;*

(f) *recognizing the essential role of women in health promotion and in the full range of community development concerns, while working with poor, disadvantaged, and remote populations, enabling them to break the cycle of deprivation and in this way contribute to the search for greater social justice and advocacy.*

This study conclusion envisions a stronger NGO sector for health care sustainability and advocates for a broadly harmonious relationship between the government and NGOs for their effectiveness in health and social sector.

The study recommendations on the desired transformation of GO-NGOs partnerships can contribute to appropriateness in community systems strengthening and achieve sustainability of rural health programmes and especially can be useful for involving NGOs, for their successful innovations and scaling-up of grassroots experiences in health systems strengthening. Therefore, the influence of civil society or NGOs on health and health care depends on the recognition of its role as a partner in primary health care, on its success in the scaling up of activities, on its cooperation with the State, business sector and on networking among stakeholders from both health and non-health sectors of inter-sectoral action. In the context of health-sector reforms and new national health policy the roles of NGOs should focus on equity, social justice and advocate health as a public responsibility for achieving progressive outcome for the universal health coverage and health care sustainability. For achieving the objectives of rural health and health care system based on the principles of 'health for all' using approaches of 'primary health care' which is accessible to all members of the community, which is concerned with the promotion of health in the whole community and in which major decisions concerning health are taken and implemented by the community, the effective involvement of NGOs and their capacity building and coordinated responses with government are essentially important to achieve sustainability.

Present study can be useful to explore the changing conceptualisation of public health as a public goods itself and to argue that such cooperation and collaboration is possible with a strong public good perspective at the national level with the strengthening partnerships and effective engagement of NGOs in sustaining their credibility in local community and promoting public health specific to local needs for promoting health care sustainability. In true sense the findings moreover contributing to the transformational global call for "Health for All" at the national level through a sustained practice for "Health in All" involving NGOs for achieving health care sustainability at the local level of functional health system.

With the expectations of global academic and policy discourses on sustainable health systems, the study outcomes will surely generate stimulations among academia, public health professionals and civil society groups to undertake more thorough analysis, with the hope of effecting a change in both what is researched and how it is researched. Readers will realize that the book is not merely a culmination of current concern over sustainability of rural health and health care involving NGOs but rather a point of departure for further analysis and action within the framework of new public health and health systems in India.

Bibliography

Chapters II-III

1. Acosta, G., Flores, M., and Silva, G. (1994) 'Los Servicios Legagel y las Campãnas de Fin de Singlo: Preguntas y Propuestas', El Otro Derecho, vol. 5(3), pp. 75-88.
2. Aga Khan Foundation (1988) The Enabling Environment, report of Nairobi Conference, London: Aga Khan Foundation.
3. Ainskow, M. (1994) 'supporting International Innovation in Teacher Education', in H. Bradley (ed.), Developing Teachers, Developing Schools, London: David Fulton.
4. AKF/NOVIB (1993) Going to Scale: the BRAC Experience 1972-1992 and Beyond, The Hague: Aga Khan/NOVIB.
5. Anangwe, A. (1995) 'NGO-State Relations in Kenya', mimeo, University of Nairobi.
6. ANGOC (1988), 'NGOs and International Development Cooperation', Lok Niti, Journal of the Asian NGO Coalition, vol. 5(4), Manila: Asian NGO coalition.
7. Annis, S. (1987) 'Can Small-Scale Development be a Large-Scale Policy? The Case of Latin America', World Development, vol. 15, Supplement, pp. 129-34.
8. Antonios, R. (1994) 'Strategies for Action for NGOs and the Notion of Civil Society', paper presented to the Conference on Egyptian Society in the Light of the New World Order, Cairo: University of Cairo, May.
9. APSA (American Political Science Association) (1995) 'Preliminary Program: 1995 Annual Meeting', PS: Political Science and Politics, vol. 28(2) (June), pp. 195-406.
10. Arellano-López, S. and Petras, J. (1994) 'NGOs and Poverty Alleviation in Bolivia', Developmwnt and Change, vol. 25(3), pp. 555-68.
11. ARTI (1991) Approaches to Development: The NGO Experience in Sri Lanka, Colombo: ARTI.
12. Australian Council for Overseas Aid (1992) Aid for Change, Canberra: ACFOA.
13. A study of NGO-funding pattern by AVARD - Country paper on NGOs in DEVELOPMENT SECTOR.
14. Anubhav Series, Ford foundation Study,(India) 1990.
15. Babadji, R. (1991) 'The Associative Phenomenon in Algeria', in M. Camau (ed.), Changements Politiques au Maghreb, Paris: Centre National de la Recherche Scientifique.

16. Bebbington, A. and Farrington, J. (1993) 'Government, NGOs and Agricultural Development: Perspective on Changing Inter-Organizational Relationships', Journal of Development Studies, vol. 29(2), pp. 199-219.
17. Bebbington, A. and Farrington, J. (1992) Private Voluntary Initiatives and Governments, NGOs and Agricultural Development, London: ODI.
18. Bebbington, A. and Kopp, A. (1995) Bolivia Case Study: Evaluation of the Swedish NGO Support Programme, Stockholm: SIDA.
19. Bebbington, A. and Riddell, R. (1994) 'New Agendas and Old Problems: issues, options and challenges in direct funding of southern NGOs', paper presented at the Workshop on 'NGOs and Development: Performance and Accountability', University of Manchester, 27-9 June.
20. Bebbington, A. and Thiele, G. (eds.) with Davies, P., Prager, M. Riveros (1993) NGOs and the State in Latin America: Rethinking Roles in Sustainable Agricultural Development, London: Routledge.
21. Bebbington, A., Domingo, T., Kopp, A. and Quisbert, J. (1995) Peasant Federations, Food Systems and Rural Politics in Bolivia, London: IIED.
22. Bebbington, A. et al. (1991) Evaluacion Del Impacto De Los Proyectos Auspiciados Por La Fundacion InterAmaricana Con Organizaciones Indigenas En El Equador, Washington: Inter-American Foundation.
23. Bernstien, S. R. (1991) Managing Contracting Services in the Non-Profit Agency: Administrative, Ethical and Political Issues, Philadelphia: Temple University Press.
24. Bhatnagar, B. and Williams, A. (1992) Participatory Development and the World Bank: Potential Directions for Change, Washington, DC: World Bank.
25. Brodhead T. and B.H. Copley (1988) Bridges of hope, Ottawa: The North-South Institute.
26. Berman, Peter and Dave, Priti. Experiences in Paying For Health Care in India's voluntary sector.
27. Bhatia, Kavita. The NGO Movement in Health, FRCH Publication on commity Health, FRCH, Bombay, 1993.
28. Beikart, K. (1995) 'European NGOs and Democratization in Central America: Assessing Performance in the Light of Changing Priorities', in M. Edwards and D. Hulme (eds.), NGO Performance and Accountability: Beyond the Magic Bullet, London: Earthscan and West Hartford: Kumarian Press.
29. Blair, Harry (1993) 'Doing Democracy in the Third World: Developing an Applied Theory of Democracy', paper for the annual meeting of the American Political Science Association, Washington, 2-5 September.
30. Blair, Harry (1994) 'Civil Society and Democratic Development: A CDIE Evaluation Paper', Washington: USAID, PPC/CDIE/E/POA, 24 February.
31. Blair, Harry (1995) 'Civil Society and Building Democracy: Lessons from International Donor Experience', paper for the annual meeting of the American Political Science Association, Chicago, 31 August-3 September.
32. Blair, Harry and Gary Hansen (1994) Weighing in on the Scales of Justice: Strategic Approaches for Donor-supported Rule of Law Programs, USAID

program and Operations Assessment Report No. 7, Washington: USAID, Center for Development Information and Evaluation, February.

33. Boularès, N. (1993) 'Associative Life in Tunisia', paper presented to the Conference of Tunisian NGOs on the Challenges of the Future, Tunis, July.
34. Bratton, Michael (1989) 'The Politics of Government- NGO Relations in Africa', World Development, vol. 17(4), pp. 569-87.
35. Bratton, Michael (1986) 'Beyond the State: Civil Society and Associational Life in Africa', World Politics, vol. 41(3), pp. 407-30.
36. Bratton, Michael (1990) 'NGOs in Africa: Can They Influence Public Policy?' Development and Change, vol. 21(1), pp. 87-118.
37. Brautigam, Deborah (1991) 'Development, Institutional Pluralism and the Voluntary Sector', Washington D.C: World Bank.
38. Brautigam, D. (1992) 'Governance, Economy and Foreign Aid', Studies in Comparative International Development, vol. 27(3), pp. 3-25.
39. Broadhead, Tim and Herbert-Copley, Brent (1988) Bridges of Hope? Canadian Voluntary Agencies and the Third World, Ottawa: North-South Institute.
40. Brown, L. David (1988) 'Organizational Barriers to NGO Strategic Action', Lok Niti Journal of the Asian NGO Coalition, vol. 5(4), Manila: ANGOC.
41. Brown, L. David (1990) 'Policy Impacts on the NGO Sector', Washington D.C.: World Bank.
42. Brown, David L. and Korten, D.C. (1991) 'Working More Efficiently with Non-governmental Organizations', in Paul and Israel (eds), pp. 44-93.
43. Burgos, G.(1994) 'Los Servicios Legles Alternativos: Preguntas Indiscretas Ante el Nuevo Contexto Politico-Economico', Portavoz, vol. 38,pp 18-26. Clark,J. (1991) Democratizing Development, London: Earthscan.
44. Clark, J. (1991) Democratizing Development, London: Earthscan.
45. Chatterjee, Meera. Private Voluntary Health Organisation in India; Health Implementing Policy, New Delhi.
46. Cannon-Lorgan,C. (forthcoming) 'Dancing with the State: the Role of NGOs in Health Care and Health Policy', Journal of International Development.
47. Carroll, T., (1992) Intermediary NGOs: the Supporting Link in 'Grassroots Development, West Hartford: Kumarian Press.
48. Carroll, T., Humphreys. Nde. And Scurrah. (1991) ' Grassroots Support-Organisations in Peru', Development in Practice, vol. 1 (2), pp. 97-108.
49. Cernea, Michael (1998) NGOs and Local Development, Washington, DC: World Bank.
50. Chambers, R. (1992) 'Spreading and Self-Improving: a Strategy for Scaling-up', in M. Edwards and D. Hulme (eds.), Making a Difference: NGOs and Development in a Changing World, London: Earthscan.
51. Chambers, R. (1995) 'Poverty and Vulnerability: Whose Reality Counts?', IDS Discussion Paper 347, Brighton: Institute for Development Studies.
52. Chambers, Robert (1983) Rural Development: Putting the Last First, Harlow: Longman.

53. CIVICUS (1994) Citizens Strengthening Global Civil Society, Washington, D.C: Civicus.
54. Clark, John (1991) Democratizing Development: The Role of Voluntary Organizations, West Hartford: Kumarian Press.
55. Clark, J. (1993) The State and the Voluntary Sector, Human Resources Development and Operations Policy Working Paper No. 12, Washington, DC: World Bank.
56. Cohen, Joshua and Rogers, Joel (1992) 'Secondary Associations and Democratic Governance', Politics and Society, vol. 20(4) (December), 393-472. (Also the responses in this special issue of the journal).
57. Colclough, C.and Manor, J. (1991) States or Markets? Neo-Liberalism and the Development Policy Debate, Oxford: Clarendon Press.
58. Commission on Global Governance (1995) Our Common Neighborhood: the Report of the Commission on Global Governance, Oxford: Oxford University Press.
59. Covey, J. (1995) 'Accountability and Effectiveness in NGO Policy Alliances', in M. Edwards and D. Hulme (eds.) NGO Performance and Accountability: Beyond the Magic Bullet, London: Earthscan and West Hartford: Kumarian Press, 167-181.
60. Duggal Ravi; NGOs, Govt. and Private Sector in Health; Economic and Political weekly; March 26, 1988.
61. Discussion Note on Voluntary organizations in India; Society for Participatory Research in Asia; New Delhi, 1990.
62. DAC (Development Advisory Committee of the Organization for Economic Cooperation and Development) (1995) Participatory Development and Good Governance, Development Co-operation and Guidelines Series, Paris OECD.
63. De Coninck, J., with Riddell, R. C. (1992) 'Evaluating The Impact of NGOs in Rural Poverty Alleviation: Uganda Country Study', Working Paper 51, London: Overseas Development Institute.
64. De Silva, K.M. (1981) A History of Sri Lanka, Colombo: University Press.
65. Diamond, Larry (1992) 'Introduction: Civil Society and the Struggle for Democracy', in Larry Diamond (ed.), The Democratic Revolution: Struggles for Freedom and Democracy in the Developing World, New York: Freedom House, pp. 1-27.
66. Diamond, Larry (1994) 'Towards Democratic Consolidation: Rethinking Civil Society', Journal of Democracy, vol. 5(3) (July), pp. 4-17.
67. Duggal, Ravi. NGOs, Govt.and the Private Sector, the FRCH, Bombay, 1986.
68. Echenique, J. (1994) 'NGOs and Pro-Democracy Movements in Latin America', in A. Clayton (ed.), Governance, Democracy and Conditionality: What Role for NGOs? Oxford: INTRAC.
69. Economist Intelligence Unit (1994) Thailand Country Report, Third Quarter, 1994, London: EUI.
70. Edwards, M. (1994a) 'NGOs in the age of information', IDS Bulletin, vol. 25(2), pp. 117-24.

71. Edwards, M. (1994b) 'International Non-Governmental, "Good Government" and the "New Policy Agenda": Lessons of Experience at the program level', Democratization, vol. 1(3), pp. 504-515.

72. Edwards, M. and Hulme, D. (1992) Making a Difference: NGOs and Development in a Changing World, London: Earthscan.

73. Edwards, M. and Hulme, D. (1994) 'NGOs and Development: Performance and Accountability in the "New World Order", mimeo, London: Save the Children Fund (UK) and Manchester: Institute for Development Policy and Management.

74. Edwards, M. and Hulme, D. (eds.) (1995) NGO Performance and Accountability: Beyond the Magic Bullet, London: Earthscan and West Hartford: Kumarian Press.

75. El Taller (1995) NGOs and Civil Society in the Arab World, Tunis: El Taller.

76. Elliot, Charles (1987) 'Some aspects of relations between North and South in the NGO sector', World Development, vol. 15(supplement), pp. 57-68.

77. Farrington,J., and Bebbington, A., (1993) Reluctant Partners? Non-Governmental Organizations, the State and Sustainable Agricultural Development, London: Routledge.

78. Fernandez, A. P. (1987) 'NGOs in South Asia', World Development, vol. 15(supplement), pp. 39-49.

79. Fernandes, R. (1985) 'Sem Fins Lucravitos', Comunicacoes ISER, vol. 4(5), July, Rio de Janeiro: ISER.

80. Fernando, Edgar (ed.) (1982) Rural Development in Sri Lanka, Ministry of Plan Implementation.

81. Fernando, Sunimal (1991) Development of NGOs of Sri Lanka. A Directory, Colombo: IRED – Development Innovations and Networks.

82. Fisher, J. (1993) The Road from Rio, New York: Praeger.

83. Fowler, A. (1988) 'NGOs in Africa: Achieving Comparative Advantage in Relief and Micro-Development', IDS Discussion Paper 249, Brighton: Institute for Development Studies.

84. Fowler, A. (1992) 'Distant Obligations: Speculations on NGO Funding and the Global Market', Review of African Political Economy.

85. Fowler, A. (1993) 'Non-Governmental Organizations as Agents of Democratization: an African Perspective', Journal of International Development, vol. 5(3), May-June, pp. 325-39.

86. Fowler, A. (1992) 'NGOs as Agents of Democratization: An African Perspective', mimeo, (draft), May, Sussex: IDS.

87. Fox, J. (1992) 'Leadership accountability in a regional peasant organization', Development and Change, vol. 23(2), pp. 1-36.

88. Freire, P. (1972) Pedagogy of the Oppressed, London: Penguin, New York: Herder and Herder.

89. Friedmann, J. (1992) Empowerment: The Politics of Alternative Development, Oxford: Basil Blackwell.

90. Gamage, Willie and Dias, Richard (1990) Some Aspects of Government- NGO Relations in Sri Lanka, Colombo: IRED – Development Innovations and Networks.

91. GAO (United States General Accounting Office) (1994) Promoting Democracy: Foreign Affairs and Defense Agencies Funds and Activities – 1991 to 1993, Washington: GAO.

92. Garforth, C. (1993) 'Rural People Organizations and Agricultural Extension in the Upper North of Thailand: Who Benefits?', mimeo, University of Reading.

93. Garilao, E. D. (1987) 'Indigenous NGOs and strategic institutions: managing the relationship with government and resource agencies', World Development, vol. 15(supplement), pp. 113-120.

94. German, T. and Randel, J. (1995) The Reality of Aid 1995, London: Earthscan.

95. Ghazali, A. (1991) 'A Contribution to the Analysis of the Associative Phenomenon in Morocco', in M. Camau (ed.), Changements Politiques au Maghreb, Paris: Center National de Recherche Scientifique.

96. Gilson, L., Sen, P. D., Mohammed, S. and Mukinja, P. (1993) 'Assessing the Potential of Health Sector Non-Governmental Organizations: Policy Options', Health Policy and Planning, vol. 9(1), March, pp. 14-24.

97. Good, A. (1994) 'Paying the Piper, Calling the Tune? Present and Future Relationships among Northern NGOs, Southern NGOs and the ODA', paper presented at the International Workshop on NGOs and Development: Performance and Accountability in the New World Order, Manchester: Save the Children Fund (UK) and Institute for Development Policy and Management.

98. Granovetter, M. (1985) 'Economic Action and Social Structure: The Problem of Embeddedness', American Journal of Sociology, vol. 91(3), pp. 481-510.

99. Hanlon, Joseph (1990) 'New Missionaries in Mozambique', mimeo, London.

100. Hansen, Gary (1995) 'Constituencies for Reform: Strategic Approaches for Donor-supported Civic Advocacy Programs', fourth draft (revised), Washington, DC: USAID/PPC/CDIE/POA.

101. Hashemi, S. (1995) 'NGO Accountability in Bangladesh: Beneficiaries, Donors and the State', in M. Edwards and D. Hulme (eds.), NGO Performance and Accountability: Beyond the Magic Bullet, London: Earthscan and West Hartford: Kumarian Press.

102. Hawley, K. (1992) From Grants to Contracts: A Practical Guide for Voluntary Organizations, London: NCVO/Directory of Social Change.

103. Hirscman, A. O. (1970) Exit, Voice and Loyalty, Cambridge, Mass.: Harvard University Press.

104. Hirsh, P. (1994) 'The Thai Countryside in the 1990s', South-East Asian Affairs.

105. Hojman, D. (1993) 'Non-Governmental Organizations (NGOs) and the Chilean Transition to Democracy', European Review of Latin American and Caribbean Studies, vol. 54, pp. 7-24.

106. Howell, J. (1993a) China Opens its Doors: the Politics of Economic Transition, Hemel Mempstead: Harvester Wheatsheaf and Boulder, Col: Lynne Rienner Publishers.

107. Howell, J. (1993b) 'The Poverty of Civil Society: Insights from China', Discussion Paper, no. 240, School of Development Studies, University of East Anglia.

108. Howell, J. (1994) 'Refashioning State-Society Relations in China', The European Journal Of Development Research, vol. 6(1), pp. 197-215.

109. Howes, M. and Sattar, M. G. (1992) 'Bigger and Better? Scaling-up Strategies Pursued by BRAC 1972-1991', in M. Edwards and D. Hulme (eds.), Making a Difference: NGOs and Development in a Changing World, London: Earthscan.

110. Hulme, D. (1994) 'Does the World Bank have a Learning Disability? A Reply to Venkatesan', Public Administration and Development, vol. 14(1), pp. 93-7.

111. Hulme, D. and Edwards, M. (eds.) (1996) NGOs, States and Donors: Too Close for Comfort? London: Macmillan.

112. Hulme, D. and Mosley, P. (1996) Finance Against Poverty, two vols, London: Routledge.

113. Huntington, Samuel P. (1968) Political Order in Changing Societies, New Haven, Yale University Press.

114. Hyden, Goran (1995) 'Assisting the Growth of Civil Society: How Might It Be Improved?', paper for Workshop on Civil Society and Democracy, arranged by the Development Assistance Committee of the OECD, Uppsala University, Sweden, 12-13 June.

115. Irvine, G. (1987) The World Bank and World Vision: A Status Report, World Vision International Staff Paper.

116. Isenman, Paul (1980) 'Basic Needs: The Case of Sri Lanka', World Development, vol. 8, pp. 247-9.

117. Jorgensen, H., Larsen, J. and Udsholt, L. (1993) The Role Of Danish Development NGOs: Challenges for the Future, Copenhagen: Danish Volunteer Service.

118. Kandil, A. (1994) The Status of the Third Sector of the Arab Region, Tunis: El Taller.

119. Karp, A. W. (1992) 'Contracting NGOs to Implement Rural Water and Sanitation Projects in Bolivia', Waterlines; vol. 11(1), July, pp. 23-5.

120. Kendall, J. and Perri 6 (1994) 'Government and the Voluntary Sector in the United Kingdom', in Perri 6, S.K.E. E Saxon-Herald and J. Kendall (eds.), pp. 16-40.

121. Klinmahorm, S. and Ireland, K. (1992) 'Government- NGO Collaboration in Bankok', in M. Edwards and D. Hulme (eds.), Making a Difference: NGOs and Development in a Changing World, London: Earthscan.

122. Korten, D. (1987) 'Third Generation NGO Strategies: A key to People-Centered Development', World Development, vol. 15, Supplement, pp. 145-59.

123. Korten, David C. (1990) Getting to the 21st Century: Voluntary Action and the Global Agenda, West Hartford: Kumarian Press.

124. LaFond, A. (1995) Sustaining Primary Health Care, London: Earthscan/Save the Children Fund.

125. Landim, L. (1993) Para além do Mercado e do Estado? Filantropia e Cidadania no Brasil, Rio de Janeiro: ISER.

126. Lateef, K. Sarwar (1992) Governance and Development, Washington, DC: World Bank.

127. Lawson, C. and Kaluwa, B. (1992) Seven Malawian Parastatals: An Appraisal of Performance and Policy, CDS Occasional Paper 01/92, Bath.

128. Lefort, C. (1983) A Invencao Democratica – Os Limites do Totalitarismo, São Paulo: Editora Brasilence.

129. Lehmann, D. (1990) Democracy and Development in Latin America, Cambridge: Polity.

130. Levinson, M. and Wehrfritz, G. (1994) 'Some Cracks in the Wall of the Miracle Economy', Newsweek, 16th May.

131. Lewis, D., Sobhan, B. and Jonsson, G. (1994) Routes of Funding, Roots of Trust? Swedish Assistance to Non-Governmental Organizations in Bangladesh, Stockholm: SIDA.

132. MacDonald, Laura (1992) 'Turning to the NGOs: Competing Conceptions of Civil Society in Latin America', paper presented to the Annual Meeting of the Latin American Studies Association, Los Angeles, 24-7 September.

133. Makabenta, L. (1995) 'Thailand', Jakarta Post, 13 January.

134. Manila (1998) 'Asian NGO Coalition', The Manila Declaration on People's Participation and Sustainable Development, Manila, June.

135. Marc, Alexandre (1992) 'NGOs in Kyrghyzstan', mimeo, Washington, DC: World Bank.

136. Meyer, C. (1992) 'A Step Back as Donors Shift Institution Building from the Public to the "Private" Sector', World Development, vol. 20(8), pp. 1115-26.

137. Michels, Robert (1915) Political Parties, reprint, New York: Dover, 1959.

138. Ministry of Finance and Planning (1981) Public Expenditure Program, Colombo: Government Printer.

139. Montgomery, R. (1995) 'Disciplining or Protecting the Poor? Avoiding the Social Costs of Peer Pressure in Solidarity Group Micro-Credit Schemes', Papers in Development, 12, Swansea: Center for Development Studies.

140. Montgomery, R., Bhattacharya, D. and Hulme, D. (1996) 'Credit for the Poor in Bangladesh: The BRAC Rural Development Program and the Government Thana Resource Development and Employment Program', in D. Hulme and P. Mosley (eds.) Finance Against Poverty, vol. 2, London: Routledge.

141. Moore, B. (1996) The Social Origins of Dictatorship and Democracy, Boston: Beacon Press.

142. Moore, M. (1993) 'Good Government? Introduction', IDS Bulletin, vol. 24(1), pp. 1-6.

143. Mosher, S. (1991) 'Cynicism Evident in Aid to China Flood Victims: Give and Let Live', Far Eastern Economic Review, vol. 153, 8th August, p. 10.

144. Muir, A. with Riddell, R. C. (1992) 'Evaluating the Impact of NGOs in Rural Poverty Alleviation: Zimbabwe Country Study', Working Paper 52, London: Overseas Development Institute.

145. Mushi, S. S., Semboja, J. and Therkilsden, O. (1992) 'Issues of Service Provision in the 1990s in Eastern Africa" paper presented at a Seminar on 'State and Non-State Provision of Services in Eastern Africa and South Asia', Copenhagen, June.

146. NCARRD NGO Committee Sri Lanka (1980) Report of the National NGO Workshop on Follow-up to WCARRD: 5-6 September.

147. Nerfin, M. (1987) 'Neither Prince nor Merchant; Citizen', IFDA Dossier, Geneva: IFDA.

148. Norway (1995) Royal Norwegian Ministry of Foreign Affairs, 'Support for Democratic Development', Oslo: Royal Norwegian Ministry of Foreign Affairs, May.

149. The Commonwealth Foundation (1999) Citizens and Governance, London: The Commonwealth Foundation.

150. Darcy De Oliveira, M. and R. Tandon (1994) Citizens: Strengthening Global Civil Society, Washington, DC:Civicus.

151. Edwards, M. and D. Hulme (eds.) (1995) Non-Governmental Organizations – Performance and Accountability – Beyond the Magic Bullet, London: Earthscan (with Save the Children Fund)

152. Holloway, R. (ed.) (199) Rethinking Development, New Delhi: Ajanta.

153. Mehta N., W. Haque, P. Wignaraja and A. Rahman (1977) Development Dialogue: A Quarter Century of Anti Rural Development.

154. Raise,V., A.Choudhury and S.Choudhury (eds.) (1997) The Dispossessed, ARENA.

155. Salomon, L.M.et.al.(1999) Global Civil Society: Dimensions of the Nonprofit Sector, Baltimore, MA: Johns Hopkins Centre for Civil Society Studies.

156. Tandon, R. (1991) Civil Society, the State and Roles of NGOs, Boston: IDR Occasional Paper.

157. Tandon, R. (1996) 'Institutional Strengthening of NGOs in the South', ODA-BOND-CDS Workshop.

158. United Nations (1995) World Summit for Social Development, 6-12 March 1995: The Copenhagen Declaration and Programme of Action, New York, NY: UN Department of Public Information.

159. Howell, J. (1994) 'Refashioning State-Society Relations in China', The European Journal Of Development Research, vol. 6(1), pp. 197-215.

160. Howes, M. and Sattar, M. G. (1992) 'Bigger and Better? Scaling-up Strategies Pursued by BRAC 1972-1991', in M. Edwards and D. Hulme (eds.), Making a Difference: NGOs and Development in a Changing World, London: Earthscan.

161. Hulme, D. (1994) 'Does the World Bank have a Learning Disability? A Reply to Venkatesan', Public Administration and Development, vol. 14(1), pp. 93-7.

162. Hulme, D. and Edwards, M. (eds.) (1996) NGOs, States and Donors: Too Close for Comfort? London: Macmillan.

163. Hulme, D. and Mosley, P. (1996) Finance Against Poverty, two vols, London: Routledge.

164. Huntington, Samuel P. (1968) Political Order in Changing Societies, New Haven, Yale University Press.

165. Hyden, Goran (1995) 'Assisting the Growth of Civil Society: How Might It Be Improved?', paper for Workshop on Civil Society and Democracy, arranged by

the Development Assistance Committee of the OECD, Uppsala University, Sweden, 12-13 June.

166. Irvine, G. (1987) The World Bank and World Vision: A Status Report, World Vision International Staff Paper.

167. Isenman, Paul (1980) 'Basic Needs: The Case of Sri Lanka', World Development, vol. 8, pp. 247-9.

168. Jorgensen, H., Larsen, J. and Udsholt, L. (1993) The Role Of Danish Development NGOs: Challenges for the Future, Copenhagen: Danish Volunteer Service.

169. Jesani, Awar and Ganguly, Shipli; Some Issues in commity participation in Health care services; FRCH; Bombay, 1990.

170. Jesani, Amar and Anantharam, Saraswatty - Private Sector and Privatisation in the Health care Services; A review paper for the ICSSR - ICMR Joint Pavel on Health - FRCH, Bombay, 1990.

171. Kandil, A. (1994) The Status of the Third Sector of the Arab Region, Tunis: El Taller.

172. Kar, Manoj (1995) 'Role of NGOs in Health and Development Programmes in India: A Policy Analysis', M.Phil. Dissertation, Center for Social Medicine and Community Health, School of Social Sciences, Jawahar Lal Nehru University, New Delhi, India.

173. Karp, A. W. (1992) 'Contracting NGOs to Implement Rural Water and Sanitation Projects in Bolivia', Waterlines; vol. 11(1), July, pp. 23-5.

174. Kendall, J. and Perri 6 (1994) 'Government and the Voluntary Sector in the United Kingdom', in Perri 6, S.K.E. E Saxon-Herald and J. Kendall (eds.), pp. 16-40.

175. Klinmahorm, S. and Ireland, K. (1992) 'Government- NGO Collaboration in Bankok', in M. Edwards and D. Hulme (eds.), Making a Difference: NGOs and Development in a Changing World, London: Earthscan.

176. Korten, D. (1987) 'Third Generation NGO Strategies: A key to People-Centered Development', World Development, vol. 15, Supplement, pp. 145-59.

177. Korten, David C. (1990) Getting to the 21st Century: Voluntary Action and the Global Agenda, West Hartford: Kumarian Press.

178. LaFond, A. (1995) Sustaining Primary Health Care, London: Earthscan/Save the Children Fund.

179. Landim, L. (1993) Para além do Mercado e do Estado? Filantropia e Cidadania no Brasil, Rio de Janeiro: ISER.

180. Lateef, K. Sarwar (1992) Governance and Development, Washington, DC: World Bank.

181. Lawson, C. and Kaluwa, B. (1992) Seven Malawian Parastatals: An Appraisal of Performance and Policy, CDS Occasional Paper 01/92, Bath.

182. Lefort, C. (1983) A Invencao Democratica – Os Limites do Totalitarismo, São Paulo: Editora Brasilence.

183. Lehmann, D. (1990) Democracy and Development in Latin America, Cambridge: Polity.

184. Levinson, M. and Wehrfritz, G. (1994) 'Some Cracks in the Wall of the Miracle Economy', Newsweek, 16th May.

185. Lewis, D., Sobhan, B. and Jonsson, G. (1994) Routes of Funding, Roots of Trust? Swedish Assistance to Non-Governmental Organizations in Bangladesh, Stockholm: SIDA.

186. MacDonald, Laura (1992) 'Turning to the NGOs: Competing Conceptions of Civil Society in Latin America', paper presented to the Annual Meeting of the Latin American Studies Association, Los Angeles, 24-7 September.

187. Makabenta, L. (1995) 'Thailand', Jakarta Post, 13 January.

188. Manila (1998) 'Asian NGO Coalition', The Manila Declaration on People's Participation and Sustainable Development, Manila, June.

189. Marc, Alexandre (1992) 'NGOs in Kyrghyzstan', mimeo, Washington, DC: World Bank.

190. Meyer, C. (1992) 'A Step Back as Donors Shift Institution Building from the Public to the "Private" Sector', World Development, vol. 20(8), pp. 1115-26.

191. Michels, Robert (1915) Political Parties, reprint, New York: Dover, 1959.

192. Ministry of Finance and Planning (1981) Public Expenditure Program, Colombo: Government Printer.

193. Montgomery, R. (1995) 'Disciplining or Protecting the Poor? Avoiding the Social Costs of Peer Pressure in Solidarity Group Micro-Credit Schemes', Papers in Development, 12, Swansea: Center for Development Studies.

194. Montgomery, R., Bhattacharya, D. and Hulme, D. (1996) 'Credit for the Poor in Bangladesh: The BRAC Rural Development Program and the Government Thana Resource Development and Employment Program', in D. Hulme and P. Mosley (eds.) Finance Against Poverty, vol. 2, London: Routledge.

195. Moore, B. (1996) The Social Origins of Dictatorship and Democracy, Boston: Beacon Press.

196. Moore, M. (1993) 'Good Government? Introduction', IDS Bulletin, vol. 24(1), pp. 1-6.

197. Mosher, S. (1991) 'Cynicism Evident in Aid to China Flood Victims: Give and Let Live', Far Eastern Economic Review, vol. 153, 8th August, p. 10.

198. Muir, A. with Riddell, R. C. (1992) 'Evaluating the Impact of NGOs in Rural Poverty Alleviation: Zimbabwe Country Study', Working Paper 52, London: Overseas Development Institute.

199. Mushi, S. S., Semboja, J. and Therkilsden, O. (1992) 'Issues of Service Provision in the 1990s in Eastern Africa" paper presented at a Seminar on 'State and Non-State Provision of Services in Eastern Africa and South Asia', Copenhagen, June.

200. NCARRD NGO Committee Sri Lanka (1980) Report of the National NGO Workshop on Follow-up to WCARRD: 5-6 September.

201. Nerfin, M. (1987) 'Neither Prince nor Merchant; Citizen', IFDA Dossier, Geneva: IFDA.

202. Norway (1995) Royal Norwegian Ministry of Foreign Affairs, 'Support for Democratic Development', Oslo: Royal Norwegian Ministry of Foreign Affairs, May.

203. Pachauri, Saroj. Reaching India's poor Non-Governmental Approaches to commity Health, Ford foundation, New Delhi, 1994.

204. Tandon, Rajesh. The state and voluntary Agencies in Asia. In Richard Holloway (ed.), Doing Development - Govts, NGOs and the Rural Poor in Asia. Earthscan Publications Ltd; London, in association with CUSO, 1989.

205. Society for Participatory Research in Asia. Voluntary Development Organisations in India. A study of History, Roles and future challanges.PRIA, NEW DELHI, NOV.1991.

206. Jesani Amar; Gupta, Manisha and Duggal, Ravi NGOs in Rural Health Care. The FRCH, Bombay, 1986.

207. Jesani Amar; Gupta, Manisha and Duggal, Ravi NGOs in Rural Health Care, Vol.1 : overview. The FRCH, Bombay, 1986.

208. ICSSR/ICMR Health for All: An Alternative strategy - 1981.

209. Veena Soni Raleish. KEM Hospital - Rural Health Project - Anuvab series, ford fundation study, 1977.

Chapters IV-VIII

1. 1982. Henderson, R.H & Sundaresan, T. "Cluster Sampling to Assess Immunization Coverage: A Review of Experience with a Simplified Sampling Method" Bulletin of the World Health Organization 60(2) pp. 253-260.

2. 1988, Expanded Programme on Immunization, Training for mid level Managers: Coverage Survey, World Health Organization, Geneva.

3. 1989 UNICEF, UNESCO & WHO. Facts for life – A communication challenge, UNICEF, New York.

4. 1989, Diarrhea Disease Control Programme, Household Survey Manual: Diarrhea Case Management, Morbidity, and Mortality, World Helath Organization, Geneva.

5. 1990 Baseline Survey report of Seva Mandir PVOH-II Project.

6. 1990 Joint Appraisal Report of National Institute of Helath and family Welfare, New Delhi.

7. 1993 National Family Health Survey, Rajasthan.

8. 1995 The Rapid Knowledge, Practice, Coverage Survey Trainer's guide Johns Hopkins University, USA.

9. Abueva, Jose V. (1969): Administrative Doctrines Diffused in Emerging States: The Filipino Response In: Braibanti, Ralph (1969, Ed.): Political and Administrative Development. Durham: Duke University Press.

10. Aminuzzaman, Salahuddin (1998): NGOs and the Grassroots Base Local Government in Bangladesh: A study of their Institutional Interactions. In: Hossain, Farhad & Myllyla, Susanna (Eds.) NGOs Under challenge. Dynamics and Drawbacks in Develpoment. Helsinki: Ministry for Foreign Affairs of Finland, Department for International Development Co-operation.

11. Anheier, Helmut K. & Seibel, Wolfgang (Eds.; 1990): The third sector, Comparative Studies of Nonprofit Organizations. Berlin: Walter de Gruyter.

12. Background history information and related materials from BCT.

13. Background history information and related materials from BRS.
14. Baseline Survey for comprehensive rural health development project under PVOH-II, Indian Institute of Health Management Research, Jaipur, 1992.
15. Field visits, interaction with project beneficiaries, *Mahila Mandals*, VHCs, village heads, members of Panchayats, members from the government health agencies from the tehsil, and district (PHC, CHC and District hospital, Jaipur, Udaipur, Churu) and interaction with key project functionaries and members from the RHC at Kherwada, RHC at Bhorugram and RHC at Lalgarh and discussion with the secretary of the NGOs at respective offices in Udaipur, Churu and Jaipur.
16. Hossain, Farhad & Malkia, Matti (1996): Conceptualising the Organisational Field of Third World Development. The Case of Third Sector Organisations. Journal of Administration and Diplomacy, Vol. 4, No. 1.
17. IEC, Directorate of Medical and Health Department, Govt. of Rajasthan.
18. IIRR (93-2501EI): Management problems in non-governmental organisations. Manila: International Institute of Rural Reconstruction.
19. Indian Journal of Community health (ISSN –0971-7420), Volume III, 1997.
20. Institute of Development Studies, Jaipur, *Rajasthan me Swayamsevi Sansthayen Nirdesika* (Directory of NGOs in Rajasthan), 1996 (First edition)
21. Jamil, Ishtiaq (1994): Transactional Friction Between NGOs and Public Agencies in a Developing Country: Culture or Dependency? Norwegian Research Centre in Organisation and Management. Norwegian Research Centre in Organisation and Management (Bergen, 1994)
22. Kalimullah, Nazmul Ahsan (1990): Non-Governmental Organisations in Development. Some conceptual Issues. In:Development Review, Dhaka, Vol. 2, No. 2.
23. Korten, David C. (1991): The Role of NGOs in Develpoment: Changing Patterns and Perspectives In: Paul, Samuel & Israel, Arturo (Eds.): Non-governmental Organisations and the World Bank – Co-operation for Development. Washington D.C.: The World Bank.
24. Masoni, V. (1985): Non-governmental Organisations and Development. Finance and Development, Vol. 22.
25. NFHS(I & II) Rajasthan, International Institute of Population Sciences, Mumbai, 1992-93, 2000-01.
26. Participatory Evaluation Workshop (North Zone) reports PRIA, New Delhi.
27. Project Appraisal Report by NIHFW, New Delhi.
28. Project Conceptualisation document by MOH&FW and USAID.
29. PVOH-II Financial Management Plan by MOH&FW, Govt. of India.
30. Rajasthan Voluntary Health Association, Jaipur.
31. Riggs, Fred W. (1977B): The Context of Development Administration. In: Riggs, Fred W. (1977, Ed.): Frontiers of Development Administration. Durham: Duke University Press.
32. Salamon, Lester M. & Anheier, Helmut K. (1996): The Emerging Nonprofit Sector. An Overview. Manchester (UK): Manchester University Press.

33. Smillie, Ian & Helmich, Henny (Eds.; 1993): Non-Governmental Organizations and governments. Stakeholders for Development. Paris: Development Centre of the Organisation for Economic Co-operation an Development.

34. Smillie, Ian (1995): The Alms Bazaar. Altruism Under Fire. Non-Profit Organizations and International Development. London: Intermediate Technology– Publications.

35. Societies Registration Act (1860): Act No XXI of 1860, British India. 21st May 1860.

36. Towards a relationship of significance: Interim report on the study of relationships between government and NGOs in Rajasthan, PRADAN, New Delhi –1996.

37. Training Need Assessment, Training Programme Reports and Baseline survey report, Mid-term and Final Evaluation Reports for PVOH-II from BCT.

38. Training Need Assessment, Training Programme Reports and Baseline survey report, Mid-term and Final Evaluation Reports for PVOH-II from BRS.

39. Tvedt, Terje (1997): Development NGOs – actors in a new international social system. Bergen: A draft paper presented at the conference "Non-Governmental Organisations in aid. A reappraisal of 35 years of NGO assistance".

References

1. Abel Smith B. 1986. The World Economic Crisis, Part I: repercussions on health, Health Policy and Planning 1: 202-13.
2. "Sustainability Analysis", Primary Health Care Management Advancement Programme, Aga Khan Health Services, New Delhi.
3. (NANGO) National Association of Non-Governmental Organisations(1991), The NANGO Programme of Activities, to 1993/94 (Harare: NANGO).
4. ___ (1985), 'Shortcut Methods of Gathering Social Information for Rural Development Projects', in Cernea, 399-415.
5. ___ (1988), Non-governmental Organisations and Local Development, Discussion Paper No. 40 (Washington, DC: World Bank).
6. ___ (1990b),Getting to the 21st Century: Voluntary Development Action and the Global Agenda (Hartford, Conn: Kumarian Press).
7. ___ (1992), 'Development Bridging Organisations and Strategic Managers for Social Change', Institute for Development Research. 9(5), May.
8. ___ and Korten, D. (1989), Understanding Voluntary Organisations: Guidelines for Donors, Working Paper WPS 258 (Washtington, DC: World Bank).
9. ___ (1987), 'Third Generation NGO Strategies: A Key to People-Centred Development', World Development, 15, suppl. (Autumn), 145-60.
10. ___ (1990a), 'NGOs and Development: An Overview Paper', prepared for the World Bank (Boston: Institute for Development Research; mimeo).
11. ___ (1991), 'The Role of NGOs in Changing State-Society Relations: Perspectives from Eastern and Southern Africa', Development Policy Review, 9/1:53-84.
12. ___ and Hulme, D. (1992) (eds.), Making a Difference: NGOs and Development in a Changing World (London: Earthscan).
13. ___ Bebbington, A.J. and Wellard, K. (1993), Between the State and the Rural Poor: NGOs and Agricultural Development (London: Routledge).
14. ___ Hakin, P., and Peinner, L. (1988), Direct To The Poor (Boulder, Colo. and London: Westview).
15. ___ (1985) (ed.), Putting People First: Sociological Variables in Rural Development (New York: Oxford University Press for the World Bank).
16. ___ (1994), 'The Origins and Practice of Participatory Rural Appraisal', World Development, 22/7: 953-69.
17. ___ and David Korten (1991), 'Working Effectively with Non-Governmental Organisations' in Samuel Paul and Arturo Israel (eds.), Non-Governmental Organisations and the World Bank, Washington, DC.

18. ___ Pacey, A. and Thrupp, L.A. (1989) (eds.), Farmer First: Farmer Innovation and Agricultural Research (London: Intermediate Technology).
19. Alliband, T. (1993), Catalysts of Development: Voluntary Agencies in India Hartford, Kumarian Press).
20. Annis, S. (1987), 'Can Small-Scale Development be a Large-Scale Policy? The Case of Latin Americ', World Development, 15, suppl. (autumn), 129-34.
21. Armstrong, G.A. and Bridger, G.A. (1986), Cost Effectness: Appraising Projects with Non-Quantifiable Benefits (London: Crown Agents).
22. Avard (1991), 'Role of NGOs in Development: A Study of the Situation in India', New Delhi, Association of Voluntary Agencies for Rural Development (mimeo).
23. Avina, J. (1990), 'The Evolutionary Life Cycles of Non-Governmental Development Organisations', Public Administration and Development, 13/5: 453-76.
24. Bagchi, A.K., "The Political Economy of Underdevelopment",
25. Baldwin, D. (1988), Non-government Organisation and African Development: An Inquiry (Washington, DC: World Bank).
26. Banerji, D., "Family Planning in the Nineties: More of the Same or a Sharp Break?", Economic and Political Weekly, Vol. XXvii, No.17, 1992.
27. Barclay A. H., Hoskins, M.W., Njenga, W.K. and Tripp, R.B.
28. Beaudoux, E., Crombrugghe, G. DE, Douxchamps, F., Gueneau, M., and Neuwkerk, M. (1990), Supporting Development Action at Community Level: A Methodological Guide (Brussels: le Collectif d'Echanges pour la Technologie Appropriee (COTA).
29. Berg, R.J. (1987), Non-Governmental Organisations: New Force in Third World Development and Politics (Lancing, Mich.: Michigan State University, Centner for Advanced Stdy of International Development).
30. Bhatia JC. Levels and causes of maternal mortality in southern India. Studies in family planning1993, 24: 310-318.
31. Bhatt RV. Maternal mortality in India - FOGSI-WHO study. Journal of obsetrics and gynaecology 1997, 47:207-214.
32. Black, M. (1992), A Cause for our Times: Oxfam the First 50 Years (Oxford: Oxfam and Oxford University Press).
33. Bossert T.J. 1990. Can they get along without us?
34. Bowden, P. (1990), 'NGOs in Asia: Issues in Development', Public Administration and Development, 10: 141-52.
35. Bowmann, M., Bannante, J., Dichter, T., Londer, S., and Reiling, P. (1989), Measuring Our Impact: Determining Cost-effectiveness of Non-Governmental Organisation Development Project (Norwalk, Conn.: Technoserve).
36. Bown, L. (1990), Preparing the Future - Women, Literacy and Development, Action Aid Development Report No.4 (London: Action Aid).
37. Bratton, M. (1990), 'Non-governmental Organisations in Africa: Can They Influence Public Policy?', Development and Change, 21/1: 87-118.
38. Brett, E.A. (1989), 'Servicing Small Farmers under Duress: Institutional Crises and Reconstructionin Uganda' (Brighton: Institute of Development Studies; mimeo).

39. Brinkerhoff D, Goldsmith A. 1992. Promoting the sustainability of development institutions; a framework of strategy. World Development 20: 369-83.

40. Brodhead, T. and Herbert-Copley, B. (1988), Bridges of Hope? Canadian Voluntary Agencies and the Third World (Ottawa: North-South Institute).

41. Brown, David (1988), 'Private Voluntary Organisations and Development Partnerships' in P.N. Khandwala (ed.). Social Development: A New Role for the Organisational Sciences, New Delhi, Sage.

42. Brown, L.D. (1990), Bridge Organisations and Sustainable Development, Institute for Development Research, Paper No. A17 (Boston: IDR).

43. Buzzard S.1987. Development Assistance and Health Programs: Issues of sustainability. Program Evaluation Discussion, Paper No. 23, Washington DC: USAID.

44. Cameron, C. and Cocking, J. (1991), 'The Evaluation of NGO Activities, Organisations, Methodology and Results' (London: ODA, Evaluation Department; mimeo).

45. Campbell, P. (1989), 'Institutional Development: Basic Principles and Strategies' (Geneva: International Council of Voluntary Agencies).

46. Canadian International Development Agency (CIDA) (1986), Corporate Evaluation of CIDA's Non-governmental Organisations Programme (Ottawa: CIDA).

47. Carroli, T. (1992), Intermediary NGOs: The Supporting Link in Grassroots Development (Hartford, conn.: The Kumarian Press).

48. Cassen R. and Associates (1986), Does Aid Works? (London: Oxford University Press).

49. Cernea, M.M. (1983), A Social Methodology for Community Participation in Local Investiments: The Experience of Mexico's PIDER Project, World Bank Staff Working Paper No. 598 (Washington, DC: World Bank).

50. Chalker, L. (1989), 'The Role of NGOs in Today's World', Cecil Jackson Memorial Lecture delivered at the Commonwealth Institute, London, October (London: ODA; mimeo).

51. Chambers, R. (1983), Rural Development: Putting the Last First (Harlow: Longman).

52. Chenery, H., Ahluwalia, M.S., Bell, C.L.G., Duloy, J.H., and Jolly, R. (1974), Redistribution with Growth (London: Oxford University Press).

53. Clark, J. (1991), Democratising Development: The Role of Voluntary Organisations (London: Earthscan Publications).

54. Clausen A.1985. Poverty in developing countries. Washington World Bank.

55. Clayton, A. (1994) (ed.), Governance, Democracy and Conditionality: What Role for NGOs?, INTRAC NGO Management and Policy Series, No.2 (Oxford: INTRAC Publications).

56. Commonwealth Secretariat (1987), Strategic Issues in DevelopmentManagement: Learning from Successful Experiences, 3 vols. (London: Commonwealth Secretariat).

57. Conyers, D. and Kaul, M. (1990), 'Strategic Issues in Development Management: Learning from Successful Experience', Public Administration and Development, 10: 127-40.

58. Cornea, G.A., Jolly, R. and Stewart, F. (1988) (ed.), Adjustment with a Human Face, ii, Country Case Studies (Oxford: Clearendon Press.

59. Cornia, G.A., et al (eds.), "Adjustment with a Human Face: Country Case Studies", Clarendon Press, Oxford, 1988.

60. CPR (1985), 'Report on Workshop on Corporate Philanthropy', New Delhi, Ford Foundation (mimeo).

61. DANIDA (1989), Danish NGOs, Report No.1, Synthesis (Copenhagen: Ministry of Foreign Affiars, Department of International Development (Cooperation).

62. Das Gupta, B. (1977), 'India Green Revolution', Economic and Political Weekly, 12, Annual Number.

63. DE. Conince, J. with Riddell, R.c. (1992), Evaluating the Impact of NGOs in Rural Poverty Alleviation: Uganda Country Study, Working Paper No. 51 (London: Overseas Development Institute).

64. DE. Graaf, M., Moyo, S., and Dietz, T. (1991), 'Non-Governmental Organisation in Zimbabwe: Report for the Impact Study Co-Financing Organisations' (Amsterdam: 3d Concept).

65. Dighter, T. (1988), 'Insights into Cost Effectiveness from One PVO's Perspective' (Hartford, Conn.: Technoserve).

66. Dreze, J. and Sen, A. (1989), Hunger and Public Action (Oxford: Clarendon Press).

67. D'Rozario, A. (1989), 'NGOs Face stricter Control from Bangaldesh Government', Asia Focus, 14/3 (Oct.).

68. Duggal, Ravi (1986), "NGOs, Government and the Private Sector", The FRCH, Bombay.

69. Ebel B. 1991. Patterns of government expenditure in developing countries during the 1980s: the impact on social services. Innocent Occasional Papers. Economic Policy Series. 18:17.

70. Ellis, G. (1984), 'Making PVOs Count More: A Proposal' in Gorman, 201-4.

71. Else, J. (1987), NGO Activities in Income-Generating Project (IGPs) in Zimbabwe: Report of a Study Conducted under the Auspices of VOICE's Development Forum (Harare: VOICE).

72. Esman, M.J. and Uphoff, N. (1984), Local Organisations: Intermediaries in Rural Development (Ithaca, NY: Cornell University Press).

73. Ewards, M. (1989), 'Learning from Experience in Africa' (Oxford: Oxfam; mimeo).

74. Farrington, J. and Martin, A. (1988), Farmer Participation in Agricultural Research: A Review of Concepts and Practices, Agricultural Administration Unit Occasional Paper 9 (London: Overseas Development Institute).

75. Farrington, M.J. et al. (eds.) (1993), Non-Governmental Organisations and the State in Asia, London and New York, Rutledge.

76. Fowler, A. (1988), NGOs in Africa: Achieving comparative Advantage in Relief and Micro-Development, Discussion Paper No. 249 (Brighton: Institute of Development Studies).

77. Ganatra BR, Coyaji KJ, Rao VN. Community cum hospital-based case-control study on maternal mortality, K.E.M. hospital, 1996.

78. Getubig, I.P. and Ledesma, A.J. (1988) (eds.), Voices from the Culture of Silence: The Most Disadvantaged Groups in Aisan Agriculture (Kuala Lumpur: Asia and Pacific Development Centre).

79. Gillespie, N. (1990), Selected World Bank Poverty Studies: A Summary of Approaches, Coverage and Findings, Working Paper WPS 552 (Washington, DC: World Bank).

80. Goetz, A.M. and Sen Gupta, R. (1994), 'Who Takes the Credit? Gender, Power and Control Over Loan Use in Rural Credit Programmes in Bangladesh', IDS Working Paper No. 8 (Brighton: Institute of Development Studies).

81. Gorman, R.F. (1984), Private Voluntary Organisations as Agents of Development (Boulder, Colo and London: Westview).

82. Government of India. Reproductive and Child Health Progarmme.Schemes for implementation.Department of Family Welfare, Ministry of Health and Family Welfare, 1997.

83. Government of India.National Youth Policy (Draft) 1998. Department of youth Affairs and Sports, Ministry of Human Resource Development.

84. Government of India. Annual Plan 2000-2001. The Planning Commission of India.

85. Government of India. Annual Report 1999-2000. Department of Elementary Education and Literacy and Department of Secondary Education and Higher Literacy, Ministry of Human Resource Development,2000.

86. Government of India. Annual Report 1999-2000. Department of Women and Chikd Development,Ministry of Human Resource Development,2000.

87. Government of India. India's progress Towards ICPD Goals. Ministry of Health and Family Welfare, 1999.

88. Government of India. Draft Ninth Five-Year Plan.(1997-2002). Chapter on Food and Nutrition Security. The Planning Commission of India.

89. Government of India. Draft Ninth Five-Year Plan.(1997-2002). Chapter on Family Welfare. The Planning Commission of India.

90. Government of India. Reproductive and Child Health(World Bank Component). Project Proposal and Implementation Plan. Volume I. Department of Family Welfare, Ministry of Health and Family Welfare, 1997.

91. Government of India. Research Studies and Standards division. Department of Family Welfare, Ministry of Health and Family Welfare.

92. Government of India. Rural Health Statistics in India. Rural Health Division Directorate General of Health Services, Ministry of Health and Family Welfare, June 2000.

93. Government of India. Annual Report 1999-2000. Ministry of Rural Development 2000.

94. Government of India. Donor co-ordination Division. Department of Family Welfare, Ministry of Health and Family Welfare.
95. Government of India. Platform for Action. Five Years After - An assessment. Department of Women and Child Development, MOHRD, June 2000.
96. Government of India. Annual Report 1999-2000. Ministry of Health and Family Welfare.
97. Government of India. Area Projects Division. Department of Family Welfare, Ministry of Health and Family Welfare.
98. Government of India. Causes of Maternal Death. Sample Registration bulletin, 1997, 1998. Office of Registrar General of India.
99. Government of India. National Policy for the empowerment of Women (Final Draft) 1996. Department of Women and Child Development, Ministry of Human Resource Development.
100. Government of India. Report of the Sub-committee on Reproductive Health Research Needs Assessment(RHRNA). Department of Family Welfare, Ministry of Health and Family Welfare, June 1999.
101. Government of India. Survey of Causes of Death (Rural). Annual Report 1995 and 1996. Office of Registrar General of India.
102. Govt. of India Ministry of Health and Family Welfare, "Expert Group on Population Policy: Draft National Population Policy", New Delhi, 1994.
103. Govt. of India Ministry of Health and Family Welfare, "Health Information India- 1992", New Delhi, 1992.
104. Govt. of India Ministry of Health, "Report of the Health Survey and Planning Committee", New Delhi, 1961.
105. Govt. of India, (1986), "Revised Strategy for National Family Welfare Programme- A Summary". Ministry of Health and Family Welfare, New Delhi.
106. Govt. of India, (1988), "Statement of National Health Policy", Ministry of Health and Family Welfare, New Delhi.
107. Govt. of India, (1991), "Action Plan for Revamping the Family Welfare Programme in India". Ministry of Health and Family Welfare, New Delhi.
108. Govt. of India Planning commission, "Report of the Working Group on Population Policy", New Delhi, 1980.
109. Griffin, K. (1974), The Political Economy of Agrarian Change: An Essay on the Green Revolution(London: Macmillan).
110. Grifftths, G. (1987), 'Missing the Poorest: Participant Identification by a Rural Development Agency', Discussion Paper No. 230 (Brighton: Institute of Development Studies).
111. Gulder M, Rifkin S. 1993. Sustainability in the health sector, part 1: Vietnam Case Study, London: Save the Childlren Fund.
112. Gupta, Narendra et al. (1992), 'Health of Women and Children in Rajasthan', Bombay, Economic and Political Weekly, 17 October, XXVII (42), pp. 2323-2330.
113. Harris, M. and Poultion, R. (1988) (eds.), Putting People First (London: Macmillan).

114. Heijden, H. VAN DER (1986), 'Development Impact and Effectiveness of Non-Governmental Organisations: The Record of Progress in Rural Development Co-oeration' (mimeo).

115. Henderson P. 1993. Sustainability in the health sector, part 1: Nepal Case Study, London: Save the Children Fund.

116. ICSSR and ICMR, "Health For All: An Alternative Strategy", 1980.

117. India, Government of (1988c), Report of Group to Review and Simplify Procedures for Processing Proposals for Grants-in-Aid to Voluntary Agencies, New Delhi, Ministry of Personnel, Public Grievances and Pensions.

118. Institute for Development Research (1992), 'A Note on NGOs and Policy Influence'.

119. International Conference on Population and Development: Programme of Action

120. International Institute for Population Sciences. India: National Family Health Survey, 1992-93.

121. International Institute for Population Sciences. India: National Family Health Survey II, 1998-99.

122. Iyer, Ramaswamy R. (1993), 'Not Much Headway', New Delhi. The Hindustan Times, 17 November.

123. Kajese, K. (1987), 'An Agenda of Future Tasks for International and Indigenous NGOs: Views from the South', World Development, 15 suppl. (Autumn), 79-86.

124. Kar, Manoj, (1995), "Role of NGOs in Health and Development Programmes in India Since Independence: A Policy Analysis", Dissertation Submitted to the Centre of Social Medicine and Community Health, Jawaharlal Nehru University, New Delhi.

125. Karat, Prakash (1988), Foreign Funding and the Philosophy of Voluntary Organisations, New Delhi, National Book Centre.

126. Khan, M.E. and B.C. Patel (1993), 'Access to Health Care', New Delhi, Seminar 410: Population Planning, October.

127. Khanna, R.N., Mehta and A. Bhan (1991), 'Voluntary Effort in Community Health', Review of the Community Health Project of SEWA-Rural (mimeo).

128. King, Maurice, "Human Entrapment in India", National Medical Journal of India, Vol.4, No.4, 1991.

129. Korten, David (1991), 'The Role of Non-Governmental Organisations in Development, Changing Patterns and Perspectives' in Samuel Paul and Arturo Israel, Non-Governmental Organisations and the World Bank, Washington, DC.

130. Korten, D.C. (1980), 'Community Organisation and Rural Development: A Learning Process Approach',Public Administration Review, 40/5: 341-52.

131. Kothari, Rajni (1987), 'Voluntary Organisations in a Plural Society', New Delhi. The Indian Journal of Public Administration, XXXIII(3), July-September, pp. 433-53.

132. Kottack, C.P. (1985), 'When People Don't Come First: Some Sociological Perspectives from Completed Projects', in Cernea, 325-56.

133. Mukhopadyay, Alok, (1992), "Voluntary Sector and Health Care". Paper presented at the workshop on `Health and Development in India', at India International Centre, New Delhi.

134. Myrdal, Gunnar, "Asian Drama: An Enquiry into the Poverty of Nations", Twentieth Century Fund, New York, 1968.

135. Nath, N.C.B. (1989), A Survey Report on the Voluntary Sector (New Delhi: Foundation to Aid Industrial Recovery).

136. Overseas Development Institute (1989), 'NGOs in Development', Briefing Paper (London: ODI).

137. Pachauri, Saroj (1989), 'Experiences in Community Health': Anubhav Series, New Delhi, Parivar Seva Sanstha & Ford Foundation.

138. Padron, M. (1987), 'Non-Governmental Development Organisations: From Development Aid to Development Cooperation', World Development, 15, suppl. (autumn), 69-78.

139. Pandey, Shahsi Ranjan (1991), Community Action for Social Justice, New Delhi, Sage

140. Patnaik, Prabhat, "Notes on the Political Economy or Structural Adjustment", Social Scientist, Vol. 22, Nos. 9-12, Sept.-Dec., 1994.

141. PRIA (1991), 'A Study of History Roles and Future Challenges', New Delhi, Society for Participatory Research in Asia (mimeo).

142. PRIA (1989), 'Networks and their Functioning', New Delhi, Society for Participatory Research in Asia, September (mimeo).

143. Qadeer, Imrana, "Black Death, White Lies", Seminar, No.425, January, 1995.

144. Ramaswamy, Uma (1990), 'Non-Government Organisation: A Perspective', Friedrich Ebert Stiftung (unpublished).

145. Rao, G.R.S. (1990), 'Corporate Social Accountability in India', Philannthropy: Newsletter of the Centre for Advancement of Philanthropy, Bombay, Centre for Advancement of Philanthropy, 14 December, pp. 2-4.

146. Sen Siddhartha (1993), Defining the Non-profit Sector: India, working Paper 1, Johns Hopkins University Institute for Policy Studies.

147. Sen, B. (1987), 'NGO Self-evaluation: Issues of Concern', World Development, 15, suppl., 161-7.

148. Sen, Jai (1986), 'On Anti-Voluntarism', New Delhi, Lokayan Bulletin, 4(3/4): May-August, pp. 9-37.

149. Sharma, Suresh (1987), 'Voluntary Efforts and Institutional Funding', New Delhi, Lokayan Bulletin, 5:2.

150. Sheth, D.L. and Harsh Sethi (1989), 'Representations and Reality: The NGO Sector'.

151. Smillie, I. and Helmich, H. (1993), Stakeholders in Development: Non-governmental Organisations and Development (Paris: OECD).

152. Smithson P. 1993a. Health Financing and Sustainability, part 2: Financial constraints to health sector sustainability in Uganda, London: Save the Children Fund.

153. Sustainability of donor-supported health projects in Central America and Africa. Social Science and Medicine 30: 1015-23.

154. Talwar, Prem, P. (1991), "Greater Involvement of Non- Government Organisations and Recommendation". Presented at the Seminar on collaboration between Government/NGOs for Maternal Health and Family Planning Programme.

155. Tandon, Rajesh (1986), 'Regulating NGOs: New Moves', New Delhi, Lokayan Bulletin, 4(3/4), May-August, pp. 38-43.

156. Tendler, J. (1982), Turning Private Voluntary Agencies into Development Agencies: Questions for Evaluation, AID Program Evaluation Discussion Paper No.12 (Washington, DC: US Agency for International Development).

157. The Development Impact of PVOs in Kenya and Niger, Report prepared for USAID (Norwalk, Conn.: Development Alternatives Inc).

158. The World Bank. World Development Report, 1993.

159. Uphoff, N. (1985), 'Fitting Project to People', in Cernea, 359-95.

160. USAID (1985), PVOs and the Promotion of Small-scale Enterprise. AID Evaluation Study, No. 27 (Washington, DC: USAID).

161. WHO/SEARO. Regional Reproductive Health Strategy for South-East Asia, 1996.

162. World Bank, "Indian Health Sector Financing: Coping with Adjustment", Report No. 10859-IN, New Delhi, 1992.

163. World Bank, "World Development Report, 1993: Investing in Health", OUP, New York, 1993.

End Notes

Chapter II

1. Tandon, Rajesh. The state and voluntary Agencies in Asia. In Richard Holloway (ed.), Doing Development - Govts, NGOs and the Rural Poor in Asia. Earthscan Publications Ltd; London, in association with CUSO, 1989.

2. Society for Participatory Research in Asia. Voluntary Development Organisations in India. A study of History, Roles and future challanges. PRIA, NEW DELHI, NOV. 1991.

3,4,5. - A study of NGO-funding pattern by AVARD - Country paper on NGOs in DEVELOPMENT SECTOR.

6. Duggal, Ravi. NGOs, Govt.and the Private Sector, the FRCH, Bombay, 1986.

7. Jesani Amar; Gupta, Manisha and Duggal, Ravi NGOs in Rural Health Care. The FRCH, Bombay, 1986.

8. Jesani Amar; Gupta, Manisha and Duggal, Ravi NGOs in Rural Health Care, Vol. 1: overview. The FRCH, Bombay, 1986.

9. ICSSR/ICMR Health for All : An Alternative strategy - 1981.

10. Veena Soni Raleish. KEM Hospital - Rural Health Project - Anuvab series, ford fundation study, 1977.

11. Neera Kuckreja Sohoni. SEWA - Rural Project, Anubhav Series, Ford foundation study, (India) 1970.

12. Duggal Ravi ; NGOs, Govt. and Private Sector in Health ; Economic and Political weekly; March 26, 1988.

13. Jesani, Awar and Ganguly, Shipli; Some Issues in commity participation in Health care services; FRCH; Bombay, 1990.

14. Bhatia, Kavita. The NGO Movement in Health, FRCH Publication on commity Health, FRCH, Bombay, 1993.

15. Jesani, Amar and Anantharam, Saraswatty - Private Sector and Privatisation in the Health care Services; A review paper for the ICSSR - ICMR Joint Pavel on Health - FRCH, Bombay, 1990.

16. Pachauri, Saroj. Reaching India's poor Non-Governmental Approaches to commity Health, Ford foundation, New Delhi, 1994.

17. Discussion Note on Voluntary organisations in India; Society for Participatory Research in Asia; New Delhi, 1990.

18, 19. Anubhav Series, Ford foundation Study,(India) 1990.

20. Chatterjee, Meera. Private Voluntary Health Organisation in India; Health Impleventing Policy, New Delhi.
21. Berman, Peter and Dave, Priti. Experiences in Paying For Health Care in India's voluntary sector.

Chapter III

1. "Sustainability" as used in this discussion refers to sustainability of benefits at the local, project, or program levels, and has always been an implicit or explicit objective of development activiites. What is new, however, and therefore less understood at this time is the more recent discussions of "sustainable development," which have been stimulated by concerns over the environmental impact of development activities. These are not mutually exclusive, but the latter conception raises larger issues not directly or immediately relevant to Initiatives' proposed activities. For a discussion of the larger emerging "vision" of "sustainable development" see: Steven H. Arnold, "Sustainable Development: A Solution to the Development Puzzle?" *Development* 1989: nos.2/3, pp. 21-25.
2. Development Assistance and Health Programs: Issues of Sustainability," *A.I.D. Program Evaluation Discussion Paper No. 23* (Washington, DC: USAID, October 1987).
3. For a discussion of the conclusions of that review, see: Thomas J. Bossert, "Can They Get Along Without Us? Sustainability of Donor-Supported Health Projects in Central America and Africa," *Social Science and Medicine*, vol. 30, no. 9, pp. 1015-1023, 1990. The five countries were: Honduras, Guatemala, Zaire, Senegal, and Tanzania.
4. Michael Bamberger & Shabbir Cheema, *Case Studies of Project Sustainability: Implications for Policy and Operations from Asian Experience*, (Washington, DC: The World Bank, 1990), pp. 3-21.
5. See, for example, Dennis A. Rondinelli, "Planning and Implementing Development Projects: An Introduction," in Planning Development *Projects* (Stroudsburg, PA: Dowden, Hutchinson & Ross, Inc., 1977), pp. 9, 16.
6. Most approaches to sustainability are donor-driven in the sense that their central concern is with the continuation of benefits following the withdrawal of external or donor resources. See, for example, Richard Martin, *A.I.D's Child Survival Program: A Synthesis of Findings from Six Country Case Studies* (A.I.D. Program and Operations Assessment Report No. 5: October 1993), pp. 20-26. This contrasts with the approach reflected in this paper's definition — shared by the SDS and *Initiatives* Projects, which shifts the focus to the clients by emphasizing the value they ascribe to the benefits or outcomes of the services provided. This shift in emphasis may appear subtle, but it can have important consequences for how the respective approaches are implemented. The importance of the relationship between valued outcomes and institutional sustainability is not entirely neglected in current discussions of sustainability; see, for example, Derick W. Brinkerhoff & Arthur A. Goldsmith, "Promoting the Sustainability of Development Institutions: A Framework for Strategy," *World Development*, vol. 20, no. 3, pp. 369-383, 1992.

7. For example: Buzzard defines "sustainability... as a program's continuing to deliver services or sustain benefits after the donor's technical, managerial, and financial support has ended," *op.cit.* p.2ff. The difference is reflected in her distinction between sustaining project infrastructure and its "impact." Also, see: Elliott R. Morss, David D. Gow, and Christopher W. Nordlinger, "Sustaining Project Benefits," in Elliott R. Morss & David D. Gow (eds.) *Implementing Rural Development Projects: Lessons from AID and World Bank Experiences (Boulder, CO: Westview Press, 1985)*, pp. 238-239. Bossert, op.cit. p. 1016.
8. Carrie A. Meyer, "A Step Back as Donors Shift Institution Building from the Public to the "Private" Sector, *World Development*, vol. 20, no. 8, pp. 1115-1126, 1992.
9. Bossert, *op.cit.*, suggests smallpox erradication as an example of a health benefit that does not require continuing activities for its impact on subsequent generations. Even here, however, it is possible to argue that there are continuing, albeit transformed, activities directly associated with that achievement, i.e. the maintenance of samples of the samllpox virus in selected laboratories against the possible reemergence of the disease in the future. Another example of the argument that benefits can be divorced from activities is the proposition that, "Low knowledge, poor motivation and poor health habits are threats to sustainability. High levels of KAP [about primary health care services and healthful behavior] can reduce the need for continued services." Jack Reynolds, *et. al., Sustainability Analysis* [Primary Health Care Management Advancement Programme, Module 9] (Washington, DC: Aga Khan Health Services, 1993), p. 24. Again, it can be argued that even "high levels of KAP" will, in the absence of reinforcement, deteriorate, as will their benefits. Here too, then, benefits are unlikely to be sustained in the absence of some form of supporting activity, even if different from the activities which initially produced the benefit. To expect otherwise is to believe in the social equivalent of a "perpetual motion machine."
10. For example, Reynolds, *ibid.*, pp. 51*ff.*
11. This approach was much in evidence in the early exchanges in the on-line conference on sustainability convened by Management Sciences for Health (MSH) on behalf of USAID's Office of Population. The initial discussion assumed that an organization acheived sustainable op-erations by passing through a series of stages modeled on the pattern of human development. In the case of this discussion, sustainability is not only associated with a well managed organization, but with a particular form of management — namely, one that is complex, structurally differentiated, and hierarchically organized.
12. *Ibid.* Also see, for example, the discussion of "institutional function" in Jerry Van Sant, *Institutional Self-Reliance: A Framework for Assessment* (North Carolina: Center for International Development, January 1991), pp. 4*ff.*
13. This was the explicit assumption of the initial model presented for comment in the MSH on-line conference cited above in note #11. For a concise discussion of the role equilibrium plays within a system model of social organization, see: Robert Chin, "The Utility of System Models and Developmental Models for Practitioners," in Warren G. Bennis, et.al., *The Planning of Change* (New York: Holt Rinehart & Winston, 1969), pp. 301-303. For a less sanguine treatment of equilibrium in non-living systems — one that relates a system's maintenance of

equilibrium in a changing environment with an invitation for "entropy to set in— see, Tom Broersma, "In Search of the Future," *Training & Development* (January 1995), pp. 38-43.

14. For a discussion of the characteristics of a social enterprise, see: J. Gregory Dees, *Social Enterprise: Private Initiatives for the Common Good* (Boston, MA: Harvard Business School, [no. 9-395-116] November 30, 1994). In this note, social enterprises are distinguished from more traditional business enterprises in terms of two core dimensions — social objective (oriented toward social betterment), and method of operation (affiliative, non-pecuniary rewards) — and four amplifying dimensions — below market-rate financial returns on investment, the social motivation of the work force, below-cost pricing to consumers, and a mission-driven "stewardship" form of governance.
15. Many of the tools under reference originated in efforts to understand the dynamics of an individual firm. Examples of these include techniques to identify client perceptions of value, and approaches to relate organizational strategy to environmental contraints and opportunities. The importance of appreciating the dynamics of an individual firm in approaches to private sector development has long been recognized by USAID, based on its experience with such activities. See, for example, Jennifer Bremer, *et.al., A Review of AID's Experience in Private Sector Development* (USAID, Washington: AID Program Evaluation Report No. 14, April 1985), pp. 37-38.
16. Dees, *op.cit.*, pp. 10-13. The sometimes contentious issue of whether a non-profit organization's activities should generate profits is relevant here. Although just *breaking even* is a typical financial goal for not-for-profit managers, a financial surplus, i.e. a "profit," is not only legitimate but necessary in an inflationary economy to satisfy needs for working capital and capital equipment replacement. See, Robert N. Anthony & David W. Young, *Management Control in Nonprofit Organizations* (Homewood, Illinois: Richard D. Irwin, Inc., 1984), pp. 41-42.
17. For one of the most influential analytical models in use, see: Michael E. Porter, "How Competitive Forces Shape Strategy," *Harvard Business Review* vol. 57, no. 2 (March/April 1979), pp. 137-145. For contrast, see the discussion (and comparison) of both traditional system and developmental models in Chin, *op.cit.*, pp. 297-312.
18. This is Porter's "five-force model" of market competition. An adaptation to not-for-profit organizations can be found in: Sharon M. Oster, *Strategic Management for Nonprofit Organizations: Theory & Cases* (New York: Oxford University Press, 1995), pp. 29-45.
19. See, for example: Cliff Havener, "Customers Can Tell You What They Want," *Management Review* (American Management Association, December 1994), pp. 42-45.
20. The critical importance of "adaptability" for organizational survival in a turbulent and competitive environment has long been recognized. See, for example, Warren Bennis' prescient essay, "The Decline of Bureaucracy and Organizations of the Future," in his *Beyond Bureaucracy: essays on the development and evolution of human organization* (New York: McGraw-Hill Book Company, 1966), pp. 3-15. A more general framework for considering the relationship between

an organization's sustainability and the fit between its internal processes and its environment can be found in Derick W. Brinkerhoff & Arthur A. Goldsmith, *loc.cit.*

21. Howard H. Stevenson & Jose Carlos Jarillo, "A New Entrepreneurial Paradigm," in Amitai Etzioni & Paul R. Lawrence (eds.) *Socio-Economics: Toward a New Synthesis* (New York: M.E. Sharpe, Inc. 1991), pp. 193-203.

22. The organizational implications of entrepreneurial and trustee management are congruent with the characteristics of *organic and mechanistic* organizations respectively. For a concise description of the organic/mechanistic organizational continuum from an organizational development perspective, see: Wendell L. French & Cecil H. Bell, Jr., *Organization Development: behavioral science interventions for organization improvement* (Englewood Cliffs, NJ: Prentice-Hall, Inc., 1978), pp. 216-225. A concise description of how an organization's skill requirements change in relation to its growth and strategic focus can be found in: H. Michael Hayes, "Developing Managers for Strategic Management," in William d. Guth (ed.) *Handbook of Business Strategy* (New York: Warren, Gorham, & Lamont, 1985), p. 25-12.

23. The *Initiatives* Project's own work with nongovernmental health and family planning service providers is the basis for the conceptual model presented in this paper. Information about *Initiatives* and its work over the past five years can be found in its website: http:\\www.jsi.com/intl/init. *Inititiatives'* experience has been entirely congruent with that of the earlier USAID-funded *Enterprise Project*, which yielded a rich and relevant wealth of information on the characteristics that appear to enhance a nongovernmental organization's prospects for achieving sustainability. Over and above the presence of basic organizational structures and systems, were the presence of business-like management practices (or the willingness to utilize such practices). The consistent overestimation of market size, and the underestimation of competition were among the critical impediments to the sustainability of the nongovernmental family planning service providers assisted by the *Enterprise Project*. See, "Promoting NGO Sustainability: The Lessons of Enterprise," (Arlington, VA: John Snow, Inc., April 1991.) See also, Catherine Fort, "The Enterprise Program Follow-Up Study: Were Private Sector Family Planning Services Sustained?" (Arlington, VA: John Snow, Inc. - JSI Research & Training Institute, March 1994). Nevertheless, these early observations regarding the importance of entrepreneurship are seldom reflected in later disucssions of service sustainability. For example, see: Ruth E. Levine & Joanne Bennett, *Sustainability of Family Planning Programs and Organizations: Meeting Tomorrow's Challenges* (Washington, DC: The Futures Group International, January 1995). This OPTIONS Project discussion of organizational-level strengthening for sustainability does not include reference to the importance of either entrepreneurship or the marketing function. In that way, it is much closer to the traditional approach to sustainability as outlined above, than to the client-driven model applied by *Initiatives*.

24. Effective trusteeship's concern with risk reduction, resource control, and accountability places a premium on problem solving, documentation, and administration (interpretation and application) of formal rules and procedures. This emphasis figures prominently in technical assistance provided to strengthen

organizations in developing countries An example of this is training to support the development of personnel systems, e.g. formal job descriptions, compensation systems based on organizational position and responsibility. Perhaps a less obvious example of this is training directed to enhance skills related to the development and maintenance of formal strategic planning systems. Such skills are less valuable in an organization that maintains a less hierarchical and more fluid internal structure than one that is more oriented to the control and routinization of internal operations. See, J. Sterling Linvingston, "Myth of the Well-Educated Manager, in the Harvard Business School's *Paths Toward Personal Progress: Leaders are Made, Not Born* (Boston, MA: Harvard Business Review, 1983), pp. 63-73, for a discussion of formal management education's preoccupation with developing problem solving and decision making skills, which, he argues, focuses managers on explaining and defending their reasoning, not on carrying out their decisions.

Annexures

ANNEX-I

State of Health Services in Rajasthan

Salient features and Status of health services in Rajasthan.

Rajasthan is the second largest state in the country having 3.42 lakh sq.km. area. The salient features of the state are given in Table – I

Due to meagre financial resource and difficult topographical conditions it is a challenging task to provide adequate medical and health services to the people of the state. The Directorate, Medical and Health Department, Rajasthan, Jaipur undertake this task. This work involves extending medical benefit to both the urban and rural population. 77.12% of the total population lives in villages whereas the remaining 22.88% of the population is urban.

Table - 1

No.	*Item*	*Year*	*Unit*	*Particulars*
1.	Area	1991	Lakh.Sq.Km	3.42
2.	Districts	1994	Number	31
3.	Sub-divisions	1991	-do-	90
4.	Tehsils	1991	-do-	213
5.	Zila Parishads	1994	-do-	31
6.	Panchayat Samitis	1991	-do-	237
7.	Village Panchayats	1994	-do-	9,173
8.	Total villages	1991	-do-	39,810
9.	Inhabited villages	1991	-do-	37,889
10.	Towns	1991	-do-	222
11.	Population	1991	-do-	4,40,05,990
12.	Rural Population	1991	-do-	3,39,38,877
13.	Urban	1991	-do-	1,00,67,113

Source:- Economic Review 1995-96.

Status of the Health Services

In the development of a nation, the nation's health is an important element. So it needs no emphasis that health care services should reach the people in the villages also. Main objectives of the health care programme are to control and eradicate communicable and other diseases and to provide curative and preventive services to the people. Details relating to allopathic medical institutions functioning in the state are as follows: -

Table - 2

No.	*Institution*	*1993-94*	*1994-95*	*1995-96*
		Number	*Number*	*Number*
1.	Hospitals	218	218	219
2.	Dispensaries	283	273	278
3.	Primary Health Centres	1,453	1,507	1,596
4.	Community Health Centres	246	246	256
5.	Maternity and Child Welfare Centres	118	118	118
6.	Sub-centres	8,000	8,000	8,700
7.	Indoor Beds	35,142	35,663	36,712

Source:- Progress Reports of the Medical and Health Department.

For every one lakh population (1991 census) 81 beds were available in the state in 1994-95(12/94). It was also noticed that there was no increase in the number of maternity and child welfare centres. 118 centres were continuing from the year 1991-92 without any increase.

System	*Number*
Ayurvedic	3,511
Unani	80
Homeopathic	110
Naturopathy	4
Total	3,70
Mobile Hospitals	5
Grand Total	**3,710**

Source: Directorate of Ayurvedic Department, Rajasthan, Ajmer, and Performance Budget 1996-97

There are 1,186 patients beds in 663 'A' class and 3042 'B' class Hospitals out of a total of 3,705.

ANNEX-II

Health and Family Welfare NGOs in Rajasthan supported by UNFPA

1. Shri Sugan Vishwakarma Charitable Trust, Jaipur
2. Adarsh Saroj Vidhiya Mandir Samiti, Dausa
3. New Bombay Hospital Society, Jaipur
4. Centre for Development Communication, Jaipur
5. Students Relief Society, Jaipur
6. Society for Education Reserach and Voluntary Affectors, Jaipur
7. Gramin Vikas Evum Takniki Shiksha Sansthan, Jaipur
8. Gram Vikas Nav Yuvak Mandal, Jaipur
9. Gramin Vikas Sansthan, Bharatpur
10. Gram Newyojan Kendra, Bharatpur
11. Shri Jan Jeewan Kalyan Sansthan, Bharatpur
12. Rajasthan Mahila Mandal, Ajmer
13. Gramin Vikas Evum Pariavaran Sansthan, Dausa
14. Swasthya Kalyan Sansthan, Ajmer
15. R R Shikshan Sansthan, Jaisalmer
16. Chetna Arogya Mandir and Samaj Sewa Samiti, Udaipur
17. Upkar Sansthan, Alwar
18. Rajasthan Mahila Prashikshan Sansthan, Kota
19. Yuva Gramin Vikas Sansthan, Sawai Madhopur
20. Social Action for Rural Development, Sikar
21. Bharatiya Gramothan Sansthan, Churu

ANNEX-III

NGOs/Voluntary Organisations in Rajasthan: An Organogram

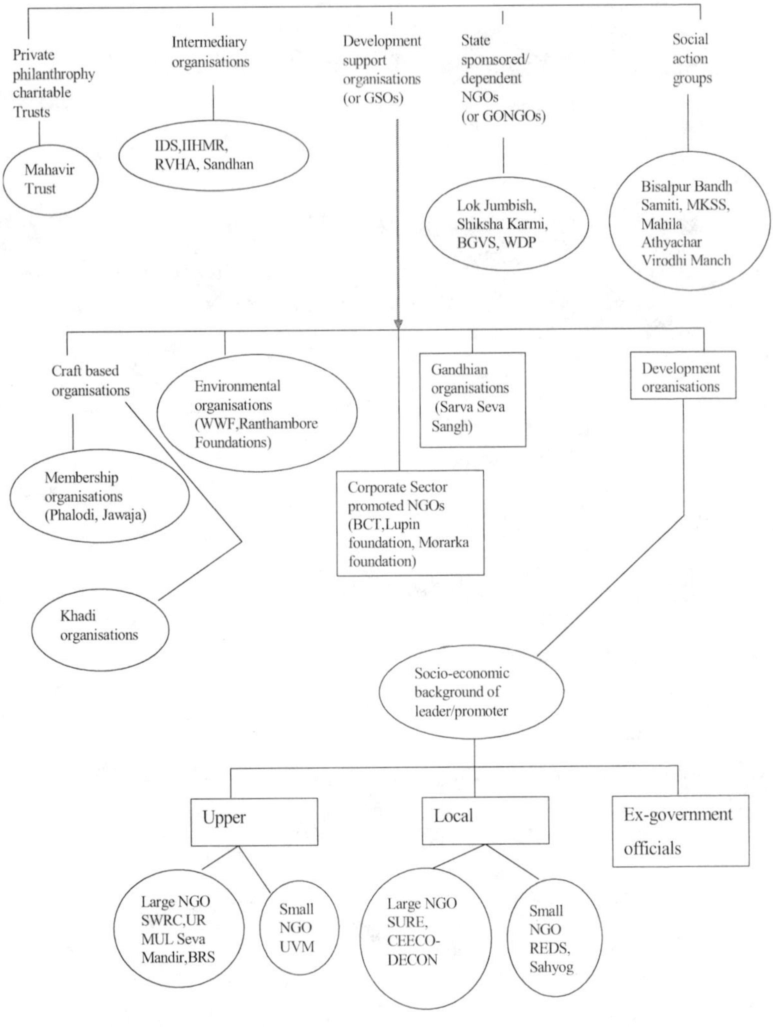

ANNEX-IV

Methodology used by Seva Mandir, Bhoruka Charitable Trust, Bal Rashmi Society under PVOH-II project for the findings of KPC(Knowledge Practice Coverage) Study and PE(Participatory Evaluation) Report.

The evaluation consisted of two components:

- KPC study to assess quantitative selected health delivery interventions
- PE Process to gauge qualitative aspects of the project activities

During the Ist phase, both KPC and PE activities including training of staff was undertaken. The KPS activities began with a 4-day training of staff members who eventually undertook the activities themselves. The training also briefly oriented the staff to the participatory evaluation exercise. The rest of the first phase was spent in field activities of KPC and PE including meetings with government officials NGOs and other PVOH-II staff.

The second phase basically saw sharing of the PE and KPC findings in the PFE. The sharing was undertaken at the following levels:

- Staff of PVOH-II
- Management of PVOH-II
- Village Community

The findings of the evaluation including the response from the various stakeholders has been incorporated in the final evaluation findings and recommendations.

Issues of Concern

At the workshop on participatory evaluation by all concerned PVOs, issues of concern for the evaluation exercise was worked jointly by the PVOs and the respective consultants.

Some of the issues were as follows:

- Whether supply of MCH related drugs and vaccines were regular?
- Whether MMU services were provided regularly?
- Whether safe deliveries were conducted by trained dais and records maintained accordingly?
- Whether training inputs provided to FHVs, dais and staff were utilised effectively?
- Whether at risk mothers and children were provided referral services by nearest referral point?

- Whether community acceptance towards services increase or not?
- Whether transportation for FP service made any significant impact?
- Whether FP services especially sterilisation, IUD, contraceptive distribution through depots done effectively?
- Whether Government support was sufficient to run the activities?
- Is there any need of nutritional programme in future?
- Whether a figure of mortality and morbidity changed?
- Whether health education activities at community level will continue?
- Whether sufficient infrastructure provided for base hospital services?
- Whether people are inclined to continue family welfare services?
- Whether local structures like *Mahila Mandals* have understood the need of MCH services?
- Whether support organizations provided help in time and adequately?
- Whether flow of funds was regular and MOHFW, NIHFW and USAID paid enough time to the project?
- Whether organisational decision-making, job description and role clarity were in tune with the project needs?
- Whether vision, mission and strategy of the project were well understood by the project staff?
- Whether PVOH-II used inputs from other projects of BCT and vice versa?
- How were monitoring and supervision done in the project and what type of data was collected?

Data Generation Methods

The Participatory Final Evaluation (PFE) involved the use of two methods of data generation:

- Knowledge Practice and Coverage (KPC)
- Participatory Evaluation (PE)

Methodology for KPC

Questionnaire

The Questionnaire was designed to collect information from mothers with children under 24 months of age. Information was elicited about the youngest child under the age of 24 months. The questions were based on a standardises survey format which USAID requires of all PVO-CSSM projects. The survey instrument, designed during a workshop of Johns Hopkin University, was appropriately adapted for the PVOH-II projects in India; field-tested, finalised and translated into Marathi.

The Questionnaire which contains 46 questions, has been designed to elicit information on the profile of mothers, and their knowledge and practices related to

- Breast feeding and child nutrition
- Growth monitoring
- Vitamin-A supplementation
- Diarrhoeal disease control
- Acute Respiratory Infection (ARI) control
- Immunisation
- Maternal health, including antenatal, intranatal and postnatal care
- Family Welfare. Determination of Sample Size

The sample size was calculated, using the formula

$$n = \frac{z^2(p.q)}{d^2}$$

where, n = Sample size

z = Statistical certainty chosen

p = Estimated prevalence / coverage

Rate / level to be investigated

q = 1-p

d = precision desired

The statistical certainty z was chosen to be 95%(c = 1.96) The value of p was defined by the coverage rate that requires the largest sample size (p = 0.5). The value 'd' depends on the precision or margin of error desired, was taken as 0.1. Given the above values, the following sample size (n) was determined, using the formula:

$$N = \frac{(1.96 * 1.96) * (0.5 * 0.5)}{(0.1 * 0.1)} = 96$$

It is tedious and time consuming to randomly select and identified individual from the survey population, and then perform the selection 96 times to identify a sample of n = 96. This was overcome by using the 30 cluster sampling technique, used in EPI programmes of WHO. However, to compensate for the bias which enters the survey from interviewing persons in clusters, rather than as randomly selected individuals, a preferred minimum sample of 210(7 per cluster) was considered, given the above values of p, d and z. For this survey, a sample size of 300 (10 per cluster) was selected, so as to ensure that sub-samples would be large enough to obtain useful management type information

Selection of the Sample

The sample consisted of 309 women with children between 0-23 months age, in a population of approximately 86,000, residing in Maval Tehsil of District Pune, Maharashtra State. 10 women residing there since over 6 months before the birth of their children were randomly in each of the 30 randomly clusters following the process described in the "EPI Coverage Survey" training manual of WHO.

Once the survey team reached the designated cluster site, initial household surveyed within the cluster, as well as the direction from the initial household, was randomly selected as suggested in the manual.

ANNEX-V

Organisation Profile

1.	Name of Organisation	:	Seva Mandir
2.	Abbreviated Name	:	SM
3.	Mission	:	Promotion of social justice through community self-reliance and mass literacy
4.	Major Scope of Activities	:	Primary education, non-formal education, linking socio-economic development of tribal community
5.	Established on	:	1968
6.	Registered/Mailing Address	:	Old Fatehpura, Udaipur Rajasthan – 313001
7.	Rural Health Centre	:	Khojwada and Saru, Kherwada BlockDistrict – Udaipur (Rajasthan)
8.	Operational Area of the Organisation	:	Jhadol, Badgaon, Girwa, Kherwada blocks in Udaipur district, Rajasthan
9.	Registration Details	:	Societies Registration Act, 1968 with FCRA permanent Registration No.
10.	Contact Person	:	Mr. Ajay Singh Mehta, Chief Executive Seva Mandir, Udaipur

ANNEX-VI

Organisation Profile

1.	Name of Organisation	: Bhoruka Charitable Trust, Churu
2.	Abbreviated Name	: BCT
3.	Mission	: Providing Integrated approach to Rural Development
4.	Major scope of activities	: Socio-economic transformation of rural areas, community groups and Institutions through community development
5.	Established on	: 1963
6.	Registered/Mailing Address	: Bhorugram (Nangal Kalan) Via Sadulpur Tehsil Rajgarh District Churu, Rajasthan-331035
7.	Rural Health Centre	: Bhorugram
8.	Operational Area of the Organisation	: Rajasthan State
9.	Registration Details	: Society Registration Act, 1961 with FCRA permanent Registration No.
10.	Contact Person	: Mr. S.P. Aggarwal, Project Director, BCT, Bhorugram, District Churu, Rajasthan-331035

ANNEX-VII

Organisation Profile

1.	Name of Organisation	: Bal Rashmi Society, Jaipur
2.	Abbreviated Name	: BRS
3.	Mission	: Save Children Save Generation
4.	Major scope of activities	: Work towards the socio-economic development of women and children particularly the children in rural and urban areas in Rajasthan
5.	Established on	: 14th November, 1972
6.	Registered/Mailing Address	: A-48, Shanti Path, Tilak Nagar, Jaipur –302004
7.	Rural Centre	: Village-Bhavasar Issarwala, Panchayar-Mansar Khedi, Bassi – 303301District – Jaipur (Rajasthan)
8.	Operational Area of the Organisation	: Rajasthan State
9.	Registration Details	: Registered under Rajasthan Society Registration Act, 1958 with FCRA permanent Registration No.
10.	Contact Person	: Mrs Alice Garg, Founder Secretary, Bal Rashmi Society, Jaipur

List of Stakeholders of NGOs under PVOH-II project

1.	Community	: Mother Children Mahila Mandal Village Groups, Gram Sabhas, Samities
2.	Project/ Organization	: FHVs, VHWs, VLWs and Health Team Dais Grass root level workers Middle Level Staff Base Hospital Staff
3.	Government Agencies	: PHCs-Primary Health Centers DHOs-District Health Officials MOHFW

4.	Other NGOs/ Institutions/ Units	: NIHFW TAUs –Technical Assistance Unit
5.	Donor	: USAID SM, BCT & BRS

Index

D

E

F

G

H

Q

T

U

V

W

Z